THE WRESTLER'S BODY

THE WRESTLER'S BODY

*Identity and Ideology
in North India*

Joseph S. Alter

UNIVERSITY OF CALIFORNIA PRESS
Berkeley • *Los Angeles* • *Oxford*

University of California Press
Berkeley and Los Angeles, California

University of California Press
Oxford, England

Library of Congress Cataloging-in-Publication Data

Alter, Joseph S.
    The wrestler's body : identity and ideology in north India /
Joseph S. Alter.
        p.   cm.
    Includes bibliographical references and index.
    ISBN 0-520-07697-4 (alk. paper)
    1. Wrestling—Social aspects—India.   2. India—Social life and
customs.   I. Title.
GV1198.71.A2A45   1992
796.8'12'0954—dc20   91-31560
                                                                                 CIP

Printed in the United States of America

1   2   3   4   5   6   7   8   9

The paper used in this publication meets the minimum requirements
of American National Standard for Information Sciences—Permanence
of Paper for Printed Library Materials, ANSI Z39.48-1984 ∞

For my parents
Robert Copley Alter
Mary Ellen Stewart Alter

Contents

Illustrations

FIGURES

Note on Translation

I have made every effort to ensure that the translation of material from Hindi to English is as accurate as possible. All translations are my own. In citing classical Sanskrit texts I have referenced the chapter and verse of the original source and have also cited the secondary source of the translated material. All other citations are quoted verbatim even when the English usage is idiosyncratic and not consistent with the prose style or spelling conventions employed in the main text. A translation of single words or short phrases appears in the first instance of use and sometimes again if the same word or phrase is used subsequently much later in the text.

Transliteration has been done with an eye toward readability and simplicity. Diacritics are excluded from the text but have been included in the glossary. Although the common language spoken in Banaras is Bhojpuri, almost everyone also speaks some version of Hindi, Urdu, or a combination thereof. All of my interviews were conducted in Hindi. Therefore, transliteration usually conforms to the standard Hindi pronunciation, but in some cases the wrestlers with whom I spoke affected a particular pronunciation of specific words, as, for example, *bethak* (deep knee bend) rather than *baithak*. In part this may be a function of the linguistic interface in eastern Uttar Pradesh, and in part because wrestlers have developed a slight accent of their own when talking about the specifics of their art among themselves. If these terms are not in common usage, and it seems that even non-Banaras wrestlers have the same pronunciation, I have conformed to the wrestlers' predilection.

Preface

This is a study of wrestling as a system of meaning, and it must be made clear at the outset that I have not undertaken to study the technical aspects of the sport. Those who look for a detailed explication of moves, countermoves, and techniques will undoubtedly be disappointed. The reason for this is quite simple. The moves, countermoves, and techniques of Indian wrestling must be filmed or photographed to be appreciated and understood fully. This monograph is not an exercise in replication or description of this exact sort; it is a work of interpretation—to adapt an old adage, 1001 words offered in place of what would otherwise be a mere picture.

I am indebted to a number of institutions and individuals for the support they have given to this project. Preliminary research funding was afforded by a Humanities Graduate Research Grant from the University of California at Berkeley for a study of the popular literature on Indian wrestling. Funding for a year of field work was provided by a Doctoral Dissertation Research Grant under the auspices of the Fulbright-Hays Foundation. The ample financial support given under this grant was much appreciated. I would also like to thank the staff officers in Washington and Delhi for their efficient work. Without their help, getting the necessary visa and academic affiliation would have been impossible. While I was in India the staff at "Fulbright House" were very helpful in many ways, which made the difficult task of research that much less arduous.

In Banaras I was granted affiliation with the Department of Physical

Education at Banaras Hindu University under the direction of Dr. S. S. Sharma. I am grateful both to the university and to Dr. Sharma for their support.

Upon completing the field research I was awarded a Mabelle McLeod Lewis Memorial Grant for a year of dissertation writing. This support proved invaluable and fulfilling, as I was able to write without distraction for an entire year—a rare situation today.

In India a number of people contributed to the success of this project. I cannot remember the names of every wrestler whose words and ideas have found their way into this text. To all of them goes my sincere gratitude for patience and long-suffering indulgence. A few wrestlers with whom I spoke extensively must be mentioned by name. In Banaras, they are: Lakshmi Kant Pande, Govardan Das Malhotra, Jatindar Kumar Pathak, Narayan Singh, Kaniya Lal Yadav, Amru Dada, Banarsi Pande, Indramani Misra, Pratap Singh, Jharkhande Rai, Krishna Kumar Singh, Kaniya, Ashok, Sohan, Manohar, Atma, Shyam, Govind, Anand, Subhash, Danesh, Ram ji, and Lal ji. I am deeply indebted also to Sita Ram Yadav, a champion wrestler of his time; Nathu Lal Yadav, a genuine *pahalwan*; and Lallu Pahalwan, a quintessential guru. I would also like to thank the owner, managers, and staff of Sandeep Hotel, where I lived for seven months. Their good humor was always appreciated. I recommend their services highly. If I have left out anyone's name it is not by design or lack of appreciation but because so many were helpful.

In Dehra Dun I express my heartfelt thanks to Kanta Pahalwan, who first introduced me to Indian wrestling. During my stay, however, Kanta was absent from Dehra Dun, and I worked closely with Yamin and his cadre of young wrestlers from Saharanpur. A special word of thanks must go to Dr. Shanti Prakash Atreya, who is by popular acclaim *the* guru of Indian wrestling. I had hoped to work closely with him in Dehra Dun but was unable to for various reasons. (The life of a fieldworker does not always accommodate itself to the obligations of a *grihastha*.) Instead I have read his numerous articles on Indian wrestling and hope to have absorbed in this way what he would rather have had me learn in his akhara at Bandarjuddha. His influence on my work is considerable.

In the Department of Anthropology at the University of California at Berkeley a number of people made valuable contributions to my research in particular, and to my academic career in general. My greatest debt is to my advisor and friend Gerald Berreman, whose support has been unstinting. Over the years his critical eye and astute judgement have broadened my appreciation and deepened my understanding of anthropology. The spirit of his work has informed much of my own thinking. William Simmons's good-natured support and insightful comments have helped to keep me on the right track. Thomas Metcalf's extensive knowledge of India has provided a necessary and much appreciated perspective.

Other people have looked over various portions of this manuscript as it went through a number of drafts. I am grateful to Burton Benedict for his comments and to the members of the dissertation-writing seminar at the University of California, Berkeley, for a chance to exchange ideas. Philip Lutgendorf has provided encouragement and has pointed out more than one *bhram*. I am indebted to Bruce Pray and Joseph Schaller for looking over the glossary. My thanks also go to Peter Nabokov, who took an interest in my work and recommended the manuscript to the University of California Press. More than one anonymous reviewer made valuable suggestions for which I am very grateful. Although not directly involved in this project, I would also like to thank Elizabeth Traube, my M.A. advisor at Wesleyan University, for getting me to ask the right questions.

Finally I am indebted to Nicole Constable, whose sharp eye for imprecision is but one mundane feature of a wholly immeasurable and invaluable contribution to the larger project.

CHAPTER 1

Search and Research

OVERVIEW

This monograph is a study of Indian wrestling as a way of life. The term *Indian wrestling* is translated directly from the Hindi phrase *Bharatiya kushti*. *Kushti* (generic wrestling) is regarded as having a uniquely Indian form. In North India there are two other terms that are used interchangeably when referring to Indian wrestling. The most common of these is *pahalwani*, which I have taken to signify two important conceptual domains within the larger framework of wrestling as a way of life. On the one hand, pahalwani defines a particular concept of self structured in terms of somatic principles; on the other hand, it articulates the values and ethics of a distinct ideology. To study pahalwani, therefore, is to understand how wrestlers make sense of who they are through the medium of their bodies.

The second term is *mallayuddha*, which may be literally translated as "wrestling combat." The term *mallayuddha* is used very infrequently and is regarded by most wrestlers as an archaic designation. On account of its classical derivation, it is used primarily by people educated in Sanskrit. The root word *malla*, translated simply as "wrestler," is used in conjunction with two other common terms. *Mallakala* is translated as the "art of wrestling," and *mallavidya* as the "knowledge of wrestling." Both terms, which are used somewhat more frequently than *mallayuddha*, indicate that wrestling is regarded as a complex system of meaning, as more than just a passive form of recreational leisure.

Wrestling in modern India is a synthesis of two different traditions: the Persian form of the art brought into South Asia by the Moguls, and an indigenous Hindu form that dates back at least to the eleventh century A.D. Although technically the two types of wrestling are identical, the culture of Muslim wrestling is formally different from Hindu wrestling. In this monograph I touch on Muslim wrestling only obliquely. For the most part this study is about the identity, ideology and way of life of the Hindu pahalwan.

Wrestling takes place in *akhara*s (gymnasia). Typically an akhara is an ad hoc institution in terms of both membership and management. An akhara may have as few as five or six members or as many as sixty or seventy who range in age from eight to sixty-five. Often wrestlers in an akhara represent a spectrum of high and low caste groups. The members of an akhara are affiliated to the institution through their allegiance to a *guru*. Every akhara is managed by a guru and a cohort of his age mates, *guru-bhais*, who are known by the junior members as *dadas*.

The physical structure of an akhara—minimally an earthen pit, an exercise floor, a well, and a temple or shrine—is maintained by public donation. Akharas do not require a great deal of financial support. Occasionally a new pavilion must be built or a new rope, bucket, or wall is required. Money is raised on demand by whomever takes responsibility, usually one of the senior members. Neighborhood residents and wealthy merchants are asked to pledge contributions, and construction or repair proceeds when enough money has been collected.

Akharas are often located on land that is owned by temple-management committees or donated by a public benefactor or patron of wrestling. Once constructed, akharas are typically regarded as public arenas, and conceptual ownership—if not legal deed—is transferred to the resident guru.

A wrestling guru is one who instructs his disciples on the fine art of wrestling. He prescribes each wrestler's individual regimen by delineating the number and sequence of exercises, the types and number of moves to be practiced, the content and quantity of diet, and the time and amount of rest. A guru is also a source of strength and wisdom, and a wrestler must be willing and able to commit himself totally to his guru in order to gain access to this strength and wisdom.

Although the majority of wrestlers tend to be in their early to mid-teens, the term *pahalwan* designates an identity that is by no means limited to the teenage wrestler. In fact, the term *pahalwan* includes men who were disciplined wrestlers in their youth and who, as married adults, continue to subscribe to the ideals, if not the strict regimen, of a wrestling way of life. These men are employed, support families, and are integrated members of their communities in every sense. However, their whole identity derives from the complex discipline of wrestling exercise and values. A wrestling identity, then, is not restricted to the context of an akhara; it is an attitude toward life in general.

PURPOSE: WHY WRESTLING?

I am often asked why I study Indian wrestling, and the answer is not straightforward. When the idea first came to me, as an undergraduate studying anthropology, I had conjured up an exotic image of extraordinary men doing strange things to and with their bodies. In other words, I fell blindly in step with an orientalist tradition intent on seeing other lives as esoteric, unfamiliar and titillating. Although I hope I have now exorcised from this picture the most malevolent of the orientalist demons, the fact remains that wrestlers view themselves as extraordinary men who do extraordinary things to and with their bodies. They project a self-consciously exotic image and thereby distort the world by way of a novel translation of normal events.

I was born and raised in India of missionary parents and educated in a Christian International School. The exotic was never far away, although not always where one might expect to find it. While no single event—exotic or otherwise—clearly marks that moment of insight when the comfortable truth of the world begins to dissolve into interesting questions, one particular event, among many, will serve to illustrate a point that has provided me with an anthropological perspective on wrestler's lives.

A traveling minstrel show, evangelicals from one of the midwestern states sponsored and funded by their mission to witness to the people of India, came to our school. Clad in blue polyester suits stitched and embroidered with white thread—the white thread sticks in my mind as particularly exotic—clean-cut and well fed, this group, a "family in Christ" who called themselves "The Potter's Clay," took the stage in front of the assembled student body. What followed was a dazzling array of folk-rock music played on a mother-of-pearl embossed accordion, a couple of electric guitars, a trombone, and a trumpet. The music was punctuated by moments of prayer and testimony when the younger members of the troupe would explain how they had gone astray—drinking, driving fast cars, womanizing (a strange world indeed)—but were ultimately saved and had been called on by the Holy Spirit to come to India and bear witness to the power of salvation.

Two sisters—twins I think—were part of this troupe and had taken it upon themselves to have someone translate their midwestern gospel-rock ballads into various Indian languages. How they did this I do not know, for they moved from state to state on a whirlwind schedule; but they would memorize the sounds of words in Tamil, Telagu, Punjabi, Hindi, or Bengali and render these in full if somewhat halting voices at the appropriate regional gospel meeting. For some reason they were exceedingly pleased and proud of the fact that they had no idea what the words meant, or, indeed, what constituted a word as distinct from a syllable or phoneme. They were blissfully comfortable with the conviction that their spiritual message was transcendent: language was reduced to a mere technological tool.

It is against this backdrop of exotic translation that I situate the question of why I have chosen to study anthropology in general and Indian wrestling in particular. In a manner suggested by Roland Barthes (1972: 15–25) I see the world of Indian wrestling as myth and the project of mythological analysis as one of translation. The best translation, as Barthes observed, does not reduce experience to some level of universal truth. To translate, in the larger, anthropological sense, is constantly to question ideology with the yardstick of history; or, to paraphrase Barthes, not to let History masquerade as Nature (ibid: 11). I have chosen to study Indian wrestling with this in mind: to offer an anthropological translation of the wrestler's somaticity and thereby, in an extended sense, to call the twin sisters' exotic bluff.

I have chosen to study Indian wrestling for more specific reasons as well. Although it is a popular sport, very little has been written about this rich cultural tradition embedded within the larger Indian cultural scene either in India or in the West. For the most part, social scientists who conduct research in India have focused on well-documented and more or less clearly articulated social and cultural institutions such as caste, economics, politics, agriculture, land tenure, marriage, kinship, ritual, and religion, to name but a few. These institutions are in fact the fabricated parts of a larger, seamless social reality. While necessary, the classification of institutions—the breaking up of the whole into manageable intellectual units—entails some distortion. For example, in order to understand "caste" one must at least temporarily take it out of its holistic context and look at it on its own terms or in conjunction with some other similarly removed category such as kinship, marriage patterns, or economic interdependence. Reification is a pitfall of this kind of analysis, when one begins to think of each category as ontologically real rather than as simply heuristically useful or analytically expedient. It is the task of any study to challenge the parameters of classification—to stretch the culturally accepted boundaries—in order to get a more complete and accurate picture of the whole by constantly reflecting its component parts against one another in new ways.

The literature on India is so vast that most topics have been analyzed numerous times from countless perspectives. Caste is probably one of the most thoroughly studied institutions (Berreman 1966, 1967, 1972, 1973; Beteille 1969; Davis 1983; Harper 1964; Hocart 1950; Kolenda 1963, 1978; Lynch 1969; Marriott 1960; Srinivas 1962, 1965, 1969; Wiser 1950). This is not to suggest that something new and interesting cannot be said about it. But because Indian institutions have been thoroughly studied in their own terms, it is necessary to ask what cultural and social phenomena transcend these traditionally defined institutions. What aspects of social life do not fit so neatly or consistently onto the existing intellectual grid? How do these phenomena provide new insight into Indian civilization? What parts of the whole have not yet been compared against one another? In pursuing such inquiry and seeking an adequate translation, I have found it necessary to situate old problems and themes in new contexts. (For recent examples of this see Carman and Marglin 1985; Daniel 1984; Gold 1988; Raheja 1988.)

Wrestling transcends the categories that anthropologists and others have traditionally used to interpret Indian society and culture. It is a sport, but it is also an elaborate way of life involving general prescriptions of physical culture, diet, health, ethics, and morality. It is not caste-specific nor directly implicated in caste hierarchy. Although it is a way of life, it is not a livelihood; it is a chosen path that is not contiguous with other life paths as defined by the Hindu life cycle. As a sport wrestling provides entertainment, but this dimension is secondary. The ethic of training and psychophysical preparation is more important than the wrestling bout itself. Wrestling is not restricted to any one class of people; it is neither rural nor urban. In general, it tends to defy simple classification. However, to say that wrestling is not primarily a caste phenomenon or that it is not completely subsumed within religious, economic, or political systems is not to say that it is irrelevant to these spheres of life; quite the contrary. My argument is that wrestling is a unique and somewhat anomalous phenomenon in Indian society. As such it can shed light on familiar institutions from a dramatically new perspective.

I chose to study wrestling in the hope that the disparity between lived experience and my interpretation of that experience could be minimized. This seemed likely because wrestling is eminently public and self-conscious. A man chooses to become a wrestler and must reflect on the implications of his decision. He must struggle with a set of ideals and values and interpret their ramifications. Wrestlers reflect on what they do and why they do it in an overtly self-conscious way. They do not simply take it for granted. This fact allowed me to build my interpretation on an already well-defined pattern of self-awareness, inquiry, personal critique, and objective analysis, thus reducing the distance between their voices and mine.

I am interested in wrestling as public performance and as a stage for self-presentation because it is on such public stages that interpretations, rationalizations, and meanings are expressed and modified (Brandes 1985; Bruner 1984; Geertz 1973; Goffman 1959). All social life is public; its cultural meaning is open to continual definition and redefinition, interpretation and reinterpretation. Wrestling, like ritual, dance, and musical performance, is a dramatically public text (Ricoeur 1971). It is unique, however, in that there are relatively few absolute semantic rules which define action within the textual framework. To use Barthes's terms, one might say that wrestling is a myth that, because of its interstitial reality, lacks a consistent grammer of its own. As such, wrestling only contingently reaffirms pervasive cultural themes such as rank and status; more significantly, it opens up the stage for a protean, maverick revision of these themes.

THE FIELDWORK

I was born in North India and lived there for twenty years. I speak and read Hindi. While in high school I became well acquainted with some wrestlers and began to wrestle in local tournaments. Although I was not a successful wrestler, I became interested in the rich culture associated with wrestling as a system of physical culture and health. In 1977 I affiliated with a wrestling gymnasium under the guruship of Dr. Shanti Prakash Atreya and was introduced to Indian wrestling as not only a sport but also a way of life, a complex system of physical fitness, exercise techniques, dietary prescriptions, personal character traits, devotion, discipline, and a host of ethical values. As a result of this experience I decided to return to India in 1987 and conduct a year of field research on the culture of Indian wrestling. My exposure to wrestling made it possible to affiliate with and quickly assimilate into a new akhara and to build rapport with a number of wrestlers.

I lived for seven months, from January to July 1987, in Banaras, Uttar Pradesh, where there are over 150 active wrestling gymnasia in the city and twenty or thirty in the surrounding villages. Because wrestling is not defined by a residential community and gymnasia are not usually residential institutions, I was not able to live with the wrestlers I studied. I was closely affiliated with one gymnasium, Akhara Ram Singh, but I did not restrict my research to this group because I did not want to become so involved with the activities of one community as to be precluded from others.

Pressure is brought to bear on all members to come to their akhara regularly. I therefore rented a room in a local hotel. This proved very satisfactory on a number of counts. The hotel was centrally located five minutes from Akhara Ram Singh and within thirty minutes of most akharas in the city. By living in the hotel I was able to maintain a necessary distance between myself and the life of the gymnasium. I was thus able to type notes and generally collect my thoughts in an isolated environment. The hotel provided food, security, mail and message service, laundry, and a regular supply of water and electricity. Rather than having to attend to these mundane concerns, I was able to spend all of my time concentrating on the research project. Moreover, I was able to entertain informants/guests on short notice and in comfort.

The term "hotel" needs to be qualified, for it may conjure up inappropriate images of luxury and leisure. I stayed at the Sandeep Hotel in Chaitganj, an "Indian Style" hotel as classified by the department of tourism, used primarily by traveling businessmen and families on pilgrimage. It was inexpensive and simply appointed to a degree unfamiliar in the West. The employees of the hotel were familiar with the wrestling scene so that wrestlers who came by to visit were not at all intimidated by the surroundings.

Banaras is not a typical Indian city (cf. Eck 1982; Freitag 1989; Lutgendorf 1991). It is one of the preeminent pilgrimage centers in India. Because of its pervasive and often intense religious atmosphere it is reputed to have a character all its own. Many people with whom I spoke—wrestlers and non-wrestlers, barbers, shopkeepers, young soldiers, policemen, students, music teachers, and others—would ask with a twinkle in their eye and a sense of pride and possessive secretiveness whether I had yet "taken in the pleasure of Banaras." What they meant was, had I bathed in the Ganga River at dawn and then gone to one of the many temples for *darshan* (spiritual "viewing"); rowed across the Ganga to the sandy south shore and spent the day washing clothes, bathing, and fixing *bhang* (hashish); been to the Bari Gaivi temple and drunk the pure well water that improves digestion? Had I been to Sankat Mochan temple on a Saturday night and offered sweets prepared in pure *ghi* (clarified butter) to Lord Hanuman; been to Ramnagar across the river to witness an enactment of Tulasi Das's *Ramacaritamanasa*? Had I been in Banaras for Holi? Had I enjoyed the unique *pan* (a betel leaf, spice, and lime-paste preparation) for which Banaras is famous (cf. Kumar 1986, 1988 for an excellent discussion of leisure and pleasure in Banaras)?

Banaras is known for many things and is unique in many ways. Wrestling in Banaras, however, is the same as wrestling in Delhi, Dehra Dun, Allahabad, and any other place in North India. Wrestling holds a special place in the Banarsi ethos (cf. Kumar 1988), but it is not defined in any unique way there. In this book I will describe what wrestling means in general in North India, using Banaras as an example, rather than what it means distinctively to people in Banaras, as Kumar has done.

After seven months in Banaras I shifted the research focus from the akhara to the competitions. For five months, from August to December 1987, I lived in Delhi and Mussoorie. Though akhara training goes on year round, the competitive season begins in July with the coming of the monsoon rains and continues through the temperate season until the Holi festival at the end of March, when the heat begins to intensify. I attended wrestling bouts in Delhi, Dehra Dun, Ramnagar, Vikasnagar, Saharanpur, Roorkee, Mangalore, and other small towns and villages to get a broader picture of this dimension of wrestling, and to insure that my interpretation was not overly specific to the Banaras experience.

METHODS AND ROUTINE

One problem I encountered in the field was how to demarcate the topical boundaries of my study. I was not sure what constituted a complete picture of wrestling from an anthropological point of view. I had thought that I would join an akhara and that the boundaries of what was and what was not wrestling would be self-evident. This was not the case. I found that there were Hindu akharas, Muslim akharas, akharas where only "English" exercise was done, akharas for "Hindi" exercise, "power lifting" akharas, akharas for relaxation where little or no exercise was done, akharas with focused religious orientations and peripheral wrestling and exercise, akharas for lifting *nal*s (stone weights), and akharas exclusively for swinging *joris* (wooden clubs) and *gadas* (maces). Some of these distinctions are sharp and exclusive, as in the case of gymnasia where members practice western-style bodybuilding. Other distinctions are more fluid, as in the case of akharas which function primarily as "health spas" but also cater to and provide facilities for wrestlers and competitive jori swingers. I focused my study on Hindu akharas that emphasized wrestling. However, I found it useful to visit akharas of all types. What goes on in an akhara where bodybuilding is the focus, for instance, sheds light on general concepts of the body in all akharas. Similarly, Muslim wrestlers provide a critical appraisal of Hindu akharas, and a jori swinger or weightlifter can speak to the general aesthetic, moral, and ethical principles of gymnasium life.

RESEARCH TECHNIQUES

One morning, soon after arriving in Banaras, I got up at 5:00 and walked over to an akhara I had located the day before. It was set back from the road under banyan and *nim* trees and demarcated by a low wall. Across the road was a park and a low marshy pond. In the center of the akhara stood a large cement structure some twenty feet tall with a flat roof supported by thin posts decorated with blue line paintings of wrestlers exercising and posturing. Within this structure was the wrestling pit: a raised rectangular platform of soft, fine earth brought in yearly from village fields and raked even and flat. Around the sides of the pit were areas of hard-packed earth. To one side was a well and cement trough for bathing. Opposite this stood a small temple decorated with paintings of Hanuman, Ram, and Sita, inside of which stood the bright vermilion, cloth-bedecked, flower-garlanded form of Hanuman, the patron deity of every akhara. Beside the temple were a number of small shrines with smaller icons of Hanuman and Shiva. Leaning up against the largest of the nim trees was a broken triptych of Hanuman figures, a Shiva *lingam*, and countless small oil lamps. Behind the pit was a shedlike veranda attached to the guru's house where wrestlers changed, exercised, and massaged one another.

As I walked by early in the morning I could see from some distance away that there were about twenty young men and boys standing around the pit. On closer examination I could see pairs of wrestlers practicing their moves in the pit. One climbed up a rope attached to the largest nim tree while others performed *dand*s (jackknifing push-ups) and *bethak*s (deep knee bends), lifted weights, and swung dumbbells and wooden clubs. Not having met these wrestlers previously, or been introduced to the akhara, my plan was simply to observe the morning activities and gradually familiarize myself with the routine. However, as I walked by, all of the wrestlers in the akhara turned on me as one, slapping their thighs and beating their chests in the aggressive challenging fashion that precedes a competitive bout. Feeling that a statement was in order, I said something to the effect that I was interested in wrestling. Immediately a number of hands were proffered in challenge. At this point I could have backed down and said I just wanted to watch, but the spirit of the moment seemed right and I accepted the challenge of one of the senior members. I did not have a *langot* (g-string), but an extra one was located and I tied it on and entered the pit. For ten minutes or so I did the best I could, which is to say not very well at all; but in the end I was, if bruised, muddy, and out of breath, at least "in the door," introduced in a dramatic way to twenty members of an akhara and on my way to understanding what wrestling was all about.

My research strategy was to become a regular member of a gymnasium and study its members and daily routine in detail through regular participant observation. Ram Singh Akhara, the first akhara I visited, turned out to be the gymnasium with which I became affiliated. Every other morning from 5:00 or 5:30 until 9:00 I practiced and exercised with the members of the akhara. Most akharas are active at a very early hour so that after practice members can go to work or school. On the mornings that I did not go to Akhara Ram Singh I would go to one of the other gymnasia in the city. Although I went to numerous akharas, I returned often to Akhara Bara Ganesh near the *loha* (metal/iron) bazaar, Gaya Seth on the Grand Trunk road near Gol Gaddha, Surya Akhara near Chauk Bazaar, Sant Ram Akhara above Manikarnika Ghat, and Akhara Karanghanta near Maidagin. In the afternoons I would try to locate other akharas and, if possible, observe their evening exercise routine.

Once I had established rapport with wrestlers at several akharas I began to conduct scheduled interviews on a range of topics. These interviews came to constitute a fair percentage of the material I gathered. I conducted thirty-five formal interviews, each between an hour and an hour and a half long. These interviews were taped and then transcribed. I did not have a key informant but rather worked with seven primary informants and ten or eleven secondary informants. I surveyed thirty-five akharas in order to discern membership, management techniques, ownership, religious foci, political affiliations, and a host of other basic census data. In informal, untaped interviews I collected short life sketches of 110 wrestlers in order to determine such factors as educational background, caste, economic-class status, residence, and family wrestling history. Although important information was collected in this way, by far the most valuable information came from attending morning practice sessions, swimming in the river and visiting temples with members of the akhara, attending weddings and parties, going to wrestling bouts, and listening to gossip while lying in the cool akhara earth after an afternoon workout.

POPULAR LITERATURE

One reason I selected wrestling as a topic of study is that it is a self-conscious public activity that people choose to do. They articulate their reasons for wrestling and reflect on what wrestling as a chosen life path means to them in particular and to all wrestlers in general. Because of this there is a considerable popular literature on wrestling, often reflexive and analytical. I have termed this literature "popular" because it is stylistically neither journalistic nor scholarly. It is popular in the dual sense of being interesting and concerned with the public interest. Most journal articles and pamphlets are not simply descriptive but advocate a particular point of view directed at a specific audience. I also refer to this literature as popular because it is largely published by small local publishing houses for a restricted audience. In this regard it is distinguished from academic texts, which enjoy a much larger circulation and currency and appear, among other places, on the accessions list of the Library of Congress and the shelves of universities both in India and in the West.

The popular literature on Indian wrestling is not easy to find unless you know where to look or are directed there by those who know: the back *galis* of Chauri Bazaar in Old Delhi, the Rangmahal area of Indor, small printing establishments in Banaras, and other equally obscure places that have yet to be discovered. While I am most familiar with the Hindi-language publications of this genre (Ali 1984; Anonymous n.d.; Changani 1958; R. Gupta n.d.; M. Lal n.d.; G. Y. Manik 1964; K. Manik 1939; Mathur 1966; Patodi 1982; Sarma 1934; A. K. Singh 1983; H. Singh 1981, 1984a, 1984b; Sivnathrayji 1955), it should be

noted that there are also a number of other regional-language publications by Soman (1963, 1974) and Suryavamshi (1966) in Marathi, and
Basu (1934) and Bhadudi (1964) in Bengali.

The most significant literature of this type is published by the Bharatiya Kushti Prakashan (The Indian Wrestling Publishing House) under
the editorship of Ratan Patodi. The publishing house was established in
1968 when the editor was forced to choose between his job as a journal-
ist in Indor and his avocation of writing and publishing material on
Indian wrestling. Since 1968 some forty-five editions of the quarterly
journal *Bharatiya Kushti* (Indian Wrestling) have been published. This
journal is a source of invaluable information. Consider some of the
articles: "Physical Education in Rural Areas" by Atreya (1971); "At
What Age to Begin Wrestling" by K. P. Singh (1975); "How to Stay
Healthy During the Rainy Season" by N. Pathak (1980); "Poverty and
Health" by Atreya (1986a); "Eat Greens, Stay Healthy" by M. R.
Gupta (1973); and "A Vegetarian Diet to Increase Your Weight" by
O. P. Kumawath (1987). In addition to numerous articles on diet, health
care, exercise techniques, celibacy, morality, and religion, there are over
a hundred articles that outline the life histories of as many famous wrestlers. There are also over a hundred accounts of wrestling tournaments
in India. In short, *Bharatiya Kushti* is a remarkable source of information.

One of the most significant features of this journal is that it provides
a cross section of views on various topics by authorities on the subject
of Indian wrestling. Through a reading of the articles by Atreya, K. P.
Singh, Pathak, Malhotra, Patodi, Guru Hanuman, and others, I am able
to compare their views with those of the wrestlers I talked with and
interviewed. I have treated popular texts on wrestling in the same way
that I have treated interviews and observations. Although the voices
which speak from the written texts are voices of authority, to the extent
that they represent wrestling to a reading public, I have read these texts
as simply other voices speaking in a common public arena. Written texts
may speak more loudly and with clearer articulation, but they do not
define some objective truth; they merely add authority to the discourse.

The existence of a self-reflexive, indigenous commentary on cultural
life raises a number of interesting and problematic questions concerning
the role of the anthropologist as foreign observer. For, in effect—to
overstate the point slightly—the anthropologist is rendered impotent
and somewhat redundant when the wrestlers write their own ethnography. Or, alternatively, would I classify myself as but another wrestler

writing in a somewhat different context, to a different audience, in a different language, but with no more or less legitimacy than any other wrestler? Certainly I have more at stake as an academic scholar but less invested as a wrestler. In any case, what is somewhat blurred here is the relationship between observer and observed and this, as Clifford (1983) and Clifford and Marcus (1986) among others (Fabian 1983; Rabinow 1977; Tyler 1986) have pointed out, raises the problematic question of ethnographic authority.

Traditional anthropological exegesis is based on both eyewitness accounts and hearsay, an epistemology that almost by definition makes a sharp dichotomy between the written word and the heard word or seen event. This is simply no longer tenable, given the fact that anthropologists can no longer study isolated, illiterate groups. In an article published in *Bharatiya Kushti* entitled "Brahmacharya," Atreya quotes Goethe and the Swedish theologian Swedenborg as well as the *Bhagavad Gita* and other classical Indian texts (1973b: 24). An early text entitled *Jujitsu and Japanese Wrestling* by a Banaras resident named Kalidas Manik (1932) compares wrestling in India with wrestling in Japan. Manik admonishes young Indian wrestlers to learn Japanese moves. Banarsi Pande, a well-known wrestler in the Banaras area, was trained as an international referee at the National Institute of Sport in Patiala. He is conversant on a range of topics that includes the Swedish gymnasium movement of the early twentieth century. When I asked him to talk about the history of Indian wrestling he spoke of classical Greece and ancient Rome and referred to notes he had taken on hand-to-hand combat described in the *Mahabharata* and *Ramayana* epics. Indrasan Rai, who comes from a family of famous wrestlers, has written a doctoral dissertation for the department of Ancient Indian History, Culture and Archeology, Banaras Hindu University, on the art of wrestling in ancient India (1984). About one-sixth of the references cited in his dissertation are of works in English about western philosophy and physical education. I was introduced to Indrasan Rai by an illiterate wrestler who directed me to textual sources—newspaper clippings and commemorative souvenir volumes—when I asked him to recount his life story.

As Marcus and Fischer have rightly pointed out, it is incumbent on anthropologists to make sense of this polyphony of voices and texts (1986: 37). The goal of such an endeavor would be to produce what Clifford refers to as dialogic texts which seek to evoke meaning in an ongoing process of creative praxis (1983). The anthropologist's voice is introduced into the arena not as any sort of final authority on represented truth but as yet another redactor of partial knowledge. A number of anthropologists have experimented with various techniques to try to reorient the anthropologist's voice in the larger discourse of ethnographic work (cf. Crapanzano 1980; Narayan 1989; M. Rosaldo 1980). The world of Indian wrestling affords a unique opportunity to examine the theoretical implications for anthropology of textual intersubjectivity. If Goethe and Swedenborg can be quoted as sources on Indian wrestling, and if wrestlers write about themselves in objective, self-reflexive intellectual terms, then where do we draw the line between text, context, and author? And who draws it?

HISTORICAL TEXTS AND THE PROBLEM OF HISTORY

It is now accepted in anthropology that cultural analysis must somehow be contexualized within a historical framework (Cohn 1987; Fabian 1983; R. Rosaldo 1980; Sahlins 1981, 1986). This is not to say that ethnography must be predicated upon historical reconstruction. History must be integrated into a holistic understanding of institutions and groups. It is not enough to make reference to the past without a critical evaluation of how the history of an event is as much a reflection of current concerns as it is an objective, impartial description. Conversely, a reevaluation of history can shed significant light on the way in which ethnography is interpreted and analyzed. In this study a lack of historical information prevents me from using history in this way.

One of the greatest frustrations in dealing with wrestling is the paucity of historical material. There are a number of cultural histories of various epochs that mention wrestling in passing but say little beyond an indication that it was a popular pastime of kings and princes (Chopra 1963; Dayal 1981: 40; Suryavanshi 1962: 63, 64). A brief account is given in *The Encyclopedia of Sport* (Pollok 1911: 353), and a short synopsis appears in *Man* (Hornblower 1928: 65) where reference is made to an earlier account in the *Times* of March 2, 1928. There are brief accounts of wrestling during the Mogul period in the *Babur Nama* (Beveridge 1921: 656, 660, 683), the *Akbar-Nama* (Blochmann 1904: [I] 456–487, [III] 482) and the *Ain-i-Akbari* (Blochmann 1873–1948: [I] 263). Wrestling is described in *Dharmamangala*, a Bengali poem by Chanaram Chakravarty (1900: 51). Wrestling, along with other sports, is described by Tridib Nath Roy in "Indoor and Outdoor Games in Ancient India" (1939), and by Dr. V. Raghavan in *Festivals, Sports and*

Pastimes of India (1979). Short accounts of wrestling during the epic ages are given by S. Bhattacharya in *Mahabharata Kalin Samaj* (Society in the Mahabharata Era; 1966), and S. K. N. Vyas in *Ramayana Kalin Samaj* (Society in the Ramayana Era; 1958). L. Singh discusses wrestling as a martial art in *Ramayankalin mein Yuddhakala* (Martial Arts in the Ramayana Era; 1982–1983). M. Rai situates wrestling in a larger context of royal entertainment in his *Prachin Bharatiya Manoranjan* (Entertainment in Ancient India; 1956). The problem with all of these secondary sources on wrestling is that they are based on the same limited corpus of primary texts. There is much repetition but little elaboration.

In his doctoral dissertation entitled *Prachin Bharat mein Mallavidya* (Wrestling Knowledge in Ancient India), Indrasan Rai (1984) has synthesized historical references to wrestling into a comprehensive analytical survey. Rai has systematically gone through Hindu, Buddhist, and Jain texts and painstakingly compiled a historical picture of wrestling. However, because most texts deal with wrestling only marginally, the historical picture of wrestling is partial and opaque. Moreover, Rai's study treats history in a scheme of "now" and "then," with "then" representing a vast, unchanging, primordial past. Through no fault of his own, Rai's work provides a thin description of wrestling in this generalized past, without depth or sense of change because there is simply not enough material to suggest any process of development.

Balbir Singh's study of wrestling history, *Bharat de Pahalwan: 1635–1935* (Wrestlers of India: 1635–1935; 1964) is a more focused and therefore comprehensive work. Written in Punjabi, it is a catalogue of famous wrestlers and their accomplishments, which, though extremely useful in its own right, simply extends the boundary of the present into the past and does not provide a historical understanding of what constituted a wrestling way of life in, for instance, the eighteenth century. In any case there is no historical connection among accounts of wrestling in the *Ramayana* (thirteenth-century Gujarat), *Mahabharata* (twelfth-century South India), and *Jataka Tales* (eighteenth-century Delhi). The texts that deal with these periods do not provide us with a comprehensive history of wrestling, but with static, dated accounts.

Two of these deserve special mention: the *Malla Purana* and the *Manasollasa*. The *Malla Purana*, edited by B. J. Sandesara and R. N. Mehta (1964), is a caste purana dating most likely to the thirteenth century A.D. (ibid: 6). The purana is a dissertation on, and description of, the Jyesthimallas—a "caste" of professional wrestlers—in medieval Gujarat. It categorizes and classifies types of wrestlers, defines necessary physical characteristics, and describes types of exercise and techniques of wrestling as well as the preparation of the wrestling pit. The text of the *Malla Purana* is Sanskrit, but the editors have provided an English synopsis in their extensive introduction. Veena Das has studied the *Malla Purana* from a sociological perspective, focusing her inquiry on why priests, who would not usually adopt a martial art, became professional wrestlers (1968, 1970).

A second text of particular significance is the *Manasollasa* of the twelfth-century Deccan king Somesvara (Srigondekar 1959). This is a general treatise on royal fine arts and leisure and contains a detailed description of the art of wrestling. Rai (1984) has referred to this text as the wrestler's "Gita" since it is both a practical and philosophical account of wrestling as a science, an art, and a way of life. However, aside from Rai, Atreya, and a few other "academic wrestlers," not many contemporary wrestlers know of this text. Although more detailed than other texts, the *Manasollasa* only gives the names of moves and exercises but does not provide descriptions.

It is worth noting that while wrestling is regarded as a martial art, it is rarely mentioned in accounts of epic or medieval military history (Chakravarti 1972; Hopkins 1972; B. K. Majumdar 1960; Oppert 1967; G. Pant 1970; J. N. Sarkar 1984; Wilson 1979; cf. also Deopujari 1973 and Irvine 1962 for accounts of Maratha and Mogul warfare respectively). When it is mentioned it is regarded as much less important than swordsmanship, archery, equestrian skill, and the other "high" arts of military combat. One reason for this may be that wrestling, no matter how well developed and refined as a fighting skill, remained a basic form of hand-to-hand combat and did not enjoy the glory and prestige of the more technologically sophisticated arts of war. Another reason may be that wrestling was regarded more as a dueling art than as a mode of field combat. Many of the epic accounts describe wrestling as taking place in an arena rather than on the battlefield, and in this respect wrestling may be regarded as the diametrical opposite of war. Consequently, one reason why wrestling may not appear in many accounts of military history is that its ambiguous status as art/sport/combat/way of life may have made it difficult to classify.

Given the paucity of historical accounts about wrestling and the generally opaque and thin description of the sport when it is mentioned, I do not believe that an adequate history of wrestling can be written now, if what we mean by such a history is the systematic developmental analysis of an institution or point of view—what Foucault calls genealogy—rather than the objective quest for origins or the abstract construction of an uncritical chronology. Foucault has clearly pointed out the pitfalls of venturing into the arena of history with preconceived notions of what to look for and where to find it (1984*a*: 76–100). He suggests, instead, that a meticulous genealogical method must be applied to create a reformed "effective" history that "deprives the self of the reassuring stability of life and nature, and . . . will not permit itself to be transported by a voiceless obstinacy toward a millennial ending. It will . . . relentlessly disrupt its pretended continuity" (ibid: 88).

The scattered fragments of information about wrestling are interesting in their own right but do not fit together in a complete picture. For this reason, I have incorporated dated texts into this book not as genealogy or history but as voices from another time speaking on various pervasive themes. To do so is unfortunate and methodologically tenuous, but unavoidable owing to the paucity of sources. A proper genealogy of the wrestler's body must await further study.

The same situation applies on a much more abbreviated time scale. I was told in a number of interviews that wrestling was very popular during the nationalist movement (mid-nineteenth century until 1947) when the ideology of nationalism was apparently closely allied with a wrestling way of life. There are tantalizing hints at how this coalescence began and developed. For instance, Gama, the great Indian wrestler of the early twentieth century, went to London in 1920 under the sponsorship of a wealthy Bengali merchant. He soundly defeated all of the British champions at a time when Indian nationalism was reaching its full strength. He returned to India a national hero (Alter: manuscript). Madan Mohan Malaviya, Bal Gangadhar Tilak, and Moti Lal Nehru all were strong advocates of physical education and akhara culture as a necessary component of building a free India (Karandikar 1957: 48). D. C. Mujumdar's *Encyclopedia of Indian Physical Culture* (1950), and the earlier, more comprehensive, Marathi text in ten volumes on which that work is based, implicitly advocate a nationalist ideology (1950: xxiv). The references to wrestling as an ideal of physical culture during the independence movement are scant and oblique. We know, for instance, that Mahatma Gandhi said that "in the search for wisdom, physical education ought to have a status equal to that of learning" (Patodi 1973*a*: 33), but we are not told how or why. Similarly Tilak is reputed to have said, "I call on students and youth to be devoted to strength and celibacy. Without wisdom and strength we cannot foster and protect

our liberty. The freedom of the nation is dependent on the courageous"
(Patodi 1973*a*: 62).

It is clear that Indian nationalists were advocates of a wrestling way
of life, but there is not yet enough evidence to write an effective history
of their views. John Rosselli has authored a brief account of the role of
physical culture in the formation of a nationalist ideology in nineteenth-
century Bengal (1980). To fill out the picture, similar and more comprehensive studies are needed for other parts of India.

A history of Indian wrestling can and likely will be written. However,
in doing so it would be wrong to look for the roots of a nationalist
ideology in the disciplinary practices of thirteenth- or eighteenth-century
wrestling. One must begin with the body and proceed not to a "rediscov-
ery of ourselves" (Foucault 1984*a* :88) but to an exegesis of the mechanics and mythology of domination.

THE WRESTLER'S BODY: IDENTITY, IDEOLOGY, AND MEANING

As a sport, wrestling evokes images of various kinds. The most pervasive and powerful of these images in the United States and other Western
countries (cf. Barthes 1972: 15–26; Craven and Mosley 1972; Morton
1985) is professional wrestling. According to Barthes, this genre of wrestling is a "great spectacle of Suffering, Defeat, and Justice" (1972: 19).

Although morality is a central feature of Indian wrestling, it is not
professional wrestling in Barthes's sense. It is not a spectacle. Wrestling
bouts are dramatic, but they are not self-conscious performances. The
contests are not "rigged," nor do the contestants adopt burlesque roles
as cult figures. Unlike the Western professional wrestler who epitomizes
a particular moral virtue, the Indian wrestler embodies a whole ideology.
As such he is an ideal figure rather than a simple caricature, a culture
hero and not a scaramouche.

Although a complete picture of Indian wrestling will emerge in this
book, it is necessary to provide a basic frame of reference—however
cryptic—in order to give a point of comparative orientation. The rules
of Indian wrestling are very close to the rules of Olympic freestyle wrestling. As a sport, wrestling is a leisure activity. It is entertaining for
both wrestlers and spectators alike; it is a medium for relaxation and
competition. This is not to say, however, that wrestling is somehow
marginal to the core factors of "real life"—production, exchange, domestic life, politics, and religion. Leisure and entertainment are no less

real on account of their "non-utility" than is production real on account of its fundamental use value. Because sport is fun does not in any way mean that it is insignificant. As a cultural system, sport is meaningful to the same extent as systems of production and exchange. That sport is seen, in contrast to drama, dance, business, and education, as nothing more than "fun" is an unfortunate fact of cultural chauvinism. One aspect of this study is to show how one sport, Indian wrestling, is an integral and important part of everyday life. A number of people—businessmen, college professors, and peasant farmers—regarded it as the most important medium through which to think about themselves and to make sense of their world.

Wrestling is more than a sport, it is a vocation: a way of life. One chooses to become a wrestler. My focus is not on moves and countermoves, holds, takedowns, or the other skills a wrestler must master. I am interested in the ideals and values associated with wrestling as a more or less bounded system of meaning. Although much of what wrestlers do is to practice techniques and moves, they regard this aspect of their art as specialized and somewhat esoteric. In contrast to the unproblematic issue of skill and technique, the wrestler is eminently concerned with such complex questions as the relationship between moral and physical strength, abstinence and celibacy. As such, wrestlers are concerned with wrestling as a way of life that defines the boundaries of their everyday actions.

For a wrestler, wrestling and all it entails is an ideology, a partial and incomplete but nevertheless holistic ordering of the world. At the locus of this ideology is the identity of the wrestler—what it means, among other things, to be strong, skillful, celibate, devoted, dutiful, honest, and humble. In order to explain this it is necessary to work through the implications of what is meant by "system of meaning," "identity," and "ideology."

It is by now a commonplace in anthropology, following Geertz, to recognize that meaning is the central problematic in understanding culture. The project of an interpretive approach is not to unlock hidden objective truths, but to engage in an ongoing dialogue from which emerges the textured fabric of cultural meaning. The focus is not on deep structures or fundamental principles but on cultural texts: experience as lived and expressed in everyday life.

Meaning cannot be reduced to first principles or located objectively in symbolic forms, social organization or elementary structures. As Bourdieu writes, "[t]he mind is a metaphor of the world of objects which is itself but an endless circle of mutually reflecting metaphors" (1977: 91). Bourdieu would be quick to add, however, that on this level of pure pastiche there is very little significance to the meaning of metaphor. To get at the significance of cultural production and reproduction one must consider both identity and ideology.

Because meaning is a derivative of interpretation and not intrinsic to symbolic forms, the role of the interpreter becomes very significant. The place of the actor in social discourse is important for understanding how persons manipulate and produce meaning. Through interaction with others, people construct their own biographies. In turn, these biographies become the basis for further interaction. One aspect of culture is the collective memory of biographies emerging from and creating a shared history. It must be remembered, however, that one person's experience of the world through intersubjective interpretation is necessarily partial and incomplete. The self is fragmentary, and people may act in terms of a particular matrix of these fragments—as they may perform a role—but a characteristic feature of the self is that it is only partially realized. As Simmel has noted, self-knowledge is inherently imperfect (Natanson 1973: xl). What this suggests, however, is not a pejorative condition, but rather a possibility for persons to borrow from other contexts and other partial and imperfect formulations in order to redefine themselves (cf. Rabinow 1983). In this context the self is not a partial reflection of an a priori social reality but instead the locus of intersubjective reflexivity (cf. Babcock 1980; Bruner 1984; Fernandez 1980).

The creative process of inventing and interpreting meaning does not take place in a vacuum. People spin the webs of their own significance, but they are constrained in the range, direction, and extent of their own action. That people tend to define themselves in terms of common values is an expression of shared cultural tradition. It is also, however, an expression of ideological constraint and domination. By definition any cultural tradition is exclusive—holistic in terms of itself but not universal—and defines appropriate and inappropriate domains of action. In this regard any culture is necessarily partial, and when juxtaposed to another culture it is at least partially subversive. What is considered to be real and meaningful in one context may in a larger context—and therefore more political arena—be peddled as universal truth. I follow Habermas (1972) in his treatment of ideology as "distorted communication" and extend this to include the whole range of culture. An ideology is a powerful cultural system for it is regarded as an immutable paradigm for interpreting meaning and guiding action (Geertz 1973: 220; cf. Ricoeur 1986).

The value of a theory of ideology, following Giddens, is that it provides a critique of domination (1979: 187). If one speaks, as Giddens suggests, in terms of the "ideological" rather than in terms of institutionalized ideologies as such, then the concept denotes some features of what Bourdieu calls habitus, "the source of these series of moves which are objectively organized as strategies without being the product of a genuine strategic intention—which would presuppose at least that they are perceived as one strategy among other possible strategies" (1977: 73). What makes habitus "ideological" is not only its "strategic" quality but the fact that it operates in a covert manner. Those who are engaged in the practice of habitus—the replication and reproduction of various forms of domination—are not fully aware of all of the ramifications of their actions (ibid: 79).

I use ideology to mean what Raymond Williams, following Gramsci, terms the *hegemonic*. Hegemony is not a formal structure of consciousness and control; rather, it refers to "relations of subordination and domination" embedded in the commonsense world of everyday life (1977: 110). Domination of this sort can be reflected with considerable power in seemingly innocuous areas: a work of art, seating arrangements, smoking etiquette, dietary patterns, body aesthetics. Rather than adopt Williams's terminology, I will use the term *ideology* to denote the everyday relations of subordination and domination embedded in culture (cf. Barnett 1977; Barnett and Silverman 1979).

Although ideologies present themselves as totalizing and immutable, they cannot explain everything. Moreover, alternative ideologies provide different possible interpretations of a single phenomenon. Barnett has provided a detailed and flexible model for understanding how persons act in terms of their ideological stance (1977). The important point in his formulation is that while persons act in terms of one ideology they have a partial understanding of how other ideologies work. They have at least a nascent idea that something can be understood from another perspective (ibid: 276).

My argument, following the spirit if not the letter of Barnett's model, is that people can change their ideological stance given persuasive counterinterpretations of experience. In order to make sense of a situation a person may interpret the significance of particular symbols in a novel way. What is crucial, however, is that the new interpretation is not pure invention but is rather the product of symbolic domination. The forms of ideological protest and counterinterpretation are encoded in the dominant symbols themselves. Giddens has focused much of his work on this point. He argues that action emanates from structure and "that the reflexive monitoring of action both draws upon and reconstitutes the institutional organization of society" (1979: 255). Action does not follow a tangent of its own making; its course is set by pervasive structural themes (ibid: 5; cf. also Barnett and Silverman 1979: 37). Ideological form, according to Barnett and Silverman, is not structured by static categories but rather by eruptions of conflict, by disjunction rather than consensus. Domination defines the parameters of protest and interpretation. Or, as Raymond Williams puts it, "the dominant culture, so to say, at once produces and limits its own forms of counter-culture" (1977: 114).

To apply this argument to the Indian case, one may say that an effective counterinterpretation of caste hierarchy is necessarily couched in terms of the pervasive and dominant symbols of purity and pollution. Barnett has shown that dramatic ideological change takes place through the reinterpretation of blood symbolism within the context of caste identity (1977: 283). As a referent for common group identity, blood can mean either holistic interdependence and membership in a caste group, or it can come to refer to substance and evoke notions of individuality, class, and ethnicity (ibid: 283). Blood as substance, however, is charged with significance precisely because it is a dominant symbol of the holistic caste ideology. It can come to be a powerful referent for racism in India because it has significance in the domain of caste interdependence.

If this perspective is reversed, one is led to ask not what caste has come to mean in India, as Barnett has done, but rather how political protest movements against caste have been articulated. Untouchability in India has been attacked from countless perspectives: the humanism of Gandhi, the democratic socialism of Nehru, the egalitarian reform of the Arya Samaj, the proto-Buddhism of Ambedkar, and the militancy of the Dalit Panthers, to name but a few. All of these forms of protest attack the institution of untouchability and suggest reform through the promotion of ethnic pride, democracy, equality, or empowerment. Reform of this type can work, and has been shown to work in particular cases. However, the fact that untouchables become Buddhists, Muslims, or advocates of democratic equality or leftist revolution does not challenge the principles of caste ideology as such. This point must be emphasized. One ideology can displace another, but what often happens is that formal change of this sort is rendered impotent by the pervasive power of the embedded ideology.

Although religious and political reform movements can be effective, they do not, so to speak, take the bull by the horns. The encoded hegemonic forces of power are not confronted on their own terms when legislation or revolt is directed at social groups or institutions who simply manifest authority. Buddhist converts become stigmatized as untouchables; low-caste persons are denied access to education, legal process, political power, temples, tea shops, and gymnasia even when legislation and public opinion seem to be in their interest. What is to be made of this paradox? I do not presume to have the whole answer, but in confronting the problem I do not locate power in the institution of high caste groups as such, or with any group in particular. The invidious nature of deeply rooted power is manifested, among other places, in the code of purity and pollution. If, for example, stigma is located in physical contact and saliva—that which pollutes tea cups and cigarettes—then one must address questions concerning the nature of ideological power to that level. To highlight the most invidious nature of power, Foucault has drawn attention along these lines to the historically situated human body (1978, 1979).

My purpose in taking up the issue of caste ideology is to understand how invidious distinctions are encoded as dominant symbols in everyday life and how these symbols can be rendered less powerful—or equally powerful in a different way—through counterinterpretation. Barnett has shown that blood purity can translate hierarchy into, among other things, racism. My point is that key symbols such as asceticism, which tend to reinforce hierarchy, at least in the context of the dominant caste ideology, can be reinterpreted to undercut caste principles. Although it may seem that wrestling has little to do with caste hierarchy, my argument is that it does. This is not because wrestling provides a forum for social protest against stratification, but rather because it is a context in which the meaning of particular key symbols that relate to the embeddedness of caste are significantly reinterpreted through the medium of the human body.

BODY DISCIPLINE: THE MECHANICS OF REFORM

Recently the body has become a subject of interest in anthropology and the other human sciences (cf. Blacking 1977; Comaroff 1985;

Kunzel 1981; Scarry 1985; Scheper-Hughes and Lock 1987; B. Turner 1984). While much of this literature is in the area of medical anthropology, there is also an extensive literature on embodiment and sport (cf. Morgan and Klaus 1988). The literature on "things somatic" is, of course, voluminous and incorporates a host of perspectives. Recent work has been most successful, however, in demonstrating that the body is not only "good to think with" as Lévi-Strauss (1966), Leach (1958, 1976), Douglas (1970) and V. Turner (1969) might have it, but is also acted upon through what Foucault has termed a "political anatomy." (cf. Scheper-Hughes and Lock 1987). In this political anatomy the body is broken down into elemental units and physiological processes. It is made docile and subject, drained of any "natural" process so that all processes reflect neither pure biology nor pure culture but a history of power relations (Foucault 1984*b*: 182). Foucault has referred to various disciplinary regimens as "projects of docility" wherein the biomechanics of control are located in the regulation of movement—balance, precision, gesture, posture—rather than in the interpretation of signs (1979: 136).

Everyone who has studied Hindu life has to some extent noted the importance of the body in ritual, health, cosmology, and everyday life. The institution of caste rules and regulations is but one arena in which the Hindu body is made the docile subject of a pervasive political anatomy. Dumont (1970) and others have noted that Hindu society may be seen in terms of the largely somatic principles of purity and pollution. More recently Daniel, drawing in part on Marriott and Inden's theory of coded substance (1977), has suggested that caste is but one manifestation of a more basic scheme of "differentially valued and ranked substances": blood, food properties, earth qualities, spatial aesthetics, and sexual fluids (1984: 2). What is at issue in this matrix of coded substance, I think, is the relationship between identity, culture, and the political anatomy to which the body is subject. To what extent, under what circumstances, in what shape, and with what qualifications does a person emerge from the intersection of these forces?

It is against this backdrop of coded substance, rules of caste propriety, and somatic aesthetics that the body of the wrestler may be seen, not simply as a signifier of meaning, but as a subject actor in a larger drama of culture and power. Since wrestling is so meticulously concerned with a unique form of body discipline—which in Foucault's sense is more a function of mechanics than meaning—one is led to ask how this discipline affects identity. Who does the physically fit wrestler think he is, and how, by virtue of what he does, is he different from the average man on the street?

These issues revolve, I think, around the nature of the person in Hindu South Asia. Dumont was perhaps the first to clearly show how the ideology of caste structures identity. Where Dumont saw caste structure as the overarching rubric of culture and identity, others have posited a more elemental structure based on coded substance (Marriott and Inden 1977; Daniel 1984). Although Daniel has criticized the extreme ethnosociology Marriott advocates (ibid: 54), his own work is aimed, it seems to me, at the same level of analysis, even though it gets there by a different, more fluid route. Regardless, in most instances there is a good "fit" between these two modes of interpretation—caste-based principles or ethnosociologically defined codes of substance—if only because many codes are keyed to an ideology of caste. However, this is by no means always the case. As Daniel's work in particular has suggested, there are many arenas where the fit is neither good nor complete, and so the person must negotiate the rough terrain of an uncharted course. It is along these lines that the world of wrestling provides an interesting case in point.

Wrestling is unique in one respect, however. It takes direct issue with the lack of "fit" between a caste-based interpretation of the body and a distinct wrestling interpretation of the body. The exigency of close physical contact can not be ignored. That is, the wrestler does not pander to the inconsistencies of forced rationalization—he takes the bull by the horns, so to speak, and marks off, in bold steps, the terms of his own identity. He refuses to say that his world is of marginal, contingent significance. Unlike Barthes's French wrestler, the Indian wrestler does not raise moral questions only for the sake of spectacle. He cannot simply leave the akhara and safely say, this is this and that is that, for he embodies the contradictions his actions engender. In embodying moral questions the wrestler does not directly challenge caste values, but he does restructure some of the codes to such an extent as to throw into question the logic, and thereby the power, of the dominant ideology.

CHAPTER 2

The Akhara: Where Earth Is Turned Into Gold

What is an akhara? It is a place of recreation for youth. It is a shrine of strength where earth is turned into gold. It is a sign of masculinity and the assembly hall of invigorated youth. Strength is measured against strength and moves and counter moves are born and develop. An akhara should be in an open area where fresh air and sunshine mingle. It should be away from dirt and filth and in a place where the earth is soft. It should be set off by a boundary of some sort and surrounded by thick foliated trees. There should be water nearby.

One should enter the akhara after paying obeisance and offering up incense to the Lord. An akhara is where one prays and where offerings are given and distributed. Its earth is saluted and taken up to anoint one's shoulders and head. And then one wrestles and the sound of slapping thighs and pounding chests fills the air. Grunts and groans of exertion echo ominously. One trounces and in turn is trounced. Exercise is done. Laziness and procrastination are drowned in sweat. The earth is mixed and finally one salutes the pit and leaves.

Patodi 1973a: 34

AESTHETICS

The spatial layout of an akhara is important insofar as it produces a geomantic aura of invigorating peace and tranquility. The ideal location for an akhara is a cool, clean, quiet area where one can get away from both an atmosphere of domestic obligation and an environment of work. One can well imagine the importance of such a place in the crowded

26

environment of urban India. However, the aesthetic ideals apply equally to rural as well as urban akharas. On entering the compound of a number of different akharas, I was asked if I could sense an aura of *shant* (peace and tranquility). Indicating the shade of a tree, the aroma of freshly moistened earth and the coolness of a refreshing breeze, wrestling friends would abandon themselves to a revery of cathartic relaxation. Indeed, it seemed that many who came to Akhara Ram Singh and the other akharas I visited regularly did so in much the same way that one might visit a health spa. Older men came to relax before going to work and younger boys would rest on their way to school. People with minor ailments—constipation, arthritis, backaches, skin infections, bruises, and sprains—came to the akhara hoping to effect a cure. Wrestling-pit earth and akhara well water are both regarded as tonics which help to cure a host of common ailments. In many ways the earth pit functions much like a mineral bath that has a reputation for healing. Many wrestlers I spoke with claimed that they had at one time or another suffered some debilitating illness—rheumatisum, consumption, heart weakness, high blood pressure, kidney stones—and that after visiting an akhara and lying in the earth had been restored to perfect health.

Akharas have a definite aesthetic appeal. Their visual tone is picturesque. Consider, for example, Akhara Bara Ganesh in the Lohatia bazaar of Banaras. The akhara is not visible from the main street, but its location is marked by the bright green leaves of a tall pipal tree and the thicker darker mass of a young nim (see plate 1).

As the name implies, Lohatia bazaar is a metal market and the main cobblestone road which runs through the market is lined with encroaching shops that sell thick-slatted parrot cages, buffalo tethering spikes, drum-sized cauldrons for boiling milk, and ladles whose size would match the cutlery of Ravana's kitchen. Anvils, arc-welders, and rivet wrenches spark, flash, and grind as contractors turn out dozens of bathtub-size feeding troughs, evaporative air-coolers, and meter upon meter of chain link.

Heading towards Maidagin and the old central post office, one turns left off the main road down a *gali* (narrow lane) which leads toward Bara Ganesh temple. A high river-rock retaining wall parallels the left side of the gali which leads directly up to a niche-shrine dedicated to lord Hanuman. Seated in the niche, a man reads verses from Tulasi Das's epic poem *Ramacaritamanasa* and dispenses Ganga river water and *prasad* (ritually blessed food offerings) to men on scooters on their way to work and to women returning home with bottles of milk, who stop to pay homage to the Lord. Hawkers of marigold garlands, incense, jasmine flowers, and other ritual paraphernalia line the small path that turns left at the niche shrine and winds its way to the gates of Ganesh's temple. Beggars mirror the hawkers on the opposite side of the path and benevolently accept alms from those in search of grace. The path continues a short way beyond the temple gates until a short flight of stairs leads one up to the left, through an arch, and into the akhara grounds.

Bara Ganesh Akhara is situated on a flat bluff twelve meters above the main Lohatia bazaar and some six meters above Ganesh's temple. The retaining wall demarcates two edges of the compound, and buildings set off the other two sides, making a rough rectangle some forty meters long and seventeen meters wide. Although the akhara is raised above the street and the temple gate, buildings, spires, and crenellations frame the grounds and shade the pit from all but the midday sun.

Walking up the stairs and through the arch, one directly faces the main Hanuman temple of the akhara complex. The temple building itself is new: a modern, square, flat-roofed brick and concrete construction, lime-washed yellow. The image of Hanuman—who is serviced by a semiresident priest—dates back to antiquity; I was told, "There is not another one like it in Banaras." The grounds of the akhara are ample, and since the guru of Akhara Bara Ganesh is both a dairy farmer and a purveyor of sheet metal, the area in front of the temple is used as a buffalo corral and a storage area for tin tubs, water tanks, buckets, roofing material, and sundry other items. Lallu Pahalwan, the guru of the akhara, can be found every morning sitting on his cot among his buffalos dispensing fresh milk from two polished tin buckets.

Just beyond the buffalos and tin tubs is a brick water drain, which marks an important spatial boundary. On the temple side of the drain the ground is covered with stubbly grass, bits of old metal, buffalo dung, sleeping dogs, and playing children. In sharp contrast, the opposite side of the drain is smooth, flat, hard-packed earth from which playing children and wandering dogs are unceremoniously chased. This is where the akhara precinct begins.

The akhara precinct is almost completely shaded by two large trees: a thick, broad nim that hangs low over the pit and a tall pipal that rises above the well. Under the shade of these trees, in the shadow of bazaar buildings, set against the temple skyline, stands the pit. It is the focal point of the akhara complex. Seven by seven meters square and a quarter-meter high, the soft red earth forms a large raised arena. Six cement

columns stand at the four corners and at the center of two sides, supporting a tin roof which creates a canopy under the heavy branches of the
nim. The columns are thickset, made of poured concrete and painted
yellow. Each one is decorated with a mural drawing: a thickset wrestler
lifting a *nal* (stone weight) over his head; another wrestler swinging a
pair of joris; two wrestlers locked together measuring each other's
strength; Lord Hanuman flying through the air carrying a mountain in
one hand and a mace in the other; Shiva bedecked in peacock feathers
holding a flaming jori in either hand. Vases of flowers supported on the
backs of jumping monkeys decorate the inner face of the four corner
columns. Intertwined blue cobras drinking from bowls of milk are juxtaposed on the center posts.

On the temple side of the akhara, overlooking the lane where mendi-
cants and lepers beg for alms and under the thickest branches of the
nim, stands a short, thick, stone dais. Lallu Pahalwan can often be found
reclining on the cool, hard stone holding audience with merchants, men-
dicants, and members of his family while casting a benevolent yet critical
eye on his practicing disciples. As Lallu reclines and his wards grapple,
rhesus monkeys, in their haste to get a share of prasad at the temple,
occasionally abandon the branches of the nim and race thunderously
across the tin roof of the pit beating a tattoo matched only by the
laborers in the gali below, who pound sheet metal into popsicle molds,
leaf springs, and saw blades. The sound of monkeys on the roof, the
gali, horns and bicycle bells on the road, prayer gongs in the temple, and
ubiquitous loudspeakers broadcasting popular film songs and praises to
the gods all blend into a distant cacophonous refrain that both envelopes
and sets the akhara apart, if only by contrast and juxtaposition.

Across the pit from the guru's dais is a larger, wide stone bench used
by the elder members of the akhara, who come to relax and watch the
younger members practice. Behind this, and raised up half a meter, is a
one-room cement building used to store exercise equipment, house visiting wrestlers, and change clothes, and to exercise and massage when the
monsoon rains turn the hard-packed earth to mud.

Rooted at the opposite corner of the pit from the nim, the pipal tree
is set in tiered, concentric circles of poured concrete. Built onto this in
the lee of the trunk is a small, brightly painted shrine dedicated to the
memory of a neighborhood saint. As the story goes, even after the saint's
death his form could be seen wandering around after dark. Once a
curious neighbor followed the form and saw it disappear into the trunk
of the pipal. A shrine was erected in propitiation, and a few devotees

come regularly to make offerings and ask for boons. The figure of the saint, who stands behind the iron gate of the shrine in a pose of contemplative prayer, is blessed, on occasions, by the akhara priest.

The akhara well is sunk behind the pipal. Being on high ground, the well is deep and the water cool. A large bucket suspended from a cantilevered pully is used to draw water. Set into the edge of the well and along the base of the pipal is a large, green, moss-lined cement trough used to hold water drawn from the well. A spigot at the base of the trough allows the water to drain into the bathing area, and from there out through the drain that marks the boundary of the akhara precinct and into the toilet at the far edge of the compound.

To appreciate the aesthetics of the space I have described above, it is necessary to take the perspective of an akhara member. Consider, for example, Amru Dada, who owns an extensive gold and silver business with a shop in the heart of the crowded Chauk Bazaar area of old Banaras. The shop is set in a narrow, busy gali off the main road. Though large as such shops go, it is cramped and confined. It is hot, and the air is redolent with incense, smoke, raw sewage, and dust. Amru Dada tends the shop from ten in the morning until eight or nine at night. The clean, cool air, soft earth, shaded light, and cold, fresh well water of the akhara stand in sharp contrast with the thick, dense smells and harsh sounds of urban life that waft and resonate in the back galis. For Amru Dada the akhara is a retreat. It is also a much-needed escape for other wrestlers who labor as dairy farmers, clerks in government offices, cooks and waiters in hotels and sweet shops, dry-goods merchants, policemen, railway personnel, hotel managers, military recruits, and pan hawkers. The akhara is, as many were fond of telling me, eagerly in animated tones and pointed gestures and, at other times, in hushed, dreamy, relaxed voices, "a world unto itself," a place set apart from the world of work and family, a peaceful place from which to draw strength. Atreya describes the aura of his akhara at Kuthal Gate, Dehra Dun district: "Upon arriving at this place one will feel a mood of self-reflection. Thoughts will turn from instinct and mundane concerns to more philosophical questions. The place is charged with an atmosphere of metaphysical reflection" (1981: 64).

Earth, air, water, and trees are the essential features which give an akhara its aesthetic appeal. The ambiance of an akhara, however, is greater than the sum of these individual parts. Although there are no rules that govern the spatial layout and geomantic ordering of trees relative to earth, air, and water, there is a sense that together they must

comprise a picturesque integrated whole: a tableau of mutually dependent elements. The roots of the trees mingle with the water of the well;
the air is cooled by the shade of the trees and is scented by their leaves.
The earth is bound by the roots of the trees and, like the water, it draws
on the ineffable essence of the trees and imparts to them the resources
of growth. The water dampens and cools the earth, and the earth keeps
the water fresh. The interdependence of natural elements reinforces a
notion of the akhara as self-contained, an aesthetic world unto itself.

Chapter 6 of the *Malla Purana* (Sandesara and Mehta 1964) describes
in some detail the exact dimensions of various types of wrestling
pits—square, rectangular and round. This text also elaborates upon the
quality of the pit earth, emphasizing that color and texture are important
and that it must be "pleasing to see and as soft as that required for seed
laying" (ibid: 21). Sandesara and Mehta note that the *malla*s (wrestlers)
of contemporary Gujarat mix various substances—buttermilk, oil, red
ochre—into the earth to enhance its quality and texture (ibid: 26). At
various akharas I have heard wrestlers talk of times when baskets full
of rose petals and bottles of fragrant perfume would be added to the pit.
Turmeric is often mixed into the earth to enhance its healing properties
(Vaishya 1975). The earth of the pit is the nexus of the akhara complex
as a whole: it is the distillate of the compound's physical elements and
of its cultural meaning as well. The earth is the essence of strength.

The balance of earth, wind, water, and trees is best exemplified by
Akhara Bari Gaivi. Bari Gaivi is as much a "therapeutic" akhara as it
is an active wrestling gymnasium. Most people who come to the akhara
do so to drink the tonic water of the central well, which has a national
reputation for curing gastrointestinal maladies. In addition to a wrestling pit and exercise area, Bari Gaivi has a well-established temple
complex.

The akhara used to be outside the city limits in a thick forested area.
Now the city has encroached on the akhara, drawing it into a more
urban environment. Nevertheless, the akhara grounds are clearly demarcated from the surrounding area. On the periphery of the grounds is a
broad, sandy plain dotted with low scrub bushes. This plain serves a
very important function in defining the akhara space, for it is the *disha
maidan* (open area) where people go to defecate before exercising or
drinking the well water. Defecation has a very positive aesthetic appeal
in the routine of akhara attendance. It puts one in the mood to exercise
or relax, I was told, by marking off both time and space. In effect,
defecation is a form of sociosomatic punctuation that indicates a transi-

tional pause between the world of work and the world of the akhara. On a number of occasions when I visited akharas I was asked whether I would like to defecate. Such inquiries were made in a very matter-of-fact manner, much as one might expect to be asked if a cup of tea would be in order at 4:30 in the afternoon. The sandy band of ground around Akhara Bari Gaivi thus serves as a topographical boundary and as a place to move from one state of body/mind to another.

Moving in concentrically from the band of sand, one finds five or six small ponds of swampy water that encircle the akhara precinct. The water in these marshy ponds is used by those who defecate to clean themselves before coming into the akhara proper. These swampy ponds serve as an important classificatory boundary, for they mark off the clean from the unclean in terms both of a personal physical condition and geographical space.

Inside the ring of pond water, up on a bluff, is a grove of trees which shade a small *dharmashala* (pilgrim rest-house), a large marble Hanuman temple, a new cement temple dedicated to Shiva, numerous small shrines honoring saints and lesser local godlings, the tin-roofed pit, exercise area, and large cement platform used for resting, dressing, and discussion. The focal point of the akhara is a deep well from which only the presiding guru is allowed to draw water. This well water is said to be very powerful. Its draws its strength from the geomancy of the area, particularly the unique soil, the specific configuration of trees, and its proximity to the Ganga. No one may use this water for bathing. It is only for drinking, and one must drink it in litre draughts rather than by the glass. (This is said to be part of the prescription even for those who drink the water as a tonic rather than as a cure.) I was asked numerous times how I felt after drinking the water: "Has it settled your stomach?" "Do you feel different?" "Isn't it fresh and cooling?" In effect, ingestion of the well water, which is the nexus of the akhara, is an internalization of the essence of the akhara, a kind of geomantic sacrament. In this respect it provides a harmonic symmetry to the defecation in the sandy field. It further puts one in touch with the ineffable aura of the akhara space. Evacuation on the periphery of the space is balanced and re-flected—in inversion—by internalization at its hub. The body of the wrestler, or of any other akhara visitor, mirrors through its action the spatial layout of the akhara.

Next to the drinking well at Bari Gaivi is a large sunken tank from which water is drawn to dampen the ground and settle the compound dust. There is also a separate well used exclusively for washing clothes and bathing. This system of hydraulic classification—swampy water to clean one's anus, water to dampen the ground, water to wash one's self and one's clothes, and water to drink—serves to structure akhara space and one's movement through this space.

After work many men come to the akhara from all over the city of Banaras simply to defecate, drink some water, bathe, change clothes, and talk with friends. In this social context of camaraderie, the atmosphere and mood of the akhara space is everything, for it charges these "simple pleasures" with therapeutic significance. The mood and aesthetic appeal of the akhara environment is captured in the term *anand* (satisfaction) which is used to summarize the feeling that one comes to the akhara to experience (cf. Kumar 1986, 1988).

Parallel to the picturesque aesthetic of the akhara is its sanctity and purity. The akhara is not only clean and pure in a physical sense, but it is also a holy place. The soil of the akhara is most pure, as it represents the essence of Mother Earth. Water is naturally pure in Hindu cosmology, but the water of an akhara well is considered purer than most. Similarly, pipal, banyan, and nim trees have general religious and ritual importance (R. Dixit 1967; R. Sharma n.d.), but those on akhara grounds are charged with extra significance.

Every akhara has at least one shrine dedicated to Lord Hanuman. This shrine is the focus of akhara religious activity. The image of Hanuman is cleaned at least twice a week and is anointed with *sindur* (vermilion paste). His "clothes" are cleaned regularly, offerings are made to him twice a week, he is prayed to every morning when his blessing is invoked, and he is saluted whenever someone enters or leaves the akhara. Most akharas have numerous shrines and temples dedicated to a host of gods, goddesses, godlings, and saints. *Lingams* are often found either in shrines by themselves, at the base of trees, or in conjunction with small images of Hanuman.

Many akharas also have a shrine dedicated to the founding guru. For instance, the images of Munni Pahalwan in Delhi and Sant Ram in Banaras are life-size figures accorded a central position in their respective akhara pantheons (see plate 13). The founders of many akharas are reputed to have been superhuman, saintly men who possessed great spiritual and physical strength by virtue of their strict adherence to a wrestling regimen of diet, exercise, and religious faith.

Akhara temples and shrines are serviced by informal functionaries who serve as semiresident priests. Even predicated with the qualifiers "informal" and "semiresident" the term *priest* denotes a much too well-defined and structured role for what is, in fact, a purely ad hoc situation. A few examples will illustrate the point.

On Tuesdays and Saturdays, the two days sacred to Hanuman, two men come to the Akhara Ram Singh temple and offer *prasad* of crystallized sugar and soaked *chana* to the image of the Lord. This prasad is distributed among the wrestlers (who often demand a second handful) and the two men then return to their respective jobs, one as cloth merchant and the other as coal trader. The two men are "religiously disposed" to the extent that they spend a great deal of their time reading scriptures and listening to the teachings of itinerant sannyasis who hold forth in a nearby public park. That they service the akhara temple is, however, purely coincidental and is neither mandated nor expected.

Baba Bhole Das, a sannyasi, has taken up residence and responsibility for the two large and elaborately decorated images of Lord Hanuman at Gaya Seth Akhara. He goes about his task of washing and bathing the images while chanting softly to himself. Devotees who are not wrestlers come and sing with Babaji on occasion, but for the most part he goes about his business with little regard for the wrestling routine that structures akhara life. Because Babaji is a mendicant it is his prerogative to service the akhara temple, but it is also his prerogative to go on indefinite pilgrimage or to simply move on to some other place.

Sonu Maharaj of Ram Kund Akhara is a dry-goods merchant. At sixty-two he has shifted his orientation away from his small business and toward devotion and a routine of contemplative prayer. He comes to the akhara every morning with a bundle of jasmine and marigold flowers and lights a lamp and stick of incense in front of the figures of Hanuman, Shiva and Parvati, Ganesh, and Surnath. Having blessed and garlanded each image he bows to the rock bench, which symbolizes the founding guru. He then digs the pit and calls on some of the younger members to wrestle with him. Sonu affects the long hair of a mendicant, and his social orientation is clearly otherworldly.

There are many other examples of men who have taken it on themselves to serve as the guardians of akhara shrines. Many of these men, like the wrestlers themselves, have oriented their lives away from everyday concerns of wealth and property and towards spiritual contemplation. Baba Shyam Lal of Bara Ganesh donates his annual earnings as a metal merchant to the poor. Such men bring a sense of religious purpose to the akharas they serve.

To some extent it may be said that akhara temple functionaries shoulder the burden of religious duty for all akhara members. This is particularly the case at Dharmsangh, Aghornath Takiya, Bari Gaivi, and other akharas affiliated with large institutionalized religious centers. Despite the religiosity of these akharas the role of temple "priest" is surprisingly marginal to the wrestling activities. When I spoke to the *mahant* (abbot, head priest) of the Aghornath Takiya complex it was apparent that he did not pay much attention to what went on in the akhara itself. He was actively involved in philosophical contemplation and metaphysical research and came into contact with the members of the akhara only when *arti puja* was performed every evening at eight. Beyond this he was not interested in the regimen the wrestlers followed.

An akhara as a whole may be considered to be a religious environment where exercise and wrestling are acts of devotion to a way of life. This is not meant in some abstract sense, for a literal parallel is drawn between the rote recitation of prayer and the repetitive exercise routines performed every morning by wrestlers. Both require the same mindset and concentration. The very act of wrestling is charged with religious significance. As the institutionalized icons of formal religion, temples and shrines on akhara grounds serve to enhance a general feeling of commitment to an idealized way of life. All wrestlers are responsible for the akhara's environment of religiosity, and they affect this as much through exercise as through washing the temple steps or lighting a votive lamp in the niche of a shrine.

An akhara pantheon is eclectic and extensive, and there is a regular regime of obeisance and ritualized prayer. However, there is not a rich or textured mystical appreciation for "things religious." Hanuman, for instance, is a real part of the akhara complex, and as such his role is set and established. He marks certain attitudes and reaffirms precedents. For all his importance, however, he does not evoke an attitude of mystery or esoteric and problematic questions of theological faith. In a religious sense, Hanuman is a practical and pragmatic figure. Wrestlers do not discuss in any great detail or trouble themselves unduly over Hanuman's metaphysical significance. What is important about him is self-evident and is regarded by wrestlers as comfortably mundane. When I asked about the significance of sindur, for instance, I was told that it was put on Hanuman in the same way that wrestlers put on oil: as an invigorating tonic and a mark of beauty. Similarly, prayers, offerings, and salutes to Hanuman are all interpreted in a generic sense as various forms of showing respect. Such acts are neither complex nor esoteric. As such they provide a deeply felt multidimensional psychological rootedness. A wrestler's general attitude is antimystical, where devotion is a holistic, pragmatic, and unambiguous way of life.

The religious life of the akhara complex is an important part of wrestling culture; yet prayer, obeisance, and other ritual events, while emotive, are not ecstatic. Nor are acts of propitiation, in and of themselves, charged with complex significance. However much temples, shrines, lamps, garlands, and incense create an atmosphere of sanctity, these things do not indicate that formal religion subsumes akhara life. It does not define the boundaries of wrestling life, but it does, as will be shown, provide a strong baseline for the construction of personal identity. While pervasive, religion is supplementary, and so one is more often than not religious as a wrestler rather than a wrestler who happens to be religious.

DAILY ROUTINE

The details of daily routine vary somewhat from one akhara to another. Nevertheless, it is possible to discern some general patterns. Though not followed to the letter, important rules define wrestling as a comprehensive discipline. A wrestler's quotidian schedule is not strictly or dogmatically defined. Rules read more like a lexicon than a litany in the sense that what is ordered and given structure is not an outline per se but a scheme of elaboration. One is not solely enjoined to do something; how it is to be done, why it is efficacious, and where it fits, etiologically, in the larger scheme of things is equally important.

A wrestler is enjoined to wake at three in the morning, when the air is pure and cool. After drinking a glass of water with lime juice, he is to go out into a forest area or scrub jungle and relieve himself. As Ratan Patodi writes, although a wrestler is not a doctor, he should inspect his feces in order to evaluate his health. If it "is coiled like a snake about to strike" then his digestion is in good order. However, if it is loose, then he should consult his guru about a dietary change (1973a: 24–25). Daily and regular evacuation of the bowels is also prescribed by Mujumdar (1950), for "if the bowels are not clean, blood becomes impure and easily leads to disease" (ibid: 675).

Following evacuation, and before the sun rises, a wrestler should brush his teeth. This must be done before dawn because the warmth of the sun turns the food particles in the mouth into poison which can cause illness and indigestion. Moreover, the strong ultraviolet light of the sun can cause a wrestler's vision to blur while he squats down to brush his teeth. Generally speaking, the cleaner one's teeth, the sharper

one's vision (Patodi 1973a: 25). Patodi further details rules for dental
hygiene:

> One should only brush for five or six minutes otherwise the gums will be
> severely damaged. God has placed two glands beneath the tongue which
> produce saliva and aid considerably in mastication and digestion. Excessive
> brushing can cause a reduction in the amount of saliva produced, and this
> will adversely affect digestion. One can use either *babul* or *nim* twigs for
> brushing, but one should not always use nim. It is astringent and can burn
> one's mouth. The toasted skin of almonds is also a good tooth powder. I
> have seen that some people use burnt tobacco and snuff but these tend to
> tarnish the natural brightness of one's teeth. It should also be remembered
> that after brushing one side of the mouth, one should rinse before brushing
> the other side. This prevents the germs of decay on one side from spreading
> to the teeth on the other side (ibid: 25–26).

Of course, these prescriptions are not exclusively devised for wrestlers.
Much of what wrestlers do as concerns personal hygiene and diet derives
from Ayurvedic principals and other traditions of health and healing.
Here, however, I am only concerned with the mechanical aesthetic of
the acts that structure a wrestler's day, and not with the "natural economy" of health per se. For a wrestler, brushing is an important part of
an integrated daily regime. Mujumdar is no less specific than Patodi in
prescribing a regime of dental hygiene for wrestlers. The following passage illustrates the fine detail and mechanical exactness of what is a very
small part of a larger intricate system.

> The toothbrush (*Dantakashtha*) should be made of a fresh twig of a tree or
> a bush grown on a commendable tract and it should be straight, not worm-
> eaten, devoid of any knots, or utmost with one knot only and should be the
> width of twelve fingers in length and like the small finger in girth. The potency
> and strength of the twig [toothbrush] should be determined by or varying
> according to the season of the year and the preponderance of any particular
> *Dosha* in the physical temperament of its user. The twig of a plant possessed
> of any of the four tastes—sweet, bitter, astringent, and pungent—should be
> the only kind collected and used. *Nimb* is the best of all bitter trees, *Khadira*
> of the astringent ones, *Madhuk* of the sweet, and *Karanja* of the pungent
> ones. The teeth should be daily cleaned with [a compound consisting of]
> honey, powdered *tri-katu, tri-varga, tejovati, Saindhava* and oil. Each tooth
> should be separately cleansed with the cleansing paste applied on [the top of
> the twig bitten into the form of] a soft brush and care should be taken not
> to hurt the gums anyways during rubbing. . . .
>
> The use of a thin, smooth and flexible foil of gold, silver or wood, ten
> fingers in length is commended for the purpose of cleansing the tongue by
> scraping. This gives relief and removes bad taste, foetor, swelling, and numb-
> ness of the mouth (1950: 675).

A regular feature of the morning activities at Akhara Ram Singh would be for a junior wrestler to climb up the large nim tree and carefully select a number of twigs for the senior wrestlers to use. Senior wrestlers who no longer engage in wrestling practice would come to the akhara and brush their teeth with careful, if somewhat distracted, precision as they watched the younger wards grapple.

After a wrestler has brushed his teeth, he must bathe before entering the akhara. As one person put it, "One can and should bathe at any time of day, but the morning bath is the most purifying." Not only does the morning bath make a person pure enough to enter the akhara precinct, but it also "[r]emoves somnolence, body heat and fatigue. It allays thirst and checks itching and perspiration, brings on a fresh relish for food, removes all bodily impurities, clears the sense organs, gladdens the mind, purifies the blood, increases the appetising power, destroys drowsiness and sinful thoughts, and increases semen. The sight of a man is invigorated by applying cold water to the head at the time of bathing, while the pouring of warm water on the head tends to injure the eye-sight" (ibid: 679). Bathing in cold water invigorates the body in winter and cools it in the summer. One should not bathe in very cold water when the air temperature is cold, or hot water when it is hot. This upsets the balance of the bodily humors. After bathing a wrestler should rub his body lightly with oil before starting his morning regime of physical exercise and practice.

Bathing, of course, has important ritual implications as well. The akhara compound is pure, and one must wash away the impurities accrued to the body through secular everyday life—sleeping, eating, urinating, defecating—before entering the precinct. When visiting akharas I was often asked whether or not I had bathed. An answer in the affirmative ensured admittance. In the wrestler's mind there is only a very vague line, if any, between the health and ritual dimension of the morning bath. Religious qualities are somatically coded, and if one is impure, one is also unhealthy.

Physical training is the focal point of a wrestler's daily routine and will be considered in detail in a later chapter. In outline, however, a wrestler starts his regime by running a few kilometers. He then digs the pit and wrestles with a number of partners. The routine concludes with a series of gymnastic and aerobic exercises. The whole schedule takes some two and a half hours.

After exercising, a wrestler rubs his body with the earth of the akhara to dry his perspiration. This prevents his body from cooling too rapidly, and thus guards against illness. While resting, he is rubbed down. As the earth dries on his skin it is scraped off by other wrestlers. By the time the earth is scraped, the body is cool enough for the wrestler to bathe. It is vitally important that a person not bathe while still hot, for this will inevitably enrage the body and cause serious illness. A wrestler must urinate before bathing in order to relieve the body's inner heat. I was often caught out on this fine point of keeping fit as wrestlers at Akhara Ram Singh kept a more watchful eye on my movements than I was apt to do myself. On a few occasions I witnessed other wrestlers who, on the verge of bathing, suddenly realized that they had not yet urinated. They would quickly retire to a nearby wall, set things right, and thereby ensure better health.

The whole body is anointed with mustard oil after bathing. This gives the skin a glossy radiance and a soft, uniform texture. It prevents it from drying out and scaling. It also combines with the natural odors of the body to produce a pleasant, clean fragrance. The application of oil to the body is an important part of massage, an integral part of the exercise regime, and will be given due consideration in a later chapter. Some of the efficacious qualities of oil should be mentioned here, however, since anointing the body—as distinct from a full massage—is an important part of the daily routine.

> Anointing the head with oil is a good cure for the affections of the head. It makes the hair grow luxuriantly and imparts thickness, softness, and a dark gloss to them. It soothes and invigorates the head and sense organs and removes the wrinkles of the face. Combing the hair improves its growth, removes dandruff and dirt and destroys the parasites of the scalp. Pouring oil [Karna-purana] into the cavities of the ears is highly efficacious in pains of the jaw, and acts as a good cure for headache and earache. Anointing the feet with oil etc. brings on sleep. It is refreshing and invigorating to the body and sight, removes all drowsiness and sense of fatigue and softens the skin of the soles of the feet. Anointing the body imparts a glossy softness to the skin, guards against the aggravation of the Vayu [wind] and the kapha [phlegm], improves the colour and strength and gives a tone to the root-principles [dhatus] of the body. The use of oil at a bath causes the oil to penetrate into the system through the mouths of the arteries, veins of the body, as [sic] also the roots of the hair, and thus soothes and invigorates the body with its own essence (ibid: 676).

Wrestlers are enjoined to shave and cut their nails regularly. As Mujumdar notes, this leads to the "expiation of one's sins, makes a man cheerful, and tends to appease his fate, increase his energy and impart a lightness to his frame" (ibid: 678). Clearly here there is a dramatic intersection of somatic practices, personality traits, auspiciousness, and *karmic* balance. In Banaras the English term "personality" was often used to denote such an intersection of physical health, beauty, and reputable character.

Having bathed, wrestlers offer prayers to Lord Hanuman. After dressing they show their respect to the guru by touching his feet. Asking his blessing, they leave the akhara.

A person must not eat or drink for two full hours after exercising. A wrestler's diet is an integral part of his regime. From roughly nine o'clock, when the morning practice session ends, until four o'clock, when the evening exercise routine begins, a wrestler must rest, eat, and sleep. Although this is a "passive" part of the wrestler's regime, it is important for his recuperation and physical development.

As everyone is quick to point out, to relax all day long is an unrealistic prescription given modern priorities and work schedules. It is nevertheless an ideal that is taken very seriously. After morning practice most wrestlers go to work or to school. Many complain that there is not enough time for proper training and that they are too tired to study or work. Anand, a wrestler at Akhara Ram Singh, bicycles almost fifteen miles a day to attend the morning practice session. He then goes directly to school and then back to his village south of the city, where he must help out on the family farm. I would often be walking through downtown Banaras and be greeted by a wrestler working in his father's sweet shop, selling general merchandise, stacking gunnysack material, weighing coal, or checking goods at the railway station. Even national-level champion wrestlers hold jobs: Naresh Kumar is head clerk at the Delhi railway office (*Asiaweek* 1989); Chandagi Ram, the national champion of the late 1960s and early 1970s, is well known as "master ji" because of his training as a schoolteacher (*Link* 1969: 35; S. Sharma 1985). Regardless of the incompatibility of a wrestling lifestyle with the requirements and duties of working life, most who come to the akharas have adapted to accommodate the rigors of work with a modified daily schedule of exercise, diet, and sleep. Many wrestlers now argue that formal education and wrestling are somewhat compatible (Areya 1978). While the wrestler rests his body he can develop his intellect; but this is something of a forced rationalization based on an artificial dichotomy of mind and body. Even when not achieved, the ideal of a purely akhara-oriented schedule sets the tone for a wrestler's perception of his day. As such, it structures his attitude if not his time.

Having eaten, rested, defecated, and bathed, wrestlers return to the akhara at about four in the afternoon. Although the pit is dug for exercise, no wrestling is practiced in the afternoon. The workout consists of a number of exercises and lasts about three hours. After a second bath the wrestler leaves the akhara. Before going to sleep at sunset he eats and rests some more.

Although sleeping is a period of inactivity, it is an important part of the wrestler's day. As Atreya writes in an article entitled "The Place of Sleep and Rest in the Wrestling Regimen," sleep is just as important as food, air, and water (1978: 19). Sleep is particularly important because it gives strained muscles and tendons a chance to recuperate. Sleep transforms the fatigue of exertion into the vigor of stamina. It also promotes digestion and thus helps a person put on weight and gain strength. Going to sleep at a regular time and getting enough sleep establishes a psychosomatic rhythm which produces a proper chemical and mineral balance in the body. In turn, this conditions the various body mechanisms responsible for producing semen. A lack of sleep produces illness, emaciation, weakness, impotence, and the risk of premature death. In general, wrestlers sleep better than other people because they exert themselves more. Wrestlers get more rest in a shorter period of time because their sleep is deeper and less agitated with dreams and restlessness. The exact amount of sleep one needs is something one's guru must determine, but the following points apply:

> A fundamental principle of wrestling is to go to sleep at sunset and wake three hours before dawn. One must sleep with an open window near one's head and never sleep with your head covered. Never sleep in the dew or on the damp ground. Sleeping on a comfortable cot or bed produces an efficacious rest and promotes endurance. When fatigue and flatulence are expunged, then semen is produced. Sleeping on an uncomfortable bed produces bad effects. This point needs to be emphasized. One should turn over repeatedly while sleeping and never sleep flat on one's back. Also, the body will suffer if one goes to sleep on an empty stomach (ibid: 23–24).

Although a wrestler's bed should be comfortable, it should be hard rather than soft; a board is better than a rope cot. "Sleep is the natural *dharma* of the body," writes Atreya (ibid: 20), and so, for the wrestler and for all who aspire to health and long life, it is crucial that they not merely sleep, but sleep properly. When wrestlers talk of trips they have taken to tournaments away from home they often comment on the nature and quality of the accomodations provided. The senior wrestlers of Akhara Bara Ganesh told me many times how they hosted wrestlers from the Punjab and made them very comfortable in a guest house/

exercise room constructed so that, among other things, it affords a healthy place to sleep. At a tournament in Gaziabad I was told by some of my Banaras acquaintances that they had performed badly on account of having had to sleep on the floor in a stuffy, crowded room. In my very first encounter with a wrestler he showed me his sleeping accommodations and described the comfort and qualities of bed, mattress, and pillow as an indication of how complete and well appointed were the facilities at his disposal.

The daily life of a wrestler is a regime of integrated health and fitness drawn out, on, through, and in his body. In this regard the guru is both taskmaster and sculptor. As I was told by many wrestlers, a person must not so much as urinate or drink without first asking his guru's permission. A disciple's role is not to think, but to be molded and shaped, to allow himself to be cut in the pattern of perfection. Subscription to this kind of discipline requires extreme self-sacrifice—as a common aphorism has it, a willingness to "chew iron chana" or to "drink a bitter cup." Total commitment to the espoused ideals is rarely if ever realized. Nevertheless, there is a strong feeling of obligation and responsibility to live by the spirit if not the letter of one's guru's prescripts.

I have described in some detail the routine of a wrestler's daily life. Considerable license is given for idiosyncratic interpretation, and rationalizations abound for "imperfect" conduct. Some wrestlers advocate massage before practice as well as after. Others disagree on whether or not to bathe in well water during the winter. Although most agree that it is proper to get up at three in the morning, the more usual practice is to wake at four-thirty or five. Similarly, most wrestlers wait only half an hour rather than the prescribed two hours after practice before drinking water or eating food. Very few go to bed at sunset. In spite of the inexact nature and outright contradiction of some alternative practices, most wrestlers agree with the basic tenets outlined above. If there is disagreement on the sequence of a particular part of the regime, more importance is placed on the rigor of whatever one chooses to do rather than on protocol. One can do virtually anything—within the tacitly agreed-on range of interpretations that make sense—as long as it is logically rationalized and is not just a random whim. Moreover, an idiosyncratic interpretation is more likely to be regarded as generally valid if it is articulated in great detail. For instance, diet is often a topic on which there is a degree of disagreement. Some wrestlers advocate a vegetarian diet, while others do not. The minority of Hindu wrestlers who eat meat are likely to give fairly detailed reasons for why their body in particular either requires the beneficial properties which meat provides or is relatively immune to the adverse effects meat has on the body. I am almost certain that no one would explain eating meat purely in terms of taste. When a wrestler from the warm dry plains visited in the cool damp hills he explained his request for chicken in terms of the warming effect it would have on his body.

A wrestler's routine follows the pattern of a logical sequence of events built one upon the other. Sleep complements diet and exercise; bathing, dental hygiene, defecation, and sleep are all directly linked to health and strength. Themes of physical purity, strength, semen production, and aesthetic beauty run through and give continuity and texture to the day's events. As such, the regime of day-to-day life does not read so much like a catalogue with separately articulated parts in cumulative sequence as it does a recipe where each step is important and unique in its own right and the sum is a complement of interdependent parts. For this reason the spirit of the "law" is more significant than a literal interpretation. It is not so important to figure out exactly what is best in any particular situation. What is important is that the whole routine be rhythmically structured and consistent with reference to itself. Lived properly, the whole day produces a whole, healthy, and harmonically balanced body.

A wrestler's daily routine extends the world of wrestling out of the strictly defined precinct of exercise and competition. It makes the practice of wrestling a significant factor in both the domestic sphere of family life and the world of work and labor. Concepts of health and strength are necessarily projected into the home, the field, the shop, the office. Although the akhara provides a pivotal point around which the wrestler's day is organized, a wrestler must also work and raise a family. It is therefore important briefly to consider the social composition of the Banaras wrestling community.

AKHARA MEMBERSHIP AND AFFILIATION

Akhara membership is nearly impossible to determine in any objective empirical sense. Most akhara elders with whom I spoke claimed that their "irregular membership"—those who come when they have time but do not follow a strict regime of exercise—numbered in the hundreds. Some elders generalized to the point of saying that everyone in their proximal neighborhood was in theory an akhara member. Moreover, a number of people claimed membership in one akhara or another on the basis of very casual and circuitous association: friends of friends, neighbors, or hyperextended kinship.

The larger akharas—Ram Singh, Bara Ganesh, Swaminath, and Gaya Seth—estimate that their regular membership is between sixty and seventy. However, on any one day there are between twenty-five and thirty wrestlers who attend morning practice (see plate 12). At the smaller akharas—Ram Kund, Ishvarigangi, Ram Sevak, Sant Ram, and Ragunath Maharaj—regular membership is between forty and fifty, with fifteen to twenty wrestlers attending on any one day. My use of the term "member" refers to anyone who comes to an akhara regularly, however "regularly" may be defined. It is a purposefully vague formulation and is in keeping with the attitude of most wrestlers. An example will help illustrate this point.

The akhara with which I affiliated is formally known by the title *Antrashtriya, Sarwajanik Akhara Ram Singh* (The International, Public Akhara Ram Singh) which appears in bold blue letters on the pavilion's entablature. One year when the akhara was repainted there was serious disagreement as to whether the word "public" (*sarwajanik*) ought to be part of the official name. Most members say that an akhara is eminently public and that this should be made explicit. Many members are proud of the fact that anyone can come to their akhara. Exercise, they argue, is something that ought not to be restricted through exclusive membership. However, even those who aspire to such high ideals of egalitarian inclusiveness recognize that in some Hindu akharas Muslims and untouchables are either overtly excluded or covertly discriminated against. One can say that the problematic meaning of the term "public" is derived from the juxtaposition of a general ethic of equality set over and against social exclusiveness and caste chauvinism. The reason a number of akhara members were against including the word "public" in the title was that it would reify a comfortably ambiguous situation. Those in favor wanted to preempt that ambiguity by formalizing an ideal of total inclusiveness. In the end the word "public" was painted on the entablature, which played no small role in the trials and tribulations of a not-quite-postpositivist ethnographer's search for demographic statistics. "Just how many wards do you have, Guru ji?" I asked. And he replied, "Who knows, my son, it is a public place."

Although membership is free and easy, an initiation ceremony formally inducts a novice wrestler into an akhara. The ritual of initiation varies from one akhara to another but is generally as follows. After attending an akhara for some time the guru will tell a wrestler that it is time for his initiation. On the appointed day the young wrestler brings with him a new langot, a *sapha* (head cloth/turban), prasad (usually in the form of *laddus* made of *besan* [chickpea flour] and sugar), paraffin or oil, cotton to make a wick for the prayer lamp, and a garland of flowers to place around the image of Hanuman. After practice the sapha and langot are offered to the guru along with cash. The sum is usually eleven rupees but any multiple of ten plus one is acceptable. The guru then takes the garland and lights the lamp after placing the prasad in front of the figure of Hanuman. The initiate is asked to honor Lord Hanuman and to swear allegiance to the akhara and the founding guru. The prasad is then taken and distributed among the other members of the akhara. The conclusion and most important part of the ceremony is when five laddus are taken and buried in the four corners and center of the pit. There is no drama associated with this rite. The whole event is rather low-key and does not seem to mark a dramatic change of status. The initiate still comes to the akhara as before and there are no privileges attached to initiated membership. Indeed, the distinction between one who has and one who has not been initiated is rarely made. Initiation does establish a bond between guru and chela. Although a guru will instruct an uninitiated member, it is said that a person can only really understand what a guru is telling him after having been initiated. Initiation is not a marker of membership in any empirical sense, but it effects a bond of respect and obligation between teacher and disciple.

AKHARA DEMOGRAPHICS

A survey of eight akharas supports the general observation that there is little variation in the demographic profile of Banaras akharas. There does not seem to be any variation in the caste, class, or status makeup of different akharas.

Every akhara I visited had a majority of Yadavs as regular members. Yadavs are a low-caste (technically Shudra) group with considerable political, economic, and demographic strength in the Banaras area. Their social mobility and group identity is linked to a longstanding traditional association with the military (Rao 1964) and with wrestling. Although many Yadavs are lawyers, doctors, businessmen, teachers, and writers, many follow their traditional caste vocation of herding and dairy farming. Of the 118 wrestlers interviewed, thirty-five reported that they were involved in some form of dairying or milk business. While most dairy farmers are Yadavs, not all Yadavs who wrestle are dairy farmers. I would estimate that some 50 percent of all wrestlers in Banaras are Yadavs. Thakurs, including Bhumihar Rais, comprise the second-largest caste group involved in wrestling, roughly 20 percent. Brahmans make up about 15 percent of the wrestling population, with the remaining 15 percent coming from a wide range of caste groups including Dhobis, Chandals, Chamars, Nais, and others.

The clear majority of dairy farmers is explained not only by caste identity. Dairy farmers have direct access to two of the most important and otherwise expensive ingredients in a wrestler's diet: milk and *ghi*. In fact, the association between wrestling and dairy farming in Banaras is so great that men who deal in milk or milk products are called *pahalwan* irrespective of whether or not they take part in the regimen of practice and exercise.

In general, many wrestlers are in business for themselves or in government service. Apart from seven weavers, very few wrestlers with whom I spoke were employed as factory workers or simple wage laborers. This may be a function of sample error; however, it is important to note that the nature of work in a factory or commercial handicraft industry would mitigate against a rigorous and exacting extracurricular "leisure" activity such as wrestling. Workers who are paid a low daily or weekly wage may well frequent akharas in order to bathe and relax, but in my casual as well as programmatic surveys of akhara life I encountered relatively few "serious wrestlers" who would fall in this class bracket. Similarly, although most wrestlers come from a comparatively low economic class bracket, irregularly employed wage laborers—rickshaw pullers, street hawkers, and others whose income is low—tend not to be involved in wrestling. A few brief portraits help fill out the occupational profile of the wrestling community:

- Kanta Pahalwan is a railway porter who works at the Dehra Dun station. His family is from a village in northwestern Bihar to which he returns every year to help with the harvest and planting. Although porters have a fairly secure position with the railway and are government-licensed, there are few perquisites. Income is low. Kanta shares room and board with other porters and sends money back to his family in Bihar.

- Sita Ram Yadav came to Banaras as a young boy and found work with a well-known and respected wrestling patron, Ram Narian Sarien, who owns an umbrella shop in the city. Ram Narian Sarien supported Sita Ram Yadav and saw to his training as a young wrestler. After considerable success as a wrestler Sita Ram was given a job with the Banaras Diesel Locomotive Works, where he works as an office clerk.

• Dr. Shanti Prakash Atreya, one-time state wrestling champion of Uttar Pradesh, earned his M.A. and Ph.D. from Banaras Hindu University, where he has taught both yoga and philosophy. Atreya is currently affiliated as a teacher with a school in Saharanpur. He also runs an institute for the study of yoga and psychology at Kuthal Gate in Dehra Dun District. His family lives in Bandarjuddha, a large, wealthy village near Deoband in Uttar Pradesh.

• Nathu Lal Yadav, the guru of Karanghanta Akhara, is a well-known purveyor of pan. In his small shop, an extension of a shrine dedicated to Lord Shiva, there is room for one person only to sit. By his own admission Nathu Lal is more concerned with philosophical questions than he is with making money. As he points out, he enjoys what he does and it is enough to support him and his immediate family.

• Ram ji, a member of Jhalani Akhara, comes from a very well-to-do Yadav family who own a number of hotels, sweet shops, and other business interests in Banaras. Ram ji works under his brother as the junior manager of one of the family hotels in Chaitganj.

• Kaniya, a B.A. candidate at Banaras Hindu University, works at his father's small tea and sweet shop. He regrets not having been able to take his degree sooner, but as the eldest son he is responsible for the day-to-day management of the family business.

Although wrestlers come from different economic backgrounds, wealth and social status are not very important factors in daily interaction. In terms of the wrestling ethic, wealth is simply irrelevant. Money enables one to have a better diet—an important consideration in its own right—but in and of itself money is not valued. This is not to say that poor wrestlers would not rather be rich or wish a better life for themselves and their families. Given the opportunity they would certainly seek to improve their lot. However, as an ethical life path wrestling takes precedence over material concerns of class and occupation. As we shall see in a later chapter, this is in part what gives it a utopian quality.

AGE AND EDUCATION

Of 123 wrestlers interviewed from eight akharas, fifteen were under age fifteen, fifty-five were between the ages of fifteen and twenty-three, twenty-eight were between the ages of twenty-three and thirty-five, and twenty-five were over thirty-five years old. This indicates not only the obvious—that most wrestlers are teenagers or young men in their early twenties—but also that men in their mid- to late twenties and early thirties are not very involved in akhara activities. Once men marry and take on the responsibility of raising a family they tend to come to the akhara less frequently. When they have established an occupation of some sort and have children of their own, these men return to the akhara as senior members. On account of this there is a sharp generational break in the membership of most akharas. Senior members are to junior members as fathers are to sons or uncles to nephews. Respect, however, is tempered with a good deal of joking and informality. True respect is reserved for the guru.

It is also important to note that wrestlers who are between twenty-three and thirty-five years old are usually the ones who have made a name for themselves. Though numerically in the minority, as individuals they represent an ideal and have great prestige. These members are regarded as quintessential wrestlers and virtually define the quality of the akhara by their presence. Shamu Pahalwan of Akhara Ram Singh is one such wrestler, and Ashok Kumar, who has taken part in national and international competitions, is another. Krishna Kumar Singh of Bara Ganesh has won national recognition as a wrestler for the northern railway team, and Ram ji, of Jhalani Akhara, has won titles in Delhi and Uttar Pradesh state tournaments.

Educational experience corresponds to the generational split in akhara membership. Older members are not educated to the same level as younger members. Of those over thirty-five, only two had the equivalent of a high-school degree. Most were educated up to a sixth-grade level. All were literate but four had gone to school for less than two years.

In sharp contrast are the data on the educational background of the ninety-nine wrestlers interviewed who were under the age of thirty-five: as of 1987, two had M.A. degrees, fourteen had B.A. degrees, thirty had the equivalent of a high-school diploma, and one had left school in tenth grade, thirteen in the ninth, eighteen in the eighth, four in the seventh, and nineteen in the fifth. Even though these data are biased by the fact that Banaras is a cultural and intellectual center, the fact remains that a significant percentage of young wrestlers are well educated compared to their senior fellows.

Having said this, it must be pointed out that education, like wealth, is not a very significant factor in the scheme of akhara activities. Education is valuable in its own right but does not figure in the wrestling rubric as a particularly important virtue. Learning and wisdom are of great importance in the construction of a wrestler's identity, but education is not regarded as the source of these skills. Where it is seen as valuable is as a prerequisite for modern life and as a vehicle for gaining employment, but this is more by default than by design. As it is institutionalized in modern India, formal education is regarded by cynical wrestlers as a somewhat benign manifestation of modern moral decay. It does not inspire; it creates an irreverent attitude and a general lack of respect. The value of education is not in its innate virtue but in its practical utility. For instance, while generally decrying modern materialist preoccupations with status and upward mobility, one wrestler spent a hot summer day networking so that his nephew and niece would gain admission into a well-regarded elementary school.

By way of contrast, Atma Ram's father places no stock in a formal education. Instead he sent his son to the akhara, saying that there he will learn all that he needs to know. Atma Ram is illiterate, but at age twenty-two he is known in Banaras as a good wrestler. Friends have been networking to get him employment with the railway.

Anand Rai's father, a schoolteacher in Kotdwar and well-to-do land owner in Banaras district, appreciates the value of a good education but recognizes the virtue of akhara training. Anand bicycles the fifteen kilometers to Akhara Ram Singh every morning and then goes from the akhara to school. When Anand was about twenty-three, after three failed attempts, he finally passed his matriculation exams and his father invited members of the akhara and village neighbors to a banquet celebration. At the banquet Anand was admonished to keep up with his physical training and to develop himself as a good wrestler.

The following amalgam describes the typical Banaras wrestler with the least synoptic violence. He is a boy in his late teens who is nearing the end of his intermediate education. Some members of his family live in Banaras city proper while others live in a village not too far away. In the city he lives in a small, modestly appointed cement building. One or two of this typical wrestler's elder brothers used to wrestle and he had an uncle who, despite hardship, "was the champion of his village district." One of his older brothers runs a dairy enterprise and has rented space on the outskirts of the city where twelve or thirteen buffalos are tethered. The other brother works in a modest sweet shop located off a main street. The typical wrestler hopes to join the army, the police, or the railway, but his father in the village needs help managing the family's

land holdings, and so the wrestler is forced to curb his ambition in the
interest of more immediate demands.

It must be emphasized, however, that within the framework of a
wrestling way of life, family wealth and status are not important considerations. As a wrestler Atma, who can neither read nor write, is on the
same footing as Babul, who has a B.A. from Banaras Hindu University.
Similarly, Ashok, whose family owns only a few buffalos and a small
tea shop, is a better wrestler than is Ram ji, who comes from one of the
wealthiest families in Banaras.

The claim that education and wealth are unimportant factors in the
akhara would be false and acrimonious but for the fact that wrestling
is not just an extracurricular leisure activity. It is, rather, a holistic integrated way of life. As a person, a wrestler must of necessity live in a
world of social and economic obligation where status, class rank, and
educational training play a strong hand. As a wrestler, however, a person must bracket himself out of the obligations and expectations which
ensue from his involvement in this larger, divisive world. The complex
and problematic nature of this important attitude will be taken up in a
later chapter.

AKHARAS AND BODYBUILDING CLUBS

Wrestling akharas stand in sharp contrast to bodybuilding clubs in
Banaras. Bodybuilding clubs are a fairly recent phenomenon in India,
dating perhaps to the early part of the twentieth century, when Ram
Murti Naidu, among others, established institutes for physical training
and exercise. In Banaras today bodybuilding is modeled on a Western
aesthetic and on Western notions of strength and fitness. Wrestlers and
bodybuilders sharply juxtapose their respective activities. Each defines
himself against the negative backdrop of the other, self-definition
through a "we-are-not-like-them" formulation. As with any such formulation there are enough parallels between the two activities to generate
a dialectic rather than to create a situation of total rejection and disregard. In the interest of summarizing what an akhara is in terms of
aesthetic appeal, health nexus, and demographic composition, it is useful to reflect the akhara, as a whole, against its more modern analog.

The Mazdoor Health Improvement Association, established in 1931
to foster ideals of physical fitness and national self-determination among
mazdurs (wage laborers), is located down a small gali in Madanpura.
The association is almost entirely Muslim, and most of the members

come from the immediate neighborhood of Al 'lu ka Masjid. Many current members work in the area as weavers, traders, transporters, or tailors of silk and other fabrics. The gali is narrow, dark, and, as with other such galis in Banaras, littered with refuse and piles of rubble. Open doors look in on huge looms sunk into the floors of family houses, where young children sit and weave the silk saris for which Banaras is famous.

The gym is open only at night. At about 6:00 P.M. the first member to arrive picks up the key from Masoom's pan shop just across the road from the gali entrance. A sign above the gym door announces the name of the organization in English and in Urdu and Devanagari script.

The gym is a small room, six meters square, crowded with dumbbells, weightlifting bars, weights of all sizes and shapes, a set of parallel bars, and a chin-up bar hung on old rusted chains suspended from a sagging central beam. In one corner is a broken pulley and bicycle-chain contraption used to lift a stack of iron-plate weights. Next to the parallel bars is an improvised bench-press board, and in front of that, set into the hard-packed earth floor, a set of wooden stumps on which to do push-ups. Pegs are set into the lime-washed bricks on each wall. Members hold on to these and stand on polished wooden boards while doing squats and deep knee bends. The boards keep the floor dry, for otherwise sweat would quickly turn the earth to slippery mud.

The central column, decorated with mirrors, supports a ceiling sagged under the weight of three upper floors. Other mirrors decorate three of the walls. Between the mirrors and the iron-barred windows which look out narrowly onto a small dusty garden, old black and white portraits of local champions palely reflect the technicolor aura of pin-ups from American bodybuilding magazines.

A raised area two and a half meters square is set apart in the small room and on it are four large chairs and a carpet. A small ceiling fan turns above this area, cooling the club manager and others who come to watch the regular members exercise. Between two of the chairs and one wall is a two by one-half meter area used for changing. Clothes are hung on pegs above the chairs and the parallel bars. On the wall above the platform are old photos of the founding association. A few plaques, commemorating long since forgotten functions, recall a time when the club had a larger membership. A penned poster, set on a shallow ledge above a covered bucket of tap water, states the club rules in Urdu script.

If there is one word which characterizes the Mazdoor Health Improvement Association, it is compact; there is a certain aesthetic appeal to the close-fitting, womblike character of the place. Contrary to what one might expect, the air in the gym is a quite pleasant combination of musty earth, mustard oil and sweat. Exercise is done with mechanical efficiency. A person doing push-ups makes way for a person doing squats who is just beyond the arch of another person swinging on the parallel bars. No more than thirteen people can exercise in the gym at any one time, and even with nine people working out, movement must be choreographed for efficiency and safety.

The contrast with wrestling akharas is obvious. While both are clearly bounded arenas, the bodybuilding club is closed and confined while the akhara is open. Earth, water, wind, and trees have no place in the confines of the closed, covered, mechanized space of the gym.

If there is a dramatic difference in the relative aesthetic appeal of clubs and akharas, there is an even more significant difference concerning management and organization. Wrestling akharas are the essence of informality. There are few if any set duties, offices, or responsibilities. The guru is nominally in charge of all akhara facilities and activities, but in fact an ad hoc committee of elder members often serves as a decision-making body. The English term "committee" is used by akhara members to refer to any group of two or more who come to a decision on any subject; for example, taking up a collection for a new bucket and rope for the akhara well, buying fresh lime-wash for repainting the akhara buildings, negotiating for a truckload of earth for the pit, or persuading someone to paint new designs on the akhara walls. In any akhara, as in many other social contexts, there are those who take charge of situations and are able to motivate people and implement their own ideas. There are also inevitable conflicts of interest and points of view. But there is no codified structure to this kind of management and organization.

In the akhara there is an informal pecking order which ensures that things get done. At the top of the pecking order is the guru and his cohort of senior members: a very loosely defined group at best. If the guru makes a demand of some sort it is acted on immediately and without comment. The guru's age cohort, known as *dada*s, can order anyone who is a junior member to do such things as fetch incense for the morning pit benediction, get mustard oil from a nearby shop, pick up flower garlands, run various errands anywhere in town, draw water for a bath, deliver a message, sweep fallen leaves from the akhara compound, throw water on the earth to settle the dust, climb up a tree to break off a toothbrush, put equipment away, wash clothes, or chase a stray dog out of the pit.

Among the junior members beneath the dada cohort, seniority and age structure the pecking order. Older members may pass on responsibility to anyone younger and less aggressive than themselves. The ethic of respect for one's elders is used as a moral lever. There is merit in being of service. However, the pecking order is characterized as much by acrimony as by smooth efficiency, as one dada discovered when he spent a whole morning cursing the laziness and disrespect of the younger generation while fishing with a large hook for a bucket lost at the bottom of the well.

While the pecking order is hierarchically multitiered in theory, in fact it is always the youngest members with whom the buck stops. During my stay at the akhara young Kailash was always going off to get something for someone, Airi was always called upon to perform his expert massage, and Govind was chasing stray dogs and cows; unless someone younger has come along, Rajindar may still be drawing water from the well. In any case, water gets drawn and the grounds are kept clean, but often to the tune of half-meant threats, disgruntled retorts, and a great deal of joking.

The akhara is characterized by a lack of bureaucracy and by ad hoc management. By way of contrast, the following is an index of the offices of the Banaras School of Physical Culture, a bodybuilding club in Jangambari: Chief Patron, Mr. Dalip Kumar (IAS), district officer and president of the association for the advancement of physical education; Patron, Mr. N. G. Bhattacharya, regional sports officer and secretary of the association for the advancement of physical education; Physical Director, Dr. Uma Shankar Rai Chaudhuri; President, Mr. Raj Kumar; Vice-President, Mr. Ajay Sharma. The list continues with such titles as chief officer, deputy officer, secretary, chief in charge of the club, and treasurer. In addition to these permanent officers, a chief advisor was appointed to organize the club's annual bodybuilding competition. In this capacity he was supported by seven deputy advisors, an organizer, deputy organizer, organizing committee, committee in charge of the competition, and a committee in charge of prizes.

Where akharas are ad hoc, clubs seem to be obsessive about a strict division of administrative labor. I have no idea how responsibility was distributed through the administrative hierarchy of the Jangambari club, or how decisions were made at any one level. A similar hierarchy of management appears on the letterhead of the Bhelupura Vyayamshala, another bodybuilding club, which also sponsors an annual competition.

The Bhelupura Vyayamshala also illustrates another striking contrast

between akharas and clubs. Stepping into many bodybuilding clubs, the
first thing that strikes the eye is a prominently posted list of rules and
regulations. At Bhelupura Vyayamshala the rules are as follows:

1.   Non-members are not allowed in without permission.

2.   Members may not bring friends with them into the club.

3.   Every member must pay a 2 rupee membership fee by the fif-
teenth of each month.

4.   The gym will be open from 5–8 AM and from 5–11 PM.

5.   The gym will be closed every Sunday.

6.   No one is allowed to enter the "exercise temple" wearing their
shoes.

7.   No smoking or chewing tobacco in the gym.

8.   No spitting anywhere in the compound.

9.   Everyone must be careful and watch out that others are exercising safely.

10.   If someone breaks any piece of equipment he is responsible for
its replacement.

11.   Members should park their bicycles where they won't get in the
way.

Similar rules are found posted in other bodybuilding clubs, but I have
never seen a posted list of regulations at any akhara where wrestling is
practiced. Wrestling akharas are governed more by established precedent and the model of the guru than by objective rules as such. Wrestlers
would agree with the injunction against tobacco, but their abstinence
derives from moral conviction rather than a concern for regulations
per se.

While bodybuilding clubs follow the Western calendar and take Sunday off, akharas break their weekly routine on Wednesday. Unlike the
clubs, akharas are not closed on their "day off." Wednesday is a day
for massage in the akhara and is thus integral to the weekly regime.

In the akhara, spitting, flatulence, and nose blowing are restricted to
the border area of the compound where they do not threaten the purity
of the sacred space. In the club, spitting is more an issue of generic
hygiene than of moral, somatic health. In the akhara purity rather than
civic-mindedness is as much if not more of an issue. In the club, spitting
must be stipulated against, while in the akhara the same restraint is

inspired by ideological conviction and is therefore a point of common sense.

Membership is another crucial point of difference between the club and the akhara. Every exercise club I visited charged a monthly membership fee. On the other hand, akhara members consider fees to be anathema. None of the akharas I visited charged fees of any kind. Moreover, clubs often keep careful record of who has and has not paid, thus sharply defining membership. Akhara membership, as we have seen, is eminently flexible and variable. Whereas clubs are exclusive and private, wrestlers see the akhara as an inclusive, public arena.

Because of membership dues, bodybuilding clubs are able to finance building repairs, equipment improvement, and fairly lavish annual events. There are other expenses as well. The Mazdoor Health Improvement Association must pay rent on its small room and also cover the cost of electricity. In contrast to club dues, akharas draw all of their resources from *chanda*, public donations collected from members, neighborhood residents, and local businesses. Taking up chanda is an ad hoc activity. If a new rope is needed, a few of the akhara dadas get together and share the expense. Expenses are minimal. I have never known of a wrestling akhara on which rent was paid. Electricity is rarely needed, but for the occasional installation of a light or fan it is most often donated by a wealthy member. When there is a large expense, such as the annual Nag Panchami festival or construction of a new building, the chanda is more formal and structured. However, the money collected is almost always designated for a specific project. Contributing to a chanda is one way in which the larger akhara neighborhood can participate in wrestling activities. A person who contributes two thousand rupees towards a new akhara pit achieves status in proportion to his contribution. For their part, the akhara members receive public acclaim and prestige in proportion to the total amount collected. While chanda is a common way for many groups—temple associations, neighborhood committees, and union fundraisers—to raise money, it is characteristic of the akhara system of organization rather than of the bodybuilding club.

Monthly dues, though nominal, restrict membership. A few clubs, such as the well-furnished Health Improvement Association, charge a very exclusive one hundred rupees per month. Some clubs have a wealthier clientele than others. This is not the pattern in akharas, where the economic and social profile of the wrestling community is fairly eclectic. Rich and poor wrestlers meet on common ground. Although I have not collected a great deal of information on bodybuilding club membership, my general impression is that specific bodybuilding clubs restrict membership to particular groups. As noted, a large number of Muslims have become avid bodybuilders. Muslims aside, bodybuilding seems to be popular among many of the more "Westernized" urban youth. The aesthetic of the bodybuilder's sleek physique is in keeping with other Western images of fast motorcycles, high-tech sound systems, digital watches, and so forth.

Some exercise clubs, like the Mazdoor Health Improvement Association, were established to target a particular class of people such as the urban labor force. The Banaras School of Physical Culture was established in 1943 for the benefit of "lower class children." My impression is that many bodybuilding clubs were established by paternalistic upper-class patrons who felt some kind of commitment to better the health of India's masses. In other words, initial impetus and funding for groups like the Mazdoor Health Improvement Association, Banaras School of Physical Culture, and Bhelupura Vyayamshala seems to have come from wealthy doctors, bankers, and industrialists. I was shown around one of these clubs by a young, wealthy accountant who said that his family had a long-standing role in maintaining exercise facilities for the poorer, disadvantaged youth of the city. By contrast, one does not find any kind of exclusive recruitment strategy or class-based paternalism in the akhara. No particular group is targeted. Akhara members make a general appeal for everyone to join an akhara, but this is inclusive rather than exclusive and is, as we shall see, part of a broader nationalistic rhetoric.

A final point of contrast between the akhara and the club concerns the place of formal religion in the organizational scheme of daily activities. Temples give akharas an atmosphere of religiosity, and every wrestler is enjoined to take Hanuman into his heart. In contrast, bodybuilding clubs are for the most part secular institutions.

Small Hanuman shrines are found at Bhelupura Vyayamshala, the Banaras School of Physical Culture, and, as the name might imply, Hanuman Vyayamshala. In every instance these shrines are small and marginal. The members are more concerned with the "cut" of their muscles and the trimness of their waists than they are with contemplating Hanuman's service to Ram. Besides, Hanuman's physique is not that of a bodybuilder, except as portrayed in some modern calendar art, but that of a wrestler. Bodybuilders defer to Hanuman, but they draw their strength almost exclusively from "pumping iron" and not from the devotional exercise of a daily regimen.

Wrestlers in Banaras point towards bodybuilders and criticize their "balloonlike bodies," which have form but no substance. They smirk at narrow waists that would snap in two at the slightest touch, and grimace at protruding tendons wrapped tight by the work of an iron machine. One wrestler laughed at the picture of a bodybuilder, saying that he looked like separate pieces of meat slapped together in a random manner. Another, echoing a similar aesthetic critique, said that bodybuilders look as though they come in parts, each a gross protrusion disembodied from its larger corporeal context. While the bodybuilder is seen as bits and pieces of random flesh, the wrestler's body is a smooth, integrated whole; as they say, *ek rang ka sharir*, a body of one color and uniform texture (see plate 2).

Wrestlers regard bodybuilding clubs as mere pale reflections of the akhara. For their part some club members see akharas as simply anachronistic institutions following the dictates of outmoded tradition. (In general exercise-club members are far more tolerant of akharas than the other way around.)

I have made a rather sharp distinction between the akhara and the bodybuilding club. In doing so some points of overlap between the two styles of physical culture have been deemphasized. But this, too, is in keeping with the perspective of both wrestlers and bodybuilders. Somewhat like closely allied and therefore antagonistic academic disciplines, both groups prefer to define their respective paths clearly and sharply rather than blur together formal and superficial similarities. Whether motivated by strong conviction or fear that the edifice of difference will crumble once assailed, the wrestler and the bodybuilder choose to narrow their respective visions while at the same time magnifying the significance of their singular predilections. Each defines itself against a negative backdrop of the other. In the case of wrestlers, this delineation serves to make the akhara more distinct and therefore more clearly defined as the locus of a specific way of life.

CHAPTER 3

Gurus and Chelas: The Alchemy of Discipleship

When I asked him, "Guruji, why is it that you have never married?" he answered, "Who says that I am not married? I have married wrestling and the children of this marriage are my disciples."

Guru Hanuman in an interview with Rajindar Singh Munna, 1983: 39; see plate 14

GURUSHIP

The concept of "guru" has been popularized to the point of parody, and it is difficult to approach the topic without stumbling over stereotypes and misconceptions. Spiritual teachers of all persuasions abound, and even those who espouse truth with conviction suffer the stigma of fraud. Paraphrasing a verse of scripture, and putting the institution of guruship in a wrestling perspective, Atreya put it this way: "In this dark age there are many gurus who plunder their disciple's wealth, but the guru is not to be found who is able to wipe sorrow from his disciple's brow."

Wrestling is not immune to this modern malady, and there are as many charlatans in the akhara as there are in the temple, spiritual retreat, music hall, dance *gharana* (intellectual lineage or "school" of artistic style), or any other arena where the institution of guruship prevails. Nevertheless, whether realized or imagined, the persona of the guru is an important concept in the wrestling rubric. In this rubric ideals are more real than actual human experience, and the guru lives more as a figure of speech than as a flesh and blood teacher. Fraud gives way to faith which is often blind. The wrestling guru is larger than life. What he is supposed to be can transcend what he is. For instance, one of the gurus I knew in Banaras was very fond of chewing tobacco and would carefully prepare himself a tack while decrying the evils of intoxication. Another publicly advocated a vegetarian diet but ate chicken in private.

Even the few gurus who subscribe to rigid moral values are often very wealthy and find themselves unable to affect an ideal of world renunciation and nonmateriality.

Hypocrisy is not necessarily reprehensible. A distinction must be made between rationalization on the one hand and fraud on the other. As any nonpartisan will explain, every guru has blemishes; stories of avarice, greed, pride, and impropriety are as common as they are subjective. Within reason, however, vice can be tempered with virtue. A guru may not practice, to the letter, what he preaches, but as long as he upholds the ideal of the institution that he represents, then the persona of the guru remains unjaded. Purists would argue that a tainted person colors the persona he affects and that any guru worth the name must suffer no human failings. This, too, is part of the charade of affected rationalization and serves, in the final instance, to bolster an image of ideal perfection. Who, after all, will cast the first stone? Arguably, all gurus are charlatans, some more than others, but this in no way undercuts the significance of what guruship stands for in the akhara.

As I was told repeatedly, the single thing that a disciple must do in order to become a good wrestler is surrender himself completely to the service of his guru. Blind faith and absolute obedience are basic prerequisites. Banarsi Pande, a senior member of Akhara Ram Singh, graduate of the National Institute of Sports in Patiala, and licensed international referee, tells of when he would go early in the morning to massage his guru's feet, wash his clothes, and prepare his morning meal. Similar accounts were given by many other wrestlers.

On my second day at Akhara Ram Singh I was preparing to enter the pit while other wrestlers undressed, bathed and oiled themselves according to established precedent. Suddenly one of the younger wrestlers shouted out, "Guru ji, Guru ji" and the whole crowd of wrestlers—half-clothed, langots flying loose, oil bottles tipping over—moved as one body in the direction of a thinnish young man who had entered the compound from a door behind the Hanuman shrine. Airi, the one who had seen the guru first, dropped the broom with which he was sweeping the sides of the pit and threw himself prostrate at the guru's feet. Others came and touched the guru's feet with equal respect but much less drama. In the akhara the guru is regarded with absolute respect and subservience. Even the most mundane tasks—giving a massage, running errands, drawing bath water, and washing clothes—are regarded as meritorious when performed for one's guru. Touching his feet is a sign of total devotion.

The gurus I knew in Banaras did not make a pretense of perfection. This penultimate status and its attendant respect is usually deferred and attributed to the founding guru of each akhara: Babu Pande, Ram Singh, Jaddu Seth, Ragunath Maharaj, Sant Ram, Ram Sevak, Gaya Seth, Kon Bhatt' Swaminath, and so forth. In this way the perfect persona is comfortably situated in an idealized past when gurus were truly saints. Although each akhara has a guru in residence, some of whom are accorded more respect than others, a wrestler looks to the founding guru for moral, spiritual, and personal guidance. In some instances the resident guru of an akhara is a lineal descendant of the founding guru, but this is more often the exception than the rule. For instance, at Akhara Ram Singh, Jaddu Singh is the youngest brother of the founding guru. He acts out the role of guru whenever required, but he always does so in his elder brother Ram Singh's name. A large framed portrait of Ram Singh is garlanded and brought out whenever Jaddu is called upon to act as the akhara's guru. Ram Singh and Jaddu aside, many of the members of Akhara Ram Singh recognize Lakshmi Kant Pande as their guru. He is the one whose feet are touched and to whom sweets are proffered out of respect. For his part, L. K. Pande is a senior member of the akhara and recognizes Ram Singh as his guru. Kaniya Yadav and Sohan, both young men in their early thirties, also recognize Ram Singh as their guru but have taken it upon themselves to train the junior members of the akhara. Although they are not themselves referred to as gurus, they perform the role and are accorded a great deal of respect by very junior wrestlers. Akhara Ram Singh has a profusion of men who act as gurus, but all of them defer to the persona of Ram Singh.

In some respects the situation is more straightforward in other akharas. At Bara Ganesh, for instance, Lallu Pahalwan is the fifth-generation lineal guru of his akhara. However, Kaniya Lal Yadav is also recognized as a guru. Lallu and he seem to share the status while most of the actual training and instruction is given by Babul Pahalwan, a senior member. At Gaya Seth, Manohar Pahalwan fills the role of guru insofar as the other members touch his feet and show respect in various other ways. Manohar also takes a very active role in instruction. However, whenever his elder brother comes to the akhara Manohar and the other members defer to him.

Theoretically a guru's authority is unambiguous and absolute. As these examples show, in Banaras akharas at least, authority is neither rigidly established nor codified. Moreover, authority is not necessarily the primary issue (or when it is, it is a one-on-one issue between disciple and guru). As Nathu Lal Yadav pointed out, a person can learn from ten different people and may go from one teacher to another, as he sees fit, to benefit from a spectrum of knowledge. However, he must keep his "true guru's" image in his heart. To devote oneself solely to eclectic instruction is to end up with piecemeal, unsubstantial knowledge. Thus, as L. K. Pande pointed out, when he was a young boy wrestling at Ram Singh's Akhara he would regularly visit the three other akharas in the Beniya Bagh area. These three akharas, now defunct, were run by Muslim gurus (known as *ustads*) of renown, and Pande said that he would have been foolish not to avail himself of their skill. Regardless, the guru of his heart, so to speak, was without a doubt Ram Singh.

In music and dance the gharana is a formal institution structured by lineal descent wherein a disciple can trace his or her affiliation back through a long line of gurus. Each gharana has a unique style and is often associated with a particular part of the country (Neuman 1990: 145–167). One can easily classify and locate a person in the world of music and dance by discovering their gharana affiliation. Given that there are many formal parallels between wrestling gurus and gurus in other disciplines, one would expect to find that wrestling would mirror the pedagogical structure of music, dance, and other such arts. This is not the case. A wrestling disciple will know his own guru and his guru's guru, but it is rare for him to know the lineage any further than this. Wrestling gurus develop their own techniques of training and invent new moves and countermoves, but the process is both too haphazard and too public to refer to such innovations as the unique patented style of one guru or another.

No guru will divulge his particular method of training. In part this is because it is secret knowledge, but more importantly it is because a guru manipulates each wrestler's regime to accommodate idiosyncrasies and predispositions. If the wrestler is strong, the guru will develop his speed; if the wrestler is fast he will work on his strength, and so forth. A guru does not have a generic strategy which he imposes indiscriminately on his wards. He cannot, therefore, articulate his particular style as such.

In Banaras in 1987, almost all of the pedagogical situations of guru-disciple interaction were of a fairly standard type. The wrestler would apply a move or a countermove and the guru would then either do and say nothing, which was most often the case, or he would offer a critique of the move and show the wrestler how to correct his balance and grip or more effectively apply force. The same principle held true for exercise. Gurus would watch their wards and demonstrate the correct technique or else physically adjust the wrestler's body to conform to an imagined ideal. At the two akharas where gurus were regularly present, Akhara Gaya Seth and Akhara Bara Ganesh, their primary role was in telling their wards what to do, with whom, and when. That is, they set activities in motion and determined who would wrestle whom for how long and who would do how many of what kind of exercise in which order. It is interesting to note that, for whatever reasons, wrestling gurus tend to be soft-spoken and in fact say very little at all during the course of a session. They may demonstrate a move but it is incumbent on the disciple to learn through practice.

Purists may argue that this is evidence of a general decay in the guru/chela relationship, and that "true" gurus used to patrol their akharas, switch in hand, ready to punish any wrestler who failed to apply a move well or who tired too quickly. Perhaps gurus are not as strict as they once were or as skilled as before; the point is moot. My impression is that the pedagogical relationship between a guru and his disciple has always been structurally informal while spiritually and psychologically strict. As such, the institution of guruship remains intact as a guiding principle in the world of wrestling.

Irrespective of this idiosyncratic mode of pedagogy, who a guru is is far more important than how or even what he teaches. As Nathu Lal Yadav told me in an interview on the subject, "Guruship is a throne and anyone may sit on it provided he has character. Whether a person is young or old he must have character. He must have a strong will and be of a peaceful disposition so that he can listen to what ten people say and act in such a way that all ten will be happy."

A wrestler's success depends more on his attitude and comportment than on pedagogy. By keeping the image of one's guru in mind one can overcome seemingly insurmountable odds. The attitude of a disciple towards his guru is as important as the guru's own personal virtue and skill (Kesriya 1972).

The role of the disciple—blind faith and unquestioning service—is manifested in the ritual of Guru Puja, a minor calendrical festival which falls on the full moon of the Hindu month of Ashadha (June–July). Disciples are enjoined to pray and show respect for their guru on this day.

On the morning of Guru Puja I went to Akhara Ram Singh, expecting, as I had been told, to witness a formal ritual of worship. Everyone with whom I spoke said emphatically that all members of the akhara would attend the ceremony. Instead it seemed as though attendance was, if anything, less than usual. Jaddu, the nominal guru, brought out the framed portrait of his brother Ram Singh, and, lighting a stick of incense, placed the photograph at one corner of the Hanuman shrine. He then stood around the akhara waiting for members to make some sort of offering. A few, but not many, did. There was no special *puja* and everyone went about their activities as though nothing was going on. The reason for this lackluster attitude was undoubtedly the fact that the wrestlers of Akhara Ram Singh recognize a number of different men as their guru.

In the evening I went to another Guru Puja ceremony at Kashi Vyayamshala, a large gymnasium overlooking the Ganga. I was again disappointed that the guru, Parasnath Sharma, was not present. I was introduced instead to his younger brother, who was sitting in to receive the disciples. As we sat on the parapet wall overlooking the river and talked into the dusk, members came by and made cash and flower offerings. In turn, they were blessed with a vermilion *tika* placed on their foreheads.

The pujas at Kashi Vyayamshala and Akhara Ram Singh were anticlimactic and confirmed my impression that the idea of guruship is far more powerful than the enactment of any formal role. As many of my pragmatic and somewhat cynical wrestling friends remarked, it may just be a sign of the times.

Returning through the galis from Kashi Vyayamshala, I was accosted at a corner milk shop by an acquaintance from Ragunath Maharaj Akhara. He asked if I was going to his akhara to see the jori-swinging demonstration being put on as a Guru Puja celebration. I said yes, and after a glass of warm milk we set off back through the galis.

Guru Puja at Ragunath Maharaj Akhara was obviously a more formal affair than at Kashi Vyayamshala or at Akhara Ram Singh. The small courtyard was crowded with well-dressed, middle-aged men sitting and standing casually. As I came into the akhara, space was made for me to sit on a bench adjacent to the pit. The guru of the akhara sat up on a raised dais above the pit in front of a small Hanuman shrine. His pose was benevolent and paternal with an aura of divinity enhanced by countless flower garlands draped around his neck, arranged on the dais, and strewn at his feet. Quarter-kilogram paper boxes of sweets proffered in offering were arranged haphazardly in front of the guru's dais. A brass tray containing incense, holy water, vermilion paste, parched rice, and chana was situated near the guru's right knee. As disciples filed in and paid their respects the guru blessed them each with a tika.

Some disciples came only to pay their respects and make an offering, but most came to stay awhile and talk with friends. As disciples came in and the courtyard filled up, Baccha Pahalwan, one of the champions of Banaras, prepared himself to swing a pair of Ragunath Maharaj's prize joris. These joris are brought out only on special occasions and are decorated with detailed floral designs.

Jori swinging is an art akin to wrestling. Some akharas are devoted exclusively to jori swinging but are nevertheless organized along the same lines as wrestling akharas. The worldview is identical. In wrestling akharas, joris are swung for exercise as part of the larger regime. In jori akharas, swinging is an art in itself. From start to finish a swing is carefully choreographed.

An entourage of four members carefully scraped old resin from the handles of the prize joris that Baccha was to swing. Fresh rock-resin was powdered on the surface of a smooth stone. The earth of the hard-packed pit was pounded to ensure a stable, firm footing. Under the watchful eye of the guru and the appreciative gaze of the crowd, one member of the entourage oiled Baccha Pahalwan's shoulders. The oil was to ensure that Baccha's arms would be both flexible and strong.

On the smooth earth directly in front of the guru's dais three square stones were arranged: two in front, one atop the other, and a single one in back set squarely into the earth. Each member of the entourage checked and rechecked the stones to ensure their stability. The guru looked on, saying nothing. Everyone watched carefully and commented on the size of the joris, the detail of the design, and on Baccha's youthful strength.

Night had fallen and the orange light of the single bulb traced the shadows of the slowly turning fan blades over the crowd. Its light glinted off Baccha's oiled shoulders and reflected off the red earth and the yellow lime-washed walls. The guru sat in repose, cauled in the glow of green neon that emanated from the shrine behind him.

After warming up with a pair of light joris, Baccha and his entourage prepared to swing the floral jori. With his right foot on the front stones and his left on the lower rear stone, Baccha positioned the two joris to his liking. He shifted his weight forward and back until the balance seemed just right. Two members from the entourage then came forward. As one dried Baccha's underarms, forearms, thighs, and face—it was very hot despite the slowly turning fan—the other applied a thin, even layer of resin to each handle. The hum of conversation from the crowded courtyard quieted and mirrored the silence of the guru.

Baccha then looked directly at the guru and asked permission to begin. With wrists forward and his weight on his raised right foot Baccha swung the eighty-kilogram jori first forward slightly and then, with increasing pendulum motion, back and forth three times. On the fourth forward swing he lunged with the weight of the joris and jumped off the raised stone platform. Twisting wrist, elbow, and shoulder so as to stand the joris up, one on each shoulder, he landed on his knees in front of the guru who looked on benevolently as the crowded courtyard erupted in cheers and applause.

Two members of the entourage quickly took hold of the joris, and after setting them down went to work repowdering them with resin and wiping them clean of sweat. After a brief rest Baccha set his feet squarely on a neatly smoothed area of particularly hard earth. His face, arms, and legs were again wiped off and careful attention was given to ensure that the palm of each hand was dry. The joris were placed on either side and slightly in front of his legs. Two members placed the flats of their hands on top of each knobbed handle and hooked an arm under the thick end of each jori. Baccha again asked the guru for permission to begin and immediately the joris were lifted high on extended arms and lowered, each in turn, gently onto Baccha's shoulders. Taking a moment to get his balance he ensured that his grip was firmly set.

The entourage coordinator, a senior member of the akhara, stood directly in front and roughly half a meter away from Baccha. Baccha began to swing the joris behind his back in alternating pendulum arches. The senior member counted out each swing as the crowd kept empathic time. As each jori lifted up, twisted, and landed on Baccha's shoulder the crowed sighed in sympathetic encouragement. Baccha's firm stance shifted under the weight and momentum of the swinging joris. The senior member moved with him so as to keep looking directly at his face. As Baccha's strength began to wane the encouragement of the crowd swelled with each swing until the slowing momentum of each upward arch was no longer enough. First one and then the other jori crashed into the earth in front of the guru's dais.

The whole performance was explicitly staged for the benefit of the guru. It was a dramatic demonstration of strength and skill, an enactment of the relationship between guru and disciple. Throughout the performance the passive benevolence of the guru was effected with a practiced hand. He sat as an emblem, an icon of divinity, learning, wisdom and experience. The jori demonstration was, in effect, not only a staged show of physical accomplishment. Like the garlands and the sweets, it was a religious offering to the guru as god.

Gurus are human, but their persona is divine. As Nathu Lal Yadav explained, one prays to one's guru in the same way that one prays to and honors Lord Hanuman. As Atreya pointed out, teaching does not distinguish a guru. A guru is one who can show his disciples the right path to follow: the way to realize a dream. As a divine persona the guru is often an oblique rather than a direct teacher. A wrestler must practice and train but, equally important, he must "think upon his guru" and draw strength from mystical contemplation. The path of right conduct is indicated and alluded to by a guru but never revealed as such. As an attitude, devotion prepares the disciple for spiritual realization, but the final step must always be his own. In the akhara wrestlers are enjoined to keep the image of their guru set in their mind's eye. As Atreya explained, they must make themselves into empty vessels which can be filled with the guru's wisdom. A disciple cannot take knowledge; it must be given, and the exercise of learning is to prepare oneself to receive.

THE CHARACTER OF A GURU

The concepts of spiritual *shakti*, devotion, and world-renunciation are of central importance to a wrestling way of life. For a young wrestler these values are difficult to understand and harder still to reconcile with a worldly life. The guru represents these values and makes them tangible. He serves as interpreter and exemplar, as commentary and commentator, a self-reflective mediator between divine ideals and lived experience.

> Uddhava asked Krishna: "Oh Lord of hallowing glory! What kind of person is regarded as a saint by you?" Krishna replied saying:
>
> > Such a sage is compassionate; he never envies or harms any creature; is full of fortitude; firm and strong in truthfulness; of pure mind; . . . equipoised in pleasure and pain; . . . obliging unto all.
> >
> > His mind is never perturbed by desires; his senses are fully under control; he is gentle hearted; of pure (perfectly moral) conduct; devoid of all possessions; free from desires; . . . moderate in eating and drinking; serene in mind, firm in his own dharma, seeking asylum in me, and contemplative of nature.
> >
> > He is ever alert and vigilant; of deep mind; . . . full of grit (in the face of danger); free from the six worries of bodily defect (viz. hunger and thirst, grief and infatuation, old age and death); though himself indifferent to worldly honor [he] pays respect (to the worthy); possesses aptitude and willingness to impart knowledge; [is a] a sincere friend; merciful

in behavior, and endowed with spiritual knowledge (*Bhagavata Purana* 11.11.26, 29–31; Shastri's translation, 1978).

In essence this is the character of a wrestling guru. Atreya quotes sections of this passage in his article "The Place of the Guru in Indian Wrestling" (1972–1973: 21). He also references other passages which litany the virtues of saintly character (*Bhagavad Gita*, chap. 12; *Bhagavata Purana* 2.3.18–32 as referenced in *Sources of Indian Tradition*, Embree 1988: 325–326).

The best-known guru of Indian wrestling is Guru Hanuman, whose wards practice in the Birla Mill Vyayamshala near the Sabji Mandi in Old Delhi. Guru Hanuman is famous because he has trained many of India's champion wrestlers—Ved Prakash, Satpal, and Suresh, among others. For whatever reasons—his skill as a coach, the resources he has at his disposal through the aegis of his wealthy patron, or his ability to inspire greatness—Guru Hanuman is regarded as the personification of what a wrestling guru ought to be. Whenever wrestling is mentioned in the media (which is not very often) he is almost always the archetype (Bose 1967; Datta 1970; Flory 1970; *Link* 1970). A whole issue of the journal *Bharatiya Kushti* is dedicated to Guru Hanuman, and in essay after essay he is praised for having produced, as more than one author has put it, "so many shining stars which have made India bright" (Patodi 1983). Some verses from a poem about Guru Hanuman, written by Pahalwan Danesh Kumar Vishnowi, capture the essence of his iconic persona:

> The artistic skill of the Great Guru
> reverberates through a thousand worlds.
> His one and only concern is how to make
> children stronger.
> With strength, with wisdom, with his
> reputation has he made India rejoice.
> He has made India mature and wise and has
> given his experience to the young (1986: 43).

As a popular adage among wrestlers has it, a guru is like an alchemical *paras* stone: able to turn iron to gold but unable to change itself into anything else, or to change anything else into itself. A guru is a pure agent of transformation. He must by definition expect and accept the fact that ultimately his disciples will be stronger, more virtuous, more saintly, and more skilled than himself. He can set an example and only hope that it will be improved upon.

Gurus fall far short of the high standards set for them. Nevertheless, they still stand for what they do not personally achieve and can thus indicate to others the path which leads to a utopian way of life. It is not, therefore, a critical paradox—a crisis of faith, if you will—that gurus do not always practice what they preach. For what a disciple sees in a guru's action is an ideal. He can read between the lines of paradox—material wealth, social status, and rank; he can see virtues of humility and abnegation rather than the common human failings of avarice and greed. Gurus represent an ideal way of life, and in his guru a wrestler never sees hypocrisy. He sees the possibility of what he must try to become.

Along these lines, consider an extract from the biography of Swami Ustad Fakir Chand Shukla, a wrestling guru of renown:

> It must be an isolated person among the lovers of exercise who is unfamiliar with the name of the great and undefeated, Ustad Fakir Chand Shukla.
>
> As well as a wrestler, he was known as a great doctor and as a man of learning. He was the very image of renunciation. He gave hundreds of thousands of rupees for the advancement of strength, learning and wisdom. His life itself was a donation to public service. He gave everything that he had to religion and wrestling.
>
> Self-realization does not come with the success of one's family, nor with wealth or the performance of sacrifices. The nectar of self realization comes only with renunciation.
>
> The soul is not revealed through physical strength, wisdom or learning. Benevolence is above all of these, just as the season of spring brings blossoms to trees and flowers. The soul is not concerned with redemption. It is dedicated to the service of goodness and truth.
>
> This incomparably great and sinless soul has dedicated himself to the service and benefit of society.
>
> The poet Narian has written some verses to honor the sage and I quote a few lines here:
> He was a priest and a devotee of Lord Shiva.
>   He was fearless.
> He was as peaceful as a forest glade.
>   He was firm in his beliefs.
> He was a great wrestler,
>   and the shining light of the akhara.
> He was a generous benefactor,
>   and gave alms to beggers.
> He was calm of mind,
>   but his body was hard (1973: 43, 45).

The character of a guru is linked to the identity of a sannyasi who renounces the world in pursuit of enlightenment. As a sannyasi, a guru draws on his spiritual strength to bring disciples closer to ideals of religious and physical perfection. It is through the persona of the guru that the link between world renunciation and physical strength is made most strongly. The ideal of sannyas belongs, of course, to a large and extensive religious system that spans well beyond the bounds of Indian wrestling. The wrestling guru channels powerful and pervasive ideals of spiritual self-realization into very specific forms of physical energy and moral strength. As will be seen in a later chapter, the character of the guru points wrestlers in the direction of sannyas. Wrestlers translate progress along that clearly defined path into success in the world of wrestling.

A guru is a conduit to a higher state of knowledge. One must dissolve oneself into the image of the guru in order to achieve this state. There is no structured pattern that defines which path to follow. Poetic spirituality rather than rule-bound precedent is taken as the template of practical experience. As will be discussed later, Hanuman, the archetype of devotion and righteous conduct, provides a model for effecting this kind of alchemical self-dissolution.

CHAPTER 4

The Patron and the Wrestler

As institutionalized support for wrestling, public patronage is an integral feature of akhara life. It is, however, a knotty and elusive issue, because it can mean two radically different things. On the one hand is what may be called the patronage of financial support, which is fairly straightforward. A patron may build an akhara, pay his wrestlers a weekly stipend, and award them prizes for their success. On the other hand patronage requires an attitude of moral and ethical support; a kind of ideological underwriting of the wrestler's way of life. From this perspective the nature of patronage is quite different. It is neither wholly institutionalized in a particular person or office nor is it necessary that tangible material support be provided. On this level patronage is regarded more as an attitude than anything else. It remains patronage, however, to the extent that it is an attitude of explicit support for a unique way of life. In terms of levels of abstraction, patronage of this kind is akin to the disembodied persona of the guru.

On a practical level patronage fulfills a very specific function. Because wrestlers must commit their lives to training and exercise they cannot support themselves financially. Patrons take financial responsibility for a wrestler's training by providing milk, ghi, and almonds as well as some clothes and other incidentals. The patron also provides the akhara facilities: earth for the pit, ropes, buckets, cement, and bricks, as well as the land on which the pavilion is built.

Even when a patron's role is clearly defined in terms of financial responsibilities, the relationship he has with his wrestlers is not strictly utilitarian. In fact, the material aspect of the relationship between wrestler and patron is regarded as mundane almost to the point of insignificance. Far more important are the issues of status and esteem. Patrons acquire status through the success of their wrestlers, and wrestlers gain esteem through the status of their patrons. It is a mutually beneficial relationship.

Patrons are responsible for the public image of their wrestlers. It is as though the wrestler, concerned as he is with the rigors of a daily regime, can only stand for, and not elaborate, the way of life he represents. He is a mute symbol: a stark register of coded meaning which requires public interpretation. Without patronage, a wrestler can, in the language of structuralism, only signify—his body stands for morality and chastity—but he is powerless and unable to convey the story of his way of life to a larger audience. The patron gives meaning to what a wrestler simply stands for. He reads a series of elaborate themes, plots and subplots into the coded meanings of his wrestler's body.

The wrestler is an empty vessel which the guru must fill with knowledge, skill, and virtue. The patron takes this and gives it public meaning and significance. In a sense, then, the patron is sponsor, publicist, and biographer, and in all of these capacities he is the author who takes the private discipline of a wrestling way of life and makes it intelligible to a larger audience.

While what it means to be a wrestler is given public interpretation through patronage, wrestlers are not silent partners to an illegitimate (if laudatory) reading of their way of life. In the akhara, and within the world of wrestling, the symbolic components of the body convey a set of standardized meanings on which any wrestler can build and from which he can elaborate and interpret various situations. When the point of reference is changed from an exclusively wrestling context to a larger and more overtly political arena, however, then the reading of these symbols changes somewhat. In the akhara wrestlers speak their own cultural language of somaticity—the body of one color as a product of self-discipline. Patrons appropriate this language, rephrase it, manipulate its poetry, and make it their own. Nevertheless, the voices that speak from behind the patron are still those of the wrestlers themselves.

ROYAL PATRONAGE

Royal courts and princely estates have sponsored wrestlers probably since the time of Kansa, Krishna, Ravana, and the Pandava brothers.

However, there is no detailed historical record of this and no way of telling whether wrestling patronage has changed over time. In all likelihood, the formal aspect of patronage has not changed significantly (cf. Rai 1984: 221–247). Kings have kept wrestlers because the physical strength of the wrestler symbolizes the political might of the king.

In the epic poems, and in some of the Puranas, wrestlers are portrayed as warriors who not only symbolize power and prestige but also effect it as their patron's martial arm. In his many wrestling battles Hanuman may be seen as both a symbol of Ram's power and as a warrior/agent in the war on Lanka. This is also clearly the case in the Harivamsa story where Krishna and Balarama defeat Kansa's court wrestlers.

> Krishna, thus playing with Chanura for a while, adopted his own form as a chastiser of the wicked, and then the earth shook and the jewels on the diadem of Kansa fell on the ground. Krishna pressed down Chanura, and placing his knees on his breast he struck a fierce blow with his fist on his head (*Harivamsa*, chap. 86, Bose n.d.).

Krishna then proceeds to move from a symbolic to a literal victory over Kansa:

> He jumped on the royal platform, and caught hold of Kansa by the hair. This sudden attack completely overwhelmed the king. Garlands, earrings and other ornaments fell from his body. Krishna tied his neck by his cloth and dragged him down to the ground. Then he killed him (ibid).

One of the best early accounts of wrestling patronage is found in the western Chaulukya king Somesvara's (1124–1138) *Manasollasa* (Srigondekar 1959). The chapter entitled "Malla Vinod" describes the classification of wrestlers into types by age, size, and strength. It also outlines how the wrestlers were to exercise and what they were to eat. In particular the king was responsible for providing the wrestlers with pulses, meat, milk, sugar, and "high-class" sweets. The wrestlers were kept isolated from the women of the court and were expected to devote themselves to building their bodies (Mujumdar 1950: 11).

According to a number of sources (Khedkar 1959; R. B. Pandey n.d.; Suryavanshi 1962; Verma 1970; K. C. Yadav 1957; Yadavkumar 1982) the Yadava kings and nobles of the early to middle medieval period were avid wrestlers and sponsored numerous tournaments. However, few details are known beyond the fact that many of the kings who ruled the great Vijayanagar Deccan kingdom (1336–1565) practiced wrestling along with other martial arts (Mujumdar 1950: 15). Krishnadevraj is said to have drunk about a pound and a half of sesame oil every morning.

The symbolic equation between physical strength and political might is also found in more contemporary historical accounts. In a number of the Mogul court records references are found which indicate that wrestlers were part of a ruler's estate. Indications are that wrestlers were paid a regular stipend and were also given provisions for maintaining themselves (Beveridge 1921: 656, 660, 683; Blochmann 1873–1948: 253; Mujumdar 1950: 16; T. N. Roy 1939). In turn they were called upon to entertain the royal court. Bouts were organized with wrestlers from other courts.

According to Mujumdar, the great Maratha leader Shivaji established numerous akharas throughout Maharashtra at the behest of his guru Samrath Ramdas (1950: 18). During the Maratha period, Maharaja Daulatarao Shinde is said to have kept a wrestler on a daily allowance of twenty pounds of milk and a sheep (ibid: 20). The best account of a royal akhara for this period is that of Nanasaheb Peshwa. According to Mujumdar his akhara was equipped with twenty-four different pieces of exercise equipment (ibid: 21). Bajirao II also built and maintained a fully equipped akhara and established Balambhaat Dada Deodhar as the guru of this facility. Later Deodhar and his disciples moved to Banaras where they established an akhara now known as Kon Bhatt Akhara in the Bibihatia neighborhood. Although the evidence is scant it would be a fair to say that court wrestlers during the Mogul and Maratha periods were kept as entertainers and as symbols of royal power. The same is true for princely states of the more modern period of British imperialism.

In an interview on the subject of princely patronage Shri Ram Sharma ji recounts his experiences to Banarsi Das Chaturvedi:

> I had the opportunity to stay with King Rukmangad Singh and I can say with complete honesty that the government of Uttar Pradesh has not done half of what this king has done for the art of wrestling. There is a small princely state in the district of Hardowi where Raja Rukmangad Singh received a privy purse from the government in the amount of 400,000 rupees. The king would sit down with about thirty wrestlers and give them instruction every day. Each day he would spend between 150 and 200 rupees on them. . . . Every wrestler in India knew the Raja and thought of him as his guardian (Banarsi Das Chaturvedi 1961: 102).

One of Maharaja Holkar of Indor's wrestlers, Kasam Ali, is said to have broken the leg of a camel that kicked him. His wrestling *janghiya* briefs

were so big that a normal man could fit his whole body through one leg
hole. Tukojirao Holkar's wrestler, Shiva Pahalwan, broke up a fight
between two raging bulls. As the story goes he "sent one flying north and
one flying south." Many remember when Shivajirao Holkar arranged a
bout between Paridatta, the father of Gulam Kadar Pahalwan, and
Ahamed Mir Khan Pathan. After three hours of wrestling the bout was
still tied and the Maharaja called a draw. After the fight the wrestler's
legs were so swollen that their janghiya briefs had to be cut from their
thighs. There are countless other such anecdotes which are told and
retold. At each telling the power of the king is remembered as a political
manifestation of his wrestlers' pugilistic valor.

A similar situation obtains when the diet and exercise regime of a
wrestler is considered. The quantity, quality, and richness of a wrestler's
diet reflects directly on the status of the king. A wrestler's appetite was
often said to be equal to that of an elephant, and the king's strength was
as great as his wrestlers' appetites. The same holds true for exercise. A
court wrestler who could drink five liters of milk and do thousands of
dands and bethaks in a day was symbolically demonstrating the extent
of his king's power. Gama, the great wrestler of the first quarter of
this century, championed the position of Maharaja Jaswant Singh of
Jodhpur by doing more deep knee bends than any other wrestler from
a field of four hundred—and this when he was only ten years old (Ali
1984: 101). Later, when in the court of Maharaja Bhawani Singh, Gama
was provided with a daily diet of about ten liters of milk, half a liter of
ghi, a liter and a half of butter, and two kilograms of fruit.

The body of the wrestler is held up by the king as an emblem of his
rule. As the following examples clearly indicate, the wrestler embodies
the king's temporal power.

> Kasam Ali, the ninety-five-year-old disciple of Abji Ustad, was a courtier of
> Maharaja Tukojirao. Even at this age he was tall and light skinned. He had
> a pleasant disposition and never stooped. I looked at him and the breath left
> my mouth: "If these were the ruins of an old man, then the tower was as
> strong as ever." . . . Wrestlers were the glory of their king. (Patodi 1986b:
> 71)

> Brij Lal ustad, a lifelong *brahmachari*, a man of his word and a man with
> faith in god, asked his king, Shivaji, to permit him to wrestle a Punjabi
> wrestler who many other wrestlers had declined to take on. Surprised, the
> king asked Brij Lal, "Are you really going to wrestle this champion?" With-
> out batting an eye Brij Lal replied, "Lord, who am I to wrestle, it is I in your
> name who challenge this man." With that the king gave his permission for
> the bout to be fought (Patodi 1986c: 65–66).

Even though wrestlers were in some instances kept in other capacities
(as was Kasam Ali, who worked in the king's munitions department),
they were never called upon to work per se. As indicated by Ratan
Patodi, wrestlers were symbols in a strict sense of the word.

> Wrestlers had self-respect when India was a colonized country. The indepen-
> dent princes never called upon their wrestlers to do any thing which would
> undercut their self-respect. And along with self-respect, courtesy and modesty
> was ingrained in them. Wrestlers considered it their duty to be honest and
> to shun any kind of doubletalk (1973b: 11).

It was precisely because wrestlers already "stood for" the ideological
principles of a disciplined way of life—physical strength, moral virtue,
honesty, respect, duty, and integrity—that they served so well as political emblems. Kings co-opted the terms of this ideology and glorified
themselves by implicitly advocating a wrestling way of life. Wrestling
became the language of royal pomp and power. Whatever else patronage
was, it served as a public dramatization of wrestling as a way of life.
The king who bestowed a prize on his champion wrestler—gold and
silver, jeweled necklaces, crowns, cash, elephants, titles, and many other
things—implicitly advocated chastity and the attendant system of disciplined action which was part of the whole regime.

The wrestler became the archetypal citizen of the royal state. This
aspect of patronage is perhaps best exemplified by Bhawanrao Pant, the
raja of Aundh. Inspired by Balasaheb Mirajkar, raja of Miraj, Bhawanrao popularized and codified surya namaskar, a system of exercise which
synthesizes many aspects of the wrestling ethos. The raja made surya
namaskar exercises mandatory in the schools under his control (Mujumdar 1950: iii). He thus symbolically transposed his power onto the
physique of his subjects. Conversely, he saw his estate as drawing power
from the collective health of his people. Although there is very little
information to go on, it seems that earlier kings of the medieval period—the Yadavas and Somesvara, in particular—also felt compelled
to turn their subjects into disciplined wrestlers. In establishing hundreds
of gymnasia throughout Maharashtra it seems that Shivaji was also
using wrestling patronage as a model for the public administration of a
broad-based program of physical education.

The rajas of Aundh and Miraj were not the only royal patrons of the
late nineteenth and early twentieth centuries. The Maharaja of Baroda,
raja of Kolhapur, a number of the rajas of Indor, and the rajas of Patiala,
Jodhpur, and Datiya were all strong supporters of wrestling as a way of

life. They are regarded by contemporary wrestlers as the guardians of an honored tradition.

According to contemporary wrestlers, the art of wrestling would have died out completely had it not been for royal patronage. What they mean by this is not so much that wrestling needed royal financing, but that it needed public royal acclaim. It needed to be drawn out of the village akhara and writ large on the royal stage. Left to its own devices, one might say, wrestling would have flourished only as a popular sport and as a marginalized and somewhat esoteric way of life. Royal patronage served to turn a popular sport into a political discourse with nascent nationalistic undertones. Although the precise history of this development has not yet been fully researched, its implications for contemporary nationalism will be examined in a later chapter.

One context in which wrestling became associated with nationalistic ideals was during the struggle for independence in the early part of this century. The story of Gama is a dramatic case in point. In 1910, two years before he became the court wrestler of the maharaja of Patiala, and as India's struggle against British imperialism gained momentum, Gama was sent to London to fight in the John Bull World Championship Competition. Gama and his brother, along with two other wrestlers, were sponsored by Sarat Kumar Mitra, a Bengali millionaire. Unfortunately, Gama was too short to gain official status as a contestant. However, a local theater offered Gama 250 pounds sterling a week to take part in some sideshow bouts. From this unofficial venue Gama challenged any of the world-class London wrestlers to a bout. To whomever could last five minutes Gama promised to pay five pounds. On the first day Gama dispatched three English challengers in short order. The next day he took on another twelve with equal success. He thus gained access to the official tournament where he was pitted against the world champion Zbyszko. Though much smaller in size, Gama fought Zbyszko for three hours and clearly had the upper hand when the contest ended for the day. Zbyszko failed to show up the following day to continue the bout and Gama was declared the world champion. The symbolic implications of Gama's rout of England's best wrestlers in the very seat of imperial power were not lost on the subjugated Indian public. Popular accounts have it that there was not a single newspaper in Hindi or Urdu that did not herald the news of India's triumph.

In 1928, after sixteen years in the maharaja of Patiala's court, Gama again challenged Zbyszko. This bout was fought in Patiala at the height of the nationalist struggle. Though Zbyszko was not British, the bout was nevertheless a symbolic reenactment of Gama's first victory. Zbyszko was defeated in two and a half seconds in front of a crowd of over forty thousand spectators who had come from all over the country to witness the fight. Ratan Patodi recounts that the arena erupted in one voice, shouting "India has won! India has won!"

After the victory the maharaja embraced Gama, took the pearl necklace he was wearing, and placed it around the champion's neck. A parade was arranged and Gama rode on the king's elephant holding in his arms a silver mace made specially for the occasion. So that Gama's regal achievement would not be forgotten, the king gave him a whole village and an annual stipend of 6,000 rupees (Patodi 1984: 35). One can well imagine the prestige that the maharaja of Patiala derived from this contest. As the wrestling euphemism for defeat goes, the maharaja had "shown the world the sky" by pinning down an emblem of imperialism. Gama and his patron the maharaja came to symbolize the possibility of self-determination and independence.

While it is true that a wrestler reflects the power of his patron king, it is also true that a king must be equal to the status of his wrestlers. In this regard a popular adage is apropos: "A subject is only as good as his king." Wrestlers sometimes reacted against their patron if they thought he was compromising their own status.

Once while watching a wrestling bout, Maharaja Tukojirao Holkar decided that he wanted to pit his wrestler Bare Bhaiya against Kyam Pahalwan of Lahore. This was arranged, and Bare Bhaiya came into the arena shouting the praise of his sponsor and patron the Maharaja. Entering the pit he applied a "*jhar*" move on Kyam who fell flat on his back. Bowing to the Maharaja and the people who had come to watch, Bare Bhaiya left the arena.

Kyam returned to Lahore and his patron Maharaja was not pleased with his performance and told him to go and fight Bare Bhaiya again. Kyam, a wrestler of self-respect, answered his king saying: "I am a wrestler not a cock that can be fought at will." The king took offense and ordered that Kyam's stipend be stopped.

Hearing this Kyam replied: "Rescind it if you wish, for it is a miserly amount upon which no one can wrestle. Wrestling runs on a silver grind stone and on the amount you give me I can only feed grain to the pigeons."

In the end Kyam did not have to fight again and his stipend was renewed (Patodi 1973*b*: 11–12).

There is a degree of tension in the relationship between a wrestler and his royal patron. Each has a great deal riding on the image the other projects. Moreover, there is the issue of power and control. As the above examples have shown, wrestlers put a great deal of stress on self-respect.

Among other things, self-respect means self-determination and an unwillingness to subject oneself to any authority. Patronage requires a degree of subjugation. Wrestlers are uncomfortable with the obligations which ensue from sponsorship. For their part, kings are threatened by the persona of a powerful wrestler. Physical strength, self-respect, honesty, faith, and moral uprightness manifest in a wrestler can sometimes outshine the king's glory. The emblem can become too perfect, and, in a sense, surpass that which it is meant to represent. A king whose power and authority does not match up to his wrestlers' standards becomes a parody of his own pomp. In fact, a king is never in complete control of the image his wrestlers project. For although a wrestler stands for the king, a wrestler also stands for himself. The king and wrestler compete for control over the meaning of such things as strength and morality. Does the king's authority serve to advance the wrestler's status or does the wrestler's status serve to reflect the king's power? This drama is played out in the following story.

Before independence there were numerous small princely states. Under the patronage of the kings and princes of these states, Indian wrestling flourished. Wherever the kings were skilled in matters of state they were also concerned with fitness and were often no less skilled than many of their wrestlers.

During the reign of Maharaja Khanderåo in the princely state of Baroda, there were some three hundred wrestlers in the royal court. Most of these wrestlers were Punjabis, Chaubes, or Jethis.

One day Maharaja Khanderao called a special *darbar* [assembly] of his court. The reason for calling the darbar was Ramju Pahalwan's uncontested success in the Indian wrestling akharas. Ramju was a Punjabi wrestler under the patronage of Khanderao and had been defeating one wrestler after another.

Maharaja Khanderao, being a patron of Indian wrestling, was concerned that there did not seem to be any counter moves to apply against Ramju's technique. This was the issue for which the darbar had been called, and all of the court wrestlers were present. The Maharaja himself was seated on a high throne and appeared as a great sage of wrestling. His strong body and rippling muscles could be seen beneath his silken robes. As the darbar came to order, the Maharaja had only to think about Ramju and the wrestler leapt like a leopard onto the dais and stood humbly beside the throne of his patron.

The Maharaja said to him, "Ramju, you have been undefeated in every akhara where you have wrestled and many of those you have defeated have renounced wrestling on your account. Many have been subdued by self-doubt. For those wrestlers who have, on your account, removed their langot and janghiya [i.e., given up wrestling] I say, 'It is easier for you, Ramju, to defeat a wrestler of equal strength and skill than it is for a wrestler obsessed with sexual passion to lose.' This is true, and to prove it I challenge you to a wrestling match."

Hearing this announcement the whole court was surprised. In order to protect the King's honor many of the court wrestlers said, "let me fight first with Ramju, my lord."

But the king said, "It will take you a long time to be worthy and skilled enough to fight Ramju."

Hearing all of this Ramju spoke, "my lord, I am your humble servant. You are my patron. What means do I, a poor man, have that I can match my skill with yours?"

In reply to this the Maharaja said, as one versed and experienced in athletics, "wrestling is an art, and it has nothing to do with wealth and status. The bout will be held one month from now. Practice hard and spare no expense."

The Maharaja instructed the accountant to spend as much as necessary on Ramju's training and diet.

Exactly one month later the Maharaja and Ramju, surrounded by courtiers and advisors, took their places in the arena which was bedecked with rose petals and scented with perfume. Both wrestlers set upon one another like two rogue elephants bent on destruction. The Maharaja was matching Ramju's technique with his own well-crafted skill. Every move was broken quickly and with great flourish.

After one hour neither wrestler had the upper hand. The Maharaja then began to have doubts as to whether Ramju was giving his full effort and asked him to swear by god and the milk he had drunk from his mother's breast that he was putting out 100 percent.

Hearing this, Ramju felt a surge of energy, applied a "*bagal-dubba*," and forced the king down on his knees. But the king again stood up and the match went on like this for another hour.

The Maharaja then said, "Ramju, we could go on like this for three days and you could still not pin me, but now I can no longer tolerate the smell of your sweat. Let me go and I will call you the winner."

So Ramju let the Maharaja go and stood up, bowing slightly and folding his hands before the king, saying, "Lord, I am your servant. I am the one who has lost. Who am I to think that I was a match for you. I only followed your instructions."

In reply the Maharaja said, "Ask whatever you wish as a prize. What you have given me is priceless and what you have taught me today is beyond compare. What you have given me is greater even than my family can give."

Now, who could argue with a king? Ramju had been given an order, and there was nothing for it but to name his prize.

"Whatever is your wish," cried Ramju, "but if you insist, it is your humble servant's request that if you grant me the crown you are wearing I would be most honored."

Hardly had Ramju finished speaking when the king removed his crown
and some 25,000 rupees worth of jewels and gave them to his court wrestler.

About the rest of Ramju's life it is only necessary to know one thing.
When Ramju was at the zenith of his career he went one day to the Maharaja
and said, "Lord, my body is splitting because I can no longer wrestle enough
to get tired."

Hearing this, the Maharaja ordered that two glass mirrors in the shape
of hands be fixed into the wall of the akhara. He told Ramju, "After your
daily practice and exercise regime place your hands on the glass mirrors and
push until you are tired." Ramju did as he was told (Patodi 1986b: 53–56).

Ratan Patodi concludes his account of this story as follows:

Swami Baldev Misra told me that he went to Lal Akhara in Baroda and saw
for himself the glass mirror hands. With his great strength Ramju had turned
the mirror hands upside down (ibid).

There are a number of interesting points which this story brings to light.
The contest between the king and his court wrestler is a metaphor for
the struggle between royal patronage and a wrestler's own self-definition. The struggle is not of epic proportions. It is a subtle issue of identity: of who represents whom. In the contest the struggle is not defini-
tively resolved; the king gives up. There is a symbolic resolution,
however, insofar as Ramju is invested with political power manifest
in the king's crown. Conversely, the king himself is recognized as an
accomplished wrestler. Their roles are reversed and thus the tension
between physical and political strength is depicted in sharp relief
through juxtaposition.

One reading of this story would be that the king felt threatened by
Ramju's success. He felt it necessary to put Ramju in his proper place.
Having not actually defeated the king, Ramju nevertheless comes out
the winner. Thus he may keep the crown as a votive symbol of status
without power. The bout thus serves to enhance and underscore Ramju's
purely symbolic role.

In the symbolism of the glass-mirror hands, Ramju must, in effect,
wrestle with his own reflection. While in the akhara he is purely a self-
referential figure, a symbol of himself, a sign of pure strength and skill
that mirrors a way of life turned in on itself. By fixing the mirrors into
the akhara wall, the king is able to harness an ideology of physical,
moral, and psychological strength. In the akhara Ramju's incomparable
strength is spent, impotently, on itself. Only the king can translate this
energized conundrum into a reflection of political prestige. Ramju's way
of life becomes glorified only in the radiance of his patron's royal status.

As a way of life wrestling does not necessarily require royal patronage, but it does require translation and interpretation. Restricted to the isolated world of the akhara, symbols of strength and virtue only refer back to a restricted and restricting set of values—chastity, devotion, and moral duty. In this self-referential arena the wrestler can only be a good wrestler and not a hero of royal proportions. From the akhara a wrestler speaks to a small audience. From beside his patron's throne, the size of his thigh and all that it is known to mean, for instance, take on regal dimensions.

At issue in the relationship between wrestler and patron is control over public identity. By and large, the public image of the wrestler belongs to the king. This is made clear in the following example where the story is told of one wrestler who sought to reappropriate his own body and public self-image.

> An artist always follows his own mind, and Ramlal Pahalwan suffered from being particularly independent and strong willed. Maharaja Tukojirao was constantly upset with him. Why was this? It was his manner. God had out done himself when he made Ramlal. To the last detail he was a tall and beautiful youth. Everyday he would wear a clean, freshly washed head cloth and *dhoti* [loincloth]. It was his habit to decorate his hands and feet with *mehandi* [vegetable dye] and place on his forehead a small, neat *bindi* [auspicious mark]. He always went out with a *pan* in his mouth. He never came out into his house compound unannounced; but if called upon by guests, he would put on perfume and come out with affected drama and pomp. The Maharaja was certainly concerned that Ramlal account for himself. But Ramlal never felt that his actions needed justification (Patodi 1986c: 64).

Being strong-willed, Ramlal wanted to stand for himself. Through his body he sought to give his own public interpretation of his identity as a wrestler. Although Ramlal epitomizes the tensions between patron and wrestler, his personality is anomalous and out of character with most other wrestlers. The majority of wrestlers, like Ramju of Baroda and Gama of Patiala, were willing simply to stand for power and prestige rather than affect it themselves.

The passing of royal patrons is lamented by every wrestler with whom I spoke. They were seen as the guardians of a way of life that would otherwise have died out as a mute and marginalized victim of modernism. The financial backing that rajas and maharajas provided is significant. However, patrons are remembered more for having cast wrestling in a positive light by giving it public and prestigious acclaim. As heir to the legacy of royal patronage the current national government is criticized by many wrestlers on precisely this point. In the court of kings, wrestling was a royal art; under the current government it is not accorded a comparable national status.

GOVERNMENT PATRONAGE

Whereas royal patronage is glorified and its passing lamented, current government sponsorship of wrestling is loudly and publicly criticized for being inadequate. I asked Atma Ram of Akhara Ram Singh about government support, and he voiced the general consensus saying, "Yes, the government supports us; and with its support we are dying." A large number of the articles on wrestling which appear in the Indian press chastise the government for having done nothing to support akharas (Deshmukh 1979: 1; Kaushik 1979: 4; Maheshwar 1981: 9; K. P. Roy 1967; D. Singh 1988; *Statesman* 1970: 3; *Swarajya* 1973: 30).

What wrestlers are critical of, however, is not necessarily the institutionalized structure of patronage and support in modern India. Many wrestlers contrast government sponsorship of Western sports—particularly cricket—with the general lack of support given to Indian wrestling. To be fair, however, it should be noted that there is an Indian Style Wrestling Association based in Delhi (Ali 1984: 12–13), and an annual Indian Style National Championship, Bharat Kesri, is sponsored by the Indian Wrestling Federation. The state government of Maharashtra, through the auspices of the Maharashtra Wrestling Association, has established at least two permanent akharas in the Kolhapur area (Bhalekar 1978: 10). Nevertheless, the prevailing attitude among wrestlers in Delhi, Roorkee, Dehra Dun, and Banaras is that the government has turned its back on their way of life. Wrestlers are dissatisfied with the apathetic attitude and outright ignorance of the government regarding what they feel is most significant about wrestling, namely its ethical ideals and moral virtues, its character and the pride and self-respect it fosters. Wrestlers are also critical of the extent to which the sport has been corrupted by political influence. In fact there is a whole "genre" of essay in the popular literature which examines and criticizes the government's intrusive and destructive role in wrestling (Koshal 1972–1973; Munna 1979, 1982; Patodi 1972; Sangar 1982; K. P. Singh 1983).

Government support for wrestling is seen from two perspectives. On the one hand is the formal institutionalized structure of patronage. Government departments and nationalized services have a "sports quota" in their employment roster and are required to hire a percentage of qualified athletes to fill these positions. The national government, along with state administrations, has established a number of "sports hostels" where qualified young wrestlers can, with the right connections, go for three years of training and education. In the state of Uttar Pradesh, the Meerut and Bareilly hostels are particularly well known for their curricular focus on wrestling.

Western-style competitive wrestling is organized under the authority of the Delhi-based Indian Wrestling Federation, made up of representatives from a network of sixteen state branches. All national and international tournaments are organized through the aegis of this body. Patronage from the Indian Wrestling Federation is directed toward wrestlers qualified for national and international competition. The emphasis is on Western freestyle wrestling done on mats, and not Indian-style wrestling per se. Nevertheless, there is some overlap between the two forms insofar as Western-style wrestlers usually have a reputation as Indian-style champions as well. The Indian/Western style distinction is more a matter of formal contrast than an exclusive dichotomy as such. In any case, I will restrict my comments to the type of institutionalized government patronage which Indian style wrestlers actually receive or feel they should receive. I am not interested in questions concerning the nationalization and internationalization of wrestling as a sport.

NATIONALIZED SERVICES AND GOVERNMENT BOARDS

Many of the basic services in India are nationalized and organized as separate departments with regional and municipal jurisdiction. The post and telegraph, water, and electricity boards are the largest of these departments. The National Railway is a similar institution and provides employment for tens of thousands of people. The armed services are organized on a large, national scale and are, of course, directly affiliated with government. Each state of the republic has a police force. The PAC (Police Armed Constabulary) is organized on a national level. The State Bank of India is the largest of the nationalized financial institutions and has a network of offices throughout the country. All of these institutions are monolithic in size and provide employment for hundreds of thousands of people.

Each division or subdivision of these branches recruits and hires athletes to fill their "sports quota." As a result local railway offices, police precincts, banks, and post offices hire wrestlers as checking clerks, constables, filing clerks, and postmen. In some cases branch offices build akharas for their locally hired wrestlers, but more often than not wrestlers who work for a branch of the government exercise and train in their own guru's personal akhara.

Wrestlers compare these government institutions to the kings and princes of pre-independence India. The railway and police in particular, but also the water and electricity boards and State Bank of India, sponsor a number of wrestlers who have proven themselves in national competition. In Banaras, for instance, Sita Ram Yadav, Banarsi Pande, Bishambar Singh, Jharkhande Rai, Krishna Kumar Singh, and Ashok have all been national champions in their weight class and work for the Diesel Locomotive Works or other railway offices. Sita Ram Yadav and Bishambar have wrestled in international competitions, and Banarsi Pande has taken part as an international referee. Bhaiya Lal, a national-level wrestler, is sponsored by the State Bank of India, where he works as a clerk. The well-known and respected Govardan Das Malhotra, one-time national referee, is also employed by the state bank. In many ways he personifies the role of the bank as patron.

Although the government boards and the nationalized services are concerned with sponsoring wrestlers, they are not particularly interested in wrestling as a way of life. On account of this it is not surprising that many of the wrestlers who are employed by the railway board or state bank do not feel any great affinity towards their sponsors. The relationship is regarded in a very utilitarian light. Wrestlers feel no great pride in being wards of the state, but they are glad to have an income and a secure status. They turn to their guru and akhara, however, when identifying themselves as Indian wrestlers.

The patronage of the state varies in significant ways from the patronage of kings and princes. Primarily, wrestlers are not kept strictly as symbols. They are employed and are required to work. In the armed services this arrangement is compatible since a recruit has no assigned task other than what he is ordered to do. He is, in effect, recruited as a wrestler. In the railway and state bank, however, wrestlers must work as clerks, baggage inspectors, and draftsman. In the post and telegraph office they must sort mail or learn some other skill. Wrestlers in the police force are expected to direct traffic or patrol their assigned post.

Many of the wrestlers with whom I spoke did not take their work very seriously, for it conflicted with their vocation of wrestling. Sita Ram Yadav pointed out the paradox, saying that wrestlers are recruited to win championships but then are told to work seven or eight hours a day. It is impossible to practice and train given such a situation. Another well-known wrestler complained that he spent his time sitting behind a desk when, as he put it, "I was born to live in the akhara." Senior wrestlers take a cavalier attitude towards their sponsoring institutions. Whether or not they actually do what they say is not clear, but many claim that they go to work only if they feel so inclined.

The railway and the armed services arrange annual training camps, and wrestlers often take an extended leave of absence from their work to attend. The camps provide effective training for national competitions and for international tours, but they do not foster ideals and values essential to wrestling as a way of life. One wrestler expressed concern over the increasing number of men who were now bringing their wives and families to the training camps. To his way of thinking this was antithetical to the mind set required of a self-controlled wrestler.

Generally speaking, the railway board and the other service branches see wrestling as just another sport. As such it is a sport cut in a very Western mold. Wrestlers are hired for their individual prowess rather than for the ideals they represent. For the most part an Indian wrestler who is hired by the railway or state bank is stripped of his unique identity and reclothed as a skilled but otherwise regular employee of the state. In this guise wrestlers no longer stand for a way of life but for a nationalized sport. To be sure, kings wanted the best wrestlers to be in their service, but they embraced the whole regime and did not extract the wrestler, as a mere athlete, from the important context of his whole way of life.

Although wrestlers glorify royal patronage, they recognize that in many instances old wrestlers were unceremoniously put to pasture. The unfortunate example of the great Gama is a case in point. Still the "world champion," he died an all-but-forgotten, poor, sick man (Rajput 1960). In some cases rajas and maharajas gave their retiring wrestlers small land grants and stipends, but for the most part there was no established precedent for giving a pension to a retired wrestler. A wrestler's career is short lived. By the time he is thirty-five, or forty at the very latest, he is no longer competitive. Severance is an important consideration for someone who has spent his whole life wrestling. Government service is very good in this respect and the senior wrestlers who no longer compete are comfortable and secure in their tenured status.

The number of wrestlers who are sponsored by the various branches of government service is insignificant when compared to the total number of wrestlers in India who have no formal sponsorship at all. It is unlikely, however, that even the rajas, maharajas, and wealthy landlords sponsored a majority of all wrestlers. One had to be good to be a court wrestler, and most practitioners of the art never earned a rank of this order. Significantly, even those without sponsorship idealize the relationship of a patron and his wrestler. Sponsorship is, therefore, more important as a symbolic relationship than as a financial and economic one. The fact that Govardan Das Malhotra was able to negotiate a state stipend of 150 rupees per month for two old Banaras wrestlers is paltry on a financial scale, and characteristic, wrestlers tell me, of the bureaucratic somersaults which have to be performed in order to squeeze out a bare minimum of prestige. Still, the stipend was a powerful, if muted, message of validation.

On the whole, government sponsorship is not charged with the same significance as royal patronage. The railway and state bank do not have tangible prestige or political power in the same way as did wealthy kings. In state institutions there is no figurehead, no pomp, and there are few if any rituals of status for the wrestler to emblazon with his character. What made wrestlers and kings compatible was the symbolic parallel between royal power and physical-cum-moral strength. There is no such parallel between wrestlers and the modern state apparatus. The nationalized services are vast bureaucracies with which wrestlers cannot identify. On the state roster a wrestler is a grappler and an athlete. Nothing more and nothing less. Contrast the biographical profile of a state wrestler with that of a court wrestler like Ramju.

> Randhawa Singh (Punjab), featherweight: Born on February 2, 1945, Randhawa hails from Lachara village, District Muzzafarnagar, and is at present a Sub-Inspector of Police in Punjab.
> His first big achievement was the National Championships in 1965 in Kolhapur, when he was declared champion of his weight class. He repeated his performance in 1966 (D. P. Chand 1980).

The story is the same for other well-known champions such as Bishambar of the railway and Bhim Singh of the armed services. Their lives are a litany of bouts and awards, and their bodies are reduced to the stark numbers of dates and weight-class identification. Their only identity is their success. Epic, apocryphal tales of great strength and superhuman achievement are strikingly absent from the state wrestler's portrait.

Although most government sponsorship is utilitarian and deals with wrestling strictly as a sport and with wrestlers as simply athletes, there are some notable exceptions. Individuals within the state apparatus who have a personal interest in wrestling as a way of life have succeeded in taking on the role of moral patron.

Govardan Das Malhotra received his training as a wrestling referee from the National Institute of Sports in Patiala in 1963. Since then he had coached international teams and managed tournaments in Kabul and Teheran. Malhotra is active in the state bank trying to recruit young wrestlers for sponsorship. He has also helped organize local bouts in the Banaras area. Three things mark Malhotra from other modern patrons of wrestling. First, he is conscious of the need to preserve interest and provide support for Indian wrestling as a way of life. Second, he has written numerous short life sketches of famous wrestlers so as to illustrate the value of Indian wrestling as an important national heritage (Malhotra 1981: 17–96). Third, he has consciously removed himself from what he refers to as the gross politics of modern wrestling where influence is everything and skill, ability, and character count for very little.

Like Malhotra, Gupteshwar Misra has worked to preserve the tradition of Indian wrestling. Though a national level freestyle wrestler himself, and trained as a referee in Paris, Misra has remained committed to the training methods and lifestyle principles of Indian wrestling. Misra is directly responsible for the national success of most Banaras district wrestlers. He has inspired many through example. In his prime he would regularly do 2,500 bethaks and 2,000 dands, run four miles, and wrestle for an hour every day. He would then drink a liter of milk and a quarter-liter of ghi and eat half a kilo of almonds and a dozen oranges. Misra has helped organize teams for the railway, the police, and Banaras Hindu University.

Malhotra, Misra and a number of others of equal stature—Parasnath Sharma, Ram Narian Sarien, and Bishambar Singh, to name but three—are important patrons of Indian wrestling. Their best intentions are, however, not fully realized. Whatever effort these men make to hold up wrestling as a symbol of the state, they do not, by themselves, have a public image of powerful patronage. They cannot quite pull it off. In his capacity as a relatively high-rank employee, Malhotra certainly represents the stature of the state bank. But he does not represent the bank's financial power in the same way that a raja represented absolute authority and temporal power. He does not embody the government's intangible power any more than does Bishambar Singh personify the power behind the railway bureaucracy. Neither man is able to effect royal pomp and circumstance. Unlike kings, modern state officials are unable to decorate akharas with palm fronds, flowers, and rose petals, or saturate the earth of wrestling pits with buckets of oil and turmeric paste. Neither can they sprinkle their wrestler's bodies with expensive perfume. They are unable properly to champion the cause of wrestling, for they do not represent the right kind of power, wealth or authority.

The Birla Mill Vyayamshala in Old Delhi, under the tutelage of Guru Hanuman, is perhaps the only wrestling akhara in India today that has the kind of sponsorship which royal patrons provided. While the circumstances of this akhara are unique, it is representative of the kind of patronage which wrestlers envision for their way of life.

The Birlas are, in effect, kings of free enterprise in the republic of India. They are one of the wealthiest and most powerful families in the country. Jugal Kishor Birla, a contemporary of Mahatma Gandhi and financial backer of the Freedom Movement, donated money for the construction of an akhara in 1928 and established Guru Hanuman as its manager. The akhara is affiliated with one of the Birla cloth mills from which it takes its name. There is no clear indication of the financial arrangement between Birla Enterprises and the akhara. Some people have told me that all of the wrestlers there—numbering in the hundreds, but the exact figure is vague—are paid a regular monthly stipend. Room and board is available at the akhara for some wrestlers, but many others come for practice and live outside the complex. Through the person of Murlighar Dalmiya, Birla Enterprises pay for the akhara's upkeep and for new construction and improvements. There is an earthen pit as well as a Western-style "rubber" mat purchased in 1979. It is likely that the Birlas also pay for the travel and training expenses of the akhara's many national and international wrestling champions.

A story is told which exemplifies the relationship between the akhara, Guru Hanuman, and Birla Enterprises. A young wrestler had come to Delhi from Maharashtra in order to take part in a wrestling tournament. Unfortunately he ran out of money and was unable to purchase a railway ticket for the return journey. Knowing one of the wrestlers at the Birla Mill Vyayamshala, he went there to seek help. At the akhara he was well taken care of. Guru Hanuman had one of his wards prepare a glass of almond tonic for the Maharashtrian wrestler. He then wrote a note which authorized the withdrawal of fifty rupees from the mill's accounting office. This he gave to the Maharashtrian wrestler, who was put up for the night by one of the mill wrestlers with whom he was acquainted. The part of the story which is particularly emotive for most wrestlers is

Guru Hanuman's apparent ability to draw freely from the ample coffers of his industrial patron.

While the financial outlay for the akhara is, no doubt, considerable—200,000 rupees were spent on a foreign wrestling mat—there is much more to Birla patronage than money. Guru Hanuman and his wards—Suresh, Ashok, Satpal, Ved Prakash, and many others—bask in the light of an industrial giant. Their success matches the financial success of Birla free enterprise. Physical strength and skill reflects well on wealth and prestige, and wealth gives stature to a "traditional" way of life in modern India. Guru Hanuman and the numerous national champions that he has produced are more than just successful wrestlers, for they stand for something larger than themselves and on the shoulders of the likes of Ghaneshyamdas Birla, who was not only one of the wealthiest men in India in the first half of this century but was also a man who awoke three hours before dawn, exercised, ate a vegetarian diet, and religiously read the scriptures and had faith in god (Ramakrishnan 1986). Like many of the best-known royal patrons, Ghaneshyamdas Birla was himself a practitioner of what he patronized.

By sponsoring an akhara, the Birlas are not just filling a sports quota, they are making a public statement about specific ideals and values. For them the Birla Mill Vyayamshala is as much a statement about independence and national identity as was their support for Gandhi and the freedom struggle. Just as kings invited the public to see in their wrestlers an image of royal authority and power, so the Birlas invite the public to see in the person of Guru Hanuman and his akhara the benevolence of an industrial giant supporting the hope of the nation.

Although the Birla Mill Vyayamshala is a powerful example in its own right, it is unique. Of all the akharas in India it is the only one with a powerful patron who is, ironically, a private industrialist. It is held up as a model for others to follow and as a vision of what the state ought to provide so that the wrestlers can get on with the task of disciplining their bodies.

CHAPTER 5

The Discipline of the Wrestler's Body

In the dream of rational control over corporeal existence,
the picture looms of growing medicalization and technology
to such an extent that the body is controlled, not by nature
this time, but by our own inventions.

De Wachter 1988: 123

When thousands of people stop to look at a famous
wrestler, then one may say that the character of the wrestler
calls out; it beckons. So what is this character? A wrestler
has a majestic body. He has strength. He has stamina, skill,
experience, and, if he is educated and well read, then he has
knowledge and wisdom. He has humility and is well
mannered. He is skilled . . . and who knows what all else.
Any number of these traits define his character, and as long
as they are maintained they will be the reason for the
wrestler's fame. But most of all a wrestler's character is
defined by his strength. . . . Character is fostered by strength
and, in turn, strength is the aura of character. A wrestler
builds his character through his own efforts; he reaps what
he sows. Celibacy is the paramount means by which a
wrestler establishes his character. He is a disciple of
celibacy.

K. P. Singh 1972b: 21–23

INTRODUCTION

In this chapter I will outline in detail the regimens of exercise, diet,
and self-control that structure the wrestler's body. Careful attention will
be given to the precise mechanics of physical training which develop

and shape the individual body in terms of somatic ideals. Before embarking on this project, however, I must consider the nature of the relationship of the individual body to these ideals.

The notion of a fit and healthy body being an ideological construct is a fairly common theme in discourses of nationalism and power (Gallagher 1986; Jennifer Hargreaves 1982; John Hargreaves 1986; Hoberman 1984). But while the equation is simple to state, the problem is, in fact, more complex. As soon as a healthy body is made to shoulder the burden of certain ideals it also becomes subjected to a microphysics of domination and control. Technologies intrude into the body and mold perceptions of health, fitness, sexuality, and aesthetic beauty. These covert technologies present themselves in many instances as emancipatory strategies whereby the individual can free himself or herself from the mundane fact of mere biology. With specific reference to the athletic body, De Wachter points out that in trying to escape from the vagaries of nature—sickness and aging—we have subjected ourselves to a numbing array of techniques. Far from freeing the body we have simply subjected it to a different kind of determinism (1988: 123). Exercise and training produce an impression of "dynamism, differentiation, and freedom" but in fact fitness is simply another way of controlling the body. This is what Heinila (1982) has termed the "nightmare of totalization," wherein fitness manifests itself as a mode of domination acting through progressively more detailed schemes of physical regimentation (in De Wachter 1988).

Exercise and health regimens dominate and control individual bodies in the same instance that they create an illusion of self-motivated physical liberation (Crawford 1985; Zola 1972). The illusion is two-dimensional: that we have somehow superseded the natural mandate of our biological bodies, and that the regimens we adopt are emancipatory and self-inflicted rather than ideologically prescribed. The mechanics of this premise rest on a tacit acceptance of the Cartesian mind/body duality. Because the body is regarded as a mere flesh and blood object, it is conceived of as a lifeless thing which can be molded. It can be disciplined, sacrificed, branded, tattooed, reproportioned, and developed through exercise. The mind (disembodied thought) is always regarded as the master of this game of control. In other words, we attribute cultural value to certain physical features, and we regard these values as taken-for-granted "natural facts" of life. Broad shoulders, for instance, are regarded as a natural feature of the male physique. While certain dimensions of physique are regarded as natural, others are regarded as inherently mutable—weight and body fat, for instance—and therefore subordinate to aesthetic, political, moral, and religious principles. Conversely, in the logic of Cartesian dualism, that which is physical is somehow regarded as more real and more elemental. Health, for example, is thought of as a purely physical condition, and illness as a purely biomedical referent. While the mind is accorded a position of supreme power in this scheme of human nature—the source of thought, logic, disposition, and emotion—it is the body which is regarded as basic to real life: a flesh and blood existence in the here and now.

Both mind and body—perhaps because they are radically dissociated from one another in Western thought—are subjected to external controls. The body is constrained by biological nature and the mind by history and the cultural construction of reality. Significantly, the mind also molds the body. But mind in this sense is not the individual mind of free will and individuality; it is the mind of ideology and collective consciousness. In the Cartesian formula, ideological thought is associated with the mind. The body is but an instrumental object of secondary significance, a purely dependent variable. By implication the body is always subject to control and can never serve as an autonomous agent through which ideas develop and change.

In Hindu philosophy the mind and the body are intrinsically linked to one another (cf. Staal 1983–1984; Zarrilli 1989). There is no sense of simple duality. In yoga, for instance, it is pointless to try to define where physical exercise ends and mental meditation begins. If one considers Gandhi's adherence to yogic principles it is indeed difficult to draw any line between the physical, the mental, and the political.

The implications are significant. If exercise and regimens of fitness manifest themselves as ways of controlling the individual body, then in Hindu India one cannot have a disciplined body without also having a disciplined mind. In the context of Hindu schemes of discipline it is impossible completely to objectify the body. The end result of regimentation and disciplined exercise in India is therefore quite different from its Western counterpart. Rather than a "nightmare of totalization" where the body is subjected to a refined and detailed biomechanics of health and fitness, in India one has a situation where discipline endows the body/mind with a heightened sense of subjective experience and personal self-awareness. This is not to say that in India the individual experiences discipline as personal emancipation. In India, however, discipline is not simply manifest as an objectification of the body but equally as a subjectification of the self. This point may be elaborated and clarified through an example.

In American physical education and sport, strength is a purely physical phenomenon. It can be measured in objective terms: body mass, arm size, muscle-to-fat ratio, heart rate, weightlifting ability, and so forth. As such, strength is something that can be developed as purely somatic and as quantifiable and calibrated. While strength is also manifest as a physical attribute in India, it is, more significantly, linked to such ineffable cultural values as duty, devotion, and morality. It is neither purely somatic nor strictly quantifiable. A wrestler cannot be strong if he does not follow his guru's mandate. He cannot be strong and indulge in sensual pleasure. Strength is manifest not only in the size of his arm but also in the sparkle of his eye and the luster of his skin, symbols that indicate spirituality, devotion, and moral control.

In a situation of mind/body synthesis such as this it is impossible to turn the body into a mere flesh and blood instrument molded to the image of some abstract ideological construct. Strength cannot be objectified from moral duty or spiritual devotion. The regimens of health and exercise practiced in India—yoga, vyayam, dietetics—exert control over the body not only through a physical mechanics of muscular training and organic chemistry but also through a disciplined regimentation of what we would call the subjective mind. As a result, discipline in India manifests itself not in the objectification of impersonal bodies, but in the complete demarcation of the person as a thinking, feeling, and acting microcosm of ideological values. In India a person's individuality is constructed through the development of his or her body. In the West disembodied individuality is imposed onto a generic biological human form:

> The steel [of the machines and tools which bodybuilders use] depersonalizes. . . . Its homogeneity drives out the principles of individuality in the bodies that devote themselves to it. It does away with eccentricities—the dry and irritable skin, the concave faint-hearted chest, the indolent stomach. . . . On his/her contours, the bodybuilder watches emerging not the eccentricities his tastes and vices leave in his carnal substance, but the lines of force of the generic human animal (Lingis 1988: 134–135).

The physical training associated with wrestling is anything but depersonalized. Nor does the wrestler emerge, through exercise, as a generic man on a larger, stronger scale (except, as we shall see, in the synoptic arena of the tournament). The disciplinary regimens associated with wrestling produce a person charged with a heightened sense of self-awareness and moral duty. The wrestler's physical strength is but one manifestation of a larger disciplinary matrix which entails moral, spiritual, social, and physical regimentation.

EXERCISE

YOGA

To understand the nature of physical exercise in the context of wrestling it is necessary to begin with the general concept of yoga. Broadly defined, yoga informs the underlying principles of the wrestler's *vyayam* (physical exercise) regimen. Yoga is a vast topic of great complexity, and I make no pretense of discussing it in its entirety.

Technical designations aside, yoga has come to mean a particular type of physical training which serves to relax and develop the mind/body. In the classical literature yoga is classified in various ways. The most salient distinction is between *Raja Yoga* or meditation-oriented training, and *Hatha Yoga*, which focuses on kinesthetic movement. Even this distinction is, however, more schematic than real. After carefully delineating types of yoga, Atreya makes the following point:

> Here it is to be remembered that there is actually one Yoga, and not many yogas which are exclusively different from one another. The one purpose of all the yogas is to bring the body, the *prana* [vital breath], the unconscious and the sub-conscious strata of the mind, the mind and the forces of individuation, under one's control; and to be conscious of one's identity with the supreme reality which is within us as our very Self (1973*d*: 48).

In philosophy, yoga refers to the ontology of a particular system. In the *Yoga Sutra* yoga means the progressive control of the whole body. In the *Tantras* it refers to the symbiosis of the individual self with the universal soul. In *Vedanta*, yoga is the discipline through which one realizes oneself as part of the absolute *Brahman*.

The most complete dissertation on yoga is given in the *Bhagavad Gita*. While many definitions of the term are offered in this classic text, the most common and general is that yoga is the expert performance of one's duties (Atreya 1973*d*: 45). Drawing primarily on the *Bhagavad Gita*, Atreya provides the following outline definition of yoga as a moral, ethical, and physical discipline.

> The word Yoga, therefore, now stands for the methods of a) realizing the potentialities of man; b) hastening the spiritual evolution of man; c) becoming one with the Divine Being who is immanent in all creatures; d) uniting the

individual soul with God; e) realizing the highest ideal of man; f) becoming conscious of one's unconscious powers and making use of them; and, g) attaining perfect health, peace, happiness, will, immortality, omniscience, power, freedom and mastery over everything in the world (ibid: 47).

Building up to a definition of yoga which includes wrestling, Atreya argues that one of the main objectives of yoga is to harmonize the whole body. By this he means the perfect functional interdependence of all of the body systems: digestive, respiratory, circulatory, nervous, and so forth. Overlying this functional harmony of the gross body is the control which must be exercised in order to channel physical energies to achieve disciplined goals.

The natural state of the mind/body is regarded in Hindu philosophy as basically flawed. Yoga is designed to compensate for the natural irregularities of the mind/body through the application of physical and mental control. Although one may practice yogic control and achieve a high degree of harmony, one is not completely healthy, Atreya argues, until one has achieved self-realization. Self-realization requires *jivan-mukti* (release from the world; lit., having left life). In this condition ignorance is banished and replaced by spiritual consciousness and wisdom. Having achieved perfect health, a person is not plagued by emotions of any sort. One is simply no longer concerned with the sensory world of pain, pleasure, suffering, and greed.

Given such a broad definition of yoga, Atreya includes the art of wrestling within the general framework of yogic practices. Wrestlers do not necessarily perform the formal *asan*s (postures) of Hatha Yoga, but they subscribe to the tenets of the more general yogic philosophy of a disciplined life. Narayan Singh, a teacher of yoga, wrestling, and physical education at Banaras Hindu University, agrees with Atreya's point. In an interview he stated that yoga and vyayam are formally different but philosophically basically the same. Wrestling is a form of yoga because it requires that one transcend one's natural physical aptitude and apply principles of sensory and nervous control to one's own body. Wrestling is a subdiscipline of yoga since yoga is defined as a system of physical health, ethical fitness and spiritual achievement.

Pranayama (controlled breathing) is a primary aspect of yogic exercise and is also integral to wrestling. Atreya distinguishes eight types of pranayama (1965: 13). Only one of these, *kumbhak*, is employed in wrestling since it enables one to achieve great strength and stamina. The formal methods of pranayama that are refined in Hatha Yoga are not practiced by wrestlers to any great extent. However, wrestlers do recognize the general efficacy of breath control. It purifies the body and unfetters the mind. It helps cut through the maze of sensory images which obstruct the path to enlightenment. Breath control is a prerequisite for performing exercises of any kind. It is not enough just to breathe; that alone only satisfies the needs of the gross body. To breathe properly harmonizes the body with the mind: the spiritual with the physical.

A wrestler must breathe through his nose while expanding his diaphragm. A great deal of emphasis is placed on this point. If one gasps for air with an open mouth and heaving chest, it is likened to the agency of an inanimate bellows. Breathing in this fashion performs the function of putting air into the body and taking it out, but as such it is purely mechanical. Breathing through the nose—with conviction, concentration, and rhythm—transforms a mundane act into a ritual of health.

As a system of physical exercise, wrestling is integrated into the philosophy of yoga through the application of two principles: *yam* and *niyam*. As Atreya (1965: 11) explained in an interview, yam and niyam are the root principles of moral, intellectual, and emotional fitness. Yam has five aspects: *ahimsa* (nonviolence), *satya* (truthfulness), *asatya* ("non-stealing"), *brahmacharya* (continence/celibacy), and *aparigraha* (self-sufficiency and independence). Niyam also comprises five aspects: *shauch* (internal and external purification), *santosh* (contentment), *tap* (mortification and sensory control), *swadhyaya* (study), and *ishvar-pranidhan* (closeness to god through worship).

Development as a wrestler depends on the degree to which one is able to apply oneself to the realization of these principles. Wrestlers do not dwell on the philosophical complexities of yam and niyam. Nonviolence, for instance, is not considered problematic on an epistemological level. Neither do wrestlers seek to explain, or even understand, the metaphysical tenets of aparigraha, for example, or the distinction made between the external body (*sthula sharir*) and the subtle body (*sukshama sharir*). For them the intuitive application of these principles to their lives is the primary order of business. To be passive and even-tempered is in accordance with a lifestyle of ahimsa and santosh; to go to a Hanuman temple every Saturday is to be close to god. Exercise is a form of tap, and going to the akhara every morning is an act of internal and external purification. All of this is not to say that wrestlers are yogis in any strict sense of the term. They are not concerned with the metaphysics of their way of life or with spirituality as an esoteric endeavor. For them the goal is practical in both a physical and a social sense. Yam and niyam develop the wrestler's body/mind and also define for him the basic moral principles of life as health.

VYAYAM

Vyayam is a system of physical training designed to build strength and develop muscle bulk and flexibility. It is in sympathy with the concept of health and fitness articulated through yoga. Yam and niyam are central to its practice. Unlike yoga, however, vyayam emphasizes physical strength. Where Hatha Yoga concentrates on the harmonization of all aspects of the body, vyayam builds on this harmonization through calisthenic and cardiovascular exercise. As with yoga, a key concept in vyayam is the holistic, regulated control of the body. In yoga, however, the body is manipulated through the practice of relatively static postures. Vyayam disciplines the body through strenuous, patterned, repetitive movement.

K. P. Singh has delineated twelve rules of vyayam (1973). Although his list is not exhaustive, it is useful in terms of understanding how vyayam is conceptualized as a system of physical fitness: 1) One should arise before dawn, defecate, bathe, oil oneself and go to the akhara. 2) At the akhara tie on a langot and join the company of other like-minded wrestlers who have focused themselves on the task at hand. Be sure that the place for exercise is clearly demarcated, for it is no less important to define a place for exercise and physical training than for spiritual contemplation. 3) Do not start off by over-exercising. Pace yourself so that you will not be exhausted. 4) Regulate your exercise regimen by either counting the number of repetitions, or timing the duration of your workout. Only in this way will your body develop at a regular and consistent pace. 5) Do not fall into the practice of exercising at irregular intervals. Exercise every day at the same time. 6) One should breathe deeply and steadily while exercising. Each exercise should be done to the rhythm of a single breath. Needless to say, one should breathe only through the nose. 7) Beware of sweat. Oil your body before exercising. The oil will fill the pores and prevent rapid cooling. 8) Focus your mind on each exercise. If your mind wanders you will not develop strength. Consider the laborer who works all day long. He is not as strong as the wrestler for he does not concentrate on his labor but thinks about other things. 9) Do not sit down after exercising. Walk around to keep warm and loose. If you exercise inside, walk around inside. If you exercise outside, walk around outside. 10) Get enough rest. Take one day off every week. Be asleep by eight in the evening. 11) Do not exercise on either a full or empty stomach. Also do not exercise if you have not evacuated your bowels. Do not smoke or chew tobacco. 12) Drink a glass of juice before exercising, and drink milk or some other tonic after exercising. This will help to focus your mind and relax your body.

As a system of fitness, vyayam comprises specific exercise routines.

SURYA NAMASKAR

Surya namaskar (lit., salutation to the sun) is a hybrid exercise which integrates aspects of vyayam training with yogic asans. While based on formal yogic principles, surya namaskar also serves to develop physical strength. Although surya namaskars have undoubtedly been practiced for centuries (cf. Mujumdar 1950), the exercise was routinized and made popular by the late raja of Aundh, Bhawanrao Pantpritinidhi. Raja Bhawanrao believed that if everyone performed this exercise religiously, the result would be a stronger and more upright nation (Mujumdar 1950: xxiv). In a book entitled *Surya Namaskar*s, Bhawanrao's son, Apa Pant, makes the following observation:

> [*Surya namaskar*] is not a religious practice in the narrow sense of the term. But it does have a deep spiritual content and it opens up a new, more profound, more powerful dimension of awareness. Slowly but surely as one continues regularly to practice it, things change in you and around you. Experiences miraculously come to you and you feel the full force of the Beauty and Harmony, the unity, the oneness, with all that is (A. B. Pant 1970: 2).

It is precisely this kind of experience which Bhawanrao was attempting to transpose onto a national level to the end of ethical and moral reform. In the beautiful and harmonized movements of surya namaskar, Bhawanrao clearly saw the harmonized body of a united Indian polity that would turn, collectively, away from the gross sensations of modern life—sex, drugs, power, pride, prosperity (ibid: 12–14)—and toward the pure experience of self-realization.

Surya namaskar consists of ten body postures which together constitute a rhythmic flow of motion (see figures 1a, b). Each posture is punctuated by the recitation of a short mantra to the rhythmic cadence of pranayama.

To perform surya namaskar one should clear a space at least two and a half meters long by one meter wide. This space should be oriented

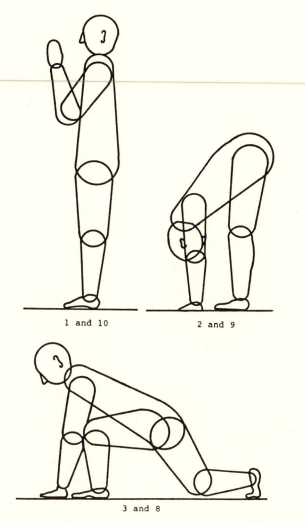

Figure 1a. Surya Namaskar

towards the rising sun. One should wear as little as possible so that movement will not be inhibited.

Position One: With feet together and back and legs straight but not rigid, bend your arms at the elbow and fold your hands in front of your chest. Breathe in deeply through your nose with full concentration. Focus your mind on your posture and your breath.

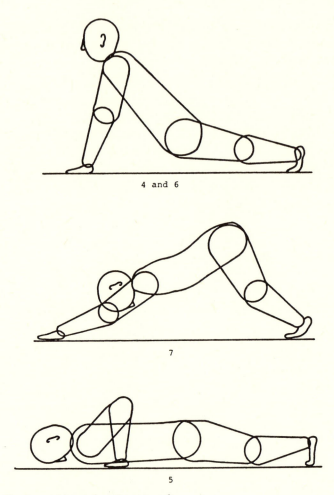

4 and 6

7

5

Figure 1b. Surya Namaskar (*continued*)

Position Two: From position one, bend and place your palms flat on the ground on either side of your legs. Your palms should be a forearm's length apart. Keep your legs straight and touch your nose to your knees. Keeping your arms straight, tuck your chin into your chest. Breathe out slowly and evenly as you reach this position. Always breathe with your stomach: in, stomach out; out, stomach in.

Position Three: From position two extend one leg back as far as it will go and touch the knee to the ground. Arch backwards at the same time and lift your head back as far as it will go. Breathe in while doing this and push your stomach out. Always be alert and concentrate on each movement, breath, and sensation. At the same time remain detached and relaxed.

Position Four: Move your second leg back so that both legs are extended backwards. Lift both knees off the ground so that your weight is supported on your palms and toes while your body is held straight. Touching your chin to your chest, look down at the ground between your palms. Hold your breath in this position.

Position Five: This is the most important and central position of the exercise. Bend at the elbows so that your body descends to the ground. Insure that your body touches the ground at only eight points: the two sets of toes, the two knees, chest, forehead, and the two palms. This part of the surya namaskar is called the *ashtanga namaskar*, or eight-pointed salutation. All eight points must touch the ground at the same time. As they come in contact with the ground you should exhale.

Position Six: In order to move from the fifth to the sixth position lift your head up and bend your neck backwards. Then, without exerting pressure on your arms, lift the trunk of your body off the ground by contracting your lower back and gradually extending your arms. Your spine should be fully arched from the top of your neck to the base of your tailbone. Breathe in while assuming this position and again concentrate on each part of your body.

Position Seven: In position seven you reverse the arch of your body by lifting your buttocks into the air as far as possible while extending your arms and legs. Your hands and feet should not move. Breathe out in this position.

Position Eight: This position is a repetition of position three. It is achieved by moving one foot forward and placing it between your palms. Arch your back and bend your head backwards. Breath in deeply.

Position Nine: Bring your other leg forward and place both feet together. Straighten your legs and tuck your chin into your chest. Breathe out with force. This is a repetition of position two.

Position Ten: This position brings you back to the starting point
of the exercise. Breath in as you stand erect and fold your hands in front
of your chest.

While doing surya namaskars one is enjoined to recite six *bij mantras*
(seed sounds). Not only does one pay obeisance to the sun by reciting
these mantras, they also reverberate through the body in an efficacious
manner. Pant points out that these reverberations invigorate the mind
(1970: 9). There are six primary bij mantras: *Om-Haram; Om-Harim;
Om-Harum; Om-Haraim; Om-Harom; Om-Hara.* In accompaniment
to the six bij mantras one should recite the twelve names of the sun:
Mitra (friend); *Ravi* (shining); *Surya* (beautiful light); *Bhanu* (brilliant);
Khaga (sky mover); *Pushan* (giver of strength); *Hiranya Garbha* (golden
centered); *Marichi* (Lord of the Dawn); *Aditya* (son of Aditi); *Savitra*
(beneficient); *Arka* (energy); and *Bhaskara* (leading to enlightenment).
    Surya namaskars integrate and harmonize all aspects of the physical,
intellectual, and spiritual body. Position two energizes the pituitary,
pineal, and thyroid glands. Position three stimulates the liver, solar
plexus, and pancreas. Position four stretches the spinal column and
facilitates blood flow to all of the organs and glands in the immediate
vicinity of the spine. Positions five and six are particularly efficacious
for the neck, chest, abdomen, and sexual glands. The regular performance of surya namaskars is intended to raise one's state of consciousness to a higher level of self-realization. As Pant notes, one can then
transpose this experience of self-realization—which he refers to as bliss,
harmony, knowledge, beauty, and awareness of the infinite—onto one's
experience of everyday life.
    Surya namaskars are more popular among older men than among
young wrestlers. While they strengthen the body, they do not strain
the muscles, bones, and organs of the body. Surya namaskars are not
vigorous, and senior wrestlers practice them in order to maintain their
physique and stature. In any case, surya namaskars are clearly associated
with physical strength and muscular prowess. Shivaji's guru, Samarath
Ramdas, was said to perform 1,200 surya namaskars every day. Shivaji
himself and Ramdas's other disciples also performed surya namaskars.
Mujumdar attributes Maratha physical prowess and military success to
this exercise (1950: 54).
    With regard to wrestling discipline, surya namaskar is important in-
sofar as it represents the formal synthesis of yoga and vyayam. This
synthesis is implicit in many of the exercises which wrestlers do. As

we shall see, the combination of dands and bethaks echoes the basic movement of surya namaskar.

DAND-BETHAK

Dands and bethaks are two different exercises, but together they constitute the core wrestling vyayam regimen. Dands are jackknifing push-ups and bethaks are comparable to Western-style deep knee bends. Although dands and bethaks are done separately, they are usually referred to as a pair. As a set they provide a complete body workout.

One starts a bethak from a standing position with feet set at forty-five degree angles and heels about fifteen to twenty centimeters apart. While squatting down one should jump slightly forward onto the balls of one's feet while lifting the heels clear off the floor. In the process of standing back up, one should jump backwards to the position from which one started. One's arms should be relaxed. They should sway with the movement of the body in order to maintain balance. One's eyes should be fixed on a point about four meters forward on the ground, so that one's head will be stationary and balanced. One should do about sixty or eighty bethaks per minute and between sixty and one hundred at a stretch (Atreya 1974: 25). All of this depends, of course, on the degree of one's strength and previous experience. Similarly, the number of bethaks one does is relative to personal strength, predilection, available time, and specific goals. Well-known champions do between two and three thousand bethaks a day. Average wrestlers often do as many as one thousand. At the very least a wrestler will do between five and eight hundred per day.

Dands are similar to certain aspects of surya namaskar. One starts a dand from a face-down, prone position with feet placed close together and palms flat on the ground directly below the shoulders about half a meter apart. To begin, one cocks the body back by lifting one's buttocks into the air while straightening both arms and legs (see figure 2). Bending at the elbows, one dives forward so that the chest glides between the palms close to the ground. One then arches up while straightening the arms and thrusting the pelvis down towards the ground. One then re-cocks the body to the starting position.

According to Atreya one should do half as many dands as bethaks (1974: 21). Once one has assumed the position of doing dands one should not move until all dands are completed. A good wrestler in the prime of life can do about 1,500 dands per hour, and many do as many

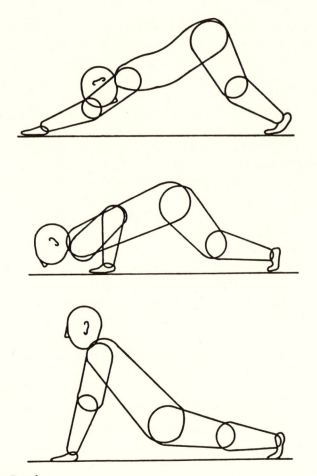

Figure 2. Dand

as 2,000 a day. Those wrestlers who swing joris and gadas as the main aspect of their routine do as many as 5,000 dands per day, but this is exceptional. Whereas bethaks are more often than not performed before *jor* (see below), dands are performed at the end of the morning practice session. However, there is no strict rule regarding the sequence of an exercise regimen. Many wrestlers do their dands and bethaks in the evening.

The most important feature of dands and bethaks is that they be done rhythmically and at a steady pace. The performance of thousands of these exercises produces a mental state not unlike that of a person who has gone into a trance through the rote recitation of a mantra or prayer.

Thus, dands and bethaks transport the wrestler into an altered state of consciousness from which he derives psychic and spiritual purification. Vyayam is very much like meditation in this respect. I was told that Jharkhande Rai, a champion wrestler who used to be a member of Akhara Ram Singh, would concentrate so hard on doing his dands that his sweat would leave a perfect image of his body as it dripped onto the earth. This and similar stories were told in order to make the point that the wrestler involved was often not even aware of the extent of his exertion. Many times I have sat on the edge of an akhara and watched a wrestler bob up and down for half an hour or more without taking his eyes off an imaginary point on the ground in front of his face. It is not surprising that the beneficial effects of dands transcend the mere physical body and strengthen aspects of moral and ethical character. Atreya points out that dands strengthen the wrists, fingers, palms, neck, chest, and back. Dands also cure all kinds of illnesses relating to semen loss (impotence, infertility, and spermatorrhoea) and faulty digestion (1974: 19). Dands strengthen the sinews of the body, and they also develop character:

> Doing dands makes a person's character and personality shine. The body takes on a powerful radiance. Not only this, but the person who does dands lives a fuller and more meaningful life. His personality is more attractive. He is liked by everyone. His whole attitude towards life is changed (ibid: 20).

As one of the central exercises in a wrestler's vyayam regimen, it is clear that dands do more than develop the gross body. They develop the personality of the wrestler as well. The wrestler's personality derives its strength—as a charismatic social force and as personal self-confidence—through the symbiosis of a personal experience akin to enlightenment and a physical experience of muscular development. With regard to both dands and bethaks Atreya makes the following observation:

> Dands and bethaks make the muscles of the body so incredibly strong that the wrestler appears divine. Dands and bethaks are the mirror in which the aura of wrestling is reflected. They are the two flowers which are offered to the "wrestling goddess." Dands and bethaks are the two sacrifices made to the goddess of wrestling. If she is pleased she will bestow great strength and turn mere men into wrestlers (ibid).

JOR

As distinct from the term *kushti*, which is used to denote competitive wrestling, *jor* is the term used for wrestling done for practice, training and exercise (see plates 7 and 8). In the same way that surya namaskar is not only a form of devotion but also an exercise, so is wrestling not only a sport but also a form of mental and physical training. Implicitly if not explicitly, therefore, jor integrates some of the basic principles of yoga into the act of wrestling.

When wrestlers come to the akhara in the morning, each spends between one and two hours practicing jor. After the pit is dug, smoothed, and blessed, two senior wrestlers take to the pit and begin to wrestle. Given the nature of wrestling as a competitive sport, each wrestler tries to throw his opponent down to the ground through the correct application of particular moves. Each move is countered by a defensive move and this sparring continues indefinitely. The nature of jor is, however, significantly different from a competitive kushti bout.

In kushti tournaments (*dangals*) the aesthetic of structured motion is achieved through a radical opposition of movements. The tone of this aesthetic is harsh, for every move is matched with a countermove. In jor, however, both wrestlers tend to work together so that the moves which are applied are executed smoothly. The dangal produces a dramatic grammar of movement with sudden moments of brilliance and, ultimately, clear superiority manifest in the success or failure of one or the other wrestler. Jor, on the other hand, tends to emphasize the harmony of the art of wrestling as it is manifest in the details of each move. The emphasis in jor is to apply a move with precision and a minimum of effort. Jor is very much like some forms of dance.

In jor you must focus your mind at once on the details of each move and on the whole of which those moves are a part. As in surya namaskar you must focus your mind on the exact posture of your body as it moves from stance to stance and from move to countermove. As pointed out earlier, it is imperative to keep one's guru's name in mind while practicing jor or any other form of vyayam. The guru's name functions as a spiritual beacon which channels the energy of enlightenment into the body of the wrestler. At Akhara Ram Singh the dadas and other senior wrestlers had a clear idea of who was concentrating on their practice and who was not. If a wrestler opened his mouth to gasp for air it was evident that his concentration had been broken. Any wrestler who appeared to be uninterested or not putting out a full effort was quickly rebuked by others.

As choreographed, regulated movement, jor has clear physical and mental benefits. It exercises every part of the body. Anyone who has wrestled for even a few minutes will soon realize that wrestling brings into play muscles which are not usually called upon to exert force or support weight. Unlike exercises like running, jumping, or lifting weights, jor does not require one to perform repetitive movements. In the course of a jor session, certain sequences of moves will, of course, be repeated. In the abstract, however, the exercise is conceived of as an unbroken chain of movement. In this regard jor is the antithesis of vyayam exercises like surya namaskar, dands and bethaks. While these exercises are mechanically repetitive, jor is almost wholly improvised.

Jor develops stamina as well as strength. As such, wrestlers place a great deal of emphasis on breath control. One should never pant or gasp. Never breathe simply to satisfy the body's need for oxygen. One must breathe in and out regularly and with deliberate, conscious thought. This serves to focus the mind on the application of specific moves. Many wrestlers with whom I spoke said that practicing jor in the morning cleared their thoughts and invigorated their bodies, allowing them to go about their lives with more vitality. What wrestlers mean by clearing their thoughts and invigorating their bodies is the same experience articulated by those who practice yoga. Through the practice of jor one is able to achieve a higher state of consciousness which is one step closer to self-realization. This self-realization can be directed towards winning in competitive bouts or, more generally, towards living a richer and more fulfilling life. As Harphool Singh writes,

> Wrestling in the earth makes the body elegant. Exercising in the earth removes pimples, unwanted hair and cures eczema while making the skin shine like gold. Exerting oneself in the earth and becoming saturated with sweat and mud makes the wrestler feel invigorated. Minor ailments aside, it is said that akhara earth can cure cholera and other serious diseases. One thing is for sure, however: after bathing, the wrestler who has exercised in the akhara earth will feel a sense of vigorous satisfaction as his mind becomes clearly focused. (1984b: 22)

Singh continues his dissertation on the efficacy of jor specifically and wrestling in general by saying that wrestlers must always be happy, and present themselves to the world as people who take great pleasure in life. The experience of jor plays no small part in enabling the wrestler to affect such an attitude.

Atreya has drawn up seven points to help define where, when, how, and with whom one should practice jor (1985: 23). Although these guidelines are not followed as rules, they do define the basic principles of jor.

1. You should begin your jor regimen by wrestling with a young

child or a wrestler who is clearly weaker than you. In this way you can warm up while the younger wrestler gets a chance to exert his full strength. You should always be careful to match strength with strength and never beat a younger wrestler simply to prove your superiority. As a senior wrestler you must draw the younger wrestler out to his full potential.

2.   After wrestling with a younger and weaker wrestler you should wrestle with someone who is your equal. This will enable you to exert your full potential. You should not try to win. Neither should you lose sight of the fine points of the art to the end of showing off your skill. You should match move for move and countermove with countermove in a balanced exchange of strength and skill.

3.   If you are called upon to practice jor with a foolish or braggart wrestler you should show him no mercy. He must be cut down to size immediately. Only in this way will he recognize that strength does not lay in conceit, but rather in the regulated practice of moves and countermoves. This must be done. Conceit clouds the mind and a wrestler will never be able to succeed or benefit from the practice of wrestling if he is ignorant of its basic tenets.

4.   When wrestling with a stronger and more senior wrestler you should exert all of your strength but at the same time show deference to his rank. This is a very difficult thing to do. It is imperative, however, if you hope to advance and improve. You should learn from a senior wrestler but apply what you learn on someone who is your equal. Thus your achievement will never challenge the seniority of the other wrestlers in the akhara.

5.   When wrestling with an old wrestler one must show respect and deference. Never wrestle as though you are stronger than him even if he is old and weak. Always seek to make the older wrestler feel good and strong.

6.   If you practice jor with a well-known wrestler you should assume the posture of a disciple at the feet of his guru. You should show respect for well-known wrestlers, and it is also important to learn from them. You should not assume that your strength or skill is a match for theirs.

7.   When wrestling with the best wrestler of an akhara you should always approach him in a forthright and confident manner. But never pin him down even if you are able. If you try to prove your strength then the practice of jor turns into a contest. As a result no one comes out of the session having gained any knowledge.

Atreya also delineates six places where one may practice jor: at your own akhara, at a competitor's akhara, at some akhara in another district, at the akhara of a village or town where one has gone to compete in a tournament, at a bus or railway station, and while on a journey. In each of these contexts there are rules for proper comportment. You should not, for instance, show your true form while wrestling in someone else's akhara. At the same time you must show respect for your host wrestlers. When at a dangal you should only practice with compatriots from your own akhara. Atreya's list of places where one may practice jor is fairly inclusive, but there are places where it is deemed inappropriate to engage in jor. One should not practice at home, for instance.

In jor a great deal of importance is placed on who one practices with. Similarly, comportment is integral to the performance of jor. Only by adhering to the above-outlined principles is one able to learn the actual techniques of wrestling. This is to say that jor properly done is as much a matter of social decorum and personal attitude towards seniority as it is a question of purely physical training. Atreya tells of a young wrestler who thought that he was stronger and more skilled than an old but well-known wrestler. He practiced jor with the senior wrestler as though they were equals. As a result he began losing wrestling bouts and became weak and unhealthy.

JORIS AND GADAS

Joris and gadas are heavy clubs which wrestlers swing in order to strengthen their shoulders and arms. At Ragunath Maharaj Akhara, Akhara Morchal Bir and other gymnasia, jori swinging is both a competitive sport and a form of exercise.

Joris are always swung in pairs (see plate 3). Those used for exercise usually weigh between fifteen and twenty-five kilograms each. They are carved of heavy wood and are weighted with bands of metal. In order to make the joris more difficult to swing, blades and nails are sometimes hammered into them.

At the beginning of the exercise, the joris are held in an inverted position. Each jori is swung alternately behind the back in a long arch. At the end of the arch each jori is lifted or flipped back onto the shoulder as the opposite jori begins its pendulum swing. Timing is an important part of this exercise. The balanced weight of one jori must facilitate the movement of the other. Jori swinging exercises the arms, shoulders, chest, thighs, and lower back. Wrestlers tend to swing fairly lightweight joris because they say that the heavier clubs cause the upper body to become rigid.

In contrast to the intricately carved silver and gold symbolic gadas (macelike clubs) depicted in art and used as wrestling trophies, gadas used for everyday exercise are rather plain. An exercise gada is a heavy, round stone, weighing anywhere from ten to sixty kilograms, affixed to the end of a meter-long bamboo staff (see plate 4). The gada is swung in the same way as a jori except that only one gada is swung at a time. A gada may be swung with either hand or both hands at once.

The swing begins with the gada balanced on one shoulder. It is then lifted and shrugged off of the shoulder and swung in a long pendulum arch behind the back until it is flipped and lifted back onto the opposite shoulder. The gada is held erect for a split second before it is swung back in the opposite direction and onto the other shoulder.

Gada and jori exercises are counted in terms of the number of *hath* (hands) that one is able to do. One gada "hand" is counted as the movement from one shoulder to the other. One jori "hand" is counted as the combined swing of both right and left clubs. Unlike dands and bethaks, which number in the thousands, wrestlers tend to swing gadas and joris for sets of relatively few repetitions. Those who swing joris and gadas on a regular basis place a higher premium on the amount of weight lifted than on sheer number of hands swung.

DHAKULI

After jor wrestlers practice *dhakuli*s (somersaults/flips). There are several variations on this exercise and all types emphasize twisting rotations. When performed in competitive bouts these twisting rotations enable a wrestler to escape from his opponent's grip.

To perform the most common dhakuli you start from a kneeling position in the pit. You lean forward and place your head on the earth. Then shift your weight from your knees to your head and neck. Standing briefly on your head, with legs bent, you twist so that you land on your knees facing in the opposite direction. This exercise requires a great deal of neck strength, and many wrestlers use their hands for balance and weight distribution.

Another dhakuli resembles a one-handed cartwheel. Standing in the pit you place your left hand on the earth. Flip your body over so that you land on your right shoulder and side. This procedure is reversed so that you get practice falling in a disciplined manner. A variation of this dhakuli is to jump and fall alternately onto each shoulder without using either hand for support.

In order to strengthen their necks, wrestlers practice "bridges" of various sorts. The most common bridge performed by Indian wrestlers is identical to the common Western form. You lie on your back in the pit, and lift your body up into a reverse arch using only your neck for leverage and feet for support. A variation of this is to lie on your back and arch off the ground enough so as to be able to roll over. As you rotate on the top of your head, your arched body rolls over and over. You cross your legs over so that you move in a circle around the axis of your head and neck.

SHIRSHASAN

Shirshasan (head stand), like surya namaskar, is an adapted form of a common Hatha Yoga technique. Wrestlers often stand on their heads—as in the dhakuli routine—both to strengthen their necks and to increase the flow of blood to their heads. This is said to clear the mind of impure thoughts and to bestow a general sense of health and well-being. It is generally recommended for all young men who suffer from spermatorrhoea or who show symptoms of emotional distress.

NALS

Nals are roughly equivalent to Western free weights and are lifted to develop arm, shoulder, and back strength. Nals are large, cylindrically carved stones which are hollowed out. A shaft of stone is left in the center of the nal's hollow core and is used as a handle. Nals usually weigh about thirty kilograms, but come in all sizes and weights. There does not appear to be any set way in which nals are lifted. The general idea is to lift the weight with one or both hands from the ground to above your head in one smooth motion. As with joris and gadas, those who lift nals place more emphasis on the weight of the stone than the number of times it is lifted. For the most part nals have been replaced by Western-style free weights.

GAR NALS

Gar nals (circular stone rings) are used to weigh down a wrestler as he does dands or bethaks. As the term *gar* (neck) would indicate, gar nals are hung around a wrestler's neck in the fashion of a giant necklace. Many akharas still have one or two gar nals on the premises, but very few wrestlers use them. It is said that Gama used to do dands while wearing such a large gar nal that a trench had to be dug between his hands so that the stone would not drag along the ground.

OTHER EXERCISES

Wrestlers do a host of other exercises, and each akhara has its own particular regimen of training techniques. Virtually all akharas advocate rope climbing and running. Many akharas are equipped with large logs or heavy pieces of lumber to which wrestlers harness themselves. Pulling these around the pit strengthens the lower back, thighs, and feet while it also develops stamina (see plate 15). Wrestlers are often instructed to run at least a few kilometers before coming to the akhara in the morning in order to build up both speed and endurance.

Some gurus advocate various games which serve to build stamina and speed. One popular game is referred to as *langur daur* (monkey's run) wherein wrestlers run around the perimeter of the pit on all fours trying to catch whoever is in the lead. To strengthen their legs and feet, wrestlers often run around the akhara weighted down with someone on their backs. To build up their arms and develop coordination and balance, they have someone hold up their legs as they run around the pit on their hands. Sometimes a wrestler will lie face down in the pit and have a heavier wrestler sit on him as he tries to stand up. Jumping rope has not been adopted by many Indian wrestlers, but jumping up and down in place or hopping around the akhara on one foot is common. Some wrestlers develop idiosyncratic exercises. I have heard of some who push cars to develop their legs. Others fill up gunnysacks with sand and lift, kick, and throw these as they see fit. In rural areas some wrestlers harness themselves to plows, grinding stones, and waterwheels. I was told of one wrestler who started his exercise regimen by carrying a buffalo calf across a river. He did this every day until after a year he was able to lift and carry a full-grown buffalo with ease.

Although formal exercises are clearly distinguished from everyday physical activities, there is a sense in which work, as physical labor, is translated by the wrestler into a form of exercise. Railway porters in particular regard carrying heavy loads as a way in which they develop their strength. Undoubtedly there are many porters who regard such hard and poorly remunerated work as simply tiring. However, the wrestling porters I know have successfully interpreted what is in fact a form of exploitation into a form of productive exertion. They have embodied their own labor power, so to speak. Similarly, many of the young wrestling dairy farmers I know speak of milking cows and buffalos as a form of exercise rather than work.

BAN

Wrestlers practice a number of "pair exercises" of which the most popular is *ban*. Ban (literally arrow) is performed as an exercise which both develops strength and which also serves as a muscle massage. The exercise resembles the movement required to draw a bow.

Two wrestlers stand facing each other about one and a half meters apart. They lean into each other and with their right hands grab hold of each other's left upper arm (see plate 5). Both wrestlers push back with their left arm and try to dislodge their partner's hand. The position is then reversed as both wrestlers push with their left hand against their partner's right arm. The idea is to resist your partner's push with as much force as possible and to dislodge his gripping hand as quickly as you can.

Ban expands the chest muscles and develops coordination. It also serves the valuable function of toughening upper arm skin. When practicing jor the upper arm is one of the areas of the body most often used as a fulcrum. As a result it is often bruised, stretched, and rubbed raw unless toughened up beforehand.

In addition to being a popular exercise for the reasons mentioned above, many wrestlers claim that ban serves to shape their upper body in an aesthetically pleasing way. It gives them the barrel-chested, turned-out arm stance characteristic of a well-built wrestler. Jori swinging and dands are also said to have this effect.

There are also various other pair exercises which some gurus place more emphasis on than others. To strengthen neck muscles and generally to toughen the head and ears, wrestlers alternately slap one another on the side of the head with their forearms. Variations on this general theme are to strike forearm with forearm, shoulder with shoulder, and chest with chest. A fairly common exercise for the neck is for two wrestlers to pull against the back of each other's head until one or the other gives up or is forced to fall forward. A popular exercise at Akhara Ram Singh is for a wrestler to get down in the pit on his hands and knees with his forehead pressed to the earth. His partner then kneels on his neck with one knee. On all fours, the wrestler tries to lift the weight of his partner, thus exercising his neck and upper back. This exercise is called *sawari* (the passenger). Variations on sawari are numerous: while doing dandas, one wrestler will have another stand on his legs; while doing bethaks one wrestler will ride on the other's back.

Group exercise, although not common, is also practiced in some akharas. One form of this exercise is for a wrestler (usually the biggest) to lie down or kneel in the center of the pit, and then a group of five or ten younger wrestlers do their best to keep him from getting up. Often such exercises are done toward the end of the jor period and will climax in a free-for-all where the senior wrestler turns the tables and sees how many junior wrestlers he can hold down at one time. Exercises such as these are as much games as they are regimented forms of physical training, but as more than one wrestler has put it, group exercises create a sense of community health among the wrestlers involved. Such group exercises are often referred to as *masti*, which, for lack of an adequate gloss, may be translated as an invigorated sense of feeling on top of the world.

The vyayam exercises mentioned above are not simply ways in which the physical body is developed as a mechanical, biological entity. One must bear in mind that vyayam is performed in an environment saturated with ideological significance. This fact becomes more explicit when massage is considered.

MASSAGE

Among wrestlers, massage is regarded as a very important exercise (see plate 6). In the akhara regimen, Wednesday of every week is set aside for massage. Being a good masseur requires a great deal of skill, and there are some wrestlers who are well known for their ability to manipulate tendons, joints, and muscles so as to relieve pain and stress. Most wrestlers, however, are not highly skilled in this regard. They are, however, familiar with some basic principles and techniques.

The first principle, as outlined by Shyam Sundaracharya, is that each muscle group or appendage must be massaged along its whole length. The masseur must stroke his hands along the wrestler's arm, back or leg. The second principle is that of pressure massage. Pressure is applied in various ways on various parts of the body, but most wrestlers simply apply pressure with the heels of their hands. This loosens the muscles and makes them flexible. The third principle is that of friction massage, wherein the skin is rubbed vigorously so that a tingling sensation permeates the body. Finally, in order to strengthen the circulatory system, there is the fourth principle of vibration. Vibration is applied through the rapid movement of the hand and wrist at the same time that pressure is brought to bear on a particular part of the body (1986b: 37).

A typical massage routine at Akhara Ram Singh is as follows. The wrestler being massaged sits on a low step with the masseur standing in front of him. Mustard oil is liberally applied to the wrestler's legs. The masseur rubs each thigh alternately from the knee up to the hip joint. He then takes the wrestler's arms and places each in turn on his shoulder. Working from the shoulders to the wrist he pulls down and away from the wrestler's body, thus rubbing, in turn, the wrestler's bicep, elbow, and forearm. The wrestler's calves are massaged in the following manner. The masseur sits on the ground with the wrestler's foot wedged between his own two feet. The wrestler's leg is bent and the masseur pulls and rubs his hands across the wrestler's calf from side to side and top to bottom.

A back massage is performed in various ways. The most common is for the wrestler to lie face down on a special wooden bench while the masseur leans over him. Using his forearm and applying his body weight, the masseur slides his arm down the wrestler's back. While the wrestler who is being massaged is face down on this bench the masseur may decide to use his feet in order to apply a great deal of focused pressure on particular parts of the body. I have seen a skilled masseur walk the full length of a wrestler's body, from ankles up to neck and out to either hand. Full body weight is not applied to all parts of the body and so a masseur must carefully gauge his own body-weight distribution relative to the type of massage required.

Every guru has his own ideas of what massage technique is best. As Atreya has pointed out (1986b: 29–30) it is fruitless to try to define rules for something which is inherently idiosyncratic. Irrespective of the fact that massage is performed in various ways, however, the virtues of massage, as an aspect of physical training, are generally agreed on.

Most significantly, massage makes the body both flexible and taut. In wrestling one must develop muscles which are supple and strong. Stiff muscles inhibit movement and prevent the application of certain moves. There is also the danger that an arm or leg may break if it is unable to bend freely. In this regard massage helps develop the wrestler's muscles in a manner suited for the practice of wrestling. On a more general level, however, massage has a calming effect on the whole body.

If one is suffering from physical fatigue or mental exhaustion, Sundara-charya notes, massage reinvigorates through structured relaxation (1986*b*: 35). In massage, as in many other vyayam exercises, there is a clear synthesis of mental health with physical fitness. One important aspect of massage is that it functions to fine-tune the body. In other words, through massage a wrestler achieves a condition where his state of mind is a direct reflection of his state of body. In this way massage serves to reiterate the tacit link between body and mind which is integral to vyayam as a whole. Through massage one is reminded, for instance, that relaxation is as much a question of attaining release from worldly concerns as it is a function of the circulation of blood through the base of one's spine, knee joints, and shoulder tendons.

Technical massage requires a detailed understanding of human physiology. Although I am not qualified to speak to this aspect of massage (nor are there any wrestlers I met who possessed such technical knowledge), my suspicion is that North Indian massage is based on a concept of the body that does not isolate body parts, organs, tissues, or skeletal structure in the same way as in comparable Western techniques of chiropractic massage. More specific and comparative data are required, but the science of Indian massage seems to be based on a logic of heat and substance flow, with substance being some combination of neuroendocrinal fluid and blood. Fluid movement along the body's various channels seems to depend on a complex equation of heat, density, and tissue depth, as well as other factors. In this regard Zarrilli (1989) has outlined the complex massage and health techniques which are part of the South Indian martial art called *kalarippayattu*. The practitioners of kalarippayattu have a fairly unique understanding of the human body and are able to effect cures for a range of ailments through the application of complex, secret methods of pressure massage. The massage technique associated with *marma prayogam* is far more sophisticated but probably not completely different from that which North Indian wrestlers practice. Both systems stem from a similar understanding of body physiology.

As a vyayam technique, massage reflects the complete symbiosis of mind and body which is also found in yoga asans, surya namaskar, dand-bethak, and jor. As an institutionalized practice in akhara life, however, massage also has very significant social implications with regard to hierarchy and purity and pollution. We have seen that jor requires a symbiosis of social rank and status concerns with practical techniques of body movement. In the same way, massage requires a reconciliation of social status with physical interaction. One cannot completely benefit from a massage without taking into account—and reconciling oneself to—what massage means in terms of personal interaction. This issue turns on the important question of who massages whom in the akhara. Atreya writes:

> Indian wrestling has never been practiced without the aid of massage. It used to be that in akharas the practice of massage was structured in a very beautiful way. As a result wrestling flourished, and India was regarded as a nation of champions. [Younger] wrestlers would massage senior wrestlers, sadhus, and the oldest men in the akhara. It was a matter of showing deference and respect. From this wrestlers received two benefits. On the one hand giving a massage was a form of exercise. On the other hand, by massaging one's guru and other senior members of the akhara one received their blessing (1986b: 28).

Atreya goes on to decry the present state of affairs where wrestlers regard it as beneath their dignity to be masseurs. Atreya's criticism is, in my experience, somewhat exaggerated. In many Banaras akharas there is a clear hierarchy of who massages whom, and this hierarchy follows the rank of seniority and age. However, rank hierarchy is not rigidly defined. Flexibility is built into the system. Two wrestlers who are roughly equal in age and skill will both be massaged by much younger wrestlers who are clearly their juniors. In turn these wrestlers will massage much more senior wrestlers who are clearly of a higher rank. Any ambiguity in rank status is displaced to a plane where status is no longer ambiguous. What is significant, however, is not so much the rank order of wrestlers, but the general principle of rank hierarchy as such. Many of the senior wrestlers with whom I spoke were very clear on this point. Massaging one's elders serves to reinforce an ethic of humility, respect, service, and devotion. Massaging one's guru's feet, is, after all, the ultimate sign of devotion.

Embedded within this system of rank hierarchy based on age and skill is a seemingly contradictory principle of inherent equality. Although the principle of rank applies to those who are clearly junior or senior, the majority of akhara members are roughly the same age. On this level wrestlers take turns massaging one another, thus reinforcing their equality. Atreya points out that this serves to underscore feelings of mutual respect.

It is important to note that massage, like wrestling itself, entails close physical contact. A masseur must not only touch another person, he must also touch that person's head and feet, which are, respectively, the purest and the most impure parts of the body. Massage is, then, a potentially dangerous activity. It poses a real threat of contagious pollution, which can have a serious impact on caste rank. Recognizing this, Atreya suggests that it is precisely because massage cuts across caste boundaries that it is important to the general condition of the akhara as a whole: "[Reciprocal massage] creates a feeling of mutual love between the wrestlers of an akhara. . . . Status, class and caste distinctions are erased. The poorest of the poor and the richest of the rich come together in the akhara. This creates a feeling of unity (1986b: 27)." Many of the wrestlers with whom I spoke expressed sentiments similar to Atreya's.

Even where massage structures a hierarchy of rank in the akhara, it is a hierarchy of status and respect based on principles other than purity and pollution. In other words, a young Brahman boy may be seen massaging the feet of a lower-caste senior wrestler. Conversely, a lower-caste boy may walk on the back and neck of a higher-caste wrestling patron. What is more significant than the fact that such events actually take place—for there are professional masseurs who are often of a lower-caste status than their customers—is that wrestlers treat massage as a critique of caste hierarchy. They appropriate it as a way of distinguishing their way of life from the dominant way of life which is structured according to rigid rules of exclusive purity. While many situations in everyday life require contact and interaction between members of different caste groups—barbers who cut their high-caste clients' hair, for instance—such activities are structured, and conceptualized, in terms of interdependent roles which preempt whatever close physical contact may be entailed. In the akhara in general, but specifically during massage, the caste-based rationale for intercaste contact is explicitly denied.

What is unique about massage, in this regard, is that a critique of caste principles is directly implicated as a factor in the collective health of the akhara. In other words, as Atreya notes, massage creates a healthy state of social unity among wrestlers. Whereas wrestling as an art tends to champion the cause of the individual, massage serves to dissolve the individual into a state of pure, embodied equality. From talking with wrestlers it is clear that general health and fitness depend, at least in part, on the extent to which one is willing and able to merge with this collectivity of feeling. As Atreya and others clearly imply, a person who is concerned with caste status, wealth, and other worldly manifestations of power cannot achieve either success or satisfaction as a wrestler. Consequently, one's attitude towards caste determines, to some extent, one's overall physical fitness. A wrestler who is not willing to massage another wrestler on the grounds that he is somehow better than him, is simply not healthy.

This sense of health again makes the point that fitness is conceptualized as a holistic integration of physical, moral, psychological, spiritual, and social elements. In the akhara the basic concept of a healthy person derives largely from a yogic concept of fitness. According to the yogic principles of *Yogavasista*, worldly, materialistic considerations divert one from the path of self-realization and perfect health. Worldly persons are unhealthy (Atreya 1973*d*: 39). What is unhealthy about a concern with purity and pollution in particular, and the caste-based body in general, is that it validates rank status as a structuring principle of worldly order. By undercutting caste principles, therefore, massage is regarded as an agency for transcending the illusionary bounds of hierarchy. Wrestlers do not fetishize this issue by turning massage into a self-conscious critique of caste every time it is performed. The power of the act and its implications are felt on a much more visceral, perhaps even psychological, level: a total surrender of the body to a world where sweat and substance mingle without grave negative consequences. What is significant, in any case, is the logic of the relationship between physical contact, caste status, moral virtue, and general health. One might say that massage promotes a form of public health by relaxing muscles as well as social and psychological boundaries.

DIET

My purpose here is to analyze the underlying structure of a wrestling diet as a regimen of health. I will show how wrestling dietetics is not only structured in terms of nutrition as a biochemical function but how it is also conceptualized in terms of moral values. In keeping with the general purpose of this chapter I will show how the disciplinary regimen of diet structures the wrestler's identity as a dimension of his overall health.

Wrestlers are distinguished not so much by what they eat as how much they eat. They are reputed to drink buckets of milk, eat kilograms of almonds, and devour large quantities of ghi per day. However, wrestlers eat many other things as well. Milk, ghi, and almonds only comprise the wrestler's specialized diet referred to as *khurak*. Like everyone else, wrestlers also eat vegetables, lentils, grains, fruit, nuts, and other items. With regard to the wrestler's dietary regimen what is significant is how each type of food is conceptualized within the larger matrix of diet, and how these concepts are applied to the discipline of wrestling.

According to Hindu philosophy, people are divided into three categories based on their overall spiritual cum moral disposition: *sattva* (calm/good), *rajas* (passionate/active), and *tamas* (dull/lethargic). In Ayurvedic theory all food categories are similarly classified (cf. Khare 1976; Beck 1969). The basic logic of this scheme is that a sattva person will tend to eat sattva food. However, a person can, through design or by accident, change his or her disposition through eating food of a different category. Khare (1976: 84) and others (Daniel 1984: 184–186; Kakar 1982: 268–270) have cautioned against a too-rigid application of this paradigm of food types to personality disposition. Although both derive from a common base, Ayurvedic healing theory finds application in the manipulation of diet, whereas the philosophical typology of physiology is largely a classificatory scheme. As Daniel has pointed out, the Ayurvedic paradigm is a flexible continuum of tendencies—more or less sattva, more or less tamas—rather than a strict scheme of absolute rules.

For the wrestler the Ayurvedic paradigm provides the basic logic for a very simple rule. Because wrestlers exercise vigorously and therefore heat up their bodies they must eat cool sattva foods in order to foster a calm, peaceful, relaxed disposition. Wrestlers do not always agree on the relative properties of specific foods. Although most will agree on whether something is hot or cold they will often disagree on which of two closely related food types is cooler or hotter than the other. For instance, butter is thought by some to be cooler than ghi. Chicken is thought to be cooler than mutton, but, like all meat, extremely hot as a general rule. The nature of milk is somewhat problematic; cow's milk tends to be regarded as cooler than buffalo milk, but both are regarded as very sattva on the whole. In order to see how wrestlers conceptualize their diet—which is to say how they work through the particular implications of both nutrition and moral disposition—it is necessary to look at some foods in detail.

MILK AND GHI

In every sense, milk and ghi are the two most important ingredients in a wrestler's diet. Although he cannot live on ghi and milk alone, a wrestler constructs his diet around them. Generally speaking, they are regarded as the most sattva of sattva foods. Ghi in particular imparts long life, wisdom, strength, health, happiness, and love (Atreya 1984:

21). Because of its eminently unctuous quality, ghi draws out the juices from other foods. It is in this capacity that ghi is able to produce resilient semen. As Atreya points out, eggs produce semen as well, but because eggs are not unctuous in the same way as ghi, their semen and strength flow out of the body as fast as they are produced (ibid: 23). Eggs are also tamas. One of the main virtues of ghi is that while it mixes with and draws out the properties of other foods, it does not lose its own properties through the process of digestion. Its sattva nature remains dominant and resilient.

Ghi is good for nearly everything (Ramsanehi Dixit 1967b). It serves as a perfect, natural health tonic. It may be consumed in any number of ways. Atreya outlines the ways in which it is most beneficial for wrestlers:

1. After exercise, place as much ghi as you are accustomed to drinking in a pan. Cover this pan with a fine cloth and sprinkle ground-sugar candy on it. Then take some milk and pour it through the cloth into the pan with the ghi. Drink this mixture.

There are a number of variations on this basic prescription. All entail the use of various specific, medicinal, tonic digestive powders referred to generically as *churan*. In all such prescriptions, churan, ground pepper, milk, ghi, and honey are mixed together in various proportions. Milk is always the final ingredient and is mixed in with the other items (Atreya 1984: 28).

2. After exercise, take powdered black pepper and mix it in with as much ghi as you are accustomed to drinking. Heat the ghi to a point where it is compatible with your strength (the "heat" referred to here is not only the temperature of the ghi but its latent energy as well). Drink the ghi in its melted form.

There are a number of variations on this prescription as well. Many of the same churan digestives are employed. The main distinguishing feature of this prescription is that milk is not mixed with the ghi.

3. In its melted form ghi is also consumed with food. It may be drunk before the regular meal or mixed in with lentils and vegetables or poured on bread and rice.

4. One of the best ways to take ghi in your diet is to mix it with dried, powdered nuts and grains. Basically anything which is dry in nature—dry in the sense of being non-unctuous—can be mixed with ghi in this way. Take whatever it is that you wish to mix—almonds, chana,

dried peas, pistachios—and grind them into a fine powder. Put this powder into an iron skillet and brown it over a fire. Add some water and continue cooking the mixture until about 150 grams of water remains. Take the iron skillet off the fire and heat up as much ghi as you are accustomed to drinking. Once this is hot, remove it from the fire, take the powdered mixture and add it to the ghi so that it is lightly and quickly browned. Drink/eat this mixture after you have finished your exercise regimen.

5. In the evening, take your usual quantity of milk and warm it. Add to this as much ghi as you are accustomed to drinking. Allow this mixture to form into yogurt through the addition of the correct culture. Drink this yogurt after your morning exercises. Be sure not to add any water.

6. Grind almonds and black pepper together with some water. Heat up as much ghi as you wish to drink and then add the almond paste to the ghi. Add some sugar and drink this mixture.

7. Mix together equal parts ghi, *gur* (hard molasses), and *besan* (chickpea) flour. Eat this mixture as a snack after exercise.

8. Mix as much ghi as you wish to drink with as much warm milk as you are able to drink. Consume this after exercise. This is different from the other prescriptions in that no digestive tonics are mixed with the milk and ghi (Atreya 1984: 30–33).

In addition to having ghi mixed into it, milk is drunk on its own. Some wrestlers argue that raw milk is best, but others claim that milk must first be boiled. Milk can be processed in various ways in order to make it more or less unctuous. In this way a wrestler can manipulate his diet in order to accommodate the variability of his digestive health. For instance, he may extract much of the butter and drink a low-fat form of milk to which might be added sugar, molasses, or salt. Alternatively, he might add yogurt to the milk and make a kind of high-fat milkshake, *lassi*, to which might be added fruit, nuts, or cream. Vedi, who has written on the various beneficial properties of lassi, buttermilk, and yogurt, observes, "Cool, fresh drinks play an invaluable role in keeping down the heat which is generated by the active body. Cool liquids [such as milk and lassi] penetrate to the innermost parts of the body and draw out heat in the form of sweat and urine. Of all liquids, milk and lassi are two in which Indians place a great deal of faith" (1973: 17).

ALMONDS

Whereas ghi produces generalized physical strength, almonds are regarded by wrestlers as a primary source of *dam kasi* (stamina) and speed
(Ramsanehi Dixit n.d.). Almonds are prepared by mashing them into a
paste and mixing this paste with milk or ghi. One wrestler explained
that almonds impart stamina and strength because they produce energy
but are not filling.

CHANA

While dried peas, chickpeas, and lentils are commonplace items in
Indian cooking, they are also accorded a special place in the dietetics
of Indian wrestling. Because almonds are so expensive (75 rupees per
kilogram in 1987), chana is regarded by many wrestlers as the poor
man's almond substitute. One of the most common tonic snacks taken
by wrestlers is made of sprouted chickpeas.

Chickpeas are soaked overnight in warm water and are then hung in
a loose cloth in a warm place. Once these peas sprout, wrestlers eat
them with salt, pepper, and lemon. In addition to being a source of
energy, strength and stamina, chana is also sattva by nature. Not
incidentally, chickpeas prepared in this way are used as the basic
prasad food offered to Hanuman and other gods on special days of
worship.

The water in which the prasad is soaked is also regarded as saturated
with the energy of the sprouted peas. When drunk, this water purifies
the blood and also increases one's strength and store of semen (Saksena
1972: 17).

Many wrestlers feel that chana is saturated with all kinds of beneficial
attributes. Western nutritional information has served to substantiate
the overall value of chana as a source of vitamins. It is regarded as a
source of energy and strength in part because it is so common and cheap.
The idea is that everyone can afford chana and therefore everyone can
be strong and healthy. Saksena writes:

> In this modern age it is difficult for the common man to receive the requisite
> daily allowance of vitamins. On account of this, the common man has be-
> come weak and a victim of disease. It is sad that we have turned away from
> chana, a cheap but nevertheless very healthy food. We have turned to West-
> ern tonics and medicines which are packaged in attractive containers and
> advertized everywhere. Who will advertise the properties of chana when the
> rich feel that it is a food fit only for animals!? (1972: 18)

Many wrestlers with whom I spoke said that when they were young and poor—and most of them emphasized that they were poor, and that being poor and strong was a virtue—they could afford to eat only a handful of chana to supplement their regular meals. On this handful of chana, however, they were able to build their bodies and generally develop their health and vitality. Even though ghi, milk, and almonds are regarded as essential to a wrestler's overall development, chana is accorded high rank. It is the food of the people and for the people, a food that potentially gives everyone access to the wrestler's health and strength.

FRUITS AND JUICES

All kinds of fruit and fruit juices are regarded as efficacious by wrestlers. The general rule is to eat whatever fruit is in season, and these are most beneficial when taken after regular meals. One should not drink fruit juice for at least two hours after exercising. One can, however, drink orange or lemon juice before one's morning regimen. Not all fruits possess the same qualities, nor is it clear exactly which properties of a fruit are regarded as particularly efficacious by wrestlers. Generally, however, fruits contain vitamins, minerals, and other nutrients which can benefit a wrestler's health. Moreover, fruit is eminently sattva.

In the journal *Bharatiya Kushti* the following fruits are recommended for having particularly valuable attributes: wood-apples (Kamal 1971), bananas (Vishwakarma 1974; A. K. Jain 1987), figs (Rajani 1974), pomegranates (Anonymous 1978), gooseberries (Rajesh Dixit n.d.; Jaini 1979; Tripathi 1981), lemons (Lal 1985), watermelons (Sundaracharya 1986a), and apples (Yogi 1986). The wood-apple, for instance, is regarded as a cure for stomach ailments and digestive problems and a remedy for sore throat and tired eyes. Mixed with honey, its juice is used to treat hepatitis. Most significantly, wood-apple is very cooling. During the summer months it is used by wrestlers as a refreshment. Similarly, orange juice is regarded as a potent tonic during the summer season. Wrestlers tend to become listless on account of exercising in the oppressive heat. Although there is not a direct correlation between air temperature, personal characteristic traits, and food classification, wrestlers tend to associate hot weather with a "hot" rajas disposition. Cooling sattva orange juice is just the thing for a hot day.

Speaking specifically about rose-apples, but implicitly about all fruit, H. Jain writes, "One will find that this fruit is very delicious. It makes the body feel light, fresh and calm. Sherbet made from the rose-apple is very cooling and it has many other attributes, one of which is that it imparts strength" (1973: 17).

REGULAR OR COMMON FOOD

Wrestlers are enjoined to eat various green vegetables not only because they contain vitamins and minerals but also because they are sattva in nature (Sundaracharya 1984: 45–51). Along with green vegetables, wrestlers may eat almost anything else that constitutes the average North Indian meal: lentils of various types; breads made of whole wheat, barley, and millet flour; rice (though in moderate proportions, for it is thought to have little nutritional value); potatoes; and other vegetables, such as cauliflower, squash, and turnips. Although these items are essential to a wrestler's health, wrestlers do not emphasize the importance of these foods when discussing their diet. Such foods—with the notable exception of chana—are mundane by virtue of their common, everyday usage and are therefore not elaborated upon in the conceptual framework of wrestling dietetics.

VOLUME: GHI, MILK, AND ALMONDS

All wrestling foods are sattva. But these foods also have other properties. Milk, for instance, helps clean out the stomach. Chana also cleans the stomach and the bowels. Vegetables provide roughage. Fruit is cooling and refreshing. Ghi, chana, milk, fruits, and vegetables all have particular healing properties which do not relate specifically to the wrestling regimen but nevertheless support more general correlations of diet with health. Thus, milk in any quantity is both sattva and a mild laxative. Ghi is sattva and can also help cure coughs, colds, and other ailments. All of these features add up to a generalized notion of good health.

Healing properties aside, wrestlers drink and eat huge volumes of ghi, milk, and almonds. It is on this level of quantity that food becomes more than just healthy: it becomes associated with physical mass and brute strength. On one level a wrestler may eat a small amount of ghi in order to maintain his sattva disposition. On this level ghi is taken as a tonic. However, by eating a large volume of ghi, say half to one liter, a wrestler can take advantage of the ghi's high fat content and increase his size and weight. Wrestlers tend to increase the volume of consumption in proportion to the number of exercises they do in their vyayam regimen. There is no simple equation for this but wrestlers who do 1,500 dands and 3,000 bethaks consume about half a liter of ghi and two liters of milk per day. Since the amount of milk, ghi, and almonds one can eat is a direct reflection of one's strength, wrestlers tend to eat increasingly larger quantities of these items. In many respects being able to eat and digest half a liter of ghi per day is regarded as a kind of exercise in its own right. One must work up to this volume gradually. It is said that Sadhiki Pahalwan, a great wrestler of the late nineteenth century, consumed a canister (five kilograms) of ghi per day.

Wrestlers realize that eating milk, ghi, and almonds makes them big and strong. However, the relationship between diet and size is not one of simple cause and effect. Therefore, when a wrestler talks about being able to eat large volumes of ghi, milk, and almonds it is primarily because he *is* big and strong and not because he seeks to *become* big and strong.

Diet is only one factor in a wrestler's overall development. As I was often told, some people can eat huge amounts of food and remain thin and weak while others eat very little and get fat. In order to become big and strong enough to eat large volumes of food one must exercise properly, be devoted to one's guru, pray to god, and, most significantly, have a calm, peaceful, and spiritual disposition.

SEASONAL VARIATION

Mujumdar suggests that one's diet must change according to the season (1950: 684–688). In my experience, few wrestlers actually change their diet in any dramatic way. There is some tendency to eat rajas and tamas foods in winter, and extra-sattva foods in the summer. For instance, *urad*, a lentil which is regarded to be quite hot, is thought of as a winter food. The same holds true for meat. Wrestlers who eat meat tend to eat less or abstain altogether in the summer.

In an article entitled "How to Stay Healthy During the Rainy Season," Pathak (1980) advocates the use of lemons, bananas, and leafy vegetables. He also suggests that during the rains digestion tends to weaken and that consequently people should eat less. It is interesting to note that the *Malla Purana* provides a fairly precise catalog of which foods to eat in each season of the year (Sandesara and Mehta 1964: 10). In general "heavy" foods are eaten in the winter and "lighter" foods in the summer, but it seems that most foods can be taken in either season, only in larger or smaller quantities.

For the most part, however, only the fringe items—fruits, lentils, vegetables—of a wrestler's diet change from one season to the next. The staples remain constant although the amount of milk and ghi may be reduced during the rains and increased in the winter months.

DIETARY PROHIBITIONS

There are very few foods that wrestlers are prohibited from eating. Many Hindu wrestlers advocate a vegetarian diet. In the journal *Bharatiya Kushti* and in other popular literature there are numerous articles which claim that a non-meat diet can produce a strong physique (M. R. Gupta 1973; Guru Hanuman 1984; R. K. Jain 1987; Kumawath 1987; Munna 1983; Sundaracharya 1984). An article in the *Hindustan Times* characterized Chandagi Ram, the national champion, as being "ninety kilograms of vegetarian muscle" (1969: 2). The argument of those who advocate a purely vegetarian diet is that a combination of grains, nuts, fruits, and vegetables not only produces a solid, big physique, but also keeps that physique cool and unagitated.

But vegetarianism is by no means a strict rule. While meat is regarded as rajas in nature, wrestlers who eat meat tend to rationalize this. They argue that one can eat meat and to some extent avoid the consequences. The trick is to neutralize the rajas nature of meat by some form of counteractivity. I was not able to determine what these counteractivities were. However, many wrestlers implied that meat would only aggravate one's passion if one were "naturally" predisposed towards excitability, anger, and hypertension. Thus anyone who ate meat could, and often did, argue that they were so sattva by nature that meat did not adversely affect them. Moreover, by virtue of their naturally aggressive "military" disposition, Rajputs are thought to thrive on meat (cf. Carstairs 1958; Minturn and Hitchcock 1966; Seesodia 1915; Steed 1955). Some Rajput wrestlers argue that meat is good for them because they should, in a sense, eat what they are.

For wrestlers, vegetarianism is not so much a moral issue—in the sense of being a more "sanskritized," nonviolent way to live—as it is an issue of personal disposition and predilection. People choose to eat meat or not eat meat on the degree to which they see it affecting their state of body/mind.

As a rule wrestlers do not drink liquor or smoke tobacco. Liquor is extremely hot and is thought to enrage passion and make one dull, listless, and weak. Moreover, intoxication is a sure sign of moral depravity and lack of willpower. Even more so than meat, it is regarded as ultrahot and may be classified as the antithesis of ghi. Liquor is the essence of evil just as milk is the elixir of life, and wrestlers attribute many modern problems to the growing popularity of alcohol. In a sense, liquor serves as the black backdrop against which the virtues of a milk and ghi diet stand out in pure, sharp relief. This important point will be taken up again when the issue of moral nationalism is considered in chapter 10.

Tobacco is regarded in much the same way as liquor: it is hot. Its use is also a sure a sign of moral weakness. Moreover, it is thought to make the body vulnerable to disease. Wrestlers realize that among other things smoking reduces their lung capacity and overall performance.

Caffeine, ingested in the form of tea, is regarded by wrestlers as a mild but dangerous narcotic. As such it is juxtaposed against purer, more efficacious drinks like warm milk, sherbet, fruit juice, *thandai*, and pure, fresh water.

Strictly speaking, wrestlers are supposed to eat only what has been prepared for them by their family or what they have cooked with their own hands. The idea behind this, as Atreya pointed out, is that psycho-emotional disposition is thought to be mildly contagious. An erotic woman can seduce a man by feeding him food that she has prepared. Similarly, if a man who is sexually aroused cooks food, the wrestler who eats it might also become sexually excited. As a safeguard, wrestlers are enjoined not to eat any food which is prepared for public sale. In fact, however, this rule is rarely if ever observed. I have never met a wrestler, with the exception of Atreya himself, who does not eat food prepared in market stalls or restaurants.

Wrestlers are supposed to avoid sour and excessively spiced foods. Meals are best eaten lightly spiced with garlic, cumin, coriander, and *haldi*. *Chatni*s (spicy syrups), *achar*s (pickled spices, vegetables and roots), *chat*s (savories), and pickles in any form are thought to cause either sensual arousal or lethargy. As with meat, however, many wrestlers rationalize the occasional use of pickles by saying that they have a surplus of sattva nature and can therefore accommodate and neutralize the occasional pickle or plate of savory chat.

As a rule wrestlers do not chew tobacco or *pan* (a mildly intoxicating betel nut, betel leaf, and lime-paste concoction.) However, pan is so prevalent in Banaras, where chewing it is regarded almost as a criterion of Banarsi identity, that many wrestlers indulge themselves. Even those wrestlers who chew it, however, say that it is wrong because it is addicting and dulls the senses. However, it is so common as to be almost regarded as a necessary evil of social life.

BRAHMACHARYA

It is a common belief among Hindus that the essence of life is contained in semen (cf. Carstairs 1958; Edwards 1983; Kakar 1982; Obeyesekere 1976; Spratt 1966). Consequently, there is a good deal of anxiety concerning the need to prevent semen from being discharged either voluntarily or involuntarily. For wrestlers the concern is magnified. Not only do they regard semen as the quintessential fluid of life, they also regard it as the very cornerstone of their somatic enterprise. It is the source of all strength, all energy, all knowledge, all skill. Semen fuels the fires of self-realization just as ghi fuels the lamps of devotional worship. Moreover, semen is regarded as a distillate of most other body fluids and substances—blood, marrow, and bone, in particular—and is therefore thought to contain the essence of the whole body within itself (Zimmer 1948). It would not be an exaggeration to say that the single most important aspect of a wrestler's regimen is his subscription to the absolute tenets of *brahmacharya*: celibacy and self-control. Atreya makes the following analogy: "Brahmacharya is the essence of life. Just as there is ghi in milk, oil in the *til* seed and syrup in sugar cane, so is there semen in the body. Like syrup and oil, semen is an essential sap of the human body. A person should guard his semen just as a jeweler guards his most valuable diamonds" (1972*b*: 25).

In an interview on the subject of brahmacharya, Narayan Singh observed:

> We emphasize brahmacharya—never to lose one's semen. It is the essence of power; the essence of strength; the essence of endurance; the essence of beauty. These days people use powder and all sorts of things to make themselves look good . . . but there is something . . . there must be something to Vivekananda [the missionary of Vedantic Hinduism and devout follower of Ramakrishna]. . . . I think if you stand in front of a statue of Gotham Buddha [perhaps the most perfect exemplar of brahmacharya] you will see some light in his face. After all, what is beauty? If there is beauty, then it must attract god. Brahmacharya gives something special to the lips, a special light to the body, a shine to the eyes, and something special to the cheeks.

The disciplinary mechanics of maintaining brahmacharya are clearly articulated by wrestlers. The basic premise is *virya nirodh* or *kamdaman* ("the protection of semen") and the control of sensual desire (Ravindra-

nath 1975: 19). A common metaphor used to describe a wrestler's strict
adherence to the path of brahmacharya is *kase langot ke* (tight/firm g-
string). The langot symbolizes celibacy, for it binds the genitals up between the legs. However, wrestlers are cautioned against wearing a langot for too long a period of time. Excessive constriction can lead to
arousal, it is thought, and so it is best to loosen or remove one's langot
soon after exercising.

In order to protect one's semen one must neither think, speak, nor
hear any evil. One should never think amorous thoughts. Ravindranath
expands on this by saying that one should not look at a woman, never
speak to a woman, never touch a woman, never think about a woman,
never listen to a woman, never be alone with a woman, never joke
around with a woman, and, of course, never have intercourse with a
woman (ibid). Lest there be any doubt, Ravindranath and many wrestlers with whom I spoke pointed out over and over again that women
pose a threat to the young wrestler's self-control. Sensuality of any kind,
and heterosexual lust in particular, is to be avoided at all costs.

Brahmacharya is not an easy path to follow. This is particularly so
in the modern world where temptations loom large. Moreover, for the
wrestler at least, the discipline involved is doubly hard. It is thought that
because he is so strong, he must contain a larger than normal reserve of
semen. The problem is how to contain this vast pool of virility. In part
the problem itself suggests its own solution. Exercise and a proper diet
in conjunction with a regimented program of bathing, sleeping, and
resting ensure that semen will be built up and channeled appropriately
(Atreya 1973c: 22–23, 25). However, wrestlers also subscribe to other
methods of maintaining brahmacharya. Atreya outlines some of these.

1. *Satsang (fellowship with good men).*   The company of like-
minded men makes the observance of brahmacharya easier. Moral support is provided and one is motivated by a sense of collective duty.
Communion with other brahmacharis fosters peace of mind and helps
to cut through the shrouds of delusion which distract and mislead. The
company of good men also creates an environment where wisdom can
develop. The exchange of ideas based on religious works allows for the
growth of knowledge (ibid.: 29). It is clear that akhara fellowship is
envisioned as just such a satsang.

2. *Isolation from Sensual Depravity.*   In order to be a brahmachari and practice self-control, one must not associate with those things
which will foster emotional feelings of love and desire. Austerity is,

therefore, the brahmachari's watchword. Films and magazines must be avoided. Animals must be kept locked up so that one will not see them copulating. One should close one's ears to lewd remarks and foul language (ibid: 21–23).

3. *Thought.* It is through our thoughts that we can change the environment we live in. But thoughts are also dangerous. It is for this reason that one must not fraternize with people whose minds are corrupted by greed, lust, and so forth. Pure thoughts foster a pure environment where the practice of brahmacharya may flourish (ibid: 23–25).

4. *Austerity.* The brahmachari must subscribe to three basic forms of austerity: of body, speech, and thought. Through the practice of these austerities one is able to destroy desire manifest in either physical, verbal, or psychological form (ibid).

5. *Reading Scriptures and Chanting Hymns.* One way to protect one's semen is to read the works of learned men. The scriptures will raise one's consciousness to a higher level, thus making the practice of brahmacharya more meaningful (ibid: 26–27).

6. *Faith in God.* The brahmachari should always remember that whatever he has achieved is through the power of god and the instruction of his guru. The brahmachari who has faith in god has no worries (ibid).

These guidelines for the practice of brahmacharya are further elaborated in a number of popular handbooks on the subject (Saraswati n.d.; J. Shastri n.d.; Shivananda 1984). Shivananda devotes special chapters to a range of central themes: The parent's duty to set a good example for the young brahmachari; control of desire, mind and emotion; and married life and brahmacharya, for example. The body of Shivananda's book is concerned with an elaboration of twenty-five rules for the practice of brahmacharya. Many of these rules overlap with those outlined by Atreya. For example, Shivananda expands on the idea of cleanliness by saying that a brahmachari must bathe and evacuate his bowels twice a day (1984: 109). Although bathing and defecating have general implications regarding health and fitness, the brahmachari wrestler bathes and defecates in order to ensure absolute control of his semen.

Although brahmacharya is a hard path to follow—and undoubtedly many fall by the wayside—most wrestlers take seriously the common injunction: brahmacharya is life and sensuality is death. Wrestlers try very hard to control their sexuality. They may not subscribe to the rigorous guidelines outlined by Atreya, Shivananda, and others, but they do respect the general theory which underlies the practice. They have an abject fear of semen loss.

Wrestlers, on the whole, avoid the company of women assiduously. Women, when encountered, are to be treated as mothers and sisters. The very idea of intercourse for the sake of pleasure is a danger of such magnitude that it is almost unthinkable. Similarly, masturbation is regarded as such an abominable waste of semen that it is antithetical to everything that brahmacharya stands for. This is not to say that no young wrestlers masturbate. However, the moral injunction against masturbation is so great that the issue itself, like sexual intercourse, is never seriously considered as posing an ongoing threat to celibacy. The practice and discipline of brahmacharya begins, essentially, where the most basic expression of sensuality ends. That one not have intercourse or masturbate are only the most basic prerequisites for brahmacharya.

A less controllable threat to celibacy than masturbation is the involuntary loss of semen through *svapna dosh* (lit., dream error, night emission). Night emission is involuntary insofar as it is thought to be caused by dream imagery or some other unconscious force (J. Shastri n.d.: 12). Many advocates of strict brahmacharya claim, nevertheless, that dream imagery is ultimately stimulated by conscious feelings of sensuality and lust. The person who has a night emission is held accountable and must work toward reforming his unconscious by means of "cleaning out" his conscious mind. In a book on the subject of brahmacharya, Shastri analyzes in great detail the problems associated with night emission. He describes the type of person who suffers from night emission as one who is conceited and thinks of himself as the essence of masculinity (ibid: 37). While the basic solution to the problem is therefore a reform of moral character, Shastri also provides a list of helpful remedies: washing one's feet with warm water before going to sleep, eating extra-cool sattva foods, thinking more deeply on god, and so forth. Most of these prescriptions are by now familiar. However Shastri outlines a host of ancillary techniques (101, to be exact) which may be employed to aid against the scourge. Do not get in the habit of riding as a passenger on someone else's bicycle. Do not sleep with your head covered. Do not drink excessive amounts of water. Do not hold back when you need to urinate. Do not sleep naked. Chew your food thoroughly. Occasionally place a wet cloth on your stomach. Wash your genitals regularly with cool water, and with salt water at least once a week. Always keep your genitals cool and fresh. Do not warm yourself by an open fire. Always keep your lower back straight. Wear clean clothes.

The basic principle of these rules is to structure the brahmachari's life to such an extent that every minute facet of daily life comes to play a role in the larger scheme of semen control. Many wrestlers I have spoken with point out that it is important to keep busy and never sit around daydreaming. Every minute of every day must be structured, even if it is structured as leisure.

Many of the popular handbooks on brahmacharya, as well as the various articles on the subject in the wreslting literature, prescribe wrestling exercise as a way to maintain celibacy. My sense is that a number of young wrestlers come to the akhara burdened with a sense of guilt regarding their adolescent emotions. In the akhara they find a release for these emotions and also a powerful means by which to control their sexuality. The akhara is not a cure-all by any means, but it does provide a regimented structure which serves to release anxiety. Wrestlers often tell stories of how some wrestler they knew was almost seduced by a woman but managed to turn his mind either to his exercise or his guru and thereby prevent a catastrophe.

While the power of celibacy is recognized as absolute, most of the wrestlers I spoke with were not able or did not feel it necessary to articulate a theory of how semen is related to psychosomatic strength. Such theories do exist, of course, within the texts of classical medicine and also in the popular literature on the subject. Such theories are themselves part of much larger systems of medical knowledge (Obeyesekere 1976; Zimmermann 1983). For the wrestler, however, what is important is not so much the theory as the practical application of rules. What is also important is an integrative poetics of power and strength. In this regard brahmacharya is talked about and written about in a language of rich metaphor.

> A brahmachari is righteous. He is not a slave to his senses, nor is he guided by mere self-indulgent thoughts. He takes no pleasure or satisfaction in worldly things. He has complete control over his thoughts, and stands firm on the limits he has set for himself. He stands as huge as a mountain: firm and grand. His seriousness reflects the depth of the ocean. He is a beacon of light and therefore brilliant and resolute. Like a lighthouse he prevents the ship of

life from wrecking itself on the rocks of desire. The brahmachari does not
break his vow. His life is pure and untainted. His roots run deep and he does
not fall like a stone from a mountain—No: he is an immovable granite ridge!
(K. P. Singh 1972a: 26–27)

Sita Ram Yadav explained the complex relationship between dietetics,
exercise, and brahmacharya thus: "Because ghi is hidden in milk there
is strength in milk. But if the butter is taken out of milk then there is no
strength left in it. In the same way, when semen leaves the body the
body becomes useless."

I was told that it is evident from the look on a person's face, the light
in his eyes, and the glow of his skin whether he is celibate. On one
occasion I went to a wedding of a sister of one of the wrestlers from
Akhara Ram Singh. The guru of the akhara was also invited. After the
meal had been served, the guests were invited to an "audience" where the
bride and groom were seated on thrones in order to receive the blessing of
various family members and guests. After watching for some time, the
guru of the akhara turned to me, shaking his head in dismay. The groom,
he said, was clearly not a brahmachari, and he proceeded to run through
an index of telltale signs: a dark, sallow complexion; a drawn face; sunken
eyes; a thin, "dried-out" physique and stooped shoulders.

Some wrestlers are more critical than others, but in talking with
senior wrestlers it became clear that many felt, figuratively as well as
quite literally, that the potential energy of youth is being sapped, drawn
out by the sensuality of the modern, materialist world. Liquor in particular is directly implicated in this demise. It is distilled from grain which
could be otherwise used as food. Moreover, liquor neutralizes food and
is therefore doubly wasteful. Specifically, liquor is regarded as a poison
in terms of what it does to the body. In the wrestler's conceptual framework we have seen that food is regarded as the building block of semen.
Liquor, it is thought, attacks semen and is thus antithetical to food.
Wrestlers are uniformly vehement in their advocacy of temperance
(Atreya 1974–1975: 17). They literally cringe at the thought of so much
energized semen—and all that it represents by way of the nation's potential energy for growth and development—going to waste. In a long
serial poem entitled Goshala (lit., cow/protection/home), "Dwivedi"
contrasts the virtues of milk with the evils of liquor.

The night turns slowly to day
    as the taverns are robbed.
Children are robbed of their youth;
    those who drink are robbed.

Seeing the light of dawn,
    the tavern turns in shame.
But my goshala welcomes the dawn
    of a new day (1972: 37).

Ultimately, the power of seduction manifest in the poison of liquor is no match for the power of brahmacharya manifest in milk and ghi—or at least that is the wrestler's sincere hope.

A common sentiment among akhara members is that the power of brahmacharya is so great that it can turn the weakest and most decrepit boy into a powerful champion. Even if all he eats is dry bread or a handful of chana, a brahmachari wrestler will develop a more magnificent and resilient physique than a wrestler who carelessly consumes buckets of milk. Clearly, then, there is a direct and unambiguous connection which exists between morals, social ethics, psychological well-being, and the strength and health of the somatic body as a whole (see plate 2). Through strict discipline, the akhara regimen provides for a holistic integration of these elements.

CHAPTER 6

Nag Panchami: Snakes, Sex, and Semen

Nag Panchami (Snake's [Cobra's] Fifth) is a minor festival celebrated throughout North India in the latter half of July on the fifth day of the light half of the Hindu month *Shravan*. As the name implies, Nag Panchami is a festival in honor of snakes. In Banaras and many parts of northwestern India, Nag Panchami is also a time when akharas hold special functions to celebrate wrestling as a way of life. Akharas are cleaned and repainted. Priests are called in to give special blessings. Gurus are honored, patrons are recognized, and wrestlers demonstrate their skill and strength before crowds of people. It is said that even people who are not usually interested in wrestling take this opportunity to get involved. Although most people get involved only as spectators, at many akharas the pit is turned into a public arena where anyone may challenge anyone else regardless of whether they know how to wrestle or not. As one man put it, on Nag Panchami everyone is a wrestler.

Why is Nag Panchami associated with wrestling? What does a festival in honor of snakes have to do with a wrestler's public presentation of self? By addressing this question I will offer an interpretation of the symbolic structure of wrestling as a way of life.

As has been pointed out, wrestlers are seriously preoccupied with their sexuality. Every effort is made to control erotic emotion and sensual desire. A wrestler must not only abstain from sex, he must also build up his stock of semen and ensure that once built up it is as potent and strong as it can possibly be. The basis for this preoccupation is a belief that physical, personal, and intellectual strength emanates from semen. Semen is the locus of a person's moral character and physical prowess. Given this emphasis, it is logical to assume that the symbolic cosmology of wrestling is structured around a theme of contained sexuality. Nag, the king cobra, is a key symbol in this scheme of coded virility.

Before beginning this analysis of coded and embodied virility, it is necessary to outline the events which make up the ceremony of Nag Panchami.

THE CELEBRATION

On Nag Panchami, snake charmers line the streets of towns and cities displaying an array of snakes. Pythons, rat snakes, and cobras mingle in deep baskets and are brought out, each in turn, to dance to the tune of their charmer's flute. Alternatively they hang, listlessly limp, around his neck as crowds of people gather to witness the drama. At temples dedicated to Nag Raja (the King of Snakes), offerings are made to sacred "pet" cobras who represent the deity. Even at temples not directly associated with Nag, cobras are often brought in by snake charmers in order to enhance the spirit of the festival. These common snakes—which otherwise languish in their charmer's basket—are also made the object of ritual worship (cf. Kitts 1885).

The main ritual event of Nag Panchami is to offer milk and crystallized sugar to a cobra. As Premlata Vatsyayan writes, "On Nag Panchami one fasts and feeds milk or *khir* [rice pudding] to snakes. A white lotus flower is placed in a silver bowl. One then takes a brush made either of clay, wood, silver or gold, and using either turmeric or sandalwood paste draws the image of a five hooded snake on the floor. People then pray to this image" (1985: 66).

In rural areas people often go to anthills or other places where snakes are thought to live. They make their offerings by lighting incense in front of the snake's hole. Milk is placed in a bowl to entice the snake out and is later poured down the hole as a libation (cf. Fuller 1944). As a number of authors have noted, feeding milk to snakes is a common motif in myth and folklore (La Barre 1962: 94; Thompson 1955–1958: B391.1.3, B784.2.1.0, B765.4.1, Q452; Vogel 1926: 174–175).

Nag Panchami is a day to pray to snakes so as to avoid being bitten. Pandit Rakesh (1986: 61), referencing the *Garuda Purana*, points out that praying to snakes is an auspicious act which can make wishes come true. He also says that after having made an offering to a snake one must follow the common ritual injunction of feeding a Brahman (ibid). Having done these things, Rakesh concludes, one will encounter no major difficulties in life.

On a commonsense level snakes are regarded as dangerous. Nag Panchami is a festival which functions on a symbolic plane to subvert any possible danger of being poisoned. Taking ritual action to avoid being poisoned is translated into a general condition which insures auspicious health and longevity.

In addition to the salient points outlined by Rakesh, many people I spoke with in Banaras said that plowing or digging is forbidden on Nag Panchami because one might inadvertently kill a snake. Vatsyayan writes that one should not dig or plow for the whole month of Shravan. But she adds that this is somewhat extreme and may not be followed strictly (1985: 66).

On Nag Panchami many people decorate their doorways and walls with pictures of snakes (cf. Fuller 1944; Vogel 1926: 277–280). They either draw these themselves, or purchase them from vendors who sell posters at streetside stalls. A typical poster shows a coiled snake surrounded by other snakes in wriggling configuration. Auspicious mantras caption these posters which, in addition to being decorative, are designed to ward off dangerous snakes.

An important dimension of Nag Panchami has to do with the telling of folktales and myths about snakes. One of the most common is recorded by Vatsyayan:

> In a kingdom lived a farmer and his family. The farmer had two sons and a daughter. One day while plowing, the farmer accidentally killed three young snakes. At first the mother of the three dead snakes raged in anger but then vowed to avenge her children's murder. That night the snake entered the farmer's house and bit the farmer, his wife and their two sons. They all died. Early the next day, having seen what happened, the farmer's daughter offered a bowl of milk to the mother snake and folded her hands asking forgiveness for what her father had done. She asked that the snake restore her parents and brothers to life. Pleased with the milk offering the snake did as the farmer's daughter asked (1985: 67).

Many other tales are also told. Vogel's collection (1926), though dated, is the most complete and includes most of those catalogued by Thompson and Balys (1951). Though none of these folktales make an explicit reference to wrestling, they do express symbolic themes of continence and contained sexuality, themes of general importance to wrestling. "The Maiden Who Wedded a Snake" (Vogel 1926: 174–175), offers a clear example of the snake as a symbol of erotic sexuality. "The Story of the Jealous Nag" (ibid: 177) illustrates the danger of a woman's insatiable passion. In this tale the female snake and her human lover are burnt to death by the jealous snake husband. In another tale (Vatsyayan 1985: 67), a man and his wife are made to promise their firstborn daughter to a snake. When they do not fulfill their promise the snake kidnaps the daughter by enticing her into a lake and pulling her down into the depths.

While most of the stories told on Nag Panchami are folktales, passing reference is made to snake myths in the epics. Krishna's defeat of the Nag King, Kaliya (*Harivamsa*, chap. 68), is the most popular. In this story Krishna falls into a part of the Yamuna river where Kaliya lives. After being overcome by poison, Krishna rallies and ends up beating the snake king into submission, thereby purifying the waters of the holy river. Kaliya is relegated to live in the ocean, and the Yamuna river—likened in the text to the beautiful body of a maiden—is made safe for the cowherds among whom Krishna lives. One wrestler told a version of this story in which Krishna dives into the still waters of the Yamuna and defeats Kaliya by sticking his flute through the snake king's nose. As H. Zimmer points out (1946: 87), it is significant that Krishna does not kill Kaliya. In the myth, passion is symbolically controlled but not neutralized. Nag's power to ravish—which he does to the river maiden Yamuna—is harnessed by the cooling agency of the ocean. The energy of sexuality is not smothered; it is simply put in its proper place. This, as we shall see, is an important theme in the akhara celebration of Nag Panchami.

The folktales and myths about snakes that are told on Nag Panchami generally reinforce a notion that snakes represent sex as dangerous. The ritual of Nag Panchami, as will be seen, is designed to address the problem of sexual danger.

Nag Panchami is celebrated in various ways throughout India (cf. Banerjea 1956; Crooke 1926: 381–399; Fuller 1944; Mandlik 1868; Panda 1986: 105–113; Vogel 1926; Wadley 1975). However, the basic practice of propitiating snakes by offering them milk is almost certainly a universal aspect of the festival throughout India.

NAG PANCHAMI AT THE AKHARA

Although I have never seen wrestlers offer milk to snakes, the general motif is nevertheless common in the wrestling milieu. Akharas are often decorated with figures of snakes, many of which are depicted drinking from bowls of milk. I was told that if a snake were to appear in an akhara on Nag Panchami or any other day, it would be offered milk. At Narsingh Akhara there is a special shrine dedicated to Nag Raja. A bowl is suspended in the middle of this shrine as a permanent symbol of the annual milk offerings made on Nag Panchami.

Most of what occurs in the Banaras akharas on Nag Panchami does not relate to snakes explicitly. To the best of my knowledge no snake charmers are called, no posters of snakes put up, and no folktales or myths recounted. The akhara festivities simply do not make reference to what is generally regarded as the most common and popular dimension of the Nag Panchami celebration. At first this appeared paradoxical. It soon became clear, however, that while snakes are not formally manifest in akhara celebrations, the symbolic meanings associated with snakes are, nevertheless, invoked in various other ways. There are clear symbolic parallels between wrestling as it is ritualized in akharas on Nag Panchami and the more general significance of the festival as it relates to snakes. Much of the sexual meanings encoded in Nag Panchami ritual are also found encoded in the symbolic life of the wrestler. The wrestler embodies the cosmic structure of Nag Panchami ritual and folklore.

On Nag Panchami akharas are cleaned, repaired, and repainted. Temples are refurbished and colored flags and mango leaves are hung on strings around the pit. Special earth is brought in from rural areas, usually from the bottom of dried-out ponds, river banks, or other places where the soil is fine-grained and soft. Oil and turmeric, and occasionally perfumes and nim leaves, are mixed with the earth as it is added to the pit. Chairs are set up and rugs laid out for guests who are invited to watch the day's events. Everyone tries to wear new or clean clothes. Devotional hymns and popular film tunes are played over rented public-address systems.

Priests are hired to perform a special puja at the akhara. The ritual puja is not directed at any deity in particular but at the pit. The names of Hanuman, Ram, and Shiva (but not Nag) are invoked, but the object of devotion is not these deities but the earth. There are two primary parts to the pujas I have seen. First, the priest and his assistant prepare a large brass plate of soaked chickpea chana and *batasa* (crystallized sugar). Water is sprinkled on this prasad offering. The priest chants a prayer over the plate as it is placed in front of Hanuman. A fire is lit in

front of Hanuman's image and he is anointed with sandalwood or turmeric paste.

The second part of the ritual begins when the priest lights a bunch of
incense sticks and walks with these around the periphery of the pit. As
he walks in a clockwise direction, the priest takes handfuls of earth and
allows the smoke from the incense to mingle with the new soil. This
stage of the ritual is identical with the blessing/invocation done every
morning before practice. The smoke from the incense transfers Hanuman's blessing into the pit. The incense is planted in the middle of the pit
and everyone gathers around and chants some version of the following
common invocation: "Speak the praises of King Ram Chandar! Praise
be to Ram's devout disciple Hanuman! Praise be to the great God
Shiva!" The priest then takes the incense around to each member, who
cups the smoke in his hand and draws it to his chest or face in an act of
communion with the pit.

The priest carries the plate of prasad around the akhara and offers a
handful to each member. As the wrestlers eat the prasad the priest puts
a tika of vermilion paste on each person's forehead.

While the priest and his assistant prepare the prasad and incense, the
members of the akhara undress and put on their langots. By the time
the invocation is chanted, the pit is encircled by a large number of
wrestlers clad only in their g-strings. Those who are not wrestlers and
have come only to watch stand out distinctly as a crowd of clothed
people on the periphery of the akhara. Attention is clearly drawn to the
wrestlers' bodies. While wrestlers feel comfortable in their langots and
there is usually no self-consciousness about one's body in the akhara,
Nag Panchami tends to force the wrestler's subjective awareness of
his physique into an objective projection of what it means to be a
wrestler. The wrestler is always aware of his body as a meaningful
and significant part of his identity. On Nag Panchami, however, his
body takes on special significance by becoming an objective and
somewhat depersonalized representation of a whole way of life. During
the ritual the wrestler is on stage and his body becomes emblematic
of what he does.

Once the puja is completed, wrestlers pair up and put on brief demonstration bouts. At some point during the festivities each wrestler makes
a cash offering to the guru of the akhara. In 1987 Jaddu Singh, the
acting guru, sat on a chair in the corner of the pit holding a framed
portrait of his elder brother Ram Singh. The members came by and
placed garlands on the portrait as they touched Jaddu's feet.

While the blessing of the pit and the formal recognition of the guru are important parts of the festivities, Nag Panchami is primarily an occasion for many akharas to sponsor *dangal*s (wrestling tournaments). Nag Panchami dangals are unique and must be distinguished from more common, "secular" tournaments. Nag Panchami dangals take place within akhara precincts, while most other dangals are held in larger, secular public arenas. As distinct from regular wrestling bouts, Nag Panchami dangals should be seen as the extension of more general religious themes of propitiation. On Nag Panchami wrestling is an act of obeisance to Ram, Hanuman, Shiva, and the earth of the pit. Just as the body of the wrestler becomes an emblematic object of celibacy, moral virtue, and strength, so are the religious and symbolic aspects of wrestling writ large on the occasion of Nag Panchami. While all dangals are dramatic, Nag Panchami dangals dramatize a particular code of symbolic meaning associated with the power and danger of sexual energy as it relates to physical strength.

Nag Panchami is an occasion for everyone to see how much a wrestler has developed and improved over the previous year. As one person put it, a wrestler eats, exercises, and practices for a full year and then puts himself on display to bear witness to the virtue of his endeavor. One wrestler compared the public presentation of self on Nag Panchami to a farmer's proud perusal of his carefully nurtured crops. Like a well-rooted and irrigated plant, a wrestler grows and develops out of the akhara earth. On Nag Panchami the wrestler's body takes on the symbolic properties of nurtured growth which is associated with fertility and the agricultural cycle.

The significance of contained sexuality will be analyzed through an examination of eight motifs: rain and water, snakes, milk, ghi, almonds, earth, trees, and exercise. On Nag Panchami the wrestler's body—situated, significantly, at the locus of these eight motifs—represents a powerful scheme of contained sexuality manifest as growth and increasing physical prowess.

RAIN AND WATER

Nag Panchami is celebrated during the early weeks of the monsoon season. After the long, hot months of summer the rains, which move up the Gangetic Plain from the Bay of Bengal, bring much-needed relief. The rains mark a distinct seasonal change that is of greatest importance to farmers who must plow and plant their fields. Wrestlers also recognize the significance of the rains. For them they mark the beginning of the wrestling season. They also bring them out of torpid dormancy. Cooler weather enables wrestlers to exercise with renewed vigor. The meaning of rain in the context of wrestling is parallel to the significance rain has to the agricultural cycle. Moreover, Dundes has noted that throughout the Indo-European world, water and moisture in general are regarded as life-giving (1980: 109). Rain in particular helps wrestlers grow, and so, too, does the regimen of daily bathing. Water falls on the fertile ground of the wrestler's body and brings forth dormant strength and skill. Nag Panchami is a time when wrestlers bloom.

The Vedic term for season, *retu*—most often associated with *vrsa retu*, the rainy season—is etymologically very close to the vedic term for semen, *retas* (O'Flaherty 1980: 20). With regard to rain and semen there is another theme which points up an interesting parallel between rain and wrestling. *Vrsti* (rain) and *vrsan* (a powerful, virile, lustful man or a bull) are both derived from *vrs* (to rain or pour forth; ibid.). There is a clear parallel between rain and semen, particularly if one bears in mind the obvious role of the monsoon rains in agricultural growth and generation. The theme of virility as symbolically linked to rain and strength provides a strong case for why wrestlers celebrate their identity at the beginning of the monsoon season.

In Hindu mythology and folklore snakes represent rain (Maity 1963: 124–125; *Rig Veda*: 1.22.2; Vogel 1926: 34). In a more general sense they are often regarded as the deities of ponds and rivers (Crooke 1926: 390; *Harivamsa* chap. 68; Maity 1963: 154). H. Zimmer writes: "Like a river winding its way, the serpent creeps along the ground: it dwells in the earth and starts forth like a fountain from its hole. It is an embodiment of the water of life issuing from the deep body of mother earth" (1946: 74–75).

In this respect snakes represent two aspects of water: masculine rain as semen and feminine water as nurturing essence. The snake both falls from the sky and gushes from the earth. Snakes must not, therefore, be strictly associated with either feminine or masculine attributes. Significantly, snakes represent both male and female sexual energy. They are not purely phallic (Kakar 1990: 57); neither is the dominant motif one of impregnation. Snakes symbolize a powerful form of androgynous sexuality which is clearly apparent in the reconciliation of male rain with female water.

This point may be taken a step further if we consider the oppostion of fire and water in relation to snake symbolism (O'Flaherty 1980:

214–215). While snakes are associated with water, they also represent
lightning (Vogel 1926: 3–4). As such snakes represent the fire of passion
and the danger of unbridled lust (Kakar 1990: 52–63). A common
theme in Indian folklore is the belief that an erotic woman's vagina
contains a poisonous snake (O'Flaherty 1980: 292). On the male side
of the erotic equation the snake represents instinctual passion which
must be controlled and channeled. As O'Flaherty has shown, the theme
of serpent passion-fire is clearly manifest in the mythic metaphor of the
submarine fire. Herein the cooling properties of the ocean contain the
fire of sexual energy (ibid: 214, 215). Kaliya, as one may remember,
is banished to the ocean where his poisonous passion is cooled.
Without going into this in detail, one may see that just as the ocean
controls passion, so does the rain aspect of Nag balance his or her
fiery passionate dimension.

Significantly, rain, water, and fire comprise a balanced symbol of
sexual energy. The power of sexuality, both male and female, is recognized through the metaphor of rain and water, and the danger of sexuality as lust and passion is recognized in the metaphor of lightning. Passion
is always cooled through the agency of rain and water. Sexuality thus
remains a potent symbol of power while the dangerous aspect of sex is
held in check.

In wrestling, where contained sexuality is so important, the rain of
Shravan represents both the engendering strength of semen and the cooling of fiery passion. The rainy season evokes the symbolic significance
of contained sexuality, and the wrestler's body reflects the dynamic
reconciliation of passion with strength. As we shall see, the wrestler
must never lose semen. He must turn it back into physical and moral
strength. As a result, he must translate the fiery energy of passion into
the physical energy of strength. He is thus like the huge rain clouds
that roll up the Gangetic Plain, swollen with rain and sparkling with
lightning.

An alternative of this same motif would be that cooling rain symbolizes the liquid female aspect of sexuality while the snake represents
the fiery passionate side (cf. O'Flaherty 1980: 55; 1973: 286–289).
However, in such an interpretation passion is cooled only through the
release of semen—as the rain falls from the swollen clouds onto the
earth—which is antithetical to building strength through containment.
The more appropriate interpretation with regard to Nag Panchami ritual
is that rain represents the nascent energy of semen for which the snake
is, in either a male or female guise, the potent agency of passion. By thus

relating but isolating agency from element, snake from rain, passion from sexuality, the wrestler is able to focus on his sexual energy without falling prey to passion.

SNAKES

In his analysis of snakehandling cults in the United States, Weston La Barre presents a convincing argument for the phallic symbolism and sexual significance of snakes (La Barre 1962; also, cf. Dundes 1985; Mundkar 1983). Without entering into the debate over the universality of this motif, I think it can be shown that in India in general and certainly in the world of the wrestler, snakes represent sexuality in many forms.

Lingams—phallic-shaped rock images of Shiva—are often depicted with a snake coiled around the base of the stone or etched onto the *yoni* (vagina/source/base) on which the phallic rock is seated. Along with this graphic and very common motif is the idea that the serpent goddess Kundalini is coiled around a person's spine. The practice of yoga is designed to give one control over the energy of Kundalini. In the imagery of Kundalini Yoga the seed of shakti is activated at the base of one's spine and shot upward through the serpent to the top of one's head (O'Flaherty 1980: 45). This metaphor of ejaculation (which, not incidentally, is completely self-contained) provides a symbolic graph of self-realization and metaphysical release in Hindu spiritualism.

Although snakes have a clearly male phallic dimension there is also the common motif of the dangerous poisonous female snake. The myth of Putana, who poisoned her breasts in order to destroy Krishna, symbolically reflects the dangerous side of female power in this regard. Folklore clearly supports this image of dangerous female sexuality in the form of snakes. In the story of the jealous Nag (Vogel 1926: 176) a female snake entices travelers to her bed and is ultimately killed by her husband because of her uncontrollable passion. As Kakar has noted, it would be a mistake to jump too quickly to general conclusions regarding the nature of female seductive power. At the very least one must take into account, on both a social as well as psychological level, the question of who is being seduced, under what circumstances, and by whom: father/daughter, mother/son, sister/brother or stranger/stranger. While themes of seduction and passion abound, what is most intriguing is the mix of particular sociopsychological roles with the expression of erotic emotions. How, for instance, is eroticism reconciled with the opposed roles of mother/lover or father/husband? While this is largely a psychological question, I think it is possible to draw general cultural conclusions from the symbolic logic—coded in myth, enacted in ritual, and embodied through exercise—by which means sense is made of anathema.

Thompson (1955–1958: D1837.4) and Crooke (1926: 394) give instances where the shadow of a pregnant woman can render a snake powerless (or blind). Enthovan indicates that a snake-bite healer loses his power over poison if he leads an immoral life, and particularly if he is in contact with a woman who has just given birth (1924: 138). Here the power of fertility overcomes the power of sexuality in either its male or female guise. The pregnant woman poses a threat to snakes (or to snake power transposed onto the healer) because, on a symbolic level, fertility is the inverse of erotic sexuality. Milk, then, becomes the dominant symbol, and energy is redirected away from sex to nurturing growth. The symmetry of poison and milk is intriguing, for as Enthovan shows, milk (representative of a pregnant or fertile woman) can ritually neutralize poison (1924: 135). Women are not categorically dangerous, only contingently so as either strangers or wives. It is only their erotic qualities which are snakelike; and in fact what is far more important than generic sexuality is the precise agency of eroticism reflected in fantasy and ritual. Maternity neutralizes passion, and it is in this respect, as we shall see, that milk plays an important symbolic role in a wrestler's diet.

On a conscious level, at least, wrestlers regard snakes as the symbolic equivalent of lustful women. One wrestler told me that the glance of a woman is as dangerous as the bite of a snake. Many of the young wrestlers with whom I spoke expressed an abject fear of eroticism in any form. In this aspect snakes are associated with rabid female sexual energy which, in the view of many Indian men, is both physically and psychologically debilitating (cf. Carstairs 1958; Kakar 1981). That women are not allowed to enter the akhara precinct is witness to the threat they pose.

The most powerful symbolic imagery employed in this regard is not only of poisonous fluid injected, but also of precious fluid sucked out. Here the image of the suckling snake is significant (La Barre 1962: 94–98; Thompson 1955–1958: B765.4.1; for a comparative perspective see Brandes 1981: 222–227; 1985: 80–84). From a wrestler's perspective, having sex with a women is like being sucked dry by a snake (cf. Jones 1951; Legman 1975). In this imagery the more common roles are reversed. The breast becomes the phallus from which semen rather than milk is sucked out. There is, then, an apparent ambiguity in the motif of the suckling snake. On one level the snake sucks out the mother's nurturing milk, but on a parallel symbolic plane it sucks out vital male energy. In the Indian scheme these confusing themes are, in fact, complementary. As Kakar (1981) and Carstairs (1958) have argued, the image of the sexually aggressive debilitating woman is in part structured in complementary opposition to that of the domineering authoritarian mother (cf. O'Flaherty 1980: 108). A mother who refuses to give up her milk becomes a sexually aggressive woman who saps men of their vital fluids (ibid). The bad mother is a dangerous woman on two fronts: she does not give up her fluid while she also takes fluid away. As the snake drinks milk it is associated with both the good mother's flowing milk and the bad mother's passion. On one plane the suckling snake is a potent symbol of erotic fantasy, but it is also, on another plane, emblematic of the non-erotic, symbiotic relationship between mother and child. The motif of the suckling snake raises the issue of sexuality in the same instance that it resolves it. As we shall see below, this same parallelism carries over into the ritual context of Nag Panchami in the akhara.

The sexual aspect of snakes is the most dominant motif in folklore and ritual. It is intriguing that another common motif is that of the snake guarding treasures buried in the earth (cf. Crooke 1926: 390; Enthovan 1924: 130–131; Jacobs 1899: 140–142). In many of the tales recounted by these authors, the treasure guarded by snakes is not only hidden and hoarded, but also very valuable. Given that snakes are associated with sexual energy, it is clear that the snakes' wealth is a symbol of semen. This is further evidenced by motifs of snakes spitting out lumps of gold (Thompson 1955–1958: B103.4.2.1; Jacobs 1899: 140–142). In the context of wrestling this motif is significant given the dominant theme of contained sexuality. The wrestler must guard his store of precious seminal fluid just as a snake keeps watch over the "life-energy that is stored in the earthly waters of springs, wells, and ponds" (H. Zimmer 1946: 63). As a common folktale has it (Jacobs 1899: 140–142), snakes give up their jewels in exchange for milk; that is, they give up semen/jewels for semen/milk, thus taking in essentially what they put out. Milk is changed into poison in this and other tales (cf. O'Flaherty 1980: 54) but it is, significantly, poison directed at someone who either does not offer milk or who tries to steal the treasure. In any case, the dominant motif here, as in the case of the suckling snake, is one of protected vital male fluids.

MILK

Milk is the central ingredient of a wrestler's diet. A wrestler is stereo-typed as a thickset man who can consume buckets and buckets of milk. K. P. Singh writes of the properties of milk:

> In order to reinvigorate oneself after exercise one should drink milk. . . . The strong substance of milk products imparts strength and valor. The mind becomes healthy and refurbished. Discipline is established and one becomes attentive. After a few days of exercise all other forms of satisfaction are channeled into strength. Surplus energy is sublimated and given a productive and beautiful outlet. Milk is like the anchor of a ship which allows the vessel to bob on the waves but prevents it from sinking (1973: 31).

Wrestlers clearly associate milk with both physical strength and sexual virility. Milk, however, develops virility without igniting the fires of sexual passion. As Singh points out, surplus energy is channeled away from "other forms of satisfaction." Sensual feelings are redirected into physical exercise, and milk contributes to this transformation. Milk is the essence of condensed energy: "Wanting to develop his strength, Lord Krishna went about the following procedure. He fed the milk of ten thousand cows to one thousand cows. He then milked these one thousand cows and fed their milk to one hundred other cows. He milked these one hundred and fed their milk to ten cows and finally fed the milk of these ten to one cow. Krishna then drank this cow's milk whereby he in fact ingested the combined energy of 11,111 cows" (Atreya 1972*a*: 33). On this plane there is an obvious parallel between wrestlers and snakes: both are characterized as extraordinary drinkers of milk. In order to understand what it means to feed milk to both snakes and to wrestlers it is necessary to first analyze the symbolic properties of milk.

In Hindu myth and ritual, milk—particularly cow's milk—is one of the purest fluids. In its symbolic character it is purely female (O'Flaherty 1980: 36). Significantly, milk is linked to more general themes of female fertility and creative energy. In the Vedas milk is referred to as *vrsnyam payas*, or virile "seed-like" milk (ibid: 21). The implication here is that women's milk is female seed (the idea of a female seed being quite common in Indian mythology) and that therefore it is clearly the sym-bolic opposite of male semen. In Vedic literature, semen is sometimes referred to as *sukram payas*, bright milk (ibid: 23). In general, O'Fla-herty argues that milk and semen are linked on the level of "secondary metaphorical applications" wherein they refer to "rain, water, *Soma* (ritual elixir), oblation and child" (ibid: 24). Zimmermann has also pointed out that "the thick fluidity and whiteness of milk resembles phlegm, semen and *ojas*, the vital fluid. It shares their properties, heavy, sweet, cold, unctuous" (1988: 204). Milk, however, is not just semen; it is a special kind of semen. According to the *Satapatha Brahmana*, milk is the semen of *Agni*, the god of fire (ibid: 205). Thus, again, there is a sharp distinction made between the fire of passion and the nature of semen as a sexual, though non-erotic, fluid; a dissociation of agency from substance. It is on this level in particular that the symbolic link is made between semen and milk in the everyday world of the wrestler's life. Milk is consumed by men to enhance virility (O'Flaherty 1980: 51–52). To wrestlers, for whom virility is linked to the development of physical prowess and personal character, milk contributes to one's growing reserve of semen.

While milk has important symbolic properties, the act of milking is no less significant. As O'Flaherty has pointed out, milking is likened to intercourse where semen is milked out of the male and mixed with the female seed to create life (ibid: 21, 24). This idea fits with the notion that men can be "milked" of their strength through contact with the wrong sort of passionate women. In this regard the dual properties of milk as symbolizing both male and female essence becomes important. If a man is milked of his semen/milk it is symmetrical for him to milk and consume the female milk/seed to restore the balance of his own supply. In this symbolic chemistry it is important to note that blood is the common denominator of both milk and semen. Although blood is regarded as a generative fluid associated with many aspects of the body, it is most directly linked to semen and milk. Many young wrestlers who live in fear of involuntary semen loss express the common belief that one drop of semen is equal to sixty drops of blood (cf. Carstairs 1958; Obeyesekere 1976: 213; O'Flaherty 1980: 36).

As pointed out above, the snake represents two aspects of sexuality: the phallic male and dangerous female. In this capacity, given what has been said about milk and milking, the image of feeding milk to snakes on Nag Panchami can be interpreted in two significant ways. On one level the act of milking is reversed. The phallic snake reingests, as it were, the symbolic semen that it has been milked of. As the phallus gives up semen/milk it takes it back in the form of milk/semen, just as the breast which gives up milk/semen takes in semen/milk (see Klein 1948 for a discussion of the "breast that feeds itself" [O'Flaherty 1980: 44]). Here the image of Shesha Nag or Ananta, the ouroboros serpent who holds up the world, provides a clear motif of this sexuality turned in upon itself. Ananta—the "endless one"—is depicted as a snake eating or sucking on its own tail: as the male and female dimensions of the snake collapse, milk becomes semen and energy moves in a perpetual circle. It is perfectly symmetrical in this respect that in the *Mahabharata* version of this myth (Adi-parvan, chap. 36), Ananta is depicted as a *sannyasi* who wants nothing more than to "delight in righteousness, tranquillity and asceticism" (Vogel 1926: 57). The self-contained, enlightening energy of yogic kundalini power, likened by some to internal ejaculation, is equivalent, on a symbolic plane, to the alchemical recycling of milk/semen/milk. As O'Flaherty has pointed out, the ouroboros snake is a symbol of the paradoxical Mobius universe which is infinite but self-contained (1984: 242–243).

On another level, it must not be forgotten that snakes often represent dangerous female sexuality, and in this capacity poison is one manifestation of female passion. One may argue, I think, that poison is the symbolic opposite of milk: it takes life where milk gives forth life in a number of different ways. As pointed out above, milk is the symbolic opposite of erotic passion and in this formulation it is possible to argue that feeding milk to snakes functions as a neutralizing agency. Dangerous female passion is cooled and rendered less threatening by the symbolic juxtaposition of milk and poison. The poison/milk opposition is here a restatement of the suckling snake motif mentioned above. Sexuality is invoked so as to be controlled.

In this regard it is interesting that sannyasis or yogis, by virtue of their complete control over the flow of their seed, are said to have power over snakes (O'Flaherty 1973: 279; 1980: 54). They are immune to poison by virtue of the overwhelming store of semen they have accumulated through their devout celibacy. Moreover, yogis are said to be able to turn poison into seed: to make that which is destructive into a creative force (1980: 54).

Wrestlers identify with yogis on many counts, but particularly as regards their ability to control and channel the flow of semen. In this capacity the image of the milk-drinking snake serves as a motif, albeit reversed, of the alchemy which yogis and wrestlers are meant to effect. Although wrestlers do not necessarily feed milk to snakes, the celebration of wrestling as a way of life on Nag Panchami is the symbolic transformation of destructive poisonous power into creative physical energy.

As has been noted, wrestlers drink enormous quantities of milk as part of their diet. Milk is not consumed in a ritualized way as it is by snakes on Nag Panchami, but nevertheless the parallels are clear. Milk builds up a wrestler's semen reserve, but it also cools his passion, just as milk neutralizes poison. Having built up his supply of semen, however, a wrestler is not only able to neutralize the poison of passion; like the sannyasi, he can turn poison back into semen. He is supervirile but sexually passive and controlled. Milk contributes directly to this powerful conundrum.

GHI

Having already noted the central place of ghi in the wrestler's dietary regimen, we may now consider ghi within the symbolic context of Nag Panchami ritual. In the conceptual framework of wrestling, ghi is related to semen in a specific way. Atreya makes the following point: "There are many things which are as rich and oily as ghi but they do not have resilience. The semen and strength which is produced from these things is not stable. Ghi is the only thing which can keep your strength up and produce *oj* [the aura of virility]. The strength that ghi fosters is resilient. It is not like other things which produce semen only to let it flow to destruction" (1984: 23). To a wrestler ghi represents the essence of semen which is held inside the body. This is not the semen of virile passion, it is the semen of physical, moral and spiritual strength.

In the above discussion of milk and snakes, milk was seen to have certain ambiguous qualities: purely female yet symbolic of semen. This ambiguity translates into various powerful motifs when related to the symbolic themes of consumption and control. When ghi is taken into account this motif is developed further. Even though ghi is not fed to snakes, the logic of how ghi relates to milk and semen is relevant here.

Just as ghi is the distillate of milk, its essence, so semen is thought to be the distilled essence of food and blood (O'Flaherty 1980: 49). The guru of Akhara Ram Singh drew a telling analogy. "Semen is like ghi," he said. "Just like ghi fuels the *dias* (lamps) of religious worship, so does semen fuel the fire of one's own body." Even more so than milk, ghi is consumed to enhance virility by contributing to one's store of semen (cf. Carstairs 1958: 166; O'Flaherty 1980: 52).

Although ghi is expressly seminal as it relates to the male body, it is androgynous as a gender symbol: it is the essence of masculine potency but, as the distillate of milk, ultimately female (O'Flaherty 1980: 23, 25). The agency associated with the symbolism of milk/semen is the act of milking. In the symbolism of ghi, the agency is also milking (as ghi is drawn out of milk [cf. O'Flaherty 1980: 29]), but, more significantly, also churning, wherein milk is made into butter (O'Flaherty 1976: 334–335; 1980: 28). Churning symbolism is crucial to an understanding of what ghi means as an androgynous symbol. Whereas to a certain extent milking refers to sexual union and the drawing out of essence, churning, more often than not, refers to unilateral creation wherein a male or female brings forth life by churning their own fluids (O'Flaherty 1976: 333–334). Even in instances where churning is taken as a metaphor for coitus, the image employed is of mixing together, not milking out or taking essence away. Significantly, the metaphor of milking implies only a transfer of substance, whereas churning clearly demands a change of substance, but without addition or subtraction. In this respect, then, milk symbolizes either male or female seed, whereas ghi represents a kind of mutated androgynous fluid that is potent but asexual in the sense of already having been churned.

In the *Mahabharata* it is significant that churning is associated with creation. More to the point, however, the ocean of milk, which is churned to bring forth life, is the substance of unilateral creation which flows endlessly from the udder of the earth-cow (O'Flaherty 1980: 43). To churn the ocean the gods use a parallel symbol of contained sexuality—Ananta, the endless snake.

In a number of the mythic references to unilateral procreation the child is born through the agency of thigh rubbing or thigh churning. For instance, Aurva is born from Urva's thigh (O'Flaherty 1980: 227). O'Flaherty also points out that the symbolism of thigh churning is related, etymologically, to churning butter from milk (ibid: 28). What is significant about thigh churning is that it alludes to the power of sexual potency without calling into play any form of overt sexual agency. Intercourse is preempted. Thus, with regard to wrestlers and ascetics, for whom asexuality is a physicomoral virtue, the power of sexuality is clearly recognized while chastity itself is never threatened.

Mythic reference to thigh churning suggests an intriguing parallel with wrestling. While wrestlers are concerned with the size of their body as a whole, they place a great deal of importance on the size of their thighs. This is particularly significant since wrestlers place absolutely no positive value on the size of their genitalia. In fact, wrestlers who have larger genitalia than others are considered somewhat deviant and are suspected of promiscuity and unchecked passion.

In expressing a wrestler's stature a person gestures the girth of the wrestler's thigh with his outstretched hands. More significantly, wrestlers slap their thighs as an aggressive gesture presaging a bout. They rub their thighs while exercising. (In two akharas I visited thigh slapping is prohibited, ostensibly because it aggressively challenges the founding guru to a wrestling bout, but also, on a symbolic level, because it brings sexuality too close to the akhara precinct.) One might interpret this thigh slapping/rubbing/measuring as penis fixation except for the fact that the manipulation of one's thigh is an act of androgynous agency while the manipulation of one's penis is, even in the instance of masturbation, a directed act of sexuality which is, by definition, only half of a whole: either heterosexual or homosexual but never androgynous.

As representing androgynous sexual energy, ghi serves as a neutral source of energy. It contains the vital shakti of sexuality—both male and female—without posing any real threat of erotic destruction. Milk, associated clearly with women, is implicated in contrasted sexuality: either male or female. As a distillate of milk, ghi collapses the contrast of sexual opposition. Metaphorically, a wrestler can rub his thighs all he wants, for churning represents self-contained energy, not energy spent. The case of the two akharas which prohibit thigh slapping serves as an exception which seems to support the rule.

While milk and milk products are generally regarded as "cool" in the hot/cold paradigm of food classification, ghi is regarded by many wrestlers as the essence of "coolness." I was told that a person suffering from intoxication, sunstroke, or "madness" ought to be fed ghi as this would counteract the heat causing the particular malady. I asked if milk or cream also had the same effect and was told, emphatically, no. Cream in particular aggravates intoxication by enraging one's passion. It is interesting that snakes are not fed ghi. The reason, I think, is that ghi would, in a symbolic sense, neutralize the dual sexuality of snakes. In contrast to ghi, milk can be either male semen or female seed, but never both at once. Thus a snake drinking milk symbolizes the resolution of opposites. Ghi by itself, having been churned from milk also represents this same opposition but without reference to the poisonous, dangerous aspect of sexuality. Ghi is in essence symbolically equivalent to Ananta, the endless ascetic snake. For a snake to drink ghi, therefore, would be to mix metaphors and render the act redundant at best and at worst meaningless. Ghi would, in effect, cool the snakes passion but with an end result of impotence rather than contained virility. In the instances where ghi is associated with snakes one is more likely to find that it is juxtaposed to venom spent (unleashed passion) rather than to the latent sexuality symbolized by the poison inside the snake. The poison of latent sexuality is, more often than not, juxtaposed against milk. Poison spent must be rendered harmless, while passion held in check must be contained and regenerated.

Wrestlers drink milk, but this does not mean that they are snakelike in their character. The motif of the milk-drinking snake in effect represents the logic of the wrestler's own body of contained sexuality. The snake is a sign of the wrestler's latent passion while the milk the snake drinks is the wrestler's semen. Turned in itself, passion becomes power and virtue rather than lust and greed. As has been argued, ghi duplicates this imagery without reference to the snake agency. Unlike a snake a wrestler can drink ghi without cooling his passion to the point of impotence. This is because he drinks ghi to enrich his semen, an act which symbolically preempts the whole issue of sexuality since ghi is never sucked up or milked out. It is only mixed in with or churned out from milk. As the guru of Akhara Ram Singh explained, ghi fuels the internal fire of the wrestler's body. Milk can be consumed and retained to build semen, but it can just as easily flow and be sucked out. Ghi is more resilient and therefore a more apt symbol of asexual, non-erotic virility.

ALMONDS

Along with buckets of milk and large volumes of ghi, wrestlers eat enormous quantities of almonds. Almonds are clearly masculine, for they are to the male seed as milk is to female creativity.

Almonds are used in making pharmaceutical cures for the "night emission" of semen (Ramsanehi Dixit n.d.: 13). However, most references to the almond's curing agency focus on mental disorders rather than on illnesses with an overtly somatic sexual manifestation: impotency, premature ejaculation, and the like (ibid: 11–20). In this regard there is an interesting parallel suggested between almonds and semen. Semen is said to be located in a reservoir in the head (Carstairs 1958: 86; O'Flaherty 1980: 46; Spratt 1966: 91, 95–96). I am not qualified to speak on the medical dimension of this correlation, but the symbolism is suggestive on an overt level. In many instances a person who engages in too much illicit sex is regarded as mentally unstable, and the telltale symptoms are, among other things, sunken eyes and a pallid complexion. I think it is clear that the eyes are sunken and the complexion pallid because the head has been drained of semen. The almonds play some role in restoring mental stability by revitalizing the reservoir.

Wrestlers prepare almonds in a way which is also suggestive of this

symbolic equation between semen and almonds. Along with the stereo-
type of the milk-drinking wrestler is the almond-grinding wrestler, who
spends hours with mortar and pestle (a strong sexual symbol in its own
right) mashing his almonds into a thick, rich, golden paste. He mixes
this paste with honey and milk and drinks it as a postpractice tonic.

At some akharas mashing almonds is done in tandem with the preparation of *bhang* (hashish). Almonds and bhang are often prepared in the
same way insofar as bhang has to be smashed and ground into a paste.
Many non-wrestlers associate bhang and the preparation of bhang paste
with akharas. In this context, bhang and almonds are often associated
with one another. The two pastes are occasionally drunk together when
diluted and mixed into a potion called *thandai*. (*Thandai* can also refer
to any cool drink made of mixed substances, usually milk, nuts, and
fruits.)

Popular stereotypes aside, wrestlers have a somewhat ambivalent attitude towards bhang (Negi 1987). A number of them said that bhang is
used by wrestlers for the same reason that it is used by ascetics: to
control desire. While it may be true that many ascetics use bhang in
order to enhance their divine passion, rather than inhibit sexuality, wrestlers do not put much credence in this interpretation. One wrestler said
that bhang calms and focuses a person's mind. The problem with bhang,
however, is that it has recreational uses which can undermine self-control. As many wrestlers pointed out, bhang can be dangerous because it
makes one lazy, idle, and self-absorbed. One becomes listless rather than
strong. If used properly, however, bhang is a substance that subverts
passion, and in this capacity it is associated with akharas. It is quite
possible, as both Lynch (1990: 103, 104) and Kumar (1988: 112, 113)
have pointed out, that the consumption of bhang in akharas is also an
aspect of other ideals, namely the *shauk* (hobby or passion) of affected
leisure which is part of Banarsi culture, or the passionate *mastram* identity of Mathura Chaubes. However, most serious wrestlers look on this
as a recreational and therefore dubious use of bhang.

In any case, where almonds are associated with bhang, one has, once
again, an instance of sexual power generated on the one hand while held
in check on the other. A bhang and almond thandai is essentially the
same thing as ghi: extremely potent but very resilient and stable. Drinking the thandai potion, a wrestler affects the same motif of the milk-
drinking snake.

I have never heard a wrestler draw a parallel between almond paste
and semen, but given the overarching concern wrestlers have with sex-

uality—the congruent symbolism of milk and ghi, the clear imagery of
mortar and pestle, the implicit correlation between an almond seed/nut
and the procreative male seed, and *finally*, the juxtaposition of bhang
and almonds—it is possible to say that almond symbolism contributes
to the more explicit themes of contained sexuality which structure the
conceptual framework of the akhara.

EARTH

While ghi and almonds are not explicitly linked to snakes and Nag
Panchami ritual, the underlying symbolic parallels are very clear: sexual
energy turned in upon itself in a motif of contained, recycled essence. A
consideration of the symbolic properties of earth in general and akhara
earth specifically returns us to the snake motif in wrestling life.

One need not stretch the imagination to appreciate the association
snakes have with the earth. They live in holes in the ground and by
virtue of being legless are seen as close to the earth in a literal and
metaphoric sense. The monsoon rains bring the snakes out of the earth
by flooding their holes. Vogel has pointed out that Kadru, the mother
of the Nag race of snakes, is a personification of the earth (1926: 20).
In this formulation, snakes are the "sons of the earth." As described
by Fuller (1944) and Maity (1963), people (and in particular women)
worship anthills on Nag Panchami. As protrusions of earth, anthills are
regarded as the homes of snakes. Moreover, given the phallic connotation of snakes, and their symbolic association with lingams, one may
surmise that anthills are phallic. However, anthills may also represent
breasts, since the earth is regarded as the life-giving mother. In this motif
the snake represents the latent sexuality of the nourishing mother: the
poison in the breast. Finally, snakes are associated with the earth
through their cosmic role. At the behest of Brahma (*Mahabharata*, Adi-
parvan, chap. 36), Ananta burrowed into the ground so as to hold up
the Earth.

There seems to be clear evidence that a theme of fertility links snakes
with the earth. Maity (1963), citing Barth (1932) and James (1959),
suggests that snakes in general are associated with cultivation and harvest. Plowing is prohibited on Nag Panchami since a snake's death might
render one's fields infertile.

Citing the *Rig Veda* (1.160.3), O'Flaherty has pointed out that the
earth is often compared to a cow full of milk, while heaven is conceived
of as a bull with seed (1980: 24). The earth is a cow from whom all

good things come, and the milk of this cow is "female seed" (ibid: 250). As O'Flaherty points out elsewhere (ibid: 108), the earth is a dominant female. This is not surprising, given the common maternal imagery associated with the earth. As the quintessential mother, the earth is aggressively protective as well as nurturing. The earth as fertile female makes sense in the context of Nag Panchami. Monsoon rain, associated with Nag and with semen, impregnates the earth by mixing with the female seed. In this regard a passage from the *Harivamsa* is telling: "The smell which emitted from earth due to the season's first rainfall stimulated in men the desire for union" (chap. 66, Bose n.d.).

As pointed out above, fresh new earth is brought into many akharas on Nag Panchami. This earth, though not special in any ritual respect is, significantly, brought to the pit either from fields or from the bottom of dried-out ponds. Thus it is eminently fertile earth. In the case of pond silt it is linked to the water aspect of Nag.

Wrestlers speak of the akhara earth in very maternal terms. It is nurturing, comforting, and protective. Wrestling in the akhara is likened to a child playing in his mother's lap. When a wrestler is initiated into an akhara five of the *prasad laddu*s are buried in the pit as a gesture of respect to "the nurturing mother" in whose lap the wrestlers grow. Atreya writes:

> Nothing can compare to the comfort of a mother's lap, but a mother's lap is only a fraction as comfortable as the "lap of mother earth": the akhara. The love of "mother earth" is consistent and never changes. The more that one loves "mother earth" the happier one will be. "Mother earth" absorbs all of your troubles and leaves you in a state of bliss. One who is not close to the earth does not have the strength to fight off illness. Nothing can compare with the comfort of "mother earth's" lap (1972b: 33).

The term *god* (lap) has the connotation of womb. When wrestlers massage themselves with earth and let the earth draw out the toxins from their bodies they achieve a childlike state which complements the earth's maternity. In this regard the general aura of the akhara as self-contained and peaceful contributes to the overall maternal symbolism.

The earth of the akhara is regarded by wrestlers as a cure-all. Based on Ayurvedic healing practices it is used to cure skin diseases, stomach ailments, headaches, and a host of other maladies. On a purely symbolic level, the idea of healing relates directly to the idea of the earth as caring mother.

One aspect of earth's healing properties is of direct interest here. Atreya (ibid: 23) and the editor of *Akhare ki Or* (H. B. Singh 1972: 3) both mention that akhara earth is a sure cure for snakebite. As an aspect of the hot/cold paradigm, earth is regarded as cool and it draws out heat from the body. Poison is a very hot fluid and thus can be drawn out of the body if the person bitten by a snake (or rabid dog, wasp, caterpillar, etc.) is covered with earth.

In mythology mother earth is associated with a cow full of milk. The juxtaposition of cool earth with hot poison is a repetition of the pervasive theme of contained sexuality. On Nag Panchami, when wrestlers "play in their mother's lap," they are acting out, in a sense, the cooling of passion: the control of their sexual energy. If sexual energy were not controlled one could argue that the wrestlers are dramatizing a repressed sexual desire for their mothers. If this were the case, however, wrestlers would be weakened by their contact with the earth rather than rejuvenated by it. On a conscious level, at least, the image of mother earth is primarily nurturing rather than sexual. All sexual feelings are transferred out of the akhara onto women in their non-maternal, dangerous aspect. Mother earth is the supreme mother in the sense that no bad maternal qualities are attributed to her. The milk never stops flowing from her breasts. For the wrestler the akhara earth is the perfect nurturing mother in whose lap he plays as a forever virginal, non-sexual child. As Atreya writes, "He who has enjoyed the pleasure of the earth will feel that worldly sensual pleasures pale in comparison. They seem base and cheap" (1972b: 30). Since the worldly pleasures of the flesh pale in comparison to the metaphysical and maternal pleasures of the earth, it is not surprising that the wrestler is not only compared to a child but also to a sannyasi:

> It is important to remember that a wrestler's strength must be passive and latent rather than aggressive. The wrestler who turns to the earth is a true ascetic, a true saint and a true yogi. In one Banaras akhara near Sankat Mochan temple I was fortunate enough to make the acquaintance of an 80-year-old man who said that he had achieved self-realization by exercising in the earth. He said that rolling in the earth was an act of devotion which had given him spiritual happiness (ibid: 32).

While the primary relationship of the wrestler's body to the akhara earth is one of passive non-sexuality, there is, nevertheless, a concept of substance exchange. Wrestlers draw on the energy of the earth and they give back to the earth the energy which flows from their bodies. There is an exchange of substance but no idea of impregnation. Milk products are mixed into the earth of the akhara for the same reason that milk products are often fed to a pregnant woman; namely, so that she will

give birth to a son (cf. O'Flaherty 1980: 28). The mother changes milk
into seminal fluid which contributes to her child's growth and development. It is significant that the nurturing fluid is semen made from milk.
In this formulation semen nurtures and fosters growth. It is a potent
and procreative substance but not an impregnating fluid. What a wrestler draws from the soil is the generalized energy of semen in the non-
sexual symbolic form of mother's milk/seed. Along these lines it is interesting to note that in rituals of royal coronation kings are often be-
smeared with mud (Inden 1978; Marglin 1982). This is variously interpreted as the king's marriage to the earth or his impregnation of the
earth. The king fertilizes the earth and thereby insures prosperity in his
realm. Significantly, however, the king also draws power from the earth.
Marglin has interpreted this as the king taking on the female power of
the earth (1982: 171). In other words, the flow of substance is to some
extent reciprocal in both kingly coronation and in the akhara.

Sweat from the wrestler's body is also mixed into the akhara earth
and is regarded as an important and beneficial ingredient. As O'Flaherty
has pointed out (1980: 39), in some contexts sweat is a symbolic substitute for semen. In mythology, however, sweat does not impregnate, but
brings forth life unilaterally. When wrestlers sweat the interpretation
they offer is that they are contributing to the general fertility of the soil.
Their sweat mixes with the essence of the earth. Just as the earth gives
up its milk/semen essence to build the wrestler's body, so the wrestler
returns his semen/sweat essence to mother earth. He does this, however,
in an explicitly non-sexual way: as the male symbolic equivalent of
mother's milk. As the mother feeds the child so the child feeds the
mother. This sets up a cyclical, non-sexual transfer of fluids which endlessly produces semen through reciprocal exchange.

Of the few instances in which akhara earth is used for anything other
than wrestling or healing it is used, significantly, in a ritual where a
bride is prepared for marriage. This is the only instance where women
are allowed into the akhara precinct. Women come to the akhara (usually in the middle of the day when there are few wrestlers present) and
take some of the earth out of the pit, mix it with water, and slap it on
the bride's back as she sits in a corner of the akhara. I was never given
an interpretation of this ritual, but I think it is clear that the bride is
being symbolically associated with both milk and semen: with the power
of sexuality and impending motherhood. The bride is the symbolic opposite of the wrestler. She draws on the vitality and fertility of the sweat
saturated earth in a ritualized context which is clearly sexual. She is not

nurtured: she is symbolically impregnated. At the same time, however, she is anointed with the essence of mother earth and thereby takes on the qualities of a good mother-to-be. Regardless, it is significant that the bride takes substance out of the akhara and does not put anything back—there is no symbolic parallel here of the wrestler's sweat. In and of itself this breaks the conundrum of contained sexuality by disassociating semen from milk, maternity from sexuality. The sexuality which the bride introduces into the akhara through her presence is tolerated by wrestlers only because of the parallel motif of maternity. Even so, on the few instances where I saw women take earth from the pit, the wrestlers moved well back and disassociated themselves from what the women were doing.

Psychologically speaking, I think that what is going on here is quite clear. In the pit the child wrestler has, to some extent, succeeded in having his cake—or ghi—and eating it too. He has managed to reconcile a deep emotional bond to the good mother (Kakar 1981, 1990) with a nondebilitating release of sexual energy. Emotionally the akhara substitutes for both mother and wife; and in the same way the wrestler is an emotional synthesis of progenitor and progeny. In fact, I think that the substitution/synthesis is further effected on another level on which the wrestler is androgynous. Wrestlers, after all, only play in their "mother's lap"; who they play with is other wrestlers.

On an emotional level at least, the cosmology of akhara life affords a homosexual solution to a pervasive cultural ambivalence with regard to heterosexual relations in general and mother-son relations in particular, where the son is unable to cope with the powerful sexual demands made by the mother (cf. Kakar 1981: 95). In other situations a cultural solution to this psychological problem is found in symbolic and ritual self-castration in the context of mother goddess worship (Nanda 1990: 34). Nanda has found that *hijras* take this logic to its ultimate conclusion in a ritual of actual emasculation whereby the young man becomes "neither man nor woman," thereby subverting his own male sexuality and appeasing his mother (ibid: 24–32). Although wrestlers are in many ways the antithesis of hijras, they too find psychological comfort in a ritualized synthesis of gender roles. Where the wrestler and the hijra part ways, however, is on the issue of emasculation; to deny male sexuality would be to undermine the source of physical strength, and so the wrestler effects a relationship of close physical contact with other men in order to circumvent the danger of female sexuality. To be sure, wrestlers do not engage in homosexual sex any more—and probably less–than they do in heterosexual sex. In this regard wrestling with another man is like rubbing thighs or feeding milk to snakes.

TREES

The trees of an akhara are in many ways associated with snakes and themes of fertility. Three trees in particular grow in akhara compounds: pipal (*Ficus religiosa*), banyan (*Ficus indica*) and nim (*melia azadirachta*). All of these trees have general religious significance in Hindu ritual (cf. Crooke 1926: 400–419; Enthovan 1924: 117–127; Pandey 1964; Philpot 1897; S. N. Roy 1931), but here the concern is only with their relation to two main symbols relating to Nag Panchami: milk and snakes.

Crooke (1926: 407) points out that the pipal tree is revered because it exudes a milky substance. Although snakes are said to populate many types of tree, the pipal is regarded as particularly suited for snakes to live in. They are thought to live entwined in its roots (H. Zimmer 1946: 72). Snakes are also regarded as part of the pipal because its branches are associated with Shiva, and Shiva is said to be adorned with snakes (Crooke 1926: 384, 407). Given that pipals exude a milky sap and are associated with snakes, it is not surprising that they are regarded, in some instances, as sources of fertility. Crooke reports that women circum-ambulate special pipal trees "in order to gain fertility" (ibid: 408). Women in Banaras wrap threads around the base of pipal trees and light lamps among the roots as an act of supplication or as fulfillment of a vow for a boon of fertility (cf. Enthovan 1924: 119). One of the pipal trees at Akhara Ram Singh is occasionally used for this purpose.

Along with the pipal tree, the banyan is also regarded as a dwelling place of snakes (cf. Maity 1963: 128; Hastings 1979: 417). The banyan's aerial roots which hang down and coil around each other are regarded as serpentine. Crooke points out that these roots are associated with the matted hair of sannyasis. The matted hair of sannyasis symbolizes not only snakes but also the reserve of semen which sannyasis are said to store in their heads (O'Flaherty 1980). According to Enthovan (1924: 120) the banyan tree, like the pipal, is associated with Shiva. Being of the same fig family of tree as the pipal, the banyan also exudes a milky sap. One wrestler said that the new fruit of a banyan—which is about two inches long and red with a white tip—can be broken off and eaten. Many claim it to be more nutritious than a glass of milk.

In Bombay, Crooke reports (1926: 407), women fast and pray to

banyan trees on the full moon of *Jyeshth* (May–June) in order to preserve themselves from widowhood. This theme is echoed in the story
recounted by Enthovan (1924: 120) where Satyavan died of a snakebite
under a banyan tree. He was brought back to life by his wife's entreaties
to Yama, the god of death (cf. Rakesh 1986: 43–45). The banyan in
this story is associated with life in general and fertility specifically. On
a few occasions people would come to Akhara Ram Singh and ask to
take some of the leaves of a large banyan to use as ritual ingredients.

While the banyan and the pipal are associated with snakes and fertility through their milky sap, the nim tree is juxtaposed to snakes by
virtue of its power to cure venomous bites (Crooke 1926: 391, 410;
Enthovan 1924: 137–140). The nim is not an antidote to poison but it
is nevertheless a purifying, purgative agent. Its bitterness is regarded as
symbolically parallel to poison. If a person can eat bitter nim leaves he
is said to be cured. Zimmer mentions that images of snakes are often
set up under pipal and nim trees and that these two trees are regarded
as a married couple since they often grow on the same ground (1946:
72). Pipal milk is also used for curing snakebites (R. Sharma n.d.: 6) but
in a different way from the nim; pipal milk draws poison out while the
bitter nim leaves neutralize venom. In its curing capacity pipal milk acts
like mother's milk whereas the nim fights fire with fire. While alike in
some respects, the milky sap of the pipal may thus also be juxtaposed
to the bitterness of the nim. If the trees are regarded as a matching
pair than there is a symbolic reconciliation of opposites. Through this
opposition it becomes logical for snakes to be regarded as comfortably
entwined in their roots.

If one considers pipal, banyan, and nim trees together, one is struck
by the familiar opposition between milk/fertility and poison/danger
which is but another articulation of the general theme of milk-drinking
snakes. The bitter nim is juxtaposed to the life-giving sap of the pipal
and banyan. In this respect the tree triad underscores the overall theme
of controlled sexuality in the akhara. One may see, in this triptych
scheme, the power of fertility without any real threat of unleashed erotic
passion.

As a final note in this regard let us consider the healing properties of
nim, pipal, and banyan trees. All three trees have important curative
qualities (cf. Ramsanehi Dixit 1967a; R. Sharma n.d.) and are used as
ingredients in numerous remedies (Sen 1985). All three trees, however,
are used to treat sexual disorders in men and women. This is not surprising, for many herbs and minerals in India are used for treating illnesses

relating to impotency, semen loss, and infertility (Gotham 1983). However, given that the trees grow on akhara grounds—and, as pointed out
earlier, they mix their essence with the earth, water, and wind of the
compound—one may assume that there is a tacit symbolic association
between the trees' essence and the charged sexuality of the earth, the
water, and the body of the wrestler. The sap of the pipal can help cure
semen loss and increase the flow of milk from a woman's breast; the
milky fruit of the banyan can reinvigorate an impotent person; and the
leaves of a nim can make a man virile and bring milk to a woman's
breast. In every instance the remedies derived from these trees build up
semen in men and either cause milk to flow in women or enhance fertility
in general. In this regard the milk of the banyan and the pipal can be
used as a substitute for cow's milk (Atreya 1986a: 50).

EXERCISE

Nag Panchami is not only a public display of wrestling as a particular
way of life, but also a general celebration of exercise, physical fitness,
and strength. In Banaras on Nag Panchami akharas sometimes put on
demonstrations of strength. Wrestlers lift heavy weights and swing large
joris and gadas. In the context of this discussion of snakes, milk, and
fertility, one may interpret the exercises which wrestlers do in terms of
contained sexuality and displaced passion.

A gada is a large round rock fixed to the end of a meter-long bamboo
staff which is lifted and swung for exercise. It may weigh as little as five
or as much as fifty to sixty kilograms. In the *Ramayana* and *Mahabharata* the gada is often mentioned as a weapon. In popular religious art
and iconography Hanuman is almost never depicted without one. It is
not only the symbol of his strength but also of his countenance. The
gada he carries is highly decorated and made of gold. At championship
bouts wrestlers are awarded gadas made of silver. The gada is, then,
clearly the mark of a wrestler's prowess. Given the preponderance of
phallic symbols in the akhara and the gada's general shape it is evident
that swinging a gada has clear symbolic overtones of sexual potency
and virility. Each time the gada is swung it is brought to a balanced
position, erect from the wrestler's waist.

The phallic aspect of the gada is also evidenced by its association
with snakes. In the *Harivamsa* (chap. 83) Akrura dives into the serpent
world where he sees Ananta asleep on top of a mace (Vogel 1926: 92).

As the manifestation of Baladev, "the mace carrier," Shesha Nag is also often depicted carrying a mace in one of his four arms (ibid: 196).

In shape a gada resembles the churning stick used to make butter and buttermilk. A parallel between churning and sexual energy has been drawn above. By swinging the gada one might say that a wrestler is churning his body to increase his store of semen.

Joris are swung like gadas but they come in pairs weighing between ten and forty kilograms each. Joris are often decorated with colorful designs, and many akharas have special pairs which are brought out only on such occasions as Nag Panchami and Guru Puja. In contrast to gadas, joris are named—the "white pair," the "shiny ones," the "thorny ones," the "flowery ones," the "mountainous ones" (many are named after a particular person who either made them, commissioned them to be made or swung them the most number of times). While gadas have clear phallic qualities, joris symbolize breasts (recognizing, of course, that breast and phallic symbols are highly mutable and multivocal to the point of being almost interchangeable). Not only do joris come in pairs, they are also swung from an inverted position with the wrestler holding firmly onto the titlike handle-grip as though he were milking a cow or buffalo. If churning is the dominant metaphor of swinging a gada, milking is associated with swinging a pair of joris.

Most of the wrestlers in Banaras are dairy farmers, and so the motifs of milking and churning are particularly appropriate. In fact, milking itself is referred to as an exercise by many young wrestlers who brag that they can milk ten or fifteen buffalos without tiring. In this instance the motif clearly refers to milk as a female substance which contributes to the development of male semen.

One of the most important exercises in a wrestler's regime involves digging the pit. The wrestling pit is dug with a *pharsa* (a short, heavy hoe) in much the same way that a field would be plowed. That is, a person digs the pit into furrows. A great deal of emphasis is placed on making the pit look like a well-cared-for field. I asked a number of wrestlers if there was not a contradiction in the fact that digging is prohibited on Nag Panchami while it is an integral part of pit preparation for the akhara festivities. I was told that there was no contradiction; the implication being, I think, that plowing is an overt act of planting or putting seed into the earth so as to take substance out. Digging the pit, on the other hand, enriches the soil by mixing things in. It is true that wrestlers draw strength from the soil but they are never seen as violating the earth. On a symbolic level they never pose a threat to the snake's potency. The wrestler is to the earth as a child, while the snake—as cloud, rain, and lightning—is emblematic of the sky father. A wrestler never challenges the virility of the snake but turns instead as a child to his mother's lap. All feelings of sexual attraction, either towards the mother or against the father, are sublimated beneath a symbolic cloak of non-sexual virility. It is not a question of who has sexual access to (or repressed desire for) whom, but of how sex itself can be held in check. The digging of the earth, as with many of the other symbols discussed here, represents the potential of sexual power turned into nurturing growth.

Once the earth of the akhara pit is dug it is smoothed out by harnessing a wrestler to a flat log which he drags around the pit behind him. In this exercise wrestlers are compared, through association with draft oxen, to bulls (see plate 15). Bulls are ubiquitous in Banaras and although they go on rampages and can be dangerous they are generally regarded as non-aggressive. They are, however, the very embodiment of strength and brute force.

While associated with Shiva, the bull in Hindu mythology is not a symbol of phallic aggression or erotic desire. As O'Flaherty points out, the bull represents controlled, passive sexuality: the inverse of Shiva's potent sexuality. The bull is "virility held in check" on two fronts: by Shiva's ascetic power on one hand and on the other by the mother (cow) who "overwhelms and blocks" the impulses of the bull (1980: 253). The bull is, then, the perfect image of the wrestler whose passion, like that of the snake, is cooled by mother milk, and whose seed is never spent.

One of the most common metaphors used to describe a wrestler's strength is to compare him to the oxen who draw huge leather buckets of water out of rural irrigation wells. These wells are sunk deep into the ground. An incline is built for the oxen to walk up and down as they pull the water up on a cantilevered pulley. Again, the motif of the impregnating bull is reversed, as it were, and instead the bull-like wrestler harnesses himself to the rope and draws out the life-giving milk/water fluids of the earth. Not coincidentally, the ox, as a castrated bull, is here associated with fertility and strength but not sexuality.

CONCLUSION

In this chapter I have sought to interpret some of the dominant symbols in the culture of wrestling in order to understand why wrestlers regard Nag Panchami as an important festival. My argument is that Nag Panchami symbolizes contained sexuality, either as the seed turned in on itself wherein the symbiotic energies of milk and semen merge, or as erotic snake passion cooled by milk. In either case non-sexual virility is the dominant motif in a wrestler's life. On Nag Panchami when wrestlers mix buttermilk into the akhara earth, when they play "in their mother's lap," and when they show off their nurtured bodies, they are, in essence, dramatizing the efficacy of celibacy. In their own terms they are enacting what it means to feed milk to snakes.

CHAPTER 7

Wrestling Tournaments and the Body's Recreation

At Ravana's face the *vanar* sprang,
Snatched from his head the kingly crown
And dashed it in his fury down
Straight at his foe the giant flew,
His mighty arms around him threw,
With strength restless swung him round
And dashed him panting to the ground,
Unharmed amid the storm of blows
Swift to his feet Sugriva arose.
Again in furious fight they met;
With streams of blood their arms were wet,
Each grasping his opponent's waist.
Thus with their branches interlaced,
Which, crimson with the flowers of spring,
From side to side the breezes swing,
In furious wrestle you may see,
The *Kinsuk* and the *Seemal* tree.

> *Ramayana, Yuddha Kanda, Chapter 40,*
> *R. T. H. Griffith's translation*

INTRODUCTION

Given the rich and textured quality of wrestling as a way of life and the fact that wrestlers are concerned with a dramatic presentation of self, I fully expected to find that wrestling tournaments would be, to paraphrase Geertz, an Indian reading of Indian experience: "a story they tell themselves about themselves" (1973: 448).

Anyone who writes about public sport performance does so in the shadow of Geertz's seminal article on the cockfight, in which Geertz effectively reoriented the anthropological inquiry away from questions of social utility and function toward issues of contextual meaning. Taking this perspective while reflecting on the meaning of a wrestling dangal, one is led to ask not whose interests are being served or what social function fulfilled, but rather what story is being told through a staged contest of skill and strength.

Like the Balinese cockfight, Indian wrestling dangals may be read as texts. They are interpretive templates which provide a framework for making sense of cultural experience. However, while the cockfight is a studied microcosm of "things Balinese"—status, honor, propriety, hierarchy, masculinity and antibestiality—the dangal seems to defy any like characterization for the Indian scene. In Geertz's reading, the cockfight seems to elaborate meaning through the operation of symbolic dramatization. Dangals, on the other hand, seem to strip meaning down to essentials, to first principles. Consequently, one of the most surprising things about dangals is that they are not ripe with symbolic significance—as is the case with Nag Panchami and the akhara—but are in fact thin where one would most expect to find elements for "thick" description. Building on this theme, I will here offer an interpretation of the dangal in order to explain what it says about wrestling in particular and also about Hindu Indian society in general.

Set against the textured aesthetic of the akhara, the intricate regime of day to day life, the charged relationship between patron, guru, and wrestler, and the symbolic world brought to life on Nag Panchami, the dangal is a one-dimensional, abbreviated event. This is not to say that it is insignificant or marginal in any sense. Wrestlers take tournaments very seriously. Moreover, for the majority of the non-wrestling public the dangal is synonymous with wrestling. It is the most visible and public aspect of the sport. The dangal is a focal point in the matrix of wrestling, for it is where a wrestler can make a name for himself as both a champion and as one who has lived up to the ideals of a rigorous way of life.

In the context of the akhara, the wrestler's identity is subsumed within the larger rubric of wrestling. His individuality—his public identity and unique biography—is less important than the fact that he lives by a strict code and subscribes to certain values. As noted, the body of the wrestler is objectified and symbolically reified on the occasion of Nag Panchami in particular. This situation is reversed in the arena of the dangal. When in the competitive pit, a wrestler stands alone as the distilled essence of his way of life. He stands alone with his own background, his own unique history of success and failure, his own strength and skill, and his own style and technique.

The dangal is a synoptic outline of wrestling as a way of life. All of the important elements are encoded in the act of competition and tournament organization, but it is as though they appear in a shorthand version of their more vivid and poetic guise as elaborated in other contexts. In this respect, but certainly only as a metaphoric equivalent, the dangal functions much as a dream, for, as Freud has noted, dreams are charged with epic significance even though they are "brief, meager and laconic" (1967: 313). What I mean by this is that in the dangal the concept of brahmacharya, say, is reduced to a singular aspect of strength. In the larger akhara context it is the multivocal nexus of character elaborated through the symbolic significance of such things as ghi, snakes, and milk. Similarly, when the guru and the patron are present at a dangal they take a back seat to the wrestler who is, for the duration of the bout, dramatically at center stage. They are shown respect, but it is a pale reflection of the kind of respect that is idealized and ritualized in other situations. While considered pure, the earth of the dangal pit seems only to allude to the purer essence of the akhara as emblematic of Hanuman and mother earth, and saturated with energy and fertility.

This synoptic aspect of dangals goes hand in hand with the emblematic individuality of the competitive wrestler. In a short story about a fictional, famous Orissan wrestler, Mohanty describes the moment just preceding the bout: "At that moment, Jaga Palei became a symbol, the symbol of glory and the fulfillment of the hopes and aspirations of the Oriya People. A sea of people surged forward to greet him, to meet the heretofore unknown, unheard-of wrestler" (1979: 28). Mohanty's story ends with Jaga Palei going down in ignominious defeat. He is forgotten even more quickly than his momentary fame had spread, and he returns in ignominy to his akhara to exercise, eat, and carry on with his way of life. For a brilliant moment he stands alone, only to fall back onto a regime which is as comfortably depersonalized as it is strictly disciplined.

A similar, though harsher, situation obtains in Ruskin Bond's story "The Garland on his Brow." Hassan, a young wrestler from Dehra Dun, is described by Bond as a godlike man with a chest as broad as the base of a pipal tree (1967: 151). Hassan achieves tremendous success in dangal competition. Basking in the heroic glory of his success he is first admired, then hired and finally seduced by a local princess. When the princess dies, Hassan is left with nothing but his slowly sagging body and the memories of his youthful past. Bond's story begins well into

Hassan's demise, for we are first introduced to the wrestler not as a hero but as the decrepit beggar he had become. In the final scene Hassan is found dead in a gutter beneath a culvert with his body, once radiant with the aura of akhara earth, now covered with sores and mud.

Dangal heroics are treated in both of these stories with a high degree of ambivalence. These being the only two works of fiction I have been able to find on wrestling, it is remarkable that pathos, rather than some more straightforward emotion, is used to describe the wrestler's life. It is as if to say that magnified strength and divine virtue must ultimately succumb to banal, mortal terms. The conceit of physique cannot preempt the more basic form of a rudimentary biology; it cannot stand alone.

There is a subtle shift of orientation when the wrestler steps out of the akhara and into the dangal. In the akhara a wrestler's individuality is subsumed within the larger ideology of his way of life: he is one disciple among many. In the dangal the ideology serves to bolster the individual identity of the wrestler if only through dissimilation. What I have in mind here is the symbolic logic which links, in the mind of all concerned, the moral virtue of devotion, for example, to the expression of concentration on all wrestler's faces, and this, in turn, to the particular skill of the local champion: Jaga Palei, Gunga Pahalwan, Ram Sevak, or any other great wrestler. The dangal is able to effect an immediate and meaningful link between the general and the specific, between ideology and identity.

Clearly this is a matter of perspective rather than a reified dichotomy. There is a didactic tension between the general aura of ideology on the one hand and graphic heroic individuality on the other. In effect, the dangal stands in relation to wrestling ideology in a textualized formulation of Victor Turner's structure/antistructure dialectic. The wrestler, and also those who watch the bout, slide through the experience of liminality—here the communitas of dangal experience—as a kind of social therapy of revitalization (1969: 129). Through juxtaposition and particularization, the dangal serves to reaffirm the efficacy of certain ideological points.

However, the dangal does not stand in relation to Hindu Indian culture in the same way that the cockfight does to Balinese culture. While the cockfight seems to be an allegory for a Balinese way of life, wrestling, to the Hindu, is a strange story indeed. Geertz's argument is that the cockfight is a telling of a Balinese story about such primary concerns as status, hierarchy and poise. It is a telling, however, that depicts values and ethics as fragile constructs rather than pervasive cultural edifices (1973: 447). Even though one can see, "behind the thinnest disguise of an animal mask," that jealousy lurks behind poise and envy casts its shadow on grace, the whole picture is nevertheless a picture of Balinese society. Its foibles and rationalizations are put on par with its equanimity and charm. In essence, then, the cockfight is Balinese through and through. As such it is a ratification; it makes sense.

In contrast, I suggest, the dangal is an anomaly in Hindu culture. One might say, to overstate the issue only slightly, that the story a dangal tells is a story against Hindu ideals and values. The dangal is not so much a ratification as it is a cultural critique, a lens through which one sees certain aspects of social integration and conformity thrown into sharp and disjointed relief. The focus of this lens is on the individuality of the wrestler as an anomaly in Hindu society.

Numerous authors have pointed out that Hindu culture is built on the irreducible fact of caste identity and that the salient principles of a Western ethic of individuality and freewill are not found in the Hindu worldview. Instead, hierarchy, built on the structuring principles of purity and pollution, defines a pervasive caste ethic. As Daniel (1984), Madan (1987), Marriott and Inden (1977), Moffatt (1979), Fruzzetti, Östör, and Barnett (1982), and Parry (1989), as well as earlier writers such as Diehl (1956), Dubois (1906), Dumont (1970), and Srinivas (1965) has each in his or her own way showed, the body is very much implicated in the cultural politics of propriety, auspiciousness, purity, pollution, health, transaction, ritual, and kinship. In this scheme, the individual body is the nexus of intersecting forces, and many have argued that a person's identity is the mutable, animated product of these cultural codes. In any case, the condition of a person's body is in many respects a measure of his or her place within the larger social whole, a social whole only partially circumscribed by caste rules and concern with rank and status. I contend that the dangal may be seen as an ideological commentary on the nature of this complex somatic identity.

The dangal, like the cockfight, is a "safe" situation in which to lay bare the very framework of society: fundamental questions and issues are raised, but nothing changes through a reading of these events. As with a dream, the fantasy is over when the waking day begins. When the dangal is all over everyone goes home, enriched, perhaps, but not overwhelmed by the implications of what has been witnessed. In his fictionalized account, Mohanty emphasizes the textuality of the wrestling dangal: though epic in its proportions and monumental in its seeming significance, in the end the wrestler is all but forgotten and a world turned momentarily upside down rights itself. There is critique here, but no real threat of sedition.

THE WEEKLY BOUT

Many cities, small towns and village clusters organize weekly dangals, the most basic example of tournament organization. Although they are not particularly elaborate, they capture the essence of all dangals small and large. I am most familiar with the weekly Sunday afternoon dangal held in Dehra Dun. The pattern is almost identical from one week to the next.

Walking along one of the many roads that lead from the area of the central clock tower towards the old cantonment parade ground on a Sunday afternoon, one is likely to hear the rhythmic beat of the *dhol* (double-sided drum) which announces the beginning of every dangal.

Earlier in the day, before anyone arrives, a hired laborer digs the tournament pit. It is inevitably hard-packed from a week of disuse, trampled under the feet of young neighborhood boys who play cricket nearby, and littered with the trash that all public grounds seem to attract.

Gradually, at about four in the afternoon, a crowd of people gathers around. Those who come early sit on the grass about fifteen meters from the edge of the pit. The dhol player walks around counterclockwise calling others to take their places. The mass of seated spectators expands to enclose the pit on all four sides. It then thickens to about ten people deep. A second band of standing spectators circles the seated group and expands outward as the dangal proceeds. Bicycles, scooters, motorcycles, and the odd truck park on the outer edges of the gathered crowd. From the time that the first bout is fought until the final contest the crowd builds from five hundred to over a thousand.

For the most part, working-class men and boys—rickshaw pullers, day laborers, semiskilled factory workers, railway porters, and vegetable hawkers—attend weekly bouts. Wrestling is also very popular among mechanics, truck drivers, and other such skilled professionals who have a self-image of physical prowess. A fair percentage of the spectators at a dangal own small businesses or work as clerks in the vast municipal bureaucracies, public offices, and district courts.

As the seated crowd expands around the pit and the drummer continues to beat the dhol, Sharma, one of the dangal organizers, enters the arena and begins to bless the pit. He lights a stick of incense on one side of the pit and, after circling it around a few times, plants it in the earth. While circumambulating the pit he takes handfuls of marigolds from his satchel and throws them onto the earth. His actions are perfunctory and distracted. While Sharma blesses and circles the pit, Bholu, a vegetable hawker who referees the bouts, enters the arena and breaks apart the larger clods of earth that the laborer has left in his haste. Both Sharma and Bholu stop occasionally to talk with friends, answer questions, and exchange jokes and jibes. The atmosphere is casual.

The contestants tend to arrive later than the spectators in order to make dramatic, staged entrances. Contestants usually arrive in groups. In Dehra Dun there are two main factions. One is lead by Yamin, a fairly well-to-do entrepreneur, and the other by "Lal Bal Wale" (the red-haired one) who promotes most of the wrestlers who are not in Yamin's clique. Both Yamin and "Lal Bal Wale" are Muslims, though the wrestlers in their respective cliques are Hindu and Sikh as well as Muslim. A clique, in the sense used here, is an ad hoc alliance of friends, co-workers, and neighbors who come to the dangal together and support the same wrestlers. A wrestler does not have to be allied with any clique, but alliance does tend to enhance personal prestige.

Yamin's clique is comprised of Muslim motorcycle mechanics, butchers, and fishmongers. The clique has supported numerous wrestlers over the years. During the summer of 1987 the focus of the group was exclusively on two Muslim wrestlers from Saharanpur, a district town to the southwest of Dehra Dun. The two wrestlers came by bus every Sunday and met Yamin and the rest of the group at a teashop near the motorcycle garages. As a group the clique would drive or walk to the parade ground. Along the way others who identified with Yamin would join the entourage. Led by Yamin, the clique would clear a path through the standing crowd and then purposefully make its way through the seated audience and unabashedly clear an area for themselves in the very front. Yamin would then sit down with the two wrestlers next to him and a clique of fifteen or so friends on either side.

The entrance of a clique into the arena is, to say the least, designed to draw attention to itself. As a body the clique comports itself with casual conceit and confident lack of interest. There is a definite quality of majestic pomp as the members of each clique (and to a lesser but still significant sense all members of the audience) affect an attitude of cocksure pride and self-confidence. There is something in the dangal that brings out the prince in everyone. Timing is a large part of this drama, and if a dangal is scheduled to start at, say, 4:30, a wrestler with any sort of reputation will not make an entrance before 5:00.

The cliques and individual wrestlers make their entrances with various degrees of drama. Yamin's clique is on par with that of "Lal Bal Wale," but there are others: three army wrestlers who form a small though highly regarded clique, a railway clique headed up by Kanta Pahalwan, and, occasionally, a small group of wrestlers from either Haridwar or Roorkee. There are also a number of regular "independent" wrestlers: Chiranji from Rampur, a local wrestler who is recognized because he has only one hand, and a few others from nearby towns and villages. Every so often a wrestler from as far away as Muzzafarnagar (150 km), Simla (200 km) or Chandigarh (125 km) will attend.

After he has blessed the pit, Sharma, a toothless seventy-year-old retired municipal-board clerk, calls on young wrestlers to come into the arena and accept challenges. Usually this appeal has no effect, and Sharma berates the crowd for wasting his and everyone else's time. This usually has about as much effect as the initial appeal which prompts Sharma to give one of his long—though always tongue-in-cheek—lectures on respect and the lack thereof: the spinelessness of modern youth, the need for self-respect, and the value and moral duty of public service. Sharma has been doing this for so long that even if it was once meant seriously, it is now a burlesque self-parody with the tone of slapstick overstatement. The crowd loves it and shouts back retorts only just disguised in enough respect for Sharma's age and status to prevent a real confrontation. While Sharma, acting the part of one mortally insulted, pretends to cancel the dangal for lack of interest, Bholu, a past-his-prime wrestler turned referee, enters the pit and starts exercising vigorously. The crowd's attention turns to Bholu as he parodies a self-important wrestler showing off his strength and physique while slapping his thighs, beating his chest, preening, and promenading around the pit. Sharma rises to the occasion and points out that Bholu, a father of eight and purveyor of potatoes, is the picture of health and youth. Sharma and Bholu's performance is a studied comic routine that belies the underlying seriousness of the dangal specifically, and, indeed, of wrestling in general.

While Bholu and Sharma are in charge of running the dangal, they represent a larger group of people who are responsible for the overall organization of the event. This group is known as the *dangal panchayat* and comprises three or four men in addition to Sharma and Bholu. In contrast to the comic aspect of Sharma and Bholu's role, the *pradhan* (boss/chief) of the dangal panchayat is a dignified and affectedly elite figure. He often wears the uniform of post-Gandhian Indian politics: *khadi churidar payjamas*, black leather "country-style" shoes, and a white "Nehru" cap. The pradhan and two other members of the panchayat always carry briefcases, a clear mark of their status in an otherwise primarily proletarian arena.

The panchayat is responsible for getting permission from the municipal board for the use of the parade ground, and from the police for holding a public dangal. The panchayat must also pay the dhol player and the man who digs the pit. Beyond this, however, there is little organization or management required. The pradhan does not take an active part in running the dangal. He walks around the pit but rarely gets involved in arranging or deciding the outcome of a bout. As such, he stands as a benevolent symbol of beneficence: an authority without responsibility.

One of the points that wrestlers make is that dangals are the essence of what may be called a minimalist philosophy. In modern India, as elsewhere, people are pressured to acquire things in order to be regarded as successful and happy. The dangal, I was told, is directed against this kind of modern materialist mentality. All that one needs is open space, a person to referee, a drummer, and a crowd. Laughing, one man pointed out that unlike cricketers or hockey players a wrestler hardly needs more than his underwear (i.e., langot) in order to engage in a tournament. Any patch of earth is a potential arena. From this elemental base the dangal follows its own momentum. It can be staged—and many dangals are—but popular opinion has it that the dangal is a creature of its own volition, an event that emerges through the happenstance encounter of uncommon men in an ultramundane environment. In this formulation quality entertainment is not a factor of embellished pomp—colorful canopies, taped music, posters, and comfortable seats—but rather a function of the skill of particular wrestlers. The Dehra Dun dangal is not an elaborate event, but it is often both entertaining and meaningful because of its stark contrast to the complexity of the larger materialist world.

A dangal always begins with the youngest wrestlers coming out to the pit to extend or accept a challenge. Often a pair of eight- or ten-year-olds will be the first to fight. Although audiences tend to watch these bouts with desultory interest, many point out that these junior wrestlers must be encouraged if there is to be any wrestling in the future. Once the first two boys have wrestled, there is usually a surge of interest among others of a similar age who quickly take to the pit and try to match themselves with someone of equal age and stature.

Sharma and Bholu move these junior bouts along as quickly as possible. Sometimes more than one bout is fought at a time, and for pre-teenage wrestlers the time limit is never more than three minutes per bout.

While the junior contestants are wrestling, young teenage wrestlers come out to the pit. In Dehra Dun, in 1987, there were not many wrestlers of this age group. At other weekly dangals, however, there are usually numerous thirteen- to fifteen-year-olds eager to challenge someone and quick to accept any challenge offered. In any case, a wrestler only really begins to gain a reputation after adolescence, and becomes well known and accomplished when he is seventeen or eighteen. It is these and the more senior wrestlers whom the spectators have come to see. All else is preamble.

After the young teenage wrestlers have fought a few bouts, Sharma and Bholu gesture to Yamin and "Lal Bal Wale" to send out their best wrestlers. Inevitably Sharma's first appeal is ignored. More often than not his more adamant second and third appeals are no more effective. Bholu is sent over to have a word with the two groups. Only when Yamin decides and gestures toward the pit with a casual though pointed shift of his eyes and head do his wrestlers take to the arena.

As with the entrance of the clique into the dangal, the entrance of a wrestler into the arena is a matter of dramatic timing and staged self-presentation. An account from the *Times* of March 2, 1928, captures the essence of this performance:

> In most places each wrestler breathes a silent prayer, then touches the sand three times and lifts some of it to his brow, after which he leaps up and down in the open, slapping his thighs with resounding smacks. . . . The experts go through an immense amount of preliminaries, even after the formal shaking of hands. They do a press-up to improve their own muscles, and a squat or two to relax their legs, and smack their biceps before facing each other in a crouching position (Hornblower 1928: 65).

Only when the top-ranking wrestlers have taken to the arena does the dangal "heat up," as one man put it. The heat is a function of the drama associated with a high rank contest. To illustrate the point we may take up the events of Sunday, September 21, 1987.

As the contest between two young wrestlers ended, Yamin leaned over to the two wrestlers from Saharanpur and indicated that it was time for them to "take a *salami* of the pit"—to go out and put forward

1. Akhara Bara Ganesha

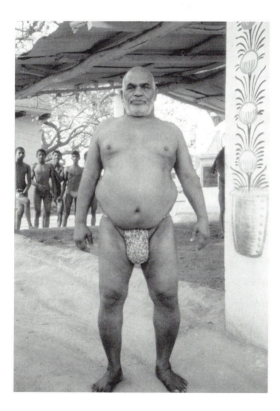

2. Lallu Pahalwan:
   A Body of One Color

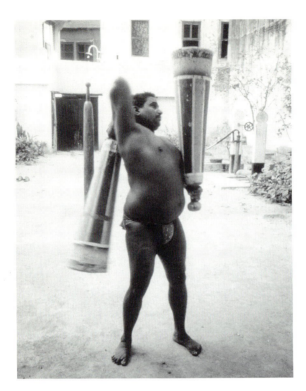

3. Jori Swinging:
   Akhara Kon Bhatt

4. Gada Swinging:
   Akhara Sant Ram

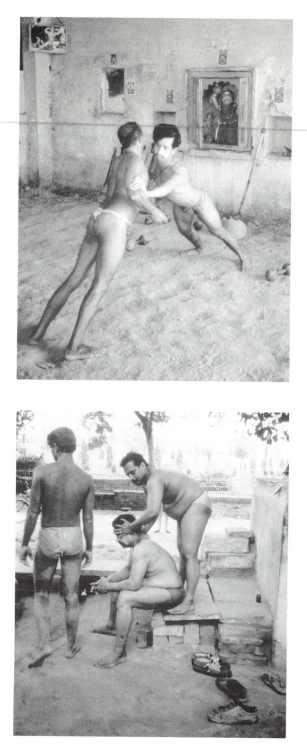

5. Ban:
   Akhara Sant Ram

6. Massage:
   Akhara Ram Singh

7. Jor: Akhara Bara Ganesha

8. Jor: Akhara Kedarnath

9. Lalji Pahalwan: A Wrestler Whose Name is Known

10. Dangal: Bout Inauguration

11. Hanuman Shrine: Akhara Gaya Seth

12. An Akhara Portrait: Akhara Gaya Seth

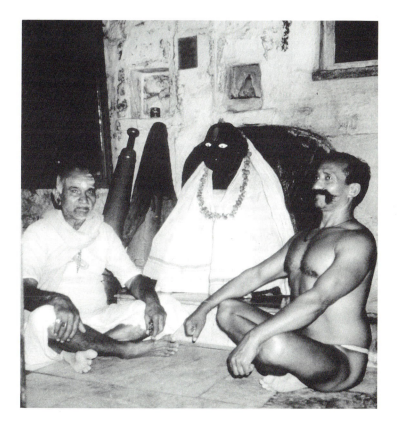

13. Sant Ram's Murti: Akhara Sant Ram

14. Guru and Chela: Akhara Ram Singh

15. Vyayam: Akhara Ram Singh

a challenge. The two wrestlers stood up slowly. To the loud applause of the crowd and the resounding rhythm of the dhol they loped out into the arena and jogged across to the near corner of the pit. To perform a *dand thonk*, both leaned over, touched the earth with their right hands and then stood up straight while gently slapping the biceps of their crooked right arms with the flats of their left hands. Faces expressionless, they stood next to each other on one side of the pit.

Seeing this, and feeling the crowd's energy surge forward with the wrestlers', one had the impression that the dangal had been building to this climax all along, a crescendo anticipated by the very first beat of the dhol's rhythm.

As the two wrestlers took to the arena, Sharma and Bholu began admonishing the crowd with renewed vigor, saying such things as, "Here are two fine wrestlers, who will challenge them? There must be someone from Dehra Dun who is up to this." Finally, and with studied casualness, Kaliya, the top wrestler of the "Lal Bal Wale" clique, sauntered out into the arena. His entry brought another loud round of applause from the crowd. Kaliya saluted the earth and stood on the opposite side of the pit.

As Kaliya came into the arena, Yamin's clique huddled together in conference as the two Saharanpur wrestlers stood and looked on. Finally, Kilo, a well-to-do butcher and vocal member of Yamin's clique, stood up and indicated that the younger of the two Saharanpur wrestlers should extend his hand to Kaliya in challenge. After a short period of confusion wherein the two Saharanpur wrestlers tried to figure out which one of them should extend the challenge, the younger one, Said, again reached down and touched the earth. Slapping the inside of his right thigh with the flat of his right hand, he leaped into the pit and ran across to face Kaliya.

Without breaking stride Said reached down and, grabbing up a handful of earth, extended his hand to Kaliya. Kaliya reacted by not reacting. As the earth ran through the fingers of Said's extended hand, punctuating, as it were, the pregnant moment of confrontation, Kaliya stood, as before, with his hands behind his back looking down at a clump of grass between his toes.

The crowd, which had to this point showed its mild enthusiasm through loud applause, all but exploded with one loud voice as Said leaped across the pit to challenge Kaliya. As he stood, hand extended, the crowd shouted out that Kaliya should take the challenge. Kaliya, however, looked over towards his clique, and reading there some sign, simply shook his head and began walking around the pit slowly. Said looked over to Yamin's camp, shrugged, and, somewhat flustered, stepped out of the pit. Kilo dashed out into the arena and started talking with Sharma and Bholu to try to do something to persuade Kaliya to take the challenge. They all tried to get Kaliya to fight, but to no avail. Frustrated, Kilo returned to Yamin's camp. The three wrestlers in the arena, now joined by four others, walked casually and with studied indifference around the pit.

Sharma and Bholu went over to the "Lal Bal Wale" camp and, judging from their gestures and the tone of their voices, told him in no uncertain terms that the match between the two wrestlers was fair and should proceed. Frustrated by a lack of immediate response from "Lal Bal Wale"—who, like any good clique leader, would not taint his poise by bowing to pressure—Sharma came over to Yamin's camp along with the pradhan of the dangal to argue that it was getting late and that if a contest was to be held it had better be soon.

As Sharma walked away in close conference with the pradhan, Kilo stood up and announced in a loud, dramatic voice that a "purse" would be collected to place as a prize for the winner of the bout. With great flourish and public demonstration Kilo collected 5 rupees from almost everyone in Yamin's clique and handed the 50-rupee purse to Bholu. Bholu danced out into the arena as the crowd shouted its approval. Holding the money over Said's head, he announced that anyone who could beat this young man stood to win the whole purse. Still standing with studied distraction, Said basked in the glory of the crowd's unchecked emotion, which seemed to counterpoise his own control.

Kaliya, who had returned to his camp while negotiations were going on, now came out to the pit again. After some hesitation, and loud encouragement from the crowd, Kaliya walked across the pit and shook hands with the young Saharanpur wrestler. Again the crowd shouted its approval as the dhol kept pace with the growing excitement.

Among Yamin's clique there was a feeling of self-satisfaction tinged with a hint of cynical mirth. As those sitting around me put it, greed had proved the strongest arm in the dramatic pre-bout negotiations. Money, they said, breaks down many barriers.

After shaking hands both wrestlers retired to their respective camps: Kaliya with his characteristic casualness and understated style of self-presentation, and Said with sudden leaps and bounds of hardly restrained excitement. With great flourish, Said unwound his langot from around his waist as Kaliya, on the opposite side of the arena, carefully took off his pants and shirt and folded them in a neat pile. As both wrestlers began to undress, those in Yamin's clique made a quick inspection of Said's new *janghiya* (briefs). Comments were made about the strength of the material, its color and pattern—purple with yellow flowers—and the fit and quality of the stitching. The leg holes were checked for flexibility and comfort while the thin ropes sewn for strength into the hems were twisted straight and smooth. The janghiya were passed from hand to hand as each member of the clique demonstrated his knowledge of such things as the texture of the cloth, the quality of the workmanship, the aesthetic of design, and the importance of fit.

Both wrestlers tied on their wrestling langots, smoothed the cloth and tested the knots around their waists before squatting down to insure a comfortable fit. Before putting on his janghiya, Said jogged up and down in front of Yamin's clique while limbering up his back, neck, and legs. Taking the janghiya and holding them by the waistband he lifted them three times to his forehead in a gesture of supplication, respect, and luck. After a few minutes Kilo helped Said into his briefs, which, in accordance with notions of correct fit, must be so tight that often more than one person must push, pull, and crimp them into place. Said shook hands with everyone in the clique and again loped into the arena and jogged slowly around the pit to keep himself warm while waiting for Kaliya to make himself ready.

Said was accompanied into the pit by Salim, the other wrestler from Saharanpur. As he stood by to offer encouragement, a local wrestler dashed across the arena and into the pit, picked up a handful of earth, and proffered it in challenge to the unsuspecting and unprepared Salim. Caught off guard, Salim backed away and refused to take the challenge. The challenger proclaimed in a loud voice that since Salim had entered the arena it was his right to extend a challenge and to have his challenge accepted. Recovering a degree of composure but losing an equal portion of patience, Salim walked to the center of the pit and announced that he had a cold and a bruised foot and would therefore subject himself to a bout only for a prize of 200 rupees. The challenger followed Salim around the pit with his hand extended and refused to listen to any excuses. This only prompted Salim to refuse more forcefully. Kilo ran into the pit and grabbed hold of Salim's sleeve and pulled him back to Yamin's camp as the crowd jeered loudly.

Having made himself ready, Kaliya sauntered into the pit and Sharma called both wrestlers to the center. Standing between them he grabbed their wrists, and holding up each wrestler's arm, in turn announced their names and hometowns. Both wrestlers introduced, Sharma indicated that the bout was set for eight minutes. He released their wrists and stepped quickly back as the dhol player, silenced only briefly for the announcements, again set to beating his drum.

Both Kaliya and Said reached down and rubbed their hands in the earth. Having already broken a sweat, Kaliya submitted to being rubbed down and dried with earth. The wrestlers faced each other, locked hands, and the contest began as Sharma, Bholu, the pradhan, Kilo, and the drummer all walked around the pit.

In striking contrast to the pre-bout vocal enthusiasm of the crowd, once a contest has begun everyone becomes quiet and attentive. This is less a natural reaction than an issue of decorum. Silence serves to focus attention on the wrestlers, and the quality of a bout is said to be reflected in the degree to which skill and strength can leave one quite literally speechless. Periods of silence are counterpoised with eruptions of vocal empathy. But silence is the mark of true appreciation.

As everyone agreed, the fight itself was lackluster. Neither wrestler had even succeeded in knocking the other down, and so, after eight minutes, Sharma declared it a draw. In spite of the anticlimax, Kilo dashed out into the arena and lifted Said onto his shoulder to carry him partway back to his clique in a gesture of recognition and accomplishment. After retiring to their respective camps both wrestlers, accompanied by a member of their clique, walked around the arena to accept money prizes offered by people in the audience. Kilo, who accompanied Said on his "round," admonished the crowd to show their appreciation by making a generous contribution. A number of people in the audience offered one or two rupees, and when Kilo and Said had completed their circuit they had collected about 100 rupees in all. This money was carefully counted and sorted into bills of like denomination. After the drummer was given two rupees (he collected that much, or a little less, from every wrestler), the rest was wrapped in a scarf and given to Yamin for safekeeping. This money was later given back to Said.

Sharma and Bholu then called on other wrestlers to compete. Soon two other bouts were arranged. However, these bouts were equally anticlimactic in both design and execution. The wrestlers were not affiliated with either of the two main cliques and were inexperienced and unskilled. During these bouts, Sharma and one of the other organizers walked through the crowd asking for contributions to ensure the dangal's regular continuance. Many people were persuaded to give up their spare change.

As the last two wrestlers fought, the crowd's interest faded with the light. Finally the smaller of the two managed to flip the other on his back. Bholu, distracted momentarily, failed to see this and Kilo dashed out shouting that the bout was over. This resulted in a degree of confusion as Bholu and the other organizers tried to figure out what had happened. The crowd, however, took this as a signal that the dangal was over and they left the parade ground en masse.

The panchayat gathered informally on the steps of a nearby building and discussed the day's dangal. Those who had wrestled and felt they were entitled to some prize money approached Sharma to ask for their winnings. The money that had been collected for the main bout between Kaliya and Said was distributed equally between them both.

DANGAL ORGANIZATION AND SPONSORSHIP

The weekly Dehra Dun dangal described above serves as a template on which to construct a more complete picture of the dynamics and practice of wrestling tournaments in general. Dangals are held on many public religious holidays such as Janamashtami, Shivaratri, Holi, Diwali, Valmiki Jayanti, Nag Panchami, and, as D. N. Majumdar has noted (1958: 304), on Anant Chaudas, Kajali Tij, Shravani, and Har Chhat. Ishwaran writes that in a South Indian village, Muharram and Basava Jayanti are occasions for three-day-long dangals (1968: 145). In fact, any holiday is an appropriate occasion for a dangal. Similarly, dangals are often held in conjunction with regional fairs. Other dangals commemorate the death anniversaries of well-known local and national leaders.

Every dangal is organized by a committee and sponsoring institution. For instance, a dangal held in New Delhi, on Shivaratri, was organized by a prominent Shiva Temple Association in East of Kailash. The dangal was part of a much larger schedule of events which culminated in a public puja on the night of Shivaratri. Another dangal, held in Pontasaheb, was organized by the local chapter of the Panther's Club—a group of young entrepreneurs and municipal leaders—to celebrate Valmiki's birthday. This dangal was a large affair. Wrestlers came from Ambala, Simla, Kurukshetra, and Chandigarh, and there were over 150 bouts organized over a period of two days. The dangal was part of a much larger celebration which included a temple inauguration, folk dances, and a bicycle race. In Banaras a dangal was organized for Nag Panchami under the auspices of a local branch of the Rashtriya Swayamsevak Sangh (RSS), a right-wing nationalist organization. Another dangal in Banaras was organized by the Cart Driver's Union—a labor organization of transport workers. A small dangal held in a village outside of Banaras was organized by local village leaders.

In sharp contrast to the weekly dangal, organizing a larger, special dangal can be an expensive proposition. For instance, there was a large dangal held across the river from Banaras in the small town of Arohra. The dangal was organized by a local group of grain merchants and mill owners. Although I do not know how much money was spent, one may imagine the capital outlay in the following list of expenses: printing of posters and newspaper announcements, transport of earth for the pit, labor for pit construction, renting and setting up the public-address system and the tent canopy over the wrestling pit, paying the salary of seven to ten policemen and the drummer's wage, and supplying flower garlands, refreshments for guests, and prizes. The largest and most important expense, of which everyone spoke, was in the form of prize money for the dangal's highest-ranking wrestlers.

At large dangals, where prizes are distributed, the younger wrestlers are awarded cash, T-shirts, drinking glasses, buckets, clocks, *saphas*, and various other items in accordance with their skill and status. These prizes are displayed on a large table in front of the dangal announcer and other members of the organizing committee.

A large dangal always has at least one major bout. A major bout is defined by the rank of the wrestlers scheduled to compete and the prize money offered. At a dangal held in New Delhi on November 19–24, 1986, Suresh, a national champion, was awarded a silver gada and 31,000 rupees. Jayprakash, the second place winner, won 15,000 rupees (Sahadev Singh 1987: 54). The large dangals in Maharashtra are said to offer purses of 100,000 rupees to the best-known wrestlers in India. In the past, national champions such as Denanath, Lal ji, Mehar Din, and Chandagi Ram have been awarded sums over 75,000 rupees. Dangals on this national scale do not take place very often. Far more common are local regional dangals to which one or two well-known wrestlers are invited. The prize money at these dangals ranges anywhere from 1,000 to 10,000 rupees. The amount is established prior to the bout and is a way of attracting well-known wrestlers.

There are various ways in which money is collected to hold a dangal. A common practice is to sell tickets, and the price of tickets varies depending on the size of the dangal and on the quality of the seats. At dangals where the prize money is under 15,000 rupees tickets sell for two to five rupees per seat.

So called "ticket" dangals are not well regarded and are sharply contrasted with *khula* (open) dangals, which are free to anyone who is interested. The main criticism of ticket dangals is that the organizers stand to make money for themselves. Ticket dangals are, in a pejorative sense, a form of business. *Thekedars* (contractors) who organize these dangals set up bouts for the explicit purpose of making money. These thekedars are not well regarded by many wrestlers who believe that their skill and status will be compromised to greed if they are required to fight *nura* or "fixed" bouts. Moreover, most wrestlers with whom I spoke said that the most reprehensible aspect of fixed bouts was that the audience would be duped and thus cheated.

*Khula dangal*s are not tainted with the stigma of ticket-sale profits, exclusivity, ranked seating, or the possibility of graft. They are often sponsored by independent nonprofit groups—temple committees, village panchayats, municipal-board departments, block-development committees, and local clubs. These groups fund the dangal either through budgetary allotment or, as is more often the case, by asking members and community leaders to contribute to a public fund. For instance, a dangal sponsored by the Cart Driver's Union of Banaras asked its membership to contribute a portion of their wage to build a purse big enough to attract a well-known Delhi wrestler. Often a few well-to-do businessmen contribute most of the money required for a dangal. These men are therefore seen as the dangal's chief organizers. For example, a dangal held in Banaras under the auspices of the RSS was financially underwritten by a wealthy sweet-shop owner. Financial contributions are a way for public figures to make a name for themselves, to project themselves into the public eye.

There is always a cadre of men who are highly visible at a dangal. They are seated behind or near the announcer's table next to the prizes, garlands, and pile of head cloths. Like the pradhan of the Dehra Dun dangal these men project an aura of authority without having any responsibility. One person from the sponsoring group—but never anyone of great status—is responsible for making announcements over the public-address system. Another low-ranking member of the cadre is usually responsible for the distribution of prizes. As in the Dehra Dun dangal there are usually two referees. At larger khula dangals the referees are not affiliated with the sponsoring group and a third person may serve as an arbitrating judge.

At a khula dangal most of the bouts are not prearranged, but are arranged in the same way as in the weekly dangal described above. Many khula dangals attract a large number of wrestlers who come and sit together with their akhara clique. These cliques sit as close to the pit as possible. Often there are more wrestlers who want to wrestle than can be accommodated. It is the referee's responsibility to select a wrestler and establish him as the challenger for the next bout. Only those who shake hands in front of the referee are legitimate contestants. Despite efforts to control the number of wrestlers challenging and being challenged, there is often a great deal of confusion on the periphery of the pit as candidates for a bout converge on the referee at the end of each preceding contest.

One of the referees announces each wrestler's name, his hometown, the name of his guru, the amount of cash or type of prize that will be given to the winner, and the length of the bout. The length of a bout increases with the age, size, and status of the wrestlers competing. Similarly, the greater the amount of the prize money, the longer the bout. A bout can be any length of time and is fought without breaks until one or the other wrestler's shoulders touch the earth. Any bout worth more than 1,000 rupees is likely to be scheduled for about thirty minutes. Occasionally bouts will be scheduled for an hour, but ten to fifteen minutes is the average for a bout worth a hundred rupees. If a bout is not decided at the end of the scheduled time, the time is often simply extended. There are tales of bouts going on in this manner for hours, and even days at a time.

SWAGAT

In between dangal bouts, short ceremonies are performed which recognize and give public acclaim to men of renown. These rituals are referred to as *swagat* (honorific welcome). To give swagat is an act of respect and to receive it a mark of honor and status.

The most common form of giving swagat is for one of the members of the dangal organizing committee to invite the person to be honored into the pit. This person salutes the pit and is introduced to the audience. He is garlanded and a sapha is tied around his head. Sometimes he is given a small sum of cash as a mark of respect. Depending on the circumstances, the honored person is sometimes asked to inaugurate a bout. This entails no more than standing between the two wrestlers who are about to compete and placing one's hand over their hands as they shake to initiate a bout (see plate 9). If a photographer is present this ceremony is staged carefully and captured on film. The wrestlers who are about to compete touch the feet of the honored person, who leaves the pit and retakes his seat as the bout begins.

A wide range of people receive swagat at wrestling bouts. Although the organizers of a bout do not usually receive swagat themselves, close associates of the organizers are inevitably honored. Thus, at a dangal organized by a group of grain merchants a number of wealthy traders were honored. Similarly, at a dangal organized by a union, ranking union members were honored. And at a dangal organized by the Rashtriya Swayamsevak Sangh, members of that organization who were not directly involved in the planning of the dangal were given swagat. At a dangal organized by a temple committee, one of the main benefactors was given swagat. Swagat is not restricted to members of the organizing group. Well-known gurus and retired wrestlers are also honored and introduced to the public. Similarly, religious leaders are accorded special status and are given swagat for gracing the dangal with their presence. Those who have been asked by the organizing committee to referee or judge the dangal are also given swagat.

At some dangals the organizing committee invites a chief guest to enhance the importance and pomp of the event. At a dangal organized by the police, for instance, the district superintendent was invited. He could not attend but sent his deputy instead. At other dangals local municipal politicians or departmental chiefs are often called upon to attend. For example, R. S. Toliya, the district magistrate of Banaras, was invited to the district jori/gada dangal of 1985. A member of the Legislative Assembly was invited to a dangal organized by Akhara Bara Ganesh. Kunwar Rajindar Singh Bedi, also a member of the Legislative Assembly of Firozpur district, Punjab, is a popular figure at local and regional dangals (Ali 1984). In Delhi, Yashpal Kapur, a Congress Party leader, was one of the luminaries at the Mahan Bharat Kesri Dangal of 1977. Village pradhans, block-development officers, and local advocates are often invited as chief guests to small rural dangals.

Many wrestlers point out that the best dangals of the past were those sponsored by rajas, maharajas, and powerful *zamindars*. It was on these occasions in particular that the king's power was most clearly reflected in the body of his court wrestler.

The presence of a local luminary such as a rich merchant, respected *mahant* (abbot), or powerful politician serves to transpose the world of wrestling onto the larger world of business, institutionalized religion,

politics, and rural development. In a figurative sense the ritual of swagat
serves to link wrestling to power and prestige in other walks of life.
More than anything else, however, the ritual of swagat highlights one
of the most important aspects of dangal participation: honor, respect,
and the public display of status expressed as *nam kamana*—to make a
name for oneself.

NAM KAMANA

Making a name for oneself is another manifestation of the general
synoptic theme being traced here. It is specifically focused on the issue
of public identity (see plate 10). What is striking about a dangal, in
contrast to the akhara, is that identity is reduced to what appears to be
mundane pride and a simple narcissistic concern for fame and social
status. In the dangal pit it does not so much matter whether a wrestler
is a true brahmachari, whether he is a vegetarian, whether he massages
his guru's feet and washes his clothes, or whether he is Hindu, Muslim,
Jat, Yadav, Thakur, or Chamar. It matters only whether he wins or loses.
One can certainly surmise that a winner probably has the character of
a good wrestler, but in the drama of victory and defeat these concerns
are subordinated to the immediacy of a simple dichotomy: success or
failure. It is on this point that the dangal is dramatically different from
the akhara regimen and ritual. While dangal preamble is cloaked in
a mantle of pomp—swagat, prizes, dramatic pit entries, stylistic self-
presentation—the contest itself strips away the larger dramatic context
to reveal a simple confrontation.

A whole hierarchy of status and fame is based on this dichotomy.
There are the wrestlers who earn a name for themselves by winning.
They become well-known and respected champions, even though, like
all wrestlers, they sometimes lose. One must not underemphasize the
degree to which a wrestler benefits from fame, even though the benefits
are not necessarily material in nature. To have a name is a primary end
in itself: to be recognized while walking down the street, to be invited
in for a glass of milk, to see one's name in the newspaper, to be fawned
over, to be talked about, to be allowed to move to the front of a line at
the bank or post office, to be given free rides on public buses, and so
forth.

A wrestler's success reflects directly on his guru. Fame is directly
translated. Similarly, a wrestler's status reflects on his akhara. When he

wins his akhara brothers also win, and when he loses all of the members of the akhara sink with him.

Less explicitly linked to the fact of winning or losing, but still implicated in the quality of each bout, is the status of the dangal organizers and their guests. A bout well fought reflects well on everyone associated with it. When I asked why people organized dangals, why people were given swagat, why people donated money to sponsor dangals, why people in the crowd gave money to successful wrestlers, and why wrestlers compete, the answer was, inevitably, for public recognition, "so that one's name will be known." Whether as king, court wrestler, or village pradhan, to "have a name" is to be firmly rooted in the larger world of social, political, and economic relations.

Except for a wrestler who is regularly successful, the dangal is not a way to make a name for oneself. The dangal is more a mode of expression than a functional device to gain recognition. It is not a medium through which to achieve status, but a context in which to express identity. The names of the organizers and chief guests are writ large on the dangal stage. However, a person must already be well known and respected to be accorded the honor of swagat. Even if an unknown person puts up thousands of rupees to organize a dangal, he will be overshadowed by someone who is already a respected, powerful person in the community.

Because of the stark dichotomy of success and failure played out again and again in every bout, there is an illusion that everyone's status is at risk. In every victory there is the exhilarating possibility of unbounded fame and in every defeat the collective shudder of possible ignominy. However, the organizers and luminaries do not stand to lose status and respect any more than they can expect to achieve status and respect through a dangal. The dangal only tells a story of status by calling out a litany of names earned in other arenas.

In this drama the risk is vicarious for all but the wrestlers themselves. It is their very real success and failure which lends credence to the event as a whole and which makes the play of status and honor meaningful.

INTERMEDIARY CONCLUSIONS: FROM THICK TO THIN

In beginning with a detailed description of a fairly commonplace, weekly dangal and moving, by stages and with progressive objectification, to a consideration of dangal types, organization, swagat, and nam kamana, I have made an effort to set the stage for what follows. In doing so I have not imposed my own categories of interpretation, but have tried to remain true to the wrestler's own interpretive rubric.

The act of wrestling is the centerpiece of every dangal. As the nexus of the dangal, the wrestling event is what all other events are organized in relation to. As such, the art of wrestling—the skill involved—provides a definitive commentary on the affected preamble of dangal pomp, the ideology of wrestling as a way of life, and, by extension, on certain aspects of the Hindu ethos.

Where the pomp of the dangal builds the wrestler up to heroic proportions, the art of wrestling strips him down to the biomechanics of a singular geometry of movement. Outside of the dangal, and indeed as the wrestler affectedly enters the arena, one might say that a wrestler's identity is pregnant with meaning. His body and its interpretations are a veritable poetics of strength and virtue. This condition is dramatically inverted when the wrestler actually begins to wrestle and the crowd falls silent. In a specific and temporary sense he is reduced, in the dangal, from texture to essence: from thick to thin.

In the following sections I will trace the biomechanics of this procedure.

THE ART OF WRESTLING

The art of wrestling is composed of stance, *paintra*, and moves and countermoves, *daw* and *pech*. I have listened to many wrestlers describe at length the importance of a balanced stance, the positioning of arms, legs and head. A balanced stance puts one in position to apply a move or counter an attack. As Ratan Patodi points out, stance is a crucial aspect of the overall technique of wrestling. In his description one can see a concern for detail and precision.

> *Paintra* is the fixing of the feet on the ground after having made a move or having countered an attack. It is the art of standing in the akhara. It is the point of entry into the act of wrestling and the prelude to every dangal. One's stance puts one in a position to attack or retreat.... Every stance has an appropriate counterstance, and one must move in tandem with one's opponent. Sometimes a strong wrestler's stance will be so firm that his feet will be as fixed as Angad's. [Angad was a great wrestler in Ram's army.] All attempts to shake him will fail.
>
> Eyes and stance move together. Stance brings color to the akhara. A wrestler who is as quick as a black hawk, can, with wisdom and vigilance, move from stance to stance and confuse his opponent. He jumps, ducks,

sways, runs, lures and frightens his opponent. He may stand near or at a distance, straight or in a crouch. He may attack aggressively or retreat passively, drop down on all fours, move from side to side and turn around. All the time he has in mind the move he wants to apply and uses his stance to choreograph the attack.

In a stance, one's forward leg should be in line with one's bowed head so that the chin is straight above the knee, and one's center of balance fixed. One should move one's feet precisely and with purpose. If one's stance is like a pillar then an attack will find its mark. One should be able to shift one's weight from one leg to another so as to feint and attack without faltering.

When you set your stance, the forward leg is usually the stronger. Some people are equally strong in both legs. In any case, one must always keep one foot at least one and a quarter hand's length ahead of the other. With the feet neither too far apart nor too close together, the angle between the feet should be between forty-five and fifty degrees. . . . One's hands should neither be fully extended nor left limp at one's side. They should be bent at the elbow and held firm . . . one should be bent at the waist with shoulders somewhat hunched and neck pulled in rather than extended. One's feet and hands should be tensed so that one can be fast on the attack and firm in absorbing and turning a parry aside. With one's right foot forward and body crouched there should be enough weight in the forward lean to make for a quick attack but not so much as will imbalance the body and make it fall out of control (Patodi 1973a: 39–40).

Patodi's description of the paintra continues. He further elaborates the virtues of a firm stance and the positioning of the wrestler's body. He draws an analogy between the firmness of stance in wrestling to like "stances" in business, war, life in general, and politics. He argues for the natural importance of stance by drawing an elaborate parallel between the innate balance of animals and the requisite balance of a wrestler in the pit. A wrestler with a balanced stance is like a hawk from whom no prey can escape (ibid: 42).

Others have spelled out the importance of stance in equal if not greater detail (cf. Atreya 1972b; K. P. Singh 1974; H. Singh 1981: 75–86; 1984a: 39–41, R. Gupta n.d.: 26). Along these lines a most embarrassing event occurred at a Banaras dangal in which a wrestler from Akhara Ram Singh was pitted against a well-known wrestler from Delhi. After about two minutes of grappling the Delhi wrestler managed to kick the feet out from underneath the Banaras wrestler with such force that his head and shoulder hit the earth while his legs flailed out of control. Having failed to apply this most basic of wrestling techniques, the Banaras wrestler was humiliated.

Although stance is of preeminent importance, the art of wrestling also entails the careful execution of moves and countermoves. It is of vital importance that a wrestler have a firm grasp of a particular move in all its ineffable intricacy. When I told wrestlers that I was writing a book on Indian wrestling they assumed that it would be a descriptive catalogue of daws and pechs, a litany of feints and parries. From their perspective this is what was needed: a step-by-step, blow-by-blow description of every possible move.

It would be simply impossible to do justice to the thousands of moves and countermoves which make up the art of Indian wrestling. In any case, H. Singh (1981, 1984b), R. Gupta (n.d.), Patodi (1973a), Ram (1982), and Mujumdar (1950) have provided synopses of many of the most common moves. Almost everyone, including the authors of many of these books, agrees that their descriptions are grossly inadequate: nothing can substitute for the real thing. In any case, my purpose here is not to give a descriptive account of wrestling moves or to undertake a formal classification of types of moves. I will restrict my comments to a discussion of how any one bout is envisioned: as a whole and choreographed sequence of moves. In doing so I hope to show how the body of the wrestler is broken down, as it were, into sequences of depersonalized movement.

From a skilled wrestler's perspective every single move, glance, shift of weight and moment of motionlessness ought to be classifiable into some aspect of a paintra, daw, or pech. In a perfect encounter there should be no extraneous or arbitrary movements which do not proceed from or come as a result of some other purposeful action. A skilled wrestler is one who can read this pure grammar of movement most clearly, and who is able to take advantage of his opponent's misreading: his carelessness. A good wrestler can interrupt a movement and translate it into something for which it was not intended. He must also be able to read ahead and anticipate his opponent's moves by examining the geometry of his stance. The art of wrestling is to achieve an economy of effective motion. Because every move can be answered with a whole range of countermoves, no two bouts are ever the same. No move is predictable or established as inevitable given the configuration of previous moves; structured improvisation is the key. Wrestlers are taught moves and how to put moves together in chains of motion, but it is only through practice that one learns the art of improvisation.

Improvisation has an ineffable quality, and in order to capture it in words the bout must be broken down into distinct parts. Memory serves to amplify the ineffable by distorting the sequence into isolated events. After a dangal one can often hear groups of men recounting a particular

bout and criticizing the wrestlers on the basis of the choices they made:
"He moved back when he should have moved forward. His weight was
on the wrong foot. All he had to do was stand up and it would have
been all over. He should not have let go of the ankle." Often these
remarks center on particular moves: "He was in the perfect position for
a *dhak* but he missed his chance and left his leg open. He didn't have
his weight far enough under to make the *dhobi pat* work. He was too
far away to try a *bhakuri*."

As they are so recounted, all moves are abstractions from what is in
fact a chain of improvised motion. It is instructive, however, to understand how particular moves are conceptualized outside the framework
of a competitive bout.

The *multani* is one of the most popular moves in Indian wrestling
because it is difficult to execute correctly but spectacular when applied
properly. Ratan Patodi describes five variations of the move. The most
common one is as follows: "You are facing your opponent and both of
you have one hand on each other's neck. At this point grab your opponent's other hand with your free hand. Jump forward and pivot on your
rear foot while kicking up your front leg to catch your opponent's rear
leg" (1973a: 53).

Naturally this description is an abbreviation of what actually takes
place: a shift of weight from one leg to the other, the twist and bend of
the hips, a rotation of the shoulders, the corresponding forward pull of
one's opponent's arm and neck, and the positioning of one's body close
enough to one's opponent to enable the pivot foot to work as a fulcrum.
There are a host of other minor but crucial aspects of the multani; for
example, the correct way to grip and pull the hand and the most effective
way to pull the neck forward and down.

> The *sakhi* is another effective and popular move. You have shaken hands as
> the bout is beginning. If your opponent's right leg is forward, grab his right
> wrist with your left hand. Circle your other arm over the upper part of his
> right arm and lock it straight. Insert your right leg between your opponent's
> legs and hook it behind his right knee (ibid: 61).

Patodi completes the picture by referring to a photograph which shows
a wrestler tripping his opponent with his hooked right leg while pulling
down and pushing forward on the locked right arm.

The *kalajangh* is a common, effective, and relatively easy move to
apply. As your opponent leans forward off balance, you grab his left
arm above the elbow with your left hand. You drop onto your right

knee and simultaneously duck under your opponent's chest while sliding
your right arm between his legs, grabbing hold of his right thigh. Rolling
to your left, flip your opponent across your back so that he lands on his
back with you on top of him.

Every dangal bout is read, retrospectively, as a series of moves and
countermoves. However, not all of the moves are recalled. Only the
most glaring mistakes, the near falls, the effective tricks, and the successful parries are remembered. Ratan Patodi recounts the following bout,
for which the prize was 100,000 rupees, between Kartar, a disciple of
Guru Hanuman, and Suresh, a disciple of India's best-known wrestler,
Chandagi Ram.

> At exactly 4:45 P.M. the minister of sports introduced the wrestlers and inau-
> gurated the dangal. Having defeated the excellent wrestler Jayprakash, Sur-
> esh stood taut, fit and with an expression of self-confidence on his face.
> Kartar, trained by Raj Singh and experienced in international competition,
> stood near by, his body radiant.
>
> For twenty minutes the two wrestlers sized each other up and measured
> one another's strength and skill. Both being fresh, neither of them wanted to
> make the first move. Both wrestlers fought defensively. Sometimes Kartar
> pushed forward and at other times Suresh would advance, but after twenty
> minutes it was impossible to tell who had the upper hand. There was a
> difference however. Kartar was pacing himself and not wasting his strength
> while Suresh was putting all of his energy into defensive tactics. He was
> getting more tired by the minute.
>
> At 5:05 P.M. Kartar applied a very strong *dhak* and although Suresh was
> not quick enough to defend himself completely, he did manage to grab
> Kartar's back. This unsettled Kartar who maneuvered his way out of the
> pit while freeing himself. The referee called both wrestlers back to the
> center of the pit and the bout continued. However, Kartar was off balance
> and after two minutes he halfheartedly tried to apply another *dhak*, but
> this time Suresh got a better grip of his waist and brought Kartar to his
> knees.
>
> This moment was for Kartar a time to catch his breath while Suresh
> continued to expend his energy. Three times Suresh put his knee on Kartar's
> neck and tried unsuccessfully to flip him over. Using his strong neck Kartar
> was easily able to rotate out of danger. Each time he foiled Suresh's efforts
> the crowd in the stadium applauded such that the arena echoed their appreci-
> ation. All the while Kartar was recovering his strength for what was to be a
> bout that went on for an extra fifteen minutes.
>
> Both wrestlers were tired after thirty minutes, but they remained cautious
> and wary of each other's moves. . . . As the fans' hearts beat faster and faster
> Kartar applied a *bagal dubba* in the eleventh minute and brought Suresh
> down with lightning speed (1986a: 81–83).

Any bout can be reduced to three basic principles: strength, stamina, and skill, with skill being a function of both experience and training. The grammar of a wrestler's movement and the geometry of his stance are a direct representation of these basic factors. There is, I think, a transparent and ultramundane quality to this art that serves to root aspects of the wrestler's identity in nature and the supernatural.

NATURALIZATION AND DEIFICATION

In a dangal one is presented with the distilled essence of a whole way of life wherein the textured identity of the wrestler is flattened out and moored to gross "natural" factors of raw strength, instinctual courage, and reflex action. When two wrestlers meet in the pit it is a cultural drama of base nature. It is as though the thick, cultural construct of a wrestling way of life is suddenly—and only for the duration of the bout—made thinly transparent. Instead of a complex scheme of strength and energy based on diet, discipline and devotion, there is, in a dangal, a clear, uninhibited representation of brute force. Training, discipline and practice are momentarily subordinated to what appears to be instinct and natural ability.

This is generally true even for those who know how to wrestle, but it is particularly true for the masses of people who come to watch a wrestling tournament. As in many sports that entail aggressive, physical contest—boxing, ice hockey, American football, cockfighting—there is, in Indian wrestling, a strong undertone of barbaric violence. Here is a world where the controlling hand of cultural civility is figuratively, and very circumspectly, removed. At many of the dangals I witnessed there was a sense of nervous, almost fearful anticipation of what might happen if things got totally out of hand. In any case there is, I think, a sense in which the Indian wrestling audience feels a degree of vicarious empathy for the naked, aggressive wrestler.

The position of the epic poems, particularly the *Ramayana* and the more popular *Tulasi Ramayana*, must be recognized in this regard. In his epic vision of wrestling, Tulasi Das writes a poetics of nature into Hanuman's fierce eyes, Angad's tree-trunklike legs, and the mountainous proportions of Ravana's warriors. Lightning, thunder, wild elephants, raging bulls, and swaying trees are all terms used to describe wrestling combat. Images such as these come to life as one watches a dangal.

In a concrete sense this distillation allows both wrestler and audience to experience the tangible essence of an elaborate cultural construct: to wallow, as it were, in the primordial clay from which the whole experience of wrestling emerges. The dangal is a peeling away of the layers of a way of life to reveal the raw material from which it is made. It is, of course, an elaborate cultural illusion to make a complex art look as though it were mere instinct, brute force, and natural talent. Through this operation the tenets of strength and virtue are more firmly grounded in what appears to be the irrefutable mandate of nature. They emerge not as programs of faith or mere conviction but as inevitable and taken for granted facts of life.

Let me put this another way. When a wrestler wrestles with such consummate skill that his strength and flawless technique appear as though they are a natural gift, this serves to ground the ideological aspects of wrestling in a world outside of culture, "in the blood of all Indians," as Patodi puts it (1985: 45). Metaphoric parallels are drawn between the fixity of a wrestler's stance and the sturdiness of a tree trunk, the bulk of a wrestler's chest and the majesty of Himalayan peaks, the lightning speed of a wrestler's twists and turns and the thunder of his slapping thighs. These parallels effectively superimpose a carefully crafted art, a most intricate cultural construct, onto a primordial extrahuman world imbued with supreme power.

This point is illustrated by Ratan Patodi in a vivid description of a 1926 wrestling bout between Gunga and Kallu Gama in Kolhapur. The natural skill and strength of the two wrestlers is demonstrated by means of an oscillating metaphor—Kallu and Gunga are at once animal and divine, natural and supernatural: "Hearing their names, Kallu and Gunga jumped up and stood firm. They were quivering with anticipation and appeared as two coiled snakes ready to strike. . . . The supporters of each wrestler danced as though lost in holy rapture at the sight of god" (1985: 45).

Wrestlers are often compared to animals: as fast as a leopard, eyes of a hawk, courage of a lion, and unleashed power of a rogue elephant. The divine metaphor is also quite common and is used to describe the radiance of victory and the complete, focused concentration of a wrestler in the pit. The great Gama was often referred to as "Krishna of the *Kaliyug*." As Atreya writes in one of his articles, "the true wrestler is god" (1973a), and in virtually every akhara one can find an image of the founding guru—always a great wrestler himself—who is said to have been of divine proportions. It could not have been otherwise, I was told, since no mortal could have possibly lifted the heavy nals or swung the gigantic gadas which now gather dust in many akhara corners.

A wrestler is never just human any more than is wrestling just a cultural construct. Metaphor and analogy serve to underscore the gross aspects of dangal wrestling by writing an act of cultural performance back onto nature and by translating a wrestler's "natural" ability into an act of god. In this formulation wrestling as a way of life emerges out of the pit, as it were, animated not just by the natural fact of instinct but by divine mandate as well.

THE DANGAL AS CULTURAL CRITIQUE

A number of anthropologists have commented in passing that wrestling tournaments are anomalous cultural events because they are situations where caste concerns are explicitly laid aside (Beals 1964: 107; D. N. Majumdar 1958; Mandelbaum 1970: 182–183, 331–332; Orenstein 1965: 201, 232, 254). Majumdar writes: "No caste restrictions are observed in choosing the combatants. All feelings of superiority and inferiority are laid aside, and a Thakur can wrestle with a Chamar or Pasi" (1958: 304–305).

I was told a story of the Banaras wrestler Jharkhande Rai's wrestling bout with Vijay Kumar, the national champion from Delhi. A group of men went with Jharkhande Rai from Banaras to Delhi where the bout was to be fought. There they looked into Vijay Kumar's caste background and discovered that he was a low caste person and would not, therefore, have the necessary *buddhi* (wisdom) to wrestle with the twice-born Jharkhande Rai.

The bout began and before anyone realized what was happening Vijay Kumar grabbed Jharkhande Rai by his janghiya and in one smooth movement picked him up and threw him to the ground. At this point in the story the narrator laughed at his own conceit and explained that Vijay Kumar's body seemed to swell and glow with a bright radiance "and we all looked toward heaven wondering from where his strength had come." Undoubtedly it was rigorous self-discipline cast in the light of a transcendent supernatural ability which had enabled Vijay Kumar to overcome his "natural" caste-based inability.

Because of the staged caste confrontation that characterizes many bouts, I suggest that dangals are important commentaries on Indian social life. The commentary aspect of the dangal turns on the synoptic reification of the natural body as an icon of identity. In other words, the

stark terms of success and failure in conjunction with a particularly
somatic way of life suggest an alternative reading of Indian social organization. They suggest a critique of caste hierarchy through positing a
body politics of almost barbaric self-determination.

In practical terms this is nothing more than the very real possibility
that a Chamar wrestler may put his knee on the neck of a young Brahman and flip him onto his back and into ignominy. But the caste status
of the particular wrestlers only adds a degree of irony and poignancy to
this picture; who a wrestler is in terms of caste rank is, in fact, beside
the point. In a world based on rigid caste ascription where the individual
is subordinated to the social whole, and where much social interaction
is guided by an implicit belief in the veracity of contagious impurity,
fate, and auspiciousness, it is unnerving to see a person write his own
destiny in terms other than those prescribed by social precedent and
cultural mandate. For the spectator the question raised might be put
something like this: If the body of the wrestler can be made to march
so effectively—and with such heroic consequences—to the tune of a
different drum, than what is to be made of the rest of culture? Where is
there room for the subtle distinctions of civilization in a world where
the rules are written in terms of muscles and morals rather than rank
and status? Regardless of what category of person is in the pit, it is
intriguing, challenging, and not a little frightening to see a person turn
an established system on its head, even when everyone accepts the fact
that it is just a game.

I am referring here to an ideological commentary on an ideological
formulation. The dangal is not a form of sociopolitical protest, if by this
one means a self-conscious project of radical change. It is, as I read it,
a textual critique of an established worldview. This critique is based on
the peeling away of the wrestler's identity to reveal an essential man. In
this sense, the wrestler stands as a naked caricature of individuality, a
parody of asocial natural man stripped of all cultural trappings of any
kind, and lauded for his personal and instinctive skill. In this formulation the emphasis placed on fame and making a name for oneself is
particularly significant. In the drama of the dangal one can, for a moment, step out of the arena of ascribed status and risk a quick turn on
the stage of pure individuality. For the wrestler and the audience alike,
the dangal is a story of society in a different key. Where normally there
is strict social hierarchy, the dangal suggests the possibility of individual
achievement. In a world of strict rules of body purity wrestlers enact a
ritual of physical contact saturated in sweat, mucus, and occasionally

blood. It is not at all coincidental that there is an element of the horrific in this barbaric, anticaste drama.

CONCLUSION

Geertz argues that the cockfight is a Balinese reading of Balinese life, a way of making sense through explication and interpretive elaboration. In a way the dangal is similar to the cockfight, but it is also fundamentally different, for it systematically takes apart that which is so carefully maintained and preserved in other arenas. The dangal focuses attention on the ideological inverse of caste hierarchy by positing the individual as a social fact, and individuality as a moral—if somewhat uncivilized—value. It makes no difference that such a suggestion is, as some have argued, a conceptual impossibility given the Hindu worldview. The dangal, after all, is only really significant in the sense that dreams and other fantasies are. Its logic is not pragmatic, but cosmological in the Lévi-Straussian sense that dangals, like myths, are tools through which people think, templates for conceptual thought. The positing of a natural individual is, in this sense, just an unconscious inversion of the more protean way things normally are. In this primal dream is the intriguing possibility of another way of seeing the world.

CHAPTER 8

Hanuman: Shakti, Bhakti, and Brahmacharya

> Chiken Pahalwan's uncle Sarabjit was a great wrestler. He
> was a very devout believer in Hanuman. He would sit at the
> akhara temple and worship for two hours straight. He only
> did 200 bethaks per day but was a great wrestler. He was a
> Hanuman *pujari* and from this he derived his strength. He
> would worship with such feeling that tears would come to
> his eyes.
>
> *Atma Pahalwan, of Akhara Ram Singh*

Largely because of his prominent role in the epic *Ramayana* drama,
Hanuman is a popular deity among North Indian Hindus. When verses
from Tulasi Das's version of the *Ramayana* are sung, the most common
and popular tell of Hanuman's exploits: his leap across the ocean to
Lanka, the grandeur of his body as revealed to the captive Sita, his
singlehanded destruction of Lanka, his journey to the Himalaya and his
flying return with the mountain on which grew the medicinal root that
would cure the mortally wounded Lakshman.

In addition to his great popularity as an epic hero, Hanuman—*Mahavir* (the great courageous)—is worshipped in countless temples and
shrines. In Banaras alone one can go hardly two hundred meters in any
direction without coming across a place which is sacred to him. These
places range in size and significance from the great Sankat Mochan
mandir in the southern part of the city, where thousands of people come
to worship on Saturday evenings, to the small roadside shrine which
may appear to be nothing more than a vermilion plastered stone set into
a niche at the base of a tree. Regardless of size or aesthetic appeal, every
shrine dedicated to Hanuman is the object of someone's devotion. Every
Tuesday and Saturday morning at dawn a group of women bathe, garland, and clothe the image of Hanuman at a crossroads near Naisarak
in the Chaitganj area of Banaras. An older man sits reading the Tulasi
Ramayana on a small ledge near a Hanuman shrine in the crowded
Chauk Bazaar. A family pushes its way through the crowded courtyard
of the Sankat Mochan mandir. Unable to get close enough to the images

of Hanuman therein, a man lifts his son onto his shoulders and instructs
him to throw a garland of flowers in the general direction of the main
shrine. A rickshaw driver leaves hold of his handlebars to bow his head
and fold his hands as he passes a flower-bedecked shrine from which
emanates the aroma of incense and marigolds and the recorded music
of devotional hymns. Entering a tea shop a man touches the feet of a
faded calendar image of Hanuman around which hang the flower garlands of other suppliants.

For many who live in Banaras, and to a lesser but still significant
extent throughout north-central India, Hanuman is regarded as a tangible deity. Though phenomenal in a supernatural, heroic mode, his exploits make sense on the pragmatic level of everyday life. As anyone I
asked was quick to reply, Hanuman stands for two things: strength
(*shakti/bal*) and devotional adoration (*bhakti*). These two aspects of his
character are clearly interrelated. Hanuman's great strength is a direct
reflection of his devotion. The more perfect his bhakti, the greater his
strength; the more fabulous his strength the greater the magnitude of
his bhakti.

Despite their eminently human qualities, deities like Ram and Krishna
stand for abstract, divine grace. They inspire an aura of respect based
on the fact of their ultimately incomprehensible divinity. While it is true
that Krishna is the object of devotional worship in the tradition of bhakti
(Singer 1963) and is therefore tangible in a purely mystical sense, his
characterization in and through the *Bhagavad Gita* is much less personal. In this text Krishna is the construct and constructor of abstract
theology. Hanuman, on the other hand, does not represent some metaphysical absolute nor advocate a particular ontology. Rather, in his
relationship to Ram, Hanuman represents spiritual devotion. To the
extent that Ram represents ultimate spiritual realization, Hanuman represents the method through which that spirituality is realized: the adoration of bhakti. Hanuman is certainly supernatural, but his power is
that of a divine agent rather than a transcendental being. In this regard
Hanuman is perhaps unique in the Hindu pantheon insofar as he represents a spiritual method rather than a spiritual goal. He provides a model
for living a virtuous life.

Every akhara has at least one shrine dedicated to Lord Hanuman and
his worship is an important part of every wrestler's daily regimen (see
plate 11). In this chapter I will show how Hanuman serves as a model
for the construction of the wrestler's identity. This identity is based on
three basic themes: the relationship of *shakti* (energy) to *bal* (strength),

the concept of *brahmacharya*, and the nature of devotion as *bhakti*. Before looking at each of these themes it is necessary to outline briefly some points regarding the nature of Hanuman's divinity.

HANUMAN: AN OVERVIEW

It is surprising that although Hanuman is one of the most popular deities in North India there is very little written about him in the academic literature (cf. Bulcke 1960; G. Rai 1976; and Wolcott 1978 for notable but still marginal exceptions). Even in the commentaries on the Valmiki *Ramayana* and Tulasi Das's *Ramacaritamanasa* (cf. Allchin 1964) there is scant attention given to an analysis of Hanuman's epic role.

In contrast to the academic literature, which seems to be biased towards incarnate gods like Ram, Lakshmi, Krishna, Shiva, and Kali, there is a wealth of popular literature devoted to an elaboration of Hanuman's exploits. *Hanuman Charit* (Gotham 1980) tells the story of Hanuman's life and deeds in forty-one separate episodes. *Hanuman Jivan Charitra*, published under the auspices of Randhir Book Sales (n.d.), provides a similar rendition in forty episodes. Two different books with the same title, *Hanuman Upasna* (Rajesh Dixit 1978; S. Shastri 1986), combine a telling of Hanuman's life story with commentaries on selected verses from Tulasi Das's poems. These two volumes also give detailed instructions on the mechanics of Hanuman worship: an itemized list of ritual tools and ingredients, a description of when and how to sprinkle water on the image of Hanuman, how and with what to prepare prasad, what mantras to recite in what order, and how to perform *arti* (special puja with fire). *Hanuman Rahasyam* (S. M. Shastri 1982), *Hanuman Jyotish* (J. S. Shastri n.d.), *Shri Hanuman Stuthi* (P. Sharma 1985), and *Ekmukhi, Panchmukhi Hanuman Kawach* (Dehati Pustak Bhandar n.d.*d*) also provide detailed outlines for the performance of specific types of worship. In addition to these volumes, designed for use as practical handbooks for the propitiation of Hanuman, religious bookstores often publish selected verses from Tulasi Das's corpus of works. One of the largest publishers of works in Hindi, the Dehati Pustak Bhandar, annually reprints a collection of verses from the *Ramacaritamanasa, Hanumanbahuk, Hanuman Chalisa, Sankatmochan*, and *Hanuman Arti*. These are collectively entitled *Hanumanbahuk* (n.d.*a*). Dehati Pustak Bhandar also publishes two other pamphlets, *Hanumansathika* (n.d.*b*), and *Bajrang Ban* (n.d.*c*).

This literature bears witness to Hanuman's tremendous popularity. The fact that there is a considerable market for such religious "self-help" manuals is indicative of the fact that Hanuman remains a folk-deity in a modern context. He is accessible not only by virtue of his practical appeal but also because his worship is not regarded as esoteric or privileged. It is populist, available for mass consumption. The implications of this are significant. Publication of detailed manuals in Hindi effectively makes anyone who is able to read an expert religious functionary. The publication of knowledge also serves to personalize the nature of one's interaction with Hanuman. By no longer being dependent on ritual specialists with esoteric knowledge, one can appropriate for oneself the methods and means for worship. Although the public worship of Hanuman through the agency of temple priests and specialists remains a mainstay of religious life, I have found that among wrestlers, at least, there is a deeply felt private identification with Hanuman on a personal level. This is not, I might add, the kind of ecstatic identification found in various bhakti cults. As we shall see, this personal identification with Hanuman takes many forms. On a manifest level, however, it is evident in the daily routine of the wrestler's worship.

In the morning wrestlers clean Hanuman's shrine with buckets and buckets of water, sometimes scrubbing the marble floor until it shines. Old flower garlands and stubs of incense are removed and the image of Hanuman is bathed with fresh water. Vermilion and ocher paste are prepared and the whole image of Hanuman is painted so that it radiates with a red-orange brilliance. Flower garlands are placed around the image, incense is lighted, and Hanuman is clothed and made comfortable. Although occasionally specialists are called into the akhara to perform a ritual of grand proportions, such as Nag Panchami, usually wrestlers themselves do the puja. In response to my persistent questions on the role and importance of religious functionaries I was told that everyone in an akhara is qualified to perform puja. It is not regarded as a specialized skill. It is a public obligation based on private devotion.

Hanuman is generally regarded as the son of Anjana, a nymph who was cursed with a simian appearance, and Kesari, a high-ranking warrior in Sugriva's monkey army (Bulcke 1960: 394). However, in many mythic versions of Hanuman's birth, paternity is ascribed to Vayu, the wind. Vayu is accused of surreptitiously impregnating Anjana. Acknowledging his paternity, but in recompense for undermining Anjana's moral fidelity, he bestowed a boon of windlike speed and strength on Hanuman, his unborn son.

Hanuman's relationship to Vayu is significant on a symbolic level. Through association with *prana* (vital breath) vayu is regarded as the purest of all elements. It is also thought to be the root substance from which fire, water, and earth are derived. Following the *Yogashastras*, Aryan suggests that the vital energy of Brahma is manifest in the air, and that the power associated with air—omnipotence and immortality—is transferred to Hanuman through the wind's paternity (n.d.: 72). All of this, of course, relates to the general yogic principle encoded in wrestling vyayam where breath and proper breathing is regarded as an essential act of devotional exercise.

Hanuman is also regarded as the eleventh incarnation of Shiva (Bulcke 1960: 399; S. Shastri 1986: 13). According to one mythic version, Anjana was impregnated with Shiva's seed. In answer to Kesari's request for a child, Shiva took his seed (previously spilled at the sight of Vishnu in the guise of beautiful Mohini) and poured it into Anjana's ear. According to Aryan it was Vayu who impregnated Anjana through her ear (n.d.: 73). In any case, from this seed Hanuman was born (Gotham 1980: 7–8). Hanuman is commonly regarded as the incarnation of Shiva's Rudra form. Rudra is the manifestation of both creative and destructive cosmological forces and is often associated with fire (Aryan n.d.: 69). In this regard, Hanuman is often associated with the color red, and some wrestlers have told me that for this reason red is the color best suited for a wrestling langot. The earth of the pit is often referred to as "red," and there is a direct correlation between the wrestler's earth-besmeared body and the red ochre paste used to beautify images of Hanuman. Hanuman is similarly associated with fire and the color red in various mythic contexts: by trying to eat the sun, being a student of the sun, burning Lanka, and through the radiant brilliance of his own fiery body.

Two stories explain the nature of Hanuman's supernatural power:

Once when he was young, Hanuman flew into the sky to catch and eat the sun which he mistook for a piece of fruit. The sun only just managed to escape from Hanuman's grip and asked Indra the sky god for help. Indra agreed to help, and when Hanuman tried again to catch the sun Indra hit him on the chin and broke his jaw. Hanuman fell wounded to the earth. Angered by Indra, Hanuman's father Pavanadeva (or Vayu), the wind, stopped all life by making it impossible for anyone to breathe. To appease the wind, Brahma used his power to heal Hanuman, and in addition gave him a boon of immortality and divine knowledge. On account of breaking his jaw, Indra gave Hanuman his name: *Hanu* meaning chin or jaw. Indra also gave Hanuman a boon of incomparable strength. In his turn the sun bestowed on

Hanuman a boon of unsurpassed wisdom, radiant brilliance and the ability to change form at will. Yamraj gave to Hanuman a boon of perfect health. Kuber bestowed on him victory in all battles. Varuna promised that Hanuman would never suffer any harm from water. Vishvakarman gave Hanuman the boon of long life and protection against all kinds of dangerous weapons. In his turn Shiva gave Hanuman immunity from his trident. Yama bestowed on Hanuman a boon of unchanging youth (Rajesh Dixit 1978: 31).

In this way all of the gods gave to Hanuman either a portion of their power or else protection from their power. One version of the story concludes with Brahma making the following sage remarks:

Now hear this Pavanadeva, this son of yours will have the quickest and sharpest mind of all, he will be faster than anyone can imagine and he will be able to change his form at will. He will have tremendous courage and will be known by everyone. During the time of the battle between Rama and Ravana he will take on the form of Rama's true and devout *bhakta* [one who performs *bhakti*]. In this form he will satisfy the spiritual needs of his own *bhaktas* by filling their hearts with adoration" (ibid).

One of the most striking features of Hanuman's character is that he appears to be the essence of all divine power manifest in one form. He has the speed of the wind, the radiance of fire and immunity from water. As the essence of virility, he is able to bestow fertility on barren women and potency on men. He can tell the future and cure diseases. He is a master musician, a sage interpreter of the *shastra*s, and a great grammarian (Bulcke 1960: 397). He is a warrior par excellence: immortal, tireless, and strong beyond compare. He is also capable of fervent and absolute devotion. Essentially he is all-powerful and all-loving. Each of his manifold abilities is regarded in different instances as more or less important than others. It is together, however, that they constitute an aura of generalized supernatural power. This generalized aura of shakti—inclusive of bhakti and brahmacharya—is an essential component of Tulasi Das's poetry.

One important event presages Hanuman's role in the Ramayana. While growing up, Hanuman enjoyed playing in a garden near a sannyasi hermitage. He played tricks on the hermits by spilling their holy water, pulling their beards, and disturbing them while they tried to meditate and perform yoga. Frustrated, the hermits cursed Hanuman (some versions say on the instruction of his distraught father and mother) by making him forget that he possessed phenomenal strength. Only when reminded of his abilities by someone else is Hanuman able to exercise his divine mandate of strength, speed and changing form.

The majority of stories about Hanuman derive from one or another version of the Ramayana. In summary Hanuman's role is as follows. As a devout Ram-bhakta, Hanuman goes in search of Ram's princess bride, Sita, who has been abducted by Ravana, a demon king from Lanka. Hanuman finds Sita in Ravana's garden where he gives her Ram's ring as a sign of good faith. He is captured by Ravana's guards and after engaging in a lively debate with the demon king, an oil-saturated cloth is tied to his tail and lighted. Turning this torture into a weapon of destruction, Hanuman lays waste the city of Lanka by jumping from roof to roof setting every house on fire. Hanuman returns and tells Ram of the situation. Accompanied by Sugriva's army of monkeys and bears, Ram attacks Lanka. After numerous great battles in which Hanuman defeats many of Ravana's great warriors, Ram's brother Lakshman is mortally wounded. Hanuman is sent in search of a root which will cure Lakshman. Not being able to distinguish the correct root, Hanuman carries back the whole mountain on which the root is said to grow. Lakshman is cured and Ram finally kills Ravana and everyone returns to Ayodhya where Ram is crowned king. Hanuman remains at his side as servant, suppliant, and warrior.

In all stories about Hanuman, two features stand out as the most important aspects of his character: his strength, and his devotion to Ram. Although brahmacharya is not often mentioned with regard to Hanuman's epic role, it too is an integral aspect of his character, a requisite condition for both his strength and his devotion.

SHAKTI

The primary connotation of the term *shakti* is the life force that maintains the universe. Woodroffe (1929) has provided a complete analysis of the concept through a theological interpretation of scriptural references. It is not my purpose here to enter into a discussion of the theological nature of shakti and shakti worship. My concern is with the wrestlers' conception of shakti as manifest in Hanuman.

Although shakti denotes a purely metaphysical concept of divine power, it is also used to articulate more basic human experiences. Shakti can refer to the abstract aura of cosmic creation and the attendant metaphors of divine procreation reflected in the union of Shiva/Shakti. More often it is used as a generic term to refer to any form of energy or power. In her discussion of shakti in village ritual life, Wadley has made this point clearly. Anything which is regarded as capable of exerting a force over human actions is thought to have shakti. What distinguishes shakti from bal (brute force and raw strength) is that shakti transcends the merely physical nature of power (1975: 55).

Wadley uses an unfortunate analogy to illustrate the distinction between shakti and bal. She says that bal is like a wrestler's strength, whereas shakti is a divine quality (ibid: 59). While in principle the distinction holds true, in fact many wrestlers associate their strength with the latent and pervasive power of divine shakti. Wrestlers often make a distinction between their strength as shakti and the mundane bal of a manual laborer such as a rickshaw puller or construction worker. As one wrestler explained, shakti is like a latent resource upon which one can draw for strength. Bal, on the other hand, is purely active energy in the sense that it is manifest only in an actual event in which force is exerted. Trying to explain the nature of shakti, J. K. Pathak, a wrestler and one-time professor of physical education at Banaras Hindu University, used the analogy of horsepower. Shakti, he said, is the potential energy of any object. Shakti can be reflected as bal, but bal is only a fraction of the sum of an object's total potential energy. Shakti itself is made manifest on those occasions when the purely physical is transcended or when bal is so great as to have supernatural proportion.

Wrestlers often use the term *shakti* very loosely, largely because from their perspective strength is never a purely physical property. For instance, a strong wrestler is said to have great shakti. A person who eats large amounts of ghi is also said to have shakti by virtue of his abnormal capacity. Nevertheless, when the term is used explicitly and self-consciously to describe a phenomenal event, it is clear that shakti is regarded as emanating from a confluence of physical strength, devotion, self-realization, and self-control. *Shakti-shali* is used to describe the radiance of a wrestler's body, the gleam in his eye, his passive and devout disposition and also the size of his neck, arms, and thighs. A strong person who does not lead a good and moral life is not regarded as having shakti. Thugs, bullies, and gang leaders—anyone who makes a spectacle of his strength or who uses strength to advance selfish interests—is regarded as physically strong but morally weak, as having bal but not shakti. (Bal is not necessarily pejorative, merely mundane.) Conversely, one does not have to have great bal to have shakti. A relatively thin wrestler may radiate shakti by virtue of his devotion to Hanuman.

Hanuman is regarded as a manifestation of shakti (Wolcott 1978: 58), and in this regard he reflects many of the vital forces associated in other contexts with Nag. Hanuman is the essence of strength and virility.

In temples and shrines Hanuman's image is often found in association with lingams which are clearly symbols of shakti as a creative life force.

The notion of shakti associated with Shiva lingams is somewhat abstract. Lingams represent the cosmic and metaphysical nature of shakti as the agency through which the dynamic force of the universe is maintained. In response to a question on the nature of this shakti, one wrestler simply took me over to a shrine and wafted the air in my direction, asking if I could feel the energy. Beyond the overt sexual symbolism of the phallic lingam—which is itself abstracted to a high degree—there is not much in the way of tangible common sense meaning associated with it. The symbolism of the lingam does not evoke a set of meanings which are easily comprehensible in terms of everyday life.

In contrast to the metaphysical and somewhat opaque nature of the energy symbolized by lingams, Hanuman evokes a notion of concrete, manifest shakti. This is not to say that Hanuman's shakti is different in kind from that of Shiva's (for Hanuman is in fact his incarnation); Hanuman's shakti is simply more tangible on a number of levels. For instance, by virtue of his boon of wisdom, Hanuman makes comprehensible the incomprehensible knowledge of Brahma. He reflects a fraction of the sun's power, thus making what is beyond compare comparable. By being as fast as the wind he gives form to what is formless. Hanuman's power falls on a liminal plane between the supernatural and the merely human. His feats are superhuman but still natural. What this means is that Hanuman functions as a mediating symbol through which human actions can be regarded in terms of divine shakti. For the wrestler this is very important. Through Hanuman he can see the divine nature of his own strength.

Hanuman is often depicted as a strong-bodied warrior-bhakta, mace in one hand, mountain in the other. Popular calendar art shows Hanuman in graphic, technicolor detail, with a golden-red, muscled body of larger-than-life proportions striking terror into the hearts of Lanka's rank and file. Wrestlers identify with these visual representations, but more than anything else it is the popular verses from Tulasi Das's *Ramacaritamanasa* which evoke the meaning of shakti.

One morning at Akhara Bara Ganesh I was introduced to a young man who performed the duties of temple priest by offering prayers and prasad and bathing and clothing Lord Hanuman. A few of the members sitting with me under the pipal tree next to the well called the priest over and asked him to sing a few verses for them. One man explained that the young priest had one of the best voices in the area and could sing praises to Lord Hanuman like no one else. The priest obliged with a rendition of some verses from the *Ramacaritamanasa*. As he sang the wrestlers reclined on the cement dais around the pipal, and, massaging one another and rubbing off the akhara earth from their bodies, receded into the revery of a vision invoked by the priest's vibrato voice. Every time the priest stopped, pleading voices asked for more, until he was finally able to make his escape. Still singing softly, now to himself, he went over to where a small gada lay and started swinging it steadily, allowing each pendulum swing to punctuate the meter of his verse until the exertion took its toll and the hymn faded into the exercise and strength that it recalled in deeds glorified by visionary poetics:

> Says Tulasi, in the sky with that
>   great tail extended shone he,
> Seeing him the warriors gibbered,
>   he was as terrible as Death,
> As a treasury of Brightness,
>   as a thousand fiery suns,
> His claws were terrifying,
>   his face all red with anger.
> (The Beautiful 5.4, Allchin 1964: 94).

> Thereupon, Hanuman became as huge as a mountain, with a body of golden hue and splendid majesty like that of a second mountain king. Roaring like a lion again and again, he cried, "I shall leap across the salt ocean; it is child's play to me! When I have slain Ravana and all his allies, I shall come back here with Mount Trikuta uprooted" (Kishkindha 4. 29, in Wolcott 1978: 658).

For the wrestler listening to these and countless other verses, Hanuman's shakti is both fabulous and yet fundamentally comprehensible in terms of everyday notions of strength, courage and bravery. As Hanuman uproots a mountain, so a wrestler lifts up his opponent. As Hanuman's body radiates with a sun like glow, so the wrestler imagines his own body to be a lustrous icon of strength. As Hanuman battles with the demon-generals of Ravana's army, so the wrestler pits himself against his opponents.

A wrestler can never hope to become as strong or courageous as Hanuman. Nevertheless, through him the terms of strength and courage are made manifest in graphic detail. Hanuman represents the translation of abstract supernatural power—the cosmic notion of shakti—into more accessible but no less dramatic terms. Hanuman's strength, while it may appear to be purely physical, is, in essence, the direct result of devotion and self-control.

BHAKTI

Like shakti, bhakti has a general meaning from which the wrestlers derive specific significance for their everyday lives. Broadly defined, bhakti is a form of spiritual devotion which entails a mystical or ecstatic experience of divine love. It is a dominant theme in Tulasi Das's *Ramacaritamanasa* (Babineau 1979: 133–192; R. K. Tripathi 1977: 125–140). Since bhakti is a highly individualized form of adoration which involves a mystical and ineffable union with god, it is difficult to say what the experience of bhakti means to the enraptured devotee. In general, however, ultimate bhakti, like the experience of mystical bliss, is total absorption into the godhead; an experience of total release and total dependence on divine grace. A *bhakta* takes great pleasure in singing the praises of god. Tulasi Das enumerates nine frames of reference for the bhakta: 1) fraternity with sannyasis; 2) concentration on the *lila* (play) of the god; 3) service to the guru; 4) singing god's praises; 5) reciting the name of god; 6) self-control and abnegation; 7) seeing the world as part of god, god in the world, and honoring the saint as greater even than god; 8) contentment with one's lot; and 9) complete, blissful but emotionless surrender to god (R. K. Tripathi 1977: 133).

What is most significant about bhakti is that it articulates a spiritual attitude which goes beyond mere supplication and ritual to define a whole religious personality. One is never just occasionally a bhakta: bhakti is a way of life. In the *Ramacaritamanasa*, Lakshman, Bharat, Vibhishan, and Sita are all said to have devotional love for Ram. However, it is Hanuman who most deeply personifies a pervasive attitude of pure bhakti (Raghaveshananda 1980; Sridattasarma 1966).

As Wolcott has pointed out, Hanuman's shakti derives directly from his adoration of Lord Ram (1978: 660). In the Tulasi *Ramayana*, Hanuman attributes everything—his jump to Lanka, his skill as a wrestler-warrior, and his wisdom—to Ram. On their first meeting in the Kishkindha forest, Hanuman falls at the feet of Ram and vows his undying devotion. Throughout the *Ramacaritamanasa* Hanuman is described as "thinking on Ram" or "keeping the image of Ram in his mind's eye" before embarking on any task. Perhaps the most telling depiction of Hanuman's bhakti is the following well-known story from the Ramayana: Sita gives Hanuman a garland which she had been given previously by Ram. Examining the gift, Hanuman finds that Ram's name is not inscribed on the garland. He proceeds to tear the garland apart and eat it. When asked why he did this he explains that nothing is of use to him unless inscribed with the name of Ram. Asked why he does not then abandon his body, Hanuman tears open his chest to reveal Ram and Sita seated in his heart.

In another scene from the Ramayana, as interpreted by Rajesh Dixit (1978: 81), Hanuman falls at Ram's feet after returning from his sojourn to Lanka. Wanting to embrace Hanuman, Ram tells him to get off his feet. But Hanuman refuses saying that he would not risk the pride that such an act would foster in his heart. He would rather remain a humble suppliant at the feet of his Lord.

For the wrestler, the lesson of Hanuman's bhakti towards Ram is very clear. Just as Hanuman is helpless without the shakti he derives from his love for Ram, so the wrestler is powerless without a similar commitment of devotion to Hanuman. Hanuman's relationship to Ram provides a model for the wrestler's general attitude of adoration towards Hanuman.

For many people Hanuman provides a conduit through which they may experience Ram's love. For the wrestler, however, Hanuman is himself the primary object of devotion and prayer. Although there are wrestlers for whom Hanuman worship is the express focus of single aspects of their lives—singing hymns, performing puja every morning, fasting on Saturdays—for the vast majority of wrestlers, bhakti is adopted as an integral but unselfconscious aspect of everyday life. It is neither restricted by time or place, nor limited to event or institution. What this means may be explained as taking on a devotional attitude towards the routine of life: a mundane, bhakti personality. The wrestler seeks to live his life as though every thought is of Hanuman and every breath a devotional prayer. However, he must do this as he goes about his daily routine: walking to work, working, exercising, resting, and eating. As previously indicated, wrestlers must keep the image of Hanuman fixed in their mind's eye when they exercise. As one wrestler explained, this gives one "peace of mind." Thinking of Hanuman, there is almost nothing that a wrestler cannot do. But should he not hold the image of Hanuman in his heart, exercise and training will be of no use. The same principle holds true for other aspects of life.

A wrestler who owns a business must conduct his affairs in a way which is in keeping with a general attitude of bhakti. For example one wrestler who owns a pan stall has transformed his shop into a quasi-shrine by painting it a holy ochre tint and filling it with pictures of Hanuman, Shiva, and other gods. More importantly, he sings hymns as he conducts his business. Other wrestlers do not affect a formal religious attitude to this extent but they do point out that as they go about delivering milk, selling coal, or trading buffalos they try to keep their heart and mind focused on Hanuman.

Bhakti entails contemplation of Hanuman's character, and Hanuman's character is revealed through his deeds as described in the *Ramacaritamanasa*. Just as Hanuman's superhuman strength provides a model for the wrestler's physical aspirations, Hanuman's bhakti provides a model for contemplation. To "think on Hanuman"—as wrestlers are want to say—is to think of the power of his love for Ram. While ecstatic bhakti entails the fervent singing of hymns, the bhakti of the wrestler's everyday life revolves around the recitation of memorized verses from the *Ramacaritamanasa* or the popular *Hanuman Chalisa*. It is common to hear wrestlers and other bhaktas reciting poetic stanzas under their breath as they sit in their shops or go about their business. The recitation of poetic stanzas not only articulates the bhakta's devotion, the verses themselves often underscore the nature of Hanuman's bhakti:

> Enraptured in Lord's deeds fore e'er thou art,
> Dwelling in Ram, Lakshman and Sita's heart.
>
> All that on earth one finds hard to do,
> Simple becomes when one is blessed with you.
>
> All suffering and all anguish of deep pain,
> End when one dwells on mighty Hanuman's name.
>
> Distress shall end, all anguish cease as well,
> When on mighty Hanuman your mind will dwell.
>
> (Verses 8, 20, 25, 36 from Tulasi Das's *Hanuman Chalisa*, S. P. Bahadur 1980: 165–168).

Hanuman's bhakti not only provides a model for the wrestler's general attitude towards his everyday life, it also provides a model for his relationship to his guru. As pointed out previously, the guru-chela relationship is paramount in the akhara. A wrestler must surrender himself to the service of his guru. Service of this sort—rubbing his feet, washing his clothes, running his errands—is not intended as an obligation but as an act of devotion. There are many stories of Hanuman's exploits which illustrate his bhakti-service to Lord Ram. One in particular will serve as an example.

Hanuman's service to Ram was so complete that Lakshman, Sita, Shatrugan, and Bharat found themselves unable to do anything for their

Lord. They were unable to show their devotion. They decided that to be fair everyone would be assigned a particular duty through which they could serve Ram. As the duties were divided up, Hanuman was left off the roster. Sita asked him how he felt about this and Hanuman said, "It is service enough that I should sing the praises of Ram whenever my Lord yawns." Everyone agreed to this. Because no one could tell when Ram would yawn, Hanuman had to stay with him at all times, a situation which pleased Hanuman to no end. The others were disgruntled since Hanuman was in the enviable position of not only being with Ram at all times but right in front of him, looking into his face to be sure that no yawn went unnoticed. Lakshman, Bharat, and the others told Hanuman that this would not do. Rather than protest, however, Hanuman went and sat in a corner of the palace and started endlessly singing Ram's praises. When asked what he was doing, he explained that since he no longer knew when Ram would yawn he simply had to sing Ram's praises all the time in order to perform his duty. Seeing Hanuman singing with such devotion, Ram was moved to tears and could not ask his bhakta to stop. When Lakshman and the others asked Hanuman to desist, he replied saying that he would comply only if no restrictions were put on his service to the Lord. The others had no option but to agree to this bhakti blackmail.

Like Hanuman and his compatriots, wrestlers compete for the honor of being of greatest service to their guru. A wonderful story is told about how, as a young disciple, Guru Ram Singh served his own guru. One day Ram Singh's guru needed some special dal and asked his ward to go and fetch half a kilogram from the market. Ram Singh dashed off and searched every store in the market but was not able to find the required item. He was told that such dal was only found in Calcutta. Off went Ram Singh to the train station and bought a ticket to the city. He returned three days later, half a kilogram of dal in hand, and went immediately to his guru's house. His guru, not a little perturbed, asked what had taken so long, and Ram Singh explained. Rather than being rebuked for his impertinence at having wasted time and money for such an insignificant amount of dal, Ram Singh was praised by his guru for having provided such selfless service.

Although service manifests itself in practical ways, it is also reflected in less tangible form through living a moral and righteous life, coming early to the akhara, and hanging on one's guru's every word.

Since the persona of the guru is divine, service to one's guru is indeed an act of supplication, a religious duty. Just as the wrestler is enjoined to keep the image of Hanuman in mind, so must he think upon his guru. One wrestler went so far as to say, "As we worship Hanuman, so we worship the guru. It is the same thing." This is, in fact, understandable, since Hanuman is not only the wrestler's *ishta devta* (primary deity) but also his *sat guru* (true or great guru). From the suppliant's perspective, the distinction between guru and deity is simply a matter of degree. In every instance that puja was done in front of the Hanuman shrine at Akhara Ram Singh, a framed portrait of the founding guru was brought out and placed next Hanuman's image. The two figures comprise an indivisible pair.

In general, Hanuman's devotion to Ram provides a clear and pragmatic model for the incorporation of bhakti into everyday life. Hanuman embodies many of the devotional virtues to which wrestlers subscribe.

BRAHMACHARYA

From the wrestler's perspective, Hanuman's most important character trait is his brahmacharya, his complete celibacy and self control. As one wrestler said: "Hanuman is the form of brahmacharya. If wrestlers are brahmacharis then they will do well. This is why Hanuman is manifest in the akhara." In one way or another every wrestler I asked about his devotion to Hanuman explained his reverence in terms of Hanuman's brahmacharya. Self-control is an arduous task, and wrestlers look to Hanuman for both guidance in how to remain celibate and also for a general validation of the virtue of brahmacharya.

While the attributes of shakti and bhakti define the largest part of Hanuman's character, his brahmacharya is taken for granted. It is only occasionally mentioned in myth and folklore. In one story (Bulcke 1960: 400; O'Flaherty 1984: 95, 96) Hanuman is approached by a demigod named Matsyaraja, otherwise known as Matsyagarbha, who claims to be his son. Hanuman protests, saying that this is impossible given that he is celibate. Matsyaraja's birth is explained, however, by the fact that drops of Hanuman's sweat were swallowed by a fish while Hanuman was bathing in the ocean. The sweat impregnated the fish and Matsyaraja was born. The only other overt mythic reference to Hanuman's chastity is found in the *Ramayana*. While in search of Sita, Hanuman finds himself in Ravana's queen's dressing chamber. The power of his brahmacharya is so great, however, that he is not distracted by desire (Bulcke 1960: 401).

Stories of Hanuman's conception and birth are also evidence of his celibate character. Many versions say that Anjana was impregnated through one ear and that Hanuman was born through the other. He is thus said to have had no direct contact with sex as such (cf. Wolcott 1978: note 661; Aryan n.d.: note 73).

To some extent these explicit statements of Hanuman's self-control are beside the point. For the wrestler there is no question but that both Hanuman's shakti and his bhakti derive directly from brahmacharya. Every reference to his strong body and incomparable devotion is a tribute to his absolute celibacy. The reverse logic applies as well. Shakti and bhakti enable Hanuman to be a perfect brahmachari. One wrestler made the following observation: "Unless one is always a brahmachari—which is to say always have a 'tight langot'—one will never do well. Only then can one be strong. In order to remain a brahmachari one must be a bhakta. If a person is not a bhakta then one's mind will wander from the goal of brahmacharya."

Shakti, bhakti, and brahmacharya constitute a powerful tautological conundrum: a spiral of ever-increasing virtue and strength based on moral control and devotion. Hanuman represents the confluence of these forces. His exploits demonstrate the veracity of their interrelationship.

Brahmacharya is taken for granted as the underlying basis for much of what Hanuman does. But while shakti and bhakti are given a concrete form in Hanuman, the concept of brahmacharya remains somewhat abstract. It is alluded to through the sexual symbolism of virility manifest in the color red and in the phallic mace which Hanuman carries, but aside from these specific signs, brahmacharya is not explicitly coded in temple images, popular art, or mythic poetics.

The rules for the practice of brahmacharya, discussed previously in the context of body discipline, complement and often underscore the devotional prescriptions for bhakti. A theme which emerges consistently in any consideration of brahmacharya, is the need to keep one's mind focused on pure and moral virtues. To sing the praises of god and to "think on god" are the best ways to insure that one does not dwell on sensual, worldly gratification. The complementary natures of bhakti and brahmacharya are clearly manifest in Hanuman. Insofar as Hanuman is completely absorbed in the contemplation of Ram, the world of sensory satisfaction pales in comparison to the invigorating bliss of service and devotion.

CHAPTER 9

The Sannyasi and the Wrestler

A recurrent theme in the preceding chapters is that of world renunciation as a moral value subscribed to by wrestlers. We have seen that wrestlers turn their backs on worldly pleasure and sensory satisfaction. There are many formal parallels between the life of a wrestler and the life of a world-renouncing sannyasi. Both are concerned with a disciplinary regimentation of the body, although in different ways; both seek a goal of self-realization, although for slightly different reasons; and both avoid many of the trappings of a social life, although, again, to different degrees and with different implications. In any case, wrestlers make an explicit comparison between their chosen life path and the life path of world renunciation. In this chapter I will explore the nature of this comparison.

The formal aspects of a wrestler's way of life have been outlined above. Therefore, I will begin with a general theoretical discussion of world renunciation so as to define the framework within which a comparison of the wrestler and the sannyasi becomes significant. In the second part of the chapter the implications of the comparison will be discussed with regard to larger questions of identity.

Wrestlers see sannyas in objective terms as a generic category with certain distinguishing characteristic traits (cf. Farquhar 1918; Ghurye 1953; Oman 1983). This is a crucial point for the argument which follows. The sannyasi of which the wrestler speaks is a figment of his ideological imagination. He is not a particular sannyasi—a Shaiva Aghori or a Vaishnava Tyagi—but an amalgam constructed to fit, analogically, with the wrestler's conception of his own somatic identity and iconic notion of self.

The thesis of this chapter is that wrestlers co-opt the values inherent in a life of asocial world renunciation and transpose these values onto their unique life path. This transposition has important implications. The sannyasi is, unlike the worldly *grihastha* (householder), an individual-outside-the-world whose orientation is egalitarian in a devotional and disciplined sense rather than hierarchical, an orientation, as we will see, towards principles of nationalism rather than principles of caste.

SANNYASI

In a well-known article Dumont (1960) argues that Hinduism, among other Indian religions, is best understood not in terms of its historical diversity and seemingly infinite permutations, but rather in terms of some basic relational categories. The categories Dumont offers are, on the one hand, the asocial world-renouncing sannyasi whose religion is based on individuality, and, on the other hand, the eminently worldly grihastha whose religion is based on sociomoral duty. Dumont argues that Hinduism emerges, as it were, through the dialogue between these two categories. The opposition is never resolved, but the dialectical tension creates situations in which the values inherent in one category are accommodated in the other. Beneath the partly "substantialized" form of popular religious movements and sects, Dumont argues, one can recognize the dynamic tension between the opposed categories (ibid: 61).

Dumont's argument has been acclaimed and criticized many times on many different levels, and my purpose is not to revive this old—and some might say tired—debate once again. Nevertheless, one point which Dumont makes must be emphasized if we are to understand the nature of the wrestler/sannyasi comparison. Although the dialogue between the sannyasi and the man-in-the-world persists as a leitmotif in Hindu development, Dumont is adamant that in terms of worldly Hinduism there is no such thing as the individual (ibid: 42). When recognized and understood as a conceptual and practical reality, individuality is strictly the province of otherworldly asceticism. To appreciate Dumont's point, it must be remembered that for him the bottom line is always relational rather than substantive or empirical. In this regard he writes: "The man-in-the-world's adoption of notions which are essentially

those of the renouncer should not conceal from use the difference between the two conditions and the two kinds of thought" (ibid: 46).

The terms of world renunciation cannot be reconciled to the terms
of caste society. The Brahman may affect the values of world renunciation, but his life of dharma is always couched in terms of the structuring
principles of hierarchy, rather than in accordance with egalitarian principles. According to Dumont's scheme, any instance where there appears
to be a reconciliation of these two domains in social life is a substantialis-
tic illusion: a superstructure of empirical form beneath which lies the
truth of a primary oppositional relationship.

The problem with Dumont's thesis, in my view, is that it defines caste,
on its most basic and inclusive, holistic level, as a closed system, one able
to subsume innovations, anomalies, rebellions, religious conversion, and
so forth within the terms of its primary relational categories. Dumont's
scheme, like the structural typologies of Lévi-Strauss, is so inclusive as
to be reductionist when applied to the narrower scope of everyday life.
Dumont's framework allows one to understand sectarian movements—bhakti, Tantrism, Buddhism, and so forth—in terms of caste
holism. He does not, however, provide a corollary scheme for making
sense of these various movements in their own terms.

While one may agree with Dumont and recognize the primacy of
purity and pollution as the basic terms of caste society, one must also
accept the fact that these are not the only terms in which social order is
conceptualized (cf. Carman and Marglin 1985; Daniel 1984; Madan
1987; Marriott and Inden 1977; also see Appadurai 1986 and Berreman
1979 for a generalized critique of Dumont in this regard). Other categories which structure significant thought and action cannot, or need not,
be conveniently reduced to Dumont's first principles. However, as Das
reminds us, though hierarchy is not an exhaustive conceptual framework for social order (1977: 51), it nevertheless defines the matrix of
social power.

This said, we may now return to the issue of the sannyasi. In a recent
book, Khare (1984) has taken a line of thinking similar to Das's but with
important modifications. Khare shows how low-caste Chamars in the
Lucknow region of Uttar Pradesh have "repossessed" the basic terms of
world renunciation in order to reconstruct an image of themselves outside of the framework of caste relations (ibid: 30). They have done this
through a radical reinterpretation of the terms of world renunciation,
and by forcing the sannyasi into a socially significant role (ibid: 67). The
Chamars have essentially constructed an ideology wherein the individu-

ality of the sannyasi—his spiritual, asocial virtue—is conceptually linked to a modern understanding of this-worldly asceticism. Where the Brahman mediates between world renunciation and householder status within a framework of caste hierarchy, the Chamars co-opt the terms of world renunciation in order to step outside of the hierarchical scheme altogether (cf. Juergensmeyer 1982 for a similar, though less explicit account, and Uberoi 1967 for an early theoretical formulation of this point in the context of Sikhism).

Khare clearly shows how certain groups have worked towards a redefinition of their identity in terms other than caste. In reading Khare's account of a burgeoning Chamar ideology, however, one is struck by the fact that it is, to an extent, an ideology built on sand. However much it may mean to the Chamars, it is not particularly persuasive as a general, nonsectarian appeal to which other groups might subscribe. Similarly, Sikhs as well as Christians and other sectarian groups (including, significantly, even ascetic monastic communities; cf. Ghurye 1953) are conscripted into a hierarchical scheme despite advocacy to the contrary. The basic problem is that any group which claims a new place for itself—as within the framework of "sanskritization" (Srinivas 1968)—or even a group which tries to step outside of the whole scheme must ultimately come to terms with its relation to other groups within a larger hierarchically structured society. When couched in terms of group identity, ideological change is doomed because its appeal is artificially circumscribed. The Chamars can construct visions of themselves as morally guided worldly ascetics, but unless these reformations are recognized by people other than Chamars, their significance is limited—limited, that is, if one is trying to understand the precise interface between Hindu ideology and other nascent ideologies.

It is at this point that wrestling becomes an important issue. Like the Chamar ideology described by Khare, the wrestling ideology reconceptualizes the relationship of the sannyasi to the world. However, the ideology of the wrestler differs from that of the Chamar in two important ways. First, the wrestling ideology is not an explicit criticism of caste status. Wrestling calls for a redefinition of sannyas in its own terms, and this has a significant impact on the understanding of caste as a conceptual framework. Wrestlers do not, however, attack caste directly: for them, caste, as a structure of signification, simply does not work as a framework for self-definition. It is inadequate and inappropriate.

Second, wrestling is an ideology that transcends caste-group affiliation. Its appeal, as I have argued, is general rather than specific; it is public, and many wrestling activities create a sense of emotional, psychological, and physical unity. Because the wrestling ideology is amorphous—to the extent that it is subscribed to by a broad spectrum of people of all castes, of many occupational backgrounds, and from different regions—it does not find expression in any institutionalized, sectarian form. Even in the akhara, where there is a strong sense of communitas based on somatic ideals, there is little sense of social solidarity. The ideology cuts through social boundaries and appeals to the individual on reconstituted somatic terms. What distinguishes the wrestler's appropriation of the terms of world renunciation from that of the Chamars and other sectarian groups is that the wrestler draws a parallel between his nascent individuality and the sannyasi's spiritual individuality. Chamars, on the other hand, seek to transpose the category of sannyas, through advocacy, onto the level of an institutionalized social group. As Dumont and others have rightly argued, on this level sectarian movements will be subsumed within the larger and more primary framework of caste.

I do not want to suggest that the wrestling ideology is a particularly powerful critique of the caste ideology. At best it is rather oblique. Unlike the partisan rhetoric of certain sectarian ideologies, however, the wrestling ideology cannot be reduced to caste terms. Because its appeal is broad, if weak through such extensive dilution, it is strong at precisely the point at which the Chamar and other sectarian ideologies are not. One primary reason for this is that the wrestler's ideology, as I have argued, is the product of a precise mechanics of body discipline. It is not an intellectual critique, at least in the first instance, and thus it does not fall into the trap of juxtaposing a discipline of the individual body/mind on the one hand to society on the other. Wrestling draws the moral value of world renunciation into the world and calls for a reform of the individual in terms of a holistic somatic synthesis. Individuality then finds expression, as we shall see in the next chapter, when it is made the object of nationalistic reform.

THE SANNYASI AND THE WRESTLER

The lives of the wrestler and the sannyasi overlap and are comparable at a number of different points. Many of these have been alluded to in previous chapters and need only be highlighted here. On a general level both wrestling and sannyas are chosen ways of life. Although sannyas is technically the final stage of the ideal Hindu life cycle, it is an elective path. Moreover, one can choose to become a sannyasi at any age or station in life (Ghurye 1953: 78). On a formal level wrestlers recognize that by joining an akhara they are making a decision which is similar to the choice a sannyasi makes when affiliating himself with a monastic order. The comparison works on a self-consciousness level rather than in terms of institutional structure. Wrestlers think of themselves as like sannyasis insofar as they share a certain mindset: a similar attitude toward the world, their consciousness, and their bodies.

Wrestlers and sannyasis are both concerned with controlling their bodies. This is not to say that they control their bodies in the same ways. For their part wrestlers regard vyayam as very much like yoga; like sannyasis, they must practice self-control in order to harness their physical energy to a higher spiritual purpose of healthy self-realization, and their diet must be regulated in order to achieve certain physical-cum-spiritual goals. The general principle of nonsensuality and a trenchant disregard for worldly pursuits link the two life paths together.

Some specific, gross features also connect the two life paths. Both wrestlers and sannyasis are known for their loincloths and near-nakedness. While sannyasis cover themselves in ashes, wrestlers cover themselves in earth. The substances are different, but they are both termed *vibhuti* (power).

Wrestlers wear their hair cropped short and sometimes have it shaved off altogether. Similarly, sannyasis either have their heads shaved or else let their hair grow long and matted. Obeyesekere has noted that hair is a complex, polysemic symbol of sexual power in the context of the ascetic's religious experience (1981). Given the wrestlers' concern with sexuality and strength, it would be safe to say that they, like the ascetic, work out some of the implications of their identity through the medium of hair. Shaved or not, the wrestler and the sannyasi are distinguishable from other men in these terms.

Sannyasis are, of course, easily distinguishable from wrestlers in a number of ways. Most significantly they do not, as a rule, wrestle. They devote their lives to wandering, begging, and pilgrimage. They eat only what is offered to them and are not supposed to own anything but a staff, a begging bowl, *rudraksha* beads, and an ocher robe (Ghurye 1953: 106). They must not fill their stomachs with food even when it is available. Except in the monsoon they must not stay in any place for more than two nights.

The issue of food is an interesting one. On the one hand, sannyasis are known for fasting and generally placing no value on the quality of food they eat. Wrestlers, on the other hand, are extraordinary eaters of very specific types of food. While this would tend to force the wrestler and the sannyasi into opposed categories, such is not the case. Sannyasis, like wrestlers, try to "cool their bodies down," so to speak, and thereby achieve a state of sattva harmony and peace. Gandhi's political dietetics was a permutation of this ascetic ideal. Both wrestlers and sannyasis are said to be supervirile; sannyasis on account of their powers of yogic meditation, and wrestlers on account of their vyayam/dietetics regimen. Therefore, they must both take extra care in channeling this energy away from passion. Where wrestlers eat ghi and milk, sannyasis tend to fast and to eat fruit and other things that are sattva.

As important as the nature of the foods eaten, is that both the sannyasi and the wrestler are supported through public donation. In direct and conscious opposition to the principles of caste purity, a sannyasi must eat only leftover food. By eating food that is "polluted" a sannyasi removes himself from the hierarchical scheme of interdependence. By accepting—in theory if not in fact—food from anyone, the sannyasi steps outside the confines of ritual food transactions which structure formal social obligations, rank status, and personal purity.

Unlike a sannyasi, a wrestler does not accept food from just anyone. A wrestler depends either on his family or a wealthy patron for support. In this regard, however, a wrestler's relationship to his family is very different from that of a typical, non-wrestling family member. Ideally a wrestler should not have to work. He is supported through the industry of his parents and siblings. Although this ideal is rarely, if ever, achieved, I was told by many wrestlers that in the best possible world—the utopia of which we will speak in the next chapter—a wrestler would be able totally to devote himself to a life in the akhara. Stories are told of great wrestlers of the past who at least approximated this ideal. In some instances, I was told, family property was sold to insure that the wrestler's diet would not be curtailed. I was also told that in the past whole villages would pool their resources to feed "their" wrestler a rich and costly diet. In this capacity the village and the family functioned much as a benevolent patron. The wrestler would be supported in much the same way as an itinerant sannyasi whose quest for self-realization is deemed worthy of generous support, the difference being that the wrestler maintains a high degree of identification with his patron, be that patron a raja, village community, or family group.

On the level of structural relations, the sannyasi and the wrestler share a common point of reference. They are both set off from the world in terms of the nature of the food they eat and by the fact that they are not directly responsible for producing—as distinct from processing—what they consume. The wrestler's dependence on his family or patron does not remove him from the world to the same degree as the sannyasi. Nevertheless, his liminal condition with regard to food serves to bracket him off from the world where reciprocal food transaction structures social relations on so many different levels (cf. Appadurai 1981).

In contemporary popular literature, folklore, and nineteenth and early twentieth-century orientalist works on the subject, sannyasis are depicted as performers of extreme austerities. The best known of these is, undoubtedly, the infamous bed of nails. Oman (1983), writing in the late nineteenth century, recounts many cases of self-inflicted pain: sitting in cold water all night; sticking skewers through tongue and cheek; extended fasting; self-flagellation; and the self-imposed atrophy of various appendages. Wrestlers do not practice such austerities. Nor, in fact, do many sannyasis. They do not usually make a spectacle of their mortification. Nevertheless, the image of the sannyasi enduring great pain and suffering to the end of self-realization is a popular image which rings true in the mind/body of the wrestler. As seen in chapter 5, the body of the wrestler is disciplined in an analogous manner.

Wrestlers often speak of shakti as a direct derivative of disciplined austerity. For example, I was told how one ascetic protested the building of a bridge across the sacred Varuna River. British engineers had proposed a construction plan but the ascetic said that Hanuman would not permit the plan to be implemented. The British civil engineer scoffed at this and asked the ascetic to demonstrate to him by what means Hanuman had this kind of power over imperial authority. The ascetic said that by himself embodying Hanuman's power he could jump across the river at the proposed bridge site. The civil engineer said that if indeed such an event occurred, he would not build the bridge. So the ascetic began his preparations and fasted and meditated for a number of months. As the story goes, his austerities were of such absolute proportions that he assimilated Hanuman's power into his own body and successfully jumped across the river. While this is but one abbreviated version of a popular tale in Banaras folk history, it illustrates the power of the ascetic's austerity, and implicitly correlates it with physical prowess in general and Hanuman's character in particular. As pointed out previously, the wrestler is said to "wear a necklace of pain" in order to achieve his goal of somatic self-perfection. Thus, the wrestler and the sannyasi both tap into the power of shakti by slightly different but equally rigorous means.

Sannyasis are generally regarded as gaunt figures whose emaciation is strikingly contrasted to the full-figured wealth of worldly Brahmans and merchants (Dumont 1960: 45). One would think that the sannyasi's body stands diametrically opposed to that of the wrestlers. As Staal has correctly observed, however, it is wrong to assume that the yogic practices of sannyas are forms of "ascetic mortification" (1983–1984: 35). Yoga is, in fact, a form of physical control aimed towards perfection and harmony rather than towards atonement or penance. Thus, as indicated earlier, wrestling is an extension of yogic philosophy even though the strength of the wrestler's bulky body appears to indicate a radically different notion of health. This fundamental commonality aside, it is important to note that there are subtle differences between wrestling and sannyas as concerns development and control of the body.

The sannyasi's orientation toward his body is transcendental. His goal is to achieve a state of mind which effectively takes him outside of his physical form. This is not a mystical trick of recognizing the inherent illusionary nature of the physical body. It is, as alluded to by Staal (ibid), a matter of coming to terms with the symbiosis of the mind/body as a unitary, multilayered principle. The sannyasi who has reached the final goal of self-realization achieves a physical state of *samadhi*. In this state his body appears lifeless but is not dead, a perfect state of transcendental consciousness.

In many temple complexes, shrines are erected around the samadhi of an ascetic. In some akharas I have seen shrines said to be the samadhis of great wrestlers. These wrestlers practiced austerities to the point of self-realization. It is not clear whether these samadhis are sannyasis who happened to be wrestlers, wrestlers who became sannyasis, or sannyasis who patronized wrestling in some way or another. The word used to define the sannyasi's austerities, *tapas* or *tap*, is also used to describe the means by which the wrestlers achieved samadhi, a situation in which it seems that two related forms of body discipline actually meet. The line between sannyasi and wrestler becomes blurred at this and other points of comparison. In the mind of a wrestler it is perfectly logical for a great wrestler to have also achieved the status of a great ascetic.

While the wrestler identifies with many of the formal attributes of sannyas, his attitude toward his body is manifest rather than transcendental. By manifest I do not mean that the wrestler regards his body as any more "real" than does the sannyasi. The wrestler, however, sees that his body is but part of a larger ethical scheme of social relations and moral responsibility. A sannyasi trains his body so as to leave the world; the wrestler trains his body to be immune to worldly things but to remain in the world. The sannyasi moves away from the world, discarding the trappings of social life; the wrestler moves through the world cloaking himself in a mantle of ascetic values. In this regard the wrestler's strength stands for many of the same things as the sannyasi's austerity. However, the wrestler's disciplinary practices—exercise, diet, self-control—are structured in manifest, social terms rather than in terms of transcendental abnegation. In defining the meaning of the ascetic practices, the referent for sannyas is *moksha*, a spiritual recognition of social life and material existence as inherently illusionary. The moral referent for the wrestler's self-discipline is an ideal of collective strength and virtue. As we shall see in the next chapter, the "illusionary" nature of the material world is confronted in terms of its decadence and depravity, but it is not discarded out of hand. In a sense, then, ascetic abnegation defines the parameters of a wrestler's moral physique. It is by virtue of the fact that the practice of sannyas has such profound spiritual, otherworldly significance that the practice of wrestling is meaningful as an ethical ideology with worldly implications. The agency through which one point of reference is translated into another is body discipline.

AKHARAS AND AKHARAS

Putting the body momentarily aside, there is also an institutional level on which wrestlers are like sannyasis: the akhara. In its broadest sense *akhara* means the social and spatial organization of any specialized group. From this general definition derive two primary commonsense denotations of the term: one is, of course, the akhara as a wrestling gymnasium; the other, the akhara as an ascetic monastery.

In its monastic sense the term *akhara* is used most often to define a subgrouping of the *Naga sannyasi* ascetic order. The Nagas are themselves a subgroup of the larger *Dasnami* order which traces its origin to Shankaracharya in the eighth or ninth century A.D. (Ghurye 1953: 6). For a sannyasi, the akhara he belongs to, rather than the larger order of which that akhara is a branch, is his primary point of reference for self-definition.

Unlike the stereotypical image of the passive, mystical sannyasi, the Dasnami Nagas were and to some extent still are known for their military exploits. Their akharas became centers for training in martial arts and weaponry. Ghurye goes so far as to translate akhara to mean "military regiment," because the Dasnami Nagas were involved in various military campaigns at different times (1953: 116; cf. also Farquhar 1925; J. Ghose 1930; Lorenzen 1978).

During the time of Akbar and through the reign of Aurangzeb, Dasnami Naga membership restrictions were relaxed in order to allow low-caste Shudras to join the order. Many Shudras were actively recruited since the Dasnami Nagas needed to increase their numbers in order to defend Hindu shrines and monastic institutions from Muslim intervention and aggression (cf. Ghurye 1953: 110–127; Orr 1940; Prasad 1982; J. Sarkar 1950). Shudras were thought to be robust and thus well suited to take up arms in defense of Hinduism. By allowing Shudras to join with Brahmans, Kshatriyas, and Vaishyas, the sheer numerical strength of the order was significantly increased.

Aside from the intercaste dynamics of the Naga order, what concerns us here is the explicit and effective incorporation of martial practices into an ascetic way of life. Naga combat was not a simple matter of sannyasis taking up arms to defend themselves. For the Nagas, fighting became an integral feature of their identity. Ghurye notes that Nagas practiced physical penance so as to make themselves physically fit and immune to pain (1953: 122). It is clear that these austerities were not purely martial—in the sense of being practiced strictly for offensive warfare—but were, in fact, methods for achieving salvation (cf. van der Veer 1989). Ghurye remarks that since many of the Nagas were Shudras, rigorous physical training, rather than spiritual contemplation, was thought to be a more appropriate form of ascetic discipline. This interpretation is suspect on the grounds that it makes a sharp and untenable distinction between physical and mental austerities. Moreover, as Chattopadhyay has pointed out, the evidence of history is that there has always been a degree of ambiguity with regard to any one caste group's monopoly on martial training. In the medieval period it was quite common for Brahmans to receive martial training at such centers as the University of Taksasila (Chattopadhyay 1966: 54). In any case, it is not accurate to say that one caste group is exclusively predisposed to physical training while another is more suited to mystical contemplation and scholarly work. Whatever factor Shudra recruitment may have played, it seems clear that Naga sannyasis, like wrestlers, translated yogic spirituality into terms more compatible with worldly action. Ghurye notes that in the post-independence era Naga sannyasis further translated their martial art into less aggressive terms. They now practice wrestling, gymnastics, and other forms of physical exercise (1953: 127).

Many of the Naga akharas have branch institutions in Banaras, and at least one of these sponsors a gymnasium on Hanuman Ghat. In this particular case the affiliation between the Naga monastic akhara and the gymnasium is tenuous and unclear. It seems that the wrestling gymnasium belongs to the monastery but is used by neighborhood residents. Oddly enough, the gymnasium is more a bodybuilding club than an akhara per se, but this is probably a fairly recent development.

There is also a defunct wrestling akhara on Manikarnika Ghat called Naga Akhara. Among the wrestling members were some Naga sannyasis. At Rang Mahal, a wrestling akhara downriver from Banaras, there is a temple complex run by Naga sannyasis. Although the majority of the wrestling members of the akhara are Muslims, Hindu merchants, Thakurs, Brahmans, and Yadavs, Naga sannyasis also practice wrestling. An annual wrestling tournament is sponsored by the Rang Mahal Akhara, but this seems to be a purely "secular" event, and to the best of my knowledge no sannyasis take part.

In his study of Ramanandi ascetics in Ayodhya, van der Veer has shown how Nagas discipline their bodies through the retention of semen (1989: 463). As with other Ramanandis (*tyagis* and *rasiks*) this practice is central to the mechanism by which emotion and passion is directed towards devotion to Ram. The Nagas of Ayodhya seem to wrestle in much the same way as "secular" wrestlers in Banaras, with the important qualification that they do so as self-proclaimed ascetics.

There are clear parallels between Naga akharas and wrestling akharas. However, I was repeatedly and without exception told that the two types of akhara have nothing to do with each other. Sannyasis who wrestle do not subscribe wholeheartedly to the lifestyle of wrestling. As a rule, according to "secular" wrestlers, they do not compete, and they do not drink milk or eat ghi and almonds. The two life paths are parallel and at points contiguous, but they are classified as distinct and separate. From the perspective of the wrestler, at least, this serves to maintain the institution of sannyas as a firm reference point, similar but different. The sannyasi who takes up arms or wrestles is never confused with his "secular" counterpart.

This point can of course be debated, and van der Veer has pointed out that in at least some Naga akharas young boys come and receive training much as they do in the "secular" akharas I have described (personal communication). Perhaps some Nagas wrestle competitively, and it is perfectly possible that some consume a diet of milk, ghi, and almonds. However, what is more important here than the objective truth of the matter, is that the secular wrestlers, absorbed in their ideological world, think of themselves as more unlike than like Nagas.

The case of the Dasnami Nagas is significant insofar as it helps define the structural relationship between wrestler and sannyasi. Obvious and formal parallels aside, wrestlers see in the practice of Naga asceticism a tacit justification for their own concern for physical fitness and moral strength. In this regard the sannyasi legitimizes the wrestler's way of life. The Naga is, in some respects, an image of what the wrestler would become if he were to renounce the world completely.

THE WRESTLER IN THE WORLD: CONTRADICTION AND PARADOX

While wrestlers recognize the moral virtue of world renunciation, they are confronted with a paradox that manifests itself in various ways. Broadly put, the problem for the wrestler is how to live a moral social life while trying to subscribe to values which define social life as basically (if not egregiously) immoral and unhealthy. Can a wrestler live with his wife and be celibate? Can he eat rich and expensive foods and still dissociate himself from sensory pleasure? Can he raise a family and be immune from concerns for prestige and social status? Can he earn a living and find time to develop himself as a devout wrestler? Can he develop his body and not become proud and conceited? One wrestler stated the problem as follows:

> A wrestler's life is like that of a sadhu. The sadhu lives in his hermitage. He worships and does his prayers. A wrestler lives in his house and is entangled in the world of *maya* (illusion). He is in the grihastha ashrama. Even in this condition he must control himself. The sadhu lives apart from the world. The wrestler lives in his house but he must dissociate himself from the concerns of a householder. He must close his eyes to it and wrestle. The wrestler is equivalent to the sadhu because they must both remove themselves from the grihastha ashrama and be absorbed in god. And yet the wrestler is tied to his family. He must live close to his wife and yet turn away from temptation. A person will never be a wrestler until he becomes like a sadhu and averts his eyes and closes his mouth to the world.

Many wrestlers expressed similar views. On the issue of food, one explained that wrestlers must be even greater, more ascetic and self-controlled, than sannyasis. Wrestlers fill their stomachs and yet control their desire while sannyasis take the easier route of quenching their desire through fasting or the consumption of bhang. Another wrestler developed this theme further by saying that wrestlers had to work harder at self-conrol than sannyasis because they ate food which produced semen in greater quantities. Some wrestlers explain that a wrestler can control his semen until he has reached the age of thirty or thirty-five, at which point he would have to marry and have children. I was told a story of the great wrestler Dara Singh, who became so strong at a young age that his family and friends quickly arranged his marriage in order to prevent the somatic equivalent of a nuclear meltdown.

It is important to note here that worldly asceticism is not intrinsically paradoxical; rationalizations of one sort or another abound. Van der Veer (1989) has noted that many Ramanandi sannyasis are wealthy, and that in an extended sense this can be seen as part of the larger program of ascetic devotion to Ram. Elements of a similar sort of worldly rationalization can be seen in the masti of the Chaube Brahmans of Mathura (Lynch 1990: 91–115). Chaubes also wrestle, but like Nagas who wrestle as ascetics, Chaubes (or at least some Chaubes) wrestle primarily as emotionally invigorated Brahmans. There is a devotional component to the Chaubes' masti, whereby aspects of ascetic ideals are given ligitimate, worldly form. What the wrestling ideology does is to force the issue of asceticism in relation to grihastha religiosity into a sharp dichotomy of either this worldly moral and physical weakness—where emotion and wealth, among other things, are false consciousness—or otherworldly health and strength, where pure consciousness is asocial. On the level of the body in particular, the wrestler is likely to see things in black-and-white, either-or terms. In this regard the wrestler would certainly agree with Dumont, even if Dumont is wrong.

Speaking on a philosophical level, one wrestler suggested that while sannyasis abide by their *karma* (moral work), wrestlers abide by their *kriya karma* (active moral work). He continued this line of thinking by saying that wrestlers and sannyasis are alike in all but the nature of the "work" that they do. From the context of the discussion it was clear that the primary distinction being made was that a wrestler's "work" is in the nature of a social avocation, or civic duty, whereas the moral work of a sannyasi is independent of any sort of social responsibility. In this regard wrestlers are clearly in step with Gandhi.

One aspect of the type of work which a wrestler is called upon to do is, in the words of K. P. Singh, to turn others into wrestlers and eventually to reform the social order through such "missionary" efforts. A wrestler is, to borrow a phrase used more often in Christendom, an "evangelical." Here the role of the guru is important, for although all wrestlers are called upon to perform their moral work, it is the guru whose missionary efforts are most important and effective. The guru, who is more often than not also a great wrestler, performs his moral work by founding an akhara. As the members grow up and achieve a level of competence, maturity, and fame, they branch off and open akharas of their own. The generalized work of all wrestlers combined thus becomes national in proportion through the compounding agency of geometric progression.

Of all the worldly concerns that a wrestler must reconcile himself to, the most important is marriage and having children. I have pointed out that intense value is placed on the strict practice of brahmacharya, which serves as a moral paradigm for the wrestler; it symbolizes his subscription to ascetic values. Significantly, it is also a unique reinterpretation of brahmacharya that serves to keep the wrestler in the world. A common phrase among wrestlers is *ek nari, brahmachari*, which means that one can be married to *one* woman and still be celibate. As I was told repeatedly, a wrestler may marry so long as his overall attitude towards sex and sensuality does not change. He may have sex with his wife, but only for reproduction and not for sensual gratification. For the wrestler, sex is work; it produces children and is justified only in this regard. There is a general sense that the children produced by the agency of moral sex will be healthier and more civic-minded than other children.

Aside from considerations of sex and sexuality, marriage draws a wrestler inextricably into the worldly status of a householder. He must earn a living, raise a family and educate his children. In an article entitled "What is a Wrestler's Home Life Like?" (1986), Munna interviews the wives of three well-known wrestlers. Not surprisingly, all three wives say that wrestling has not undermined their family status, which is to say, their husbands are good husbands and good wrestlers. They exercise and train hard and also provide for their families. Significantly, each of the three women says that the family is stronger by virtue of the husband's avocation. Because of the husband's prestige as a wrestler, the family has earned social status and public respect. The general thesis of Munna's article is corroborated by many of the wrestlers I interviewed. Wrestling improves the quality of one's family life by making the householder fit and healthy. The moral principles of wrestling are extended to include the larger family unit within the domain of worldly asceticism.

K. P. Singh develops this point in some detail. He points out that great Indian leaders like Gandhi and M. M. Malaviya were married but were nevertheless brahmacharis (1972a: 30). He argues for the integration of moral virtue into social life.

> Gandhi controlled himself, kept himself in check and was a brahmachari. He was a great saint and a reformist. He freed the nation. And Gandhi's discipline of self-control was not contrived. . . . His was the work of the world and he would shoulder his burden of work taking only the name of god for support. Gandhi was greater than Shankaracharya. Shankaracharya advocated the complete separation of men and women, but Gandhi said that all men and women should be as brother and sister. He also said that the primary relationship between a man and a woman is that of mother and son. . . . What an excellent method for uprooting the evil of sensuality! What a grand vision! What insight to turn sensuality into a feeling of respect and honor! We must all live in society and we all must purge the evils of social life from our thoughts. Morality must, instead, fill our minds. Shankaracharya did not make the common people of India his disciples whereas Gandhi had tens of thousands of followers. We must tire our bodies, focus our minds and cleanse our thoughts. We must adopt commitment and independence as our way of life (ibid: 31).

Using Gandhi as an example, K. P. Singh argues for the incorporation of ascetic values into the practices of everyday life. When so translated, the practice of brahmacharya clearly becomes an ethical practice with sociomoral implications. For the wrestler, living in the world as a householder, the appeal is to have a family which is guided by moral principles: to raise children who recognize the value of strength, honesty, devotion, self-respect, and humility, and who are able to channel their emotions away from the intoxication of self-indulgent sensual gratification and towards a feeling of obligation to society at large (Atreya 1973a: 24). Although no wrestler with whom I spoke made the association, there is a clear parallel, I think, between what wrestlers advocate and the position held by moral reformers of the late eighteenth and early twentieth century such as Sri Aurobindo and Sri Ramkrishna's missionary disciple, Vivekananda. Of particular interest in this regard are Sri Aurobindo's statements on the spirituality of physical education (A. Ghose 1949, 1954; A. Ghose and The Mother 1967).

Unlike the sannyasi who has turned his back on the ethical problems of social life (as in K. P. Singh's characterization of Shankaracharya's contrived asceticism), the wrestler has a clearly defined—though certainly visionary—social purpose. Not only is the wrestler embedded in social life, he is responsible for setting an ethical standard. He must be honest, humble, duty-bound, hard-working, principled and fair. He must be physically fit. In the process he takes personal responsibility for precisely those things which the sannyasi regards as illusionary.

EXEMPLARY LIVES

The incorporation of ascetic values into the practice of everyday life entails individual subscription to ethical principles. On account of this, it is not surprising that the wrestler is often recognized as an exemplary person. Unlike the sannyasi who is recognized for the extent and nature of his austerities and for the power of his spirituality, the wrestler is recognized for his work in the world. To be sure, wrestlers are remembered for the bouts they fight and win, but they are also recognized for the kind of men they are. A few examples are illustrative.

The following is the story of Mangala Rai as told by Parmanand Shukla of Ghazipur (n.d.). Although not an exact translation of Shukla's prose, I have sought to capture the flavor of a rhetorical, literary style that serves to embellish the facts of an exemplary wrestling biography:

> As peaceful and sincere as the full moon, deeper than the ocean itself and more brilliant than the sky above, Mangala Rai, the essence of wrestling and well-known pahalwan, established such a high national standard, and gave Ghazipur and Uttar Pradesh such eminence, that he will not soon be forgotten, much less equalled. This wonder of Ghazipur and Uttar Pradesh was born on the pure and eternal soil of the holy Ganga. Champion wrestlers like Kamar, Amir Phutte, Hori Nariyan Singh, Hanuman Pande and Raj Nariyan Rai as well as others, were all born in Ghazipur, have glorified the earth of that district, and have advanced the nation's pride through their art.
>
> In Ghazipur Vijaya Dashmi is a grand festival which commemorates Ram's victory over the southern Kingdom of Lanka. On this occasion Ram heroically defeated the forces of Ravana's demonic culture and established a new standard of respectability and truth throughout the country. People break from their routine and visit one another or else go to fairs on this day.
>
> I was inspired on this occasion to go and have an audience with Mangala Rai, who, with heroism, abnegation and energy had established another standard; a standard of wrestling throughout India.
>
> Along the green banks of the Ganga, where I had to go, the land is fertile and the people are well off. On this festive occasion I arrived in the village of Musahib as dusk was approaching and found Mangala Rai seated on a cot next to the door of his home reading a *Dinman* magazine. Upon catching sight of me he graciously asked that I be seated and inquired after my health. Then we began to talk.
>
> I was surprised that he was as strong and fit as ever, despite his age. There was no sign of his getting older at all. This narrow-waisted, broad-shouldered,

hard body, radiant with the glory of great achievements, seemed to throw out a challenge: Is there a wrestler in this country who is my equal?

Mangala Rai, the wrestler who showed us the gems of this art, was born in the month of Kunwar, 1916, in the village of Musahib. His father was Ramchandar Rai. Ramchandar and his brother, Radha Rai, were both great wrestlers of their time. Kamala Rai, Mangala Rai's younger brother, was also a great wrestler. Ramchandar and Radha Rai both lived in Rangoon where they practiced and exercised in an akhara. Radha Rai was the more accomplished of the two and he trained his nephews on the finer points of wrestling.

I asked Mangala Rai when he started wrestling in the akhara and when his first competitive bout was. He said that he started wrestling at age sixteen and didn't compete until a year later. He was good enough so that from the start he was matched up with good, strong wrestlers so that his skill and experience developed accordingly. The great wrestler Shiv Murat Tiwari from Vabhanpura, Jalhupur, Varanasi district was also in Rangoon at this time and Mangala Rai benefited greatly from his instruction. After some time Mangala Rai and his brother returned to their village in Uttar Pradesh.

From the very beginning these two young men led a simple and unpretentious life. They were so neat and tidy that one could not find so much as a stain on their clothes. Another feature of their character was that they always provided food and facilities for any wrestler who stayed with them.

For many years Mangala Rai did not have the opportunity to live in his village. Someone or the other was always making demands on his time. He had become so famous for his numerous victories in Rangoon that daily people would come to see him. Sri Dharam Dev Pande was one such person, a great fan of wrestling from Gorur village. Now, just as Vishwamitra called on Raja Dashrat and asked that Ram and Lakshman be sent to his ashram to pursue their training, so did Dharam Dev Pande call Mangala Rai and Kamala Rai to his own village so that they could improve their skill. There was always a crowed gathered to watch these two wrestlers working out. After gazing on their wrestling prowess, their moves and countermoves, and on their tall, hard physiques, all who came to watch were left dumbfounded.

Living on the banks of the Ganga, bathing in the Ganga and spending some time in secluded self-reflection are some of Mangala Rai's most cherished pleasures. There is always a book of one kind or another in his hands.

The people of Narayanpur, in Ghazipur district, were very keen that Mangala Rai come and stay among them. Being of a passive disposition Mangala Rai was not able to refuse the people of Narayanpur. Arrangements were made for an akhara to be constructed in a grove near the Ganga, and Mangala Rai's daily needs were also provided for. Vishwamitra's airy ashram, Buxar, is just on the other bank of the Ganga from this grove. Mangala Rai further developed his skill while living in this place by wrestling with twenty or twenty-five wrestlers, three times with each. Dukhram of Darbhanga, Sukhdev of Azamgarh, Mathura's Mohan Chaube, Kamala Rai, Brahmachari Rai, Mathura Rai, and Baleshwar Pahalwan, among many other great wrestlers, all came to stay and practice with Mangala Rai. Mangala provided for their diet and personally looked out for their welfare.

Mangala Rai's fabulous success and great national fame may be attributed to the fact that upon returning from Rangoon he fought with the great Mustafa Pahalwan of Allahabad and Varanasi. He applied his favorite moves, *tang* and *baharali*, with such perfection and power that those who were watching were awestruck. His fame spread like wildfire and in his thirty-second year he had to fight some one hundred bouts.

Mangala Rai himself explained to me his regimen: four thousand bethaks, two thousand five hundred dandas and three sessions each with twenty or twenty-five wrestlers. Sometimes he would undertake other kinds of exercise as well. Mangala Rai weighs three and a half maunds [288 pounds] and is six feet tall. In addition to bread, dal, and vegetables, he used to eat half a liter of ghi, two liters of milk, a kilogram of almonds and occasionally some fruit and juice.

Mangala Rai is fond of saying that anyone can be a guru, but the true guru is one who trains and cares for his disciples as he would his own sons. He must teach them complex and great ideas. Mangala Rai's original trainer and guru was his uncle. His true guru is the late Sri Mahadev Pande (Pandeji) of Varanasi who was like a father to him. Remembering Pandeji, Mangala Rai becomes grave and contemplative.

Mangala Rai is of the opinion that at the present time wrestlers are becoming enamored with fashion and frivolity and have lost sight of the essential principles of the art. They are caught up in a materialist, consumer culture and are dragging the art of wrestling down with them. He is an advocate of unlocking each wrestler's individual potential. He has kept clear of rural politics, and has instead worked tirelessly at developing character. Mangala Rai says that the life of a wrestler is no less than the life of a yogi. Only by engaging in this magnificent regimen can wrestling continue to develop.

Now that Mangala Rai no longer wrestles he has become a hard-working and successful farmer who owns a tractor. His discipline and industriousness can be seen in this area as well. Now Mangala Rai's good character and sage counsel is taken advantage of by those who need advice and those who need a dispute resolved.

Another exemplary life history is that of Brahmdev Pahalwan as recounted by Govardan Das Malhotra (1981: 68–70). The literary style of presentation again serves to evoke an image of greatness:

Accomplished wrestlers are regarded as saints. Just as saints and great sages renounce the world of illusion and deceit and become absorbed in god, so do wrestlers have to focus themselves and lose themselves in their art. If his concentration should even slightly waver and his pace falter then it is certain that he will end up as the lowest of low and no better than a person who grovels in the dirt.

Wrestling is unique among India's ancient arts. From the beginning wrestling practice has been done on the ground, in the soil. Among those who have practiced wrestling there are many who have made a name for themselves and have built up the nation's standard. Among these, Brahmdev Pahalwan—the Lion of Uttar Pradesh—earned a reputation for his guru, the nationally known Chandan Pahalwan. Such skill as he demonstrated is rarely seen in your average wrestler.

A devotee of Baba Gorkhanath; a nobleman of Gorakhpur; a patron of wrestling, the late Babu Purushotam Das provided Brahmdev with the venue—Pakki Bagh Akhara—in which he performed, exercised and thereby gave his admirers such satisfaction. What fame he achieved may be attributed to his true commitment, deep concentration and self-consciousness. Today this straightforward man, advocate for the poor and under-privileged, and tireless political worker is no longer with us, but those in Gorakhpur—nay, the entire state—cannot live without recalling Brahmdev's great skill.

Brahmdev was born the youngest son of Mahadev Mishra in Rudrapur, Khajni Gram, near the Bansgaon thesil of Gorakhpur district in 1917. Khajni is a veritable pilgrimage point for wrestlers. Brahmdev's grandfather, father and brothers were all wrestlers, so how could he have been anything else! He regularly went to the village akhara with his father where he rolled around and covered himself with earth. The aura of so many great wrestlers must have rubbed off on Brahmdev and served to focus his attention on wrestling.

On account of his devotion to the akhara, Brahmdev's formal education ended in middle school. However, being from a Brahman family and living in an intellectual community he learned the Ramayan very well and was able to quote Sanskrit verses with great proficiency. In addition to being a wrestler, Brahmdev took an interest in politics and was an accomplished public speaker. As a village *pradhan* [head man] and Block Officer he served the public well.

Brahmdev enjoyed his life in the peaceful environment of the village akhara. He exercised and ate to his heart's content. In the city akhara of Pakki Bagh he became a disciple of Chandan Singh and thereby followed a more rigorous regimen and improved his skill. In local tournaments he sought out wrestlers bigger and stronger than himself and regularly defeated them. When he defeated the great Surti Pahalwan in a Gorakhpur tournament the fans' excitement was unbounded. He also defeated a European wrestler in Gorakhpur.

Brahmdev's daily work-out consisted of two thousand five hundred bethaks and one thousand six hundred dands. After running he would wrestle with twenty-five good wrestlers. He was most accomplished in the *nikal, tang,* and *multani* moves. Any opponent who was subjected to these moves would most certainly "see the sky."

His diet included one *seer* (a quarter measure) of ghi, six seers of milk, and thandai made from half a seer of almonds. He also enjoyed fruit and was a vegetarian. In Calcutta he exercised in the akhara at Mochi Pari Thana in Bara Bazaar where he instructed many great Bengali wrestlers.

According to Indian tradition he wore a *dhoti* and *kurta* with a *dopatta* around his neck and shoulders. With huge mustachios Brahmdev cut a very impressive figure. When he walked through the bazaar thousands of people would stand and watch while his many disciples would compete for the honor of touching his feet.

Brahmdev was married very young but had no children. However, he regarded his nephews as his own sons and personally looked out for them. He admonished the children of his family to pay particular attention to their studies. As someone who advocated education he was a model citizen until his death in 1975.

As indicated in chapter 3, Guru Fakir Chand Shukla is characterized by Ramkumar Shukla as "the embodiment of renunciation" (1973: 43). In fact, the ideal persona of a guru is perfectly congruent with the wrestler's vision of worldly asceticism. Many of the founders of well-known akharas are remembered for their exemplary lifestyle of total devotion to hard work and rigorous self-discipline. In addition to establishing a well-known wrestling akhara, Fakir Chand Shukla gave away medicine to the poor and also built numerous temples. In and of itself this makes his life noteworthy. What is most exemplary about his life is "that he worked for development by disregarding the formal manifestations of life and turned instead to a reform of the "inner man" (ibid: 47). Heroism and courage of this sort is achieved not through grand aspirations but rather through personal application on the level of everyday, mundane situations. As Ramkumar Shukla points out, Fakir Chand Shukla's greatness was a manifestation of his small achievements (ibid). Although not at all diminutive, he was a quotidian hero.

Mahadev Pahalwan is also known for his worldly asceticism. Govardan Das Malhotra writes: "Mahadev Pahalwan was born to a *gwal* [dairy farming] family but he was born for wrestling and wrestling alone, and he died doing the work of a wrestler. This exemplary wrestler who embodied self-respect was regarded as a saint by the people of Kanpur" (1981: 30). There are numerous other wrestlers who are referred to as saints or sadhus; for instance, Bhagwan Singh Narayan Wale, a follower of Swami Dayananda who lived in a community of wrestlers in the forest outside of his village (Atreya 1979; Sinha 1978: 12), and Mangaldas, who renounced the world at age eleven and later became the "spiritual teacher" of other wrestlers (Malhotra 1981: 19). Atreya tells the story of Ramsanehi Pahalwan of Kakare, a village near Moradabad. At the age of thirty-two Ramsanehi left his family and spent eight years practicing the "extreme austerities" of wrestling. No one in his village saw him until he emerged from seclusion to defend his father, who was embroiled in a village dispute. For all his austerities, however, Ramsanehi was a Jat farmer whose life revolved around the mundane tasks of irrigation, plowing, and planting.

One of the many stories told about Gama, the world-champion wrestler, reaffirms the value placed on austerity and simplicity as an exemplary virtue. Gama was asked by a young man what he should do to achieve great strength and skill. Reflecting on the question and considering the great discipline required of a wrestler Gama said, simply, "do eleven dands and bethaks a day, eat a handful of chana, and think on god." Exemplary wrestlers, whether they be well-known gurus or local champions, have succeeded in fully integrating devotional spirituality with disciplined exercise.

All exemplary wrestlers are remembered for the extent of their self-discipline. However, it is their life in the world that is regarded as noteworthy and meritorious. Like Ramsanehi, many wrestlers are simple farmers who turned their labor into a form of spiritual exercise. They draw strength from plowing fields, pulling water from wells, and turning grindstones and oil presses (Atreya 1979: 41). Mangaldas sang hymns and read the scriptures while tending his feed store in Kanpur. Fakir Chand Shukla was, among other things, a pharmacist whose healing practice was informed by his spiritual temperament. Without wishing to romanticize, it may be noted that many of the most highly regarded senior wrestlers in Banaras—Lallu Pahalwan, Nathu Lal Yadav, Lakshmi Kant Pande, and many others—fall into this category, not because they are saints, by any means, but because they have a vision of the future, to the attainment of which they have dedicated a good part of their lives.

Trying to characterize the wrestler's personality, Atreya cites a passage from the *Bhagavad Gita* (7.11) where Krishna says, "In the strong I am strength unhindered by lust" (1971: 27, translation from Prabhavananda and Isherwood 1975: 90). In quoting this passage Atreya's point is that even when wrestlers seem to have renounced the world, the nature of their austerities are still active rather than passive. The wrestler's strength is readily translated into commonsense, everyday terms; the sannyasi's austerities are not.

From his perspective—somewhat outside and yet implicated in social life—a wrestler's vision of the world is quite different from either that of the worldly householder or the asocial ascetic. By virtue of his somewhat liminal condition as a moral individual in the world, the wrestler is able to look beyond the horizon of the taken-for-granted social order and see, or more properly imagine, a different paradigm for sociosomatic action.

CONCLUSION

As Dumont (1960) has noted, the man-in-the-world is subsumed within the framework of caste holism. Hinduism, he argued, is structured in terms of the dialectical relationship between the worldly householder and the world renouncer. Das (1977) and Heesterman (1985) have both suggested that the Brahman embodies the tension between these two categories. The Brahman remains, nevertheless, embedded within the world of caste relations. The ascetic practices of the Brahman only serve to underscore his spiritual authority and his caste purity.

As an ideology, wrestling goes beyond the bounds of a caste model by appealing to a visionary—but no less real—social ethic. Being nonsectarian, and outside the bounds of caste relations, wrestlers are not conscripted by the terms of hierarchy. By adopting the somatic practices of world renunciation, the wrestler effectively realigns the relational categories which structure the caste ideology. The regimen of wrestling juxtaposes sannyas ascetics to worldly nationalism. What is most intriguing about this relationship is that the ideology of wrestling accommodates the individuality of sannyas and defines for it a social role which transcends the bounds of caste. This works not because of an active protest against caste values, but because of a tacit and covert realignment of the dominant ideology's primary coordinates. Within the scheme of wrestling the conceptual framework of caste relations is replaced by a utopian vision of national ideals. Here, as we will see in the next chapter, the individual is accorded a preeminent position as the embodiment of moral, physical, and spiritual strength. The value of individuality is thereby recast in the light of somatic reform.

In his discussion of the Chamar ideology, Khare observes that the vocation of sannyas is like "walking on the sharp edge of a sword" (1984: 68). The sannyasi must step carefully so as not to become mired in the world of sensory illusion. When wrestlers reflect on their avocation they say it is a "bitter cup" or "like chewing iron chana." Unlike the sannyasi who steps out of the world to achieve his goal of self-realization, the wrestler takes on the world as a domain for moral action. Both walk a similar path but in different directions, in relation to different points, and with quite different consequences.

CHAPTER 10

Utopian Somatics and Nationalist Discourse

Up to this point we have been primarily concerned with the symbolic meanings and disciplinary techniques that structure the wrestler's body and give corporeal form to an ideology of regimented self-control and expressive identity. In this chapter we shall look at the way in which this somatic ideology is translated into a nationalist discourse as the wrestler is cast in the role of perfect citizen.

I was invited to the wedding of one of the wrestlers from Akhara Ram Singh. It was about 5:30 in the evening, the height of rush hour in downtown Banaras. Bicycles, rickshaws, pedestrians, motorscooters, and hawkers crowded Chaitganj along Naisarak Road as the groom's party—an entourage of over two hundred people, including two brass bands and a garland-bedecked Victorian carriage drawn by four horses—set off through the bustling city. Progress was slow, but more by design than because of the crowds.

As we walked along, one of the wrestlers shouted over the sound of the trumpets, drums, and exploding fireworks that one could easily tell that this was the *barat* (groom's wedding party) of a wrestler. "Just look at all of those wrestlers at the front of the group," he said as he threw back his head, stuck out his chest and drew his shoulders back while splaying his arms in the characteristic pose of a *mast* (invigorated) wrestler.

Leading the barat, the guru of the akhara sauntered through the crowds, flanked on either side by elders, senior members, and a host of young wards. Their gait, posture, and general aura was dramatic and self-conscious. Thick necks set on squared shoulders; straight, strong backs; twirled mustaches and short, oiled hair; eyes set in a benevolent, disinterested, yet proud and self-confident gaze: they sauntered through the crowd slowly, ignoring the bustle around them, the young men mingling in front of the local cinema waiting for the six o'clock show to begin, the gridlock of mopeds and cars at the Godaulia intersection, but conscious of the eyes that turned in recognition, admiration and, undoubtedly, not just a little annoyance as the wrestlers' parade moved against the tide of the city's ebb and flow.

A wrestler is always on stage, whether he is walking along a street, attending a wedding, praying at a temple, exercising at his akhara, or competing in a tournament. This is not to say that wrestlers are burlesque performers in a physical-cum-ethical sideshow. More in the manner of a morality play, their character *is* their virtue, and it permeates and shades all aspects of their lives. To get at the nature of the power matrix within which the wrestler's body is so cast it is necessary to consider the larger context of modern India.

Wrestlers have a specific, overtly circumscribed interpretation of modernity. Throughout my research wrestlers often provided unsolicited critical commentaries on the state of the modern world. It became apparent that these were not the usual conservative and often anachronistically nostalgic retrospectives. In fact, a refined and critical evaluation of the current moral, economic, and political state of affairs in India is central to the practice of wrestling as a way of life. From the wrestler's perspective an affliction of modernity assails the human body and thereby directly undermines the integrity of the modern state. A fairly elaborate discourse has developed that both delineates the precise nature of this affliction and offers a utopian alternative. The nature of this discourse is encoded in the body itself, but wrestlers are likely to elaborate on this somatic base with great rhetorical flourish and poetic force.

THE ENEMY WITHIN

The modern world threatens to exercise control over individual human subjects through the agency of seduction. Many times wrestlers would point to specific artifacts thought to characterize the modern era—cinema halls and popular films; mopeds, scooters, and other two-wheeled, power-driven vehicles; synthetic fabrics; liquor stores—and speak of how contemporary youth have fallen prey to crass commercialism and the lure of gross, sensual satisfaction that these artifacts of culture represent. The world of the bazaar is regarded as a den of iniquity which is sharply contrasted to the wholesome world of the pristine akhara. While the modern world is regarded as highly unnatural and immoral, wrestlers feel that individuals are inherently weak and susceptible to the seductive sensuality of a debauched way of life. That is, given half a chance, young men will gravitate toward cinema halls, tea shops, and liquor stores. Wrestling's implicit project is to throw up a moral and physical barrier to prevent this from happening.

Given the overt physicality of wrestling, it is not surprising to find that the most heinous modern afflictions are also cast in a particularly corporeal light. For instance, hairstyles are regarded as prime indicators of a person's more general moral character. Wrestlers are concerned with hair as a symbol of self-control in particular and identity in general. They wear their hair short, groomed with mustard oil, and they provide various interpretations of why this is efficacious. Many argue that it keeps the head cool, thus allowing the mind to remain focused and concentrated on practice and moral propriety. Others point out that the scalp and hair follicles absorb the oil, thus preventing baldness, dandruff, or eczema.

Given these perspectives it is not surprising that modern "hippie-cut" hairstyles are regarded as unhealthy and sensuous. In many areas of urban India one can find numerous hairstyling salons which advertise the latest in Bombay "filmy fashion." The stylists in these salons have developed haircutting to a very sophisticated and, indeed, sensuous art. Scented oils, facial creams, and aftershaves are available, as are warm facial cloth wraps, blow-dryer sculpting, tints, and dyes. A vocabulary has evolved that delineates, with considerable nuance, the difference between particular styles of haircuts, mustaches and beards. These salons are noteworthy in part for their ubiquity. They can be found at almost every turn in a crowded bazaar. But there is also the fact that they make a sophisticated, sensuous technology readily available to a broad-based consuming public. In the evening salons are often brightly lit, and shiny metal fixtures and large mirrors accentuate what is regarded as a quintessentially modern environment of plastic, vinyl, and glass. The biggest and brightest of these salons are often located near cinema halls, and crowds of young men can be seen preening in front of mirrors as they are attentively groomed to perfection.

It is precisely this sort of hedonistic self-indulgence that wrestlers criticize. What rankles many is the fact that grooming has become a narcissistic passion of meticulous precision. It is a form of self-indulgence which is expressly sensual and consciously physical. Hair length is but one dimension of this. In particular, talcs and scented aftershaves are regarded as grossly egregious insofar as they are artificial tonics that threaten to replace the natural ardor of akhara earth and well water. The wrestler's body is said to radiate with a natural, healthful glow, and talcum powder and moisturizing creams inhibit this aura. These commercial toiletries offer an alternative image of refined, effete civility, which is, quite literally, only skin deep.

Another target of the wrestlers' criticism is what might be called "public food" in the form of snacks sold at streetside stalls as well as meals served in more lavishly appointed establishments. Wrestlers are extraordinary eaters, and their diets are carefully managed. Therefore they are usually united in their vocal criticism of public food, which is, according to them, prepared in suspect circumstances by less than circumspect chefs and consumed in the chaotic environment of the market, railway station, bus stop, or cinema hall.

Although all cooked food available for immediate consumption is regarded with some trepidation, there are a few specific food items which are inherently worse than others. *Chat*—a salty, sour snack made from lentil cakes and a variety of spices and condiments—is regarded as the prototype of dangerous public food; it can throw one's bodily humors into drastic imbalance. In so doing it can enrage passion, a fact which is further exacerbated by the inherently stimulating properties of salts and spices. As with any other type of public food, one is never certain of the circumstances under which chat has been prepared. Is the condiment sauce diluted, and if so, with what? What has been added to stretch the bulk of the lentil batter? Were clean pots and pans used for preparation? In addition to concerns with purity and hygiene, wrestlers are often suspicious of the fact that they might "catch" bad emotions through the consumption of public food. Emotions such as anger, frustration, lust, and anxiety are said to be contagious and are transmitted from one person to another through the agency of food.

As with haircutting salons, purveyors of chat and other snacks are commonplace in modern urban India. The public dimension of streetside stalls is important in this context, for a well-known chat vendor can attract a large crowd. Thus, casual consumption—which, from the wrestler's critical perspective, is wholly gratuitous and unhealthy—takes on the character of a spectacle. Spectacles of such indiscriminate eating reach epic proportion as many young men congregate before and right after the showing of a popular film in a downtown cinema. In addition to the dubious dietary properties of public food, of which the wrestlers are obviously critical, public food is also maligned as leisure food eaten purely for pleasure. In this regard snacks like chat are seen as sensually self-indulgent junk food.

Tea, like chat, is vociferously criticized for a number of reasons. Because it is drunk in so many situations and in such large quantities in modern India, it is referred to sarcastically, and often in a tone of resignation, as *kaliyug ki amrit*—the elixir of the dark age. As a narcotic, tea is an artificial stimulant said to dull the senses over time. It inhibits one's appetite and can have a number of other detrimental effects on the body. Equally significant is the fact that tea has become associated with leisurely self-indulgence. Tea shops abound in the urban environment where workers, travelers, truck drivers, and government bureaucrats indulge themselves often. Because it is drunk purely for pleasure, wrestlers reason that tea drinking is a sign of idleness. It replaces the purposeful single-minded consumption of pure water or pure milk with a kind of distracted revery of the palate that serves no purpose.

Another primary dimension of the wrestler's critique of modern life has to do with clothes and sartorial fashion. Generally speaking, wrestlers feel that the healthy body is properly maintained when clothed in loose-fitting cotton garments. The rationale provided is that the body must breathe and therefore should not be artificially constricted. Some wrestlers say that a *dhoti*—a long, loosely bound loincloth—and *kurta*—a long, uncuffed shirt—are preferred apparel. However, only a minority of senior wrestlers wear this costume. Wrestlers in general wear a wide array of clothes, but for the most part they dress in a fairly conservative and unpretentious style. While it is difficult to generalize about what wrestlers wear, it is relatively easy to delineate those dimensions of fashion that they regard as particularly abhorrent. Tight-fitting tailored trousers and shirts made from synthetic, permanent-press materials are said to inhibit free movement and cause excessive perspiration as well as chafing. Bell-bottom and flared pants are regarded as self-indulgent, as are "bush shirts" with wide collars, snaps, frills, fringes, darts, and pleats. Clothes that are fashionably tight are criticized for drawing unnecessary (and usually unwarranted) attention to one's physique.

As with haircuts and public food, wrestlers feel that young men have become obsessed with fashion. Tailors, like hair stylists, have refined their sartorial art into an elaborate mechanics of subtle precision by which means they are able to cater to the proclivities of modern taste.

Clothes are, of course, closely associated with the individual body, and
for this reason wrestlers are particularly perturbed by the extent to
which consumer-oriented fashion threatens to cloak the disciplined
body in a garish, artificial, and unhealthy costume.

Wrestlers criticize a number of aspects of modern life, but nothing
is regarded as more hedonistically debauched than the modern Indian
cinema. Films are synonymous with virtually everything which is wrong
with the country. Popular film songs which can be heard, among other
places, played through amplifiers from hair salons, tea shops and chat
stalls, are regarded as obscene. Without wishing to cast aspersions on
the genius of Indian cinema, it is necessary to emphasize the degree to
which wrestlers feel that film and film fashion has undermined public
morality. Larger-than-life technicolor film billboards are regarded as a
blight on the moral landscape.

While many may be critical of the impact which popular film has
had, the exact nature of the impact is of particular importance for the
wrestler. It hits at the very heart of his identity: controlled sexuality.
Films are thought to be vulgar and erotic and therefore the essence of
seduction. Scantily clad heroines dance, tease, and otherwise entice
young men who then follow the well-groomed hero's lead and let themselves be seduced. All of which is a vicarious fantasy of course, but
daydreams can lead directly to adolescent confusion, wrestlers argue,
and impure thoughts directly presage a loss of semen.

While cinematic images impact the young man's mind, wrestlers feel
that erotic thoughts manifest themselves in certain somatic ways. An
erotic mood is said to be most visible in the eyes and the face. The initial
passionate flush is followed by a prolonged condition in which the eyes
lose their brightness and become hollow. Skin becomes dull and lackluster while cheeks become sunken. The image, appropriately, is of someone who is drained of life.

From the critical, conservative wrestler's perspective, the debauched
everyman is a fairly two-dimensional figure whose thin physique and
narcissistic fashion complement his immoral character. In addition to
the primary points outlined above, such men are criticized for numerous
other things as well—riding around on fast motorcycles, smoking cigarettes, drinking liquor, chewing tobacco, idly sitting around, or, alternatively, promenading in public with no other purpose than to show off
their clothes. Wrestlers, as well as other less dogmatic critics, use the
English term "loafer" to label anyone who affects this fashion. On this

general subject Rajkumar "Hans," writing the introduction to a wrestling manual, makes the following remarks:

> It is a matter of grave concern that people in post-independence India are
> becoming less and less interested in exercise. When I consider the question
> of why this is so I am forced to conclude that it is because we are surrounded
> on all sides by a rotten environment. The young people who should be in the
> akhara, who should be turning the pit, who should be exercising, wrestling
> and swinging gadas . . . they are today popping "mandrix pills" [a common
> tonic which is said to bestow strength], taking drugs and drinking liquor.
> They sit around and read cheap novels or flip through pornographic maga-
> zines.
>
> Who knows why this "cabaret-disco" mentality has returned to India? In
> the newspapers we read about murder, robbery and fraud. The reason for
> this is very clear: men do not practice self-control; they are afflicted with
> prejudice and mental tension (1983: 17).

THE BODY AND CIVIC DUTY

The wrestler's somatic critique of hedonistic everyday life is not restricted to the "skin-deep" level of fashion. It is also directed toward
larger issues of public, civic life. Wrestlers feel that physical health and
fitness are directly related to one's duty and ethical responsibility as a
citizen. Consequently, it is argued, the weak, debauched everyman is
not only undermining his own integrity but is, in effect, shirking his
responsibility as a modern Indian.

Wrestlers, like many others, express cynical frustration with the haz-
ards and alienation of modern life. In particular, they are vocally critical
of those things which affect them personally. A ponderous, monolithic
bureaucracy must be negotiated when seeking admission to schools. A
formidable legal apparatus must be penetrated when applying for building permits, licenses, and interstate-transportation documents. Tension
is inherent in dealing with police and other public officials. And one
feels alienated by a pervading sense of powerlessness when performing
everyday tasks such as buying rations at a state-run store, making reser-
vations for a bus or train, or waiting for a shipment of building materials
for the construction of a government-subsidized house. Accusations of
corruption are legion, and many wrestlers with whom I spoke expressed
a deep-seated distrust of police officers, railway booking clerks, local
politicians, legal advocates, school administrators, bank managers,
building contractors, and many others. Some wrestlers come from the
ranks of these much-maligned public servants, and many wrestlers know

people in high places. Despite this, however, the category of public servant, as opposed to those individuals who actually fill the role, is regarded with a great deal of suspicion and resentment. I often heard wrestlers talk of how they were unable to gain admission to school, take out a bank loan, or build an extension onto a house without first bribing someone involved; this did not solve the problem, it simply bought them access to a daunting, alienating bureaucratic maze.

While corruption is regarded as a public scourge that has penetrated almost every rung of public administration, state bureaucracy, and private enterprise, wrestlers are equally critical of a less administrative form of corruption: the practice of adulteration. Wrestlers are very suspicious of the quality of all commercial goods. Like many others, they doubt if the sugar they buy is in fact pure sugar. The same applies for flour, milk, salt, ghi, molasses, oil, or any other household commodity. Cement, coal, petrol, kerosene, and diesel fuel are all thought to be "cut" with some inferior product in order to increase profits by way of inflated volume. For wrestlers in particular, ghi and milk have become the symbols of once pure and pristine products which are now rendered less valuable through adulteration. I was told that it would be impossible for me to buy pure milk, and this from a wrestler whose family business was dairying. One of the elders at Akhara Ram Singh arranged for "pure" ghi to be made available to me through the aegis of a "reputable" dealer. Left to my own devices, he said, and others concurred, I would probably have ended up buying some half-and-half mixture adulterated with cheap vegetable shortening. One can only imagine the apoplectic effect this would have had on my digestive tract.

The inchoate world of suspicion, public distrust, and corruption shadows the parallel world of seductive self-indulgence. Thus, in the wrestler's view, it is the young man who primps, preens, drinks tea, and watches films or television who is also most likely to take bribes and adulterate products. A satirical verse in a popular wrestling journal (Dwivedi 1974–1975: 33) captures this notion:

> There is no product now which is not adulterated
> And no official will "move" unless well remunerated
>
> Yes, we can live without the aid of television
> But without the mandate of T.V.
> is there a national mission?

Immorality extends directly out from the unhealthy body to influence the ethics of public life. In part this equation is effected through a particular logic of responsibility and duty. Narcissism is manifest self-interest. As a person's attention is drawn narrowly to himself, the degree of his responsibility to the common good diminishes. In this formula, corrupt power—whether it be the ability to influence ticket sales or building contracts—is concentrated in the individual and serves self-interest. It is significant that power, morality, and fitness are linked so closely in this logic. In a very real sense an individual is thought to be more susceptible to vice if his body is not fortified through exercise and disciplined training.

THE RHETORIC OF SOMATIC REFORM

The wrestler's way of life may be seen as a form of protest against self-indulgence and public immorality. By disciplining his body the wrestler is seeking to implement ethical, national reform. This formal somatic ideology finds most powerful and explicit expression in the popular literature on wrestling. By way of the printed page this literature makes public an ideology which is otherwise strictly encoded in the regimen of akhara practice. Those who write about exercise, diet, and training seek to interpret the discipline of wrestling so as to make it intelligible and accessible to the lay person. Moreover, this literature is explicitly designed to thwart the affliction of modernity: to provide a medium by which means the degenerate everyman might find his own salvation. Essays, letters, and poems call on wrestlers to champion the cause of their way of life in order to bring about moral and physical reform.

A few right-wing organizations in India take a similarly dim view of, among other things, moral decay and cosmopolitan, secular modernism. While the ideology of such groups as the militant Hindu Rashtriya Swayamsevak Sangh is in some ways similar to various aspects of the wrestling ideology, there are significant differences (see appendix). Although some of the rhetoric may sound the same, the points of view are quite different.

Despite the overtly nationalistic and patriotic tone of many essays and poems, most of the literature on wrestling does not call for direct political action through group organization or formal advocacy. The literature on wrestling parallels the practice of wrestling itself by casting national reform in a specifically individualistic and somatic light. The ultimate goal of somatic discipline is a reformed collective consciousness of national morality and health. Consider the following passage, typical of many commentaries which contain both an exaggerated lament and a utopian prospective:

> Today independent India is blinded by its freedom. Wrestling, which once made India strong beyond compare and which made our soldiers the strongest in the world, is now practiced by only five or ten people. Guru Hanuman has a had a great deal to do with keeping the tradition of wrestling alive. But what can one Guru Hanuman do? We should have one Guru Hanuman born in every village in the nation; if not, then wrestling will no longer run in the blood of the Indian people. There are only a few villages which have akharas, and one can count on one's fingers the number of city akharas. . . . There was a time when every village had an akhara. . . . This sport, which costs nothing, has made India great in terms of strength and fitness. . . . Not until every man in India has spent ten to twelve years in the earth of an akhara can we hope to regain our national strength. . . .
>
> These days the strength of society—not only in the villages, but everywhere—is being spent on intoxicants of all kinds. Our energy should be spent building strength and wisdom. In this way we can prevent the wastage of our national wealth. The health of the nation will increase. The character of the nation will grow strong.
>
> It is my prayer that the people of India send their children to the akharas. Send your children to learn the knowledge of wrestling. Without the people's effort, no progress will be made. . . . Ninety percent of our problems can be solved through wrestling. We can rescue ourselves from the problems which face us. The true wrestler is god. He is a true person (Atreya 1973a: 21–24).

Another example of this powerful rhetoric is found in the preface to *The Art of Wrestling* by Rajesh Gupta. He articulates quite clearly both the nature of the problem as well as its possible solution:

> Who does not know that the health of our people has fallen to a low ebb? These are our children with sunken cheeks, hollow eyes and wrinkled skin. Youth?—Yes! The very youth who will . . . build the future of the nation on the pattern of our cultural heritage. Can these thin, dry-boned youth protect the country, the race, our religion and our people? How can they when there is no light in their eyes and no life in their hearts? And why is this? . . . It is not laziness, it is the fact that no one follows the path of brahmacharya. . . .
>
> Brothers! It is time for us to renounce our poisonous desires and follow the path of brahmacharya with a pure heart. We must make our bodies fit, strong, and radiant. We must set our minds on the rules and attitudes which will ensure that our bodies will be healthy, beautiful, taut, and invigorated so that we can do the work that we are called on to do (n.d.: 3–4).

Here the appeal is emotional and general. There is no specific program to be followed other than that offered by the akhara regimen. The idea is that strong wrestlers are moral citizens who will produce strong, healthy children. Eventually, it is thought, the whole country will exercise and eat its way toward a civic utopia of propriety and public service.

In this rubric all that is artificial about the modern world is contrasted to the wholesome coordinates of the akhara environment. The earth of the akhara in particular is regarded as the most natural of natural substances. Wrestlers explain that close contact with the earth ensures good health. It is a potent symbol of national strength. An essay entitled "The 'Earth' Akhara is Heaven and the 'Mat' Akhara is Hell" (Atreya 1972b) sharply contrasts modern Olympic wrestling with traditional Indian wrestling. The author extols the virtues of earth as does H. B. Singh in his introduction to the journal *Akhare ki Or* (1972). Singh speaks of modern Indians as those who no longer feel the fertile earth between their toes.

> They do not even remember that their bodies are the product of the earth. We see that they are reticent to pick up their playful, dust-covered children, for fear of soiling their fancy, tight-fitting, mill-cloth clothes. And yet these same people blindly smother their children in powder and perfume. They do not realize that the wrestler who grapples in the earth, the farmer who plows the earth and the child who plays in the earth are all far healthier than those who are alienated from the soil (ibid: 2).

Patodi charts the various healing properties of akhara earth and concludes,

> The earth will make you great. The Indian wrestler puts on his g-string and wrestling shorts and enters this earth. Upon doing so his body takes on a radiant aura. Can the office clerk—effete proclivities, flabby physique, white clothes and all—decked out in the very finest cloth milled in Bombay and Ahmadabad compare with this half-naked wrestler's radiant magnificence? Never! Absolutely not! (1973a: 35)

A number of poems quite forcefully express the general ideological attitude of personal responsibility. In the following poem by Ram Chandar "Kherawda" Kesriya entitled "We Will Advance the Glory of India" (1978: 25), wrestlers—the diamonds of the red earth—are enjoined to become moral reformers.

> Virtuous, we will teach the world true duty.
> As the diamonds of the red earth
>   we will build the Nation's pride.
> As the burning lamps of energy
>   we will teach peace.
> Tearing asunder the veil of darkness
>   we will call forth a new day of brightness.

Weakness shall be removed from the earth.
Strength and manhood will be fostered.
The shadow of fraud, conceit and deceit
   will be removed.
As the diamonds of the red earth
   we will make the Nation proud.
We shall water the forest of bay trees with
   pure faith.
Pearls of humility will grow from the earth.
Ethics, fraternity and moral pleasure will be
   fostered.
There will be no more eroticism.
The veil of illusion will be removed.
And the lesson is: "The body is the vehicle of
   right living."
As the diamonds of the red earth
   we will advance the Nation's pride.
We will worship the source of energy.
The lesson of fitness will be taught.
Through teaching the lesson of self-control
   the troubles of the government will be solved.
Business will be profitable.
Blemishes shall be removed from beauty.
Society will be neither rich nor poor.
With the power of the individual
   we will make the nation great.
As the diamonds of the red earth
   we will make the Nation proud.

Of particular interest is the fact that the individual, as a wrestler, is called upon to shoulder the burden of national pride. Reform is clearly situated in the body, as both agent for, and example of, reconstitution. When the claim is made that self-control can solve "government" problems, Kesriya is referring to overpopulation and the related scourges of poverty, unemployment, overcrowding, and pollution. To the wrestler's way of thinking, rapid population growth can be curtailed, quite simply, through the practice of celibacy. Given the importance of celibacy within the wrestling ideology, it is not at all unreasonable to assume—from the wrestler's perspective—that people will recognize the intrinsic value of self-control. A solution is found to a national problem, almost coincidentally, by making everyone think and act like a wrestler. Similarly, it is reasoned, poverty will fall before an inspired work ethic fueled by the natural energy of the wrestler's good health. Grain will be abundantly available once it is not used to distill liquor and ferment beer. Pollution will be eradicated when wrestlers realize that they need clean air to breathe, clean water to bathe in, and clean earth upon which to exercise. However fantastic and visionary this logic may seem, many wrestlers feel that their way of life would set in motion a chain of events extending out from each individual body and gradually bringing into line all aspects of public policy.

GOVERNMENT PATRONAGE: THE STATE AS KING OF KINGS

At least in part the government is held responsible for the weak moral and physical character of Indian youth. It has failed in its paternal, moralistic duty. As such, many wrestlers feel that the state must take a leadership role in championing the cause of civic reform. "What can the government do?" asks K. P. Singh.

> For its own sake it can do much. It can be the leader. It can organize and provide encouragement. The government has shakti; it has resources. What can it do? It can do anything and everything (1972c: 40).

> The government was quick to uproot the rajas and landlords who were the guardians and sponsors of wrestling. It should be as quick to take over responsibility for this art and do as well, if not better, than did the patrons of the past. If the government demands school diplomas from its youth—the same youth who look to public service for status, money and respect—then it stands to reason that along with these high standards the government must also require strength and physical fitness (1986: 27–28).

In many ways wrestlers see in the government the possibility of quintessential royal patronage: the government as king of kings, with unlimited resources and unbounded stature. The utopian government imagined by such writers as K. P. Singh, S. P. Atreya, and R. Patodi is not the bureaucratic and impersonal leviathan of the modern state; it is a paternalistic institution of almost divine proportions, an enlightened body of good works and moral purpose. In Banaras I would often hear wrestlers talking of how they wished the government would provide them with food, clothes, and akhara facilities, thus enabling them to concentrate singlemindedly on the immediate task at hand. If the government would only take care of mundane concerns, the citizen wrestler would be that much less encumbered by obligations, responsibilities and temptations of the material world. If the government were to give each village a "fitness account" of 100 rupees, writes K. P. Singh, then "[H]earts which have been still will burst with life, and the villages will revive. The rural masses will be reinstated as the real citizens of the nation. A fresh breeze will animate the country. . . . The youth of India will be flooded with pride in their bodies. They will be united with the government and the government's popularity will grow" (1972*c*: 41).

The utopian government of which the wrestler speaks is dramatically different from the government that sets "sports quotas" but does not otherwise take an interest in the wrestler's way of life. The line between government responsibility toward wrestlers becomes blurred with the wrestler's responsibility toward the nation. As the wrestling ideal expands, national leaders will be drawn into the ranks of the wrestling citizenry. National concerns are wrestling concerns, and the perfect leader is the perfect everyman who is the perfect wrestler. There is a sense here in which the perspective on polity and responsibility changes as wrestlers move from a minority position to a majority status. Paternalism shades into communal self-help. As such the need for patronage is preempted; or rather, the citizen wrestler is his own patron. Patronage and governance dissolve into civic responsibility, a kind of romantic, bucolic anarchy of the collectively fit.

THE UTOPIAN VISION

Utopia is a corollary to ideology, and the ethical nationalism of wrestling presages an anachronistic image of India as a country of villages and akharas populated by men of great physical strength and moral stature. The image is as pure as it is necessarily vague and visionary. While there are obviously elements of nostalgia built into this utopia—the golden age of past perfection—it is for the most part an image of progressive change. The utopia which the wrestler/writers herald is sharply juxtaposed to the dystopia of modernity. Akharas replace tea shops and cinema halls, milk replaces tea as the drink of choice, earth replaces facial cream, mustard oil replaces scented hair tonic, and the tight langot replaces all that is vulgar in the world of sensual, sartorial fashion.

From the perspective of someone who does not appreciate the wrestler's view of the body, such an image of progressive change would seem shallow and misguided. It does not deal with the larger issues of policy, planning, and economic development, which is to say that it seems more fanciful than functional. The wrestler's utopian vision does not contain a formula for revolutionary changes in social structure or civic organization. Having become disciplined wrestlers, it is argued, people will otherwise go about their lives in a normal fashion. The citizen wrestler is called upon to change his attitude and way of living rather than the type of work he does or the practical goals he envisions for himself and his children. Subtle subversion is regarded as the means by which immorality and deceit are to be leached from the national fabric. Thus, a wrestling politician will be less susceptible to corruption and will work for the common good; a wrestling police officer will sacrifice his personal gain to the end of greater social justice; a wrestling dairy farmer will not dilute the milk he sells, thus insuring the better health of all concerned; and so on, through the ranks of all occupations, roles, and institutions.

The utopian future is, admittedly, a two-dimensional place conceived of by wrestlers in primarily somatic terms. They almost wholly ignore questions of economic growth, political power, and development, as well as other national concerns. Theirs is a circumscribed utopia, but not one bounded by ideals of communal living and isolated simplicity. The future is cast in terms of picturesque rural beauty: fertile fields, fresh air, shade trees, and cool streams. Although pro-rural, the utopian future is not expressly anti-urban. In fact, given the poetic and visionary nature of wrestling rhetoric, it is fairly easy to cast urban life in rural terms. Airy, cool, earthy urban akharas are in many ways rural microcosms. In keeping with the image of rural simplicity, wrestlers speak of the future as a time when good, pure food will be available to everyone. As one wrestler put it, "There will be enough milk and almonds for everyone to eat." Self-sufficiency is an aspect of this gastro-utopia, for in the best possible world each hard-working family group would own enough cows and buffalos to have an unlimited supply of milk and ghi.

In order to bring about the utopia envisioned and presaged by the ideology of wrestling, it is the moral duty of every wrestler to convert others to his chosen life path.

> If every wrestler were to train two wrestlers every five years, then every fifth year the number of wrestlers would at least double. . . .
>
> It can be said that a wrestler is not a wrestler unless he makes others into wrestlers. The wicked and the corrupt are quick to swell their ranks with converts, while the pure and honest sit back quietly. Is goodness cowardly and shy? Is it selfish? It is essential that we put our lives behind goodness. Today! Now! . . .
>
> A wrestler must have a missionary spirit. He must be obsessed with the advancement of wrestling. He must get excited about his art. He must be interested in spreading the word throughout the nation. He must make wrestling contagious; not as a disease, but as a way of life (K. P. Singh 1972–1973: 11–12).

A number of poems glorify the nature of the wrestler's nationalistic duty. One entitled "Duty" by Ram Chandar "Kherawda" Kesriya (1973: 25) is typical:

> Duty calls, stand up oh youth of India.
> Lift up the nation's name today, oh youth.
>
> It is lost, oh listen youth of India.
> Go and find the wrestling which is lost,
>   oh youth.
>
> With the strength of shakti
> Krishna lifted up the mountain.
> With the strength of shakti
> Bali defeated Ravana.
>
> Only by worshiping shakti
>   was Ram able to pull Shiva's bow.
> Steadfast duty enabled these three
>   to have shakti.
>
> Duty is one of God's voices.
> It is the law of manhood.
>
> Duty is behind all courageous achievements.
> Behind all manifest power is the hand of duty.
>
> It is the call of duty, awaken oh youth of India.
> Rekindle the lamp of youth.
>
> Recognize the strength of shakti,
>   oh youth of India.
> It is the time, raise up oh youth of India.

Shantilal Chajherd, another wrestling poet, has written a number of poems. In one, entitled "We Will Make it Heaven," he admonishes India's youth to throw off the veil of darkness, light the lamps of national pride, lovingly embrace spirituality, and turn away from passion so that "there will be no more hunger and no more thirst; and so that all people will have understanding" (1973: 30). In a song entitled "Vital Life" (1972: 77) the same poet laments the passing of wrestling champions and criticizes an attitude of complacency which characterizes the modern scene:

> Some say, "What are you doing friend?"
> "Why exercise and stop eating chat?"
>
> We eat like indiscriminate animals, and are sick.
> By the thousands in hospitals we rot.

Another poet, who calls himself "Dwivedi," has written a long serial poem entitled "The Cow Shed." Six new stanzas of the poem appear in each successive edition of the journal *Bharatiya Kushti*. The poem elaborates on the theme of cow protection—a powerful symbol of Hindu religiosity—and uses the symbol of the cow shed (*goshala*) as a metaphor for all that is good and moral about the traditional Indian polity. Dwivedi laments the way in which the goshala has been undermined by corrupt politics (1972–1973: 33; stanza 146); how the cow shed metaphorically stumbles at the sight of young men in foreign suits and ties (ibid: stanza 148); how temples, masjids and churches have undermined the integrity of the cow shed (1973: 19; stanza 153); how taverns and liquor stores have pitted brother against brother (1971: 19; stanza 112); and how drinking has been the downfall of fathers, husbands and sons (1972–1973: 33; stanza 145). Each set of six stanzas usually ends with an appeal for young men to uphold the values the cow shed represents. Often the correlation between the cow shed and the akhara is made explicit. One set (1973: 19; stanza 156) ends with the following verse.

> In June there is again to be a tournament in Delhi.
> Let us watch to see who will win—
> Who will carry away the prize.
>
> In a tournament one must show—
> The jewels of one's strength, courage and brilliance
> It is for this reason that the wrestler—
> Must remember the cow shed.

It is incumbent on every wrestler to read the poetics of this nationalism into the particular situation of his own life. What this means is to be able to translate personal strength into national integrity, personal health into national well-being and self-control into national discipline.

ASCETIC WRESTLERS: AGENTS OF UTOPIAN REFORM

In wrestling rhetoric the sannyasi provides a model for the duty-bound missionary wrestler. As K. P. Singh writes,

Practice self-denial. Go to the villages. Be an ascetic for your work. Spread the word and do it with missionary zeal. If a wrestler only gives a fraction of himself and goes to the villages, thousands of young people will crowd around him and dig an akhara. The roots will then run deep and it will not take long to build up a tower of moral and physical strength (1972c: 47).

As the sannyasi stands apart from the world yet is integrated into life as a spiritual teacher, so the wrestler is integrated into social life as an ethical reformer.

> It is not sufficient for a wrestler to be just a wrestler. If he does not give a portion of his strength back to society will he benefit from his selfishness? What fruit will his effort bear? Even the sannyasi who has retreated from society to the forest has given us learning in the form of scriptures (K. P. Singh 1972–1973: 12).

Perhaps the single most important aspect of the sannyasi's character is his detachment from worldly concerns. As such, he is the mirror opposite of the debauched everyman whose obsession with commodities, fashion, and sensual gratification is so expressly worldly in a gross, modern way. In this regard the sannyasi-like wrestler heralds in a new era of somatic ethics. Just as the hedonistic everyman embodies the affliction of modernity as personal narcissism, the sannyasi-like wrestler embodies reform in terms of manifestly individualistic ideals. As an eminently individualistic persona, the sannyasi-like wrestler is a perfect citizen of the utopian future.

Given the preponderance of "evils" in modern India and the very conservative interpretation of what poses a moral threat to society, the only effective response is to put the burden of responsibility on the shoulders of each individual. A community of wrestlers cannot hope to censure every film and magazine or shut down every liquor store, tea shop or chat stall. Nor could they realistically hope to organize a campaign against prostitution or shut down the mills which produce synthetic cloth. The nature of the conservatism is too diffuse and the objectionable sources of debauchery too powerful and entrenched. Following the model of the sannyasi, the wrestlers advocate a retreat from the world. Each person must turn into himself as he turns his back on what Rajkumar "Hans" has called the "rotten environment" of an afflicted nation. The idea is not to combat depravity through direct political action but to replant the seeds of reform, as it were, in the body of each person. R. K. Sharma captures this ascetic ideal when he calls on the citizens of India to return to the akharas:

> Brothers! If we are to revive our true and natural condition. If we are to shatter our naivete; if we are to champion the people's concern for ethical reform and establish programs for morality in everyday life; if we are to reestablish the primacy of the race through the revival of religious and moral values; if, more than anything else, we are to protect our national freedom, then the most important and crucial task which is before us is to banish once

and for all every vestige of carnal sensuality which we secret within us. To do this we must begin immediately to champion the cause of our own fidelity; and to do this we must not rely on the agency of our thoughts alone but on the reconstitution of our bodies as not only healthy, but strong, quick, beautiful and radiant enough to take on the difficult task of ethical reform (n.d.: 4–5).

In the utopian vision, wrestling remains a world turned in on itself where character and strength are a feature of personal identity. But as all of the people turn in upon themselves—exercising, praying, eating, drinking milk, and following the mandate of their respective guru—the nation itself becomes an akhara.

However abstract and romantic this ideal may seem, it is, in fact, put into practice by some wrestlers. Many wrestlers with whom I spoke emphasized the role they must play in drawing young boys into akharas. The future of the nation is dependent on the degree to which they are able to pass the heritage of wrestling ideals from one generation to the next. They must do this both through active recruitment as well as by straightforward example. It was always with great pride and a sense of deep satisfaction that senior wrestlers—themselves cut in a somewhat ascetic/teacher mold—would show me a group of eight- to ten-year-olds wrestling their way to a better India.

CHAPTER 11

The Individual Re-Formed

Having ended the previous chapter on a note of utopian rhetoric, I feel compelled to remind the reader that the world of wrestling is not nearly what it aspires to be. Relative to factories, temples, mosques, police stations and government offices—to say nothing of cinema halls and cloth mills—there are only a few akharas in modern India.

Along these lines of relative perspective, I heard an interesting folktale about a two-ton wrestler. It went something like this:

A two-ton wrestler, who was unbeaten in his own land, went in search of a three-ton wrestler who he had heard lived not far away. The two wrestlers met and they began to wrestle in a farmer's field. In the process they crushed six or seven goats which were part of a herd of forty or fifty which belonged to an old woman. The woman came upon the wrestlers and, seeing her goats crushed, quickly gathered up the remaining animals, put them in a bag, and slung this across her shoulder. She then picked up the two-ton wrestler and put him on one shoulder and picked up the three-ton wrestler and put him on the other. The wrestlers continued to grapple as she made her way toward home.

Along the way, however, a black vulture smelled the dead goats and swooped down, grabbed the old woman, the two wrestlers and the bag of goats, and flew off into the sky. As the vulture flew over a king's palace, the old woman, the goats and the two wrestlers fell and landed in the eye of a princess who was sitting on the palace roof.

The princess called out to her courtiers and servants, asking them to look into her eye to see what it was that caused her so much discomfort. However, no one, not even the court doctor, was able to find anything in the princess's eye. The king called a council and asked his advisors what ought to be done.

One of them suggested that a local fisherman be called in to cast his net in the princess's eye and thereby extract whatever it was that caused her such pain.

The local fisherman was called, and taking his best net he cast it into the princess's eye. He and his relatives all began to pull and pull until they were so tired that they could hardly stand. Finally, however, they pulled the net all the way through and out of the princess's eye, and there in the net was the old woman, the bag of goats, and the two wrestlers still grappling on her back as though nothing had happened.

The tale, which is constructed as a riddle, or paradox, ends with the question: who was the biggest? Was it the two-ton wrestler, his three-ton adversary, the disgruntled old woman, the black vulture, the hapless princess, or the fisherman? Ultimately, as I think the tale/riddle demonstrates, scale is not as important—or as clearly defined, and therefore as constitutive of reality—as is the nature of the universe within which the seemingly out-of-perspective events take place. In her study of the *Yogavasistha*, O'Flaherty discusses the dimensions of such a universe, which she characterizes as mobius in nature: finite, but unbounded; bigger inside than outside; where inside is outside; where things get bigger as they get smaller; and where the dreamer is dreamed (1984: 240–241). The two seemingly gigantic wrestlers grapple their way through just such a paradoxical universe; and it is in this mobius sense, I think, that we can understand how the akhara becomes the world and the wrestler's body expands to realign the coordinates of psychosomatic existence.

My argument throughout this study has been that wrestling casts the body in a particular light. Various regimens, in conjunction with certain symbolic structures, have the effect of building the body up to larger-than-life proportions. The regimentation to which the wrestler's body is subject does not produce a wholly disembodied pugilist such as might be the product of Western forms of discipline where body is radically dissociated from mind, and where the rank-and-file individual is regarded as a mere machine. Because Hindu philosophy and practice does not make the same distinction between mind and body, the individual is not objectified in the same way when subject to various forms of discipline. As Narayan Singh pointed out, and I think many other wrestlers would concur, the first step of any exercise begins with the question: Who am I, and what am I put on this earth for? It proceeds along a direct path of regimentation to a subjective experience of self as whole and healthy. Far from being clones in the growing ranks of the merely physically fit, wrestlers develop their ability to translate a bethak, a dand, a glass of milk into self-realization, and this into the subjective reform of moral problems. Such a fit person, as described by Atreya, is "free from egoism, desire, anger, vanity and attachment. Everything is under his control—the body, mind and speech. All his selfish interests get merged with the social interest. He is engaged in bringing about social welfare without any selfishness. He is really a model of ideal and pure behavior. He is not governed by anybody, but his very nature is ethical. Right actions are performed naturally by him" (1973d: 41–42).

In other words, in Hindu India—which is otherwise a world of much larger and more mutable proportions—the somatic discipline of wrestling creates an icon of the individual self. On this subject K. P. Singh provides the following observation:

> When you seek to develop your character, develop it in such a way that it becomes a treasure trove of magnetic power. Do not expect that the riches of life will fall at your feet. You must search for the true meaning of life. Whether through enterprise or through the rigid practice of vyayam, the goal is to plant the seed of human magnetism in this flesh and bone body. When milk is boiled, cream develops, and when gold is fired it shines (1972b: 23).

One of the consequences of building an iconic body charged with the power of human magnetism is that it is slightly out of step with the more protean rank and file who march to the beat of a different drum. The rhythm of everyday life gets confused in the process, as when the wrestler suggests that the health of his body is contingent not only on an ideological denunciation of caste values but also on a physical enactment of what is normally anathema. A positive interpretation of mingling sweat, among other things, is but a logical extension of what is otherwise encoded in the precise mechanics of all akhara life.

But to a large extent the Banaras wrestlers wrestle their way toward a utopian future in much the same way as the two- and three-ton wrestlers grapple their way through the mobius universe. They are oblivious to the cold, hard logic of proportion and pragmatism. They do not always know what the consequences of their actions are. Certainly the close physical proximity of dangal competition, jor, ban, and massage raises the whole issue of purity and pollution. Sometimes, as I have noted, the question is addressed directly. But for the most part the whole issue of caste propriety is analogous to the old woman's goats in the mobius riddle: a fact of life which is somewhat out of place in the arena of wrestling and which accidentally gets crushed by the larger dynamics of an epic struggle. In setting their sights on the utopian future, wrestlers

scale down and then abandon the logic of a more familiar moral environment. The iconic individuality of the sannyasi-like citizen wrestler accidentally undermines the integrity of caste holism.

When I first began to talk with wrestlers I was often told that wrestling is "a world apart." As the research continued I began to understand
how it is that wrestling is apart, and what it is apart from. It skews one's
vision of the social whole. As does a glimpse of the mobius universe, a
wrestling way of life shakes up the perspective and thereby suggests a
different way of seeing commonplace social relations—even if it is just
a mote in a princess's eye.

Appendix

THE NATURE OF WRESTLING NATIONALISM

Wrestling ideology is but one of many forms of nationalism in India today. On account of this it is necessary to situate wrestling within this larger arena of political rhetoric.

The right-wing militant Hindu organization known as the Rashtriya Sway-amsevak Sangh (RSS) advocates ideals that at first glance appear to be analogous to those held by wrestlers (Anderson 1987). The RSS advocates physical training and self-discipline. Youth camps are held in urban neighborhoods where young men and boys are taught *lathi shiksha* (a form of martial art using staves). The emphasis at these camps is on group regimentation and synchronized martial choreography. The ideology of the RSS is structured around a dogmatic interpretation of Hindu philosophy. Poetic verses and slogans commemorate the heroic glory of epic characters such as Bhim, the Pandava brother who possessed phenomenal strength, and Hanuman, whose martial exploits in the service of Ram are regarded as the essence of courageous duty and just aggression. In its pure form, RSS ideology is expressly sectarian and communal. Although the RSS has recently tried to placate non-Hindu minority groups in an effort to gain a greater degree of political legitimacy, it is still regarded by most people as militantly pro-Hindu.

There is much in the RSS ideology which seems to fit with wrestling ideals. In both arenas young men are taught self-control and physical fitness. Personal strength is regarded in both systems as an individualistic form of national strength. The focus on Hanuman as an icon of strength and self-sacrifice is found in both wrestling and RSS circles. Indeed, there are undoubtedly some wrestlers who find much to commend in the militant ideology of Hindu chauvinism. There are also probably a number of RSS sympathizers who are akhara members. Nevertheless, and despite formal parallels, I found that those wrestlers who followed a strict regimen of daily training felt a great deal of ambivalence and some outright hostility toward RSS ideals. This may be explained with reference to the following points.

First, at least in principle, wrestling is non-sectarian. In other words its use of Hindu symbols to express national ideals—sannyas and Hanuman, for example—are thought to be general enough not to alienate non-Hindu wrestlers. However naive this may be, many wrestlers claim that the Hanuman of the wrestling akhara is symbolically and morally equivalent to Ali, his heroic Islamic counterpart found in many Muslim akharas. In any case, Hindu and Muslim wrestlers strive toward an ideological compromise by which they seek to transcend formal substantive differences in order to arrive at a common utopian future where the akhara mediates between temple and mosque. While there are some akharas where Muslims and Hindus practice together, there are more where segregation along communal lines is the norm. This is often lamented by both Hindu and Muslim senior wrestlers who point out that Gama, a Muslim wrestler who became "world champion" in the early part of this century, was trained by a Hindu guru. In spite of the incipiently sectarian tone of much wrestling rhetoric—where images of Shiva, shakti, and Pandava war heroes abound—there is usually also a more pervasive tone of secular, non-communal fraternity. For example, H. B. Singh recalls the glory of Arjun and Krishna's martial exploits. He then writes that in the akhara—which is modeled on the guru/chela relationship most perfectly manifest in Ram and Lakshman's relationship with Vishwamitra and Arjun's discipleship under Dronachariya— "there should be no hint of the vile, invidious distinctions fostered by caste, religion or community" (1972: 3).

The second point of difference between the two ideologies is that RSS leaders advocate militant reform while wrestlers advocate peaceful self-sacrifice. RSS leaders argue that Hinduism has been eroded by foreign religious teachings as well as by the post-independence state policy of secular democracy. RSS leaders point to instances of affirmative action in education and legal discrimination to argue that the Hindu majority is being discriminated against. Public parades on religious holidays have become powerful arenas for militant protest. Similarly, violent confrontations occur around issues of temple and mosque construction and renovation. While the RSS leadership has toned down its militant rhetoric in recent years, one of the primary rationales for training young men in lathi drill is to prepare them for defensive and offensive confrontation. The young RSS recruit is, in this regard, a Hindu soldier. Through physical training he develops his body. But unlike the wrestler, who develops his body to a primarily moral and ethical end, the RSS recruit develops his body as a utilitarian means for a more expressly political purpose. Thus, for example, the RSS and the wrestler have quite different interpretations of Hanuman's divinity. In Hanuman's powerful physique the wrestler sees strength derived from devotion and self-control. The RSS recruit is trained to see a Hanuman who does righteous battle against the forces of evil.

A third point of difference between the two forms of nationalist ideology has to do with structural organization. The RSS is a religious organization with a clearly defined leadership and an extensive bureaucratic and administrative apparatus. It is an expressly reform-oriented movement with clear goals and explicit motives. Regional and local chapters are directly, if not always closely, linked to a centralized command structure. While the RSS is not overtly involved in state-level party politics, it does lend considerable informal support to those party factions and candidates who are sympathetic to its views. By virtue of the fact that authority is vested in a few key individuals and ideologues, RSS nationalism is clearly articulated as a kind of militant manifesto.

No wrestling institution corresponds to the RSS's structure of leadership and network of national affiliation. Each akhara is a unit unto itself. Indeed, the institutional structure of the akhara is itself fairly weak, for the primary relationship which might be said to structure the world of wrestling is the bond that exists between a disciple and his guru. The akhara is a collectivety of individuals who subscribe to a particular regimen. Wrestling ideology is, in this regard, the antithesis of the RSS ideology. Where the RSS ideology starts with a vision of Hindu reform and imposes discipline on the body of the young recruit, the wrestling ideology starts with the discipline of the individual body and works toward a somatic utopia. It is important to remember that wrestling is a sport, and many wrestlers enjoy competition for the sake of competition. The ideological dimension of wrestling grows out of a fairly innocuous base, and, as we have seen, nationalistic implications emerge through poetic interpretation. From the wrestler's perspective the moral enemy is everyman's inner susceptibility to sensual seduction. From the RSS perspective the enemy lies without in the form of "false" religious teachings and a secular state ideology. The latter requires a bureaucratic structure of organized defense, the former a regimen of self-control.

As a cautionary note it must be said that I may be accused of reifying both forms of nationalism in order to contrive a sharp dichotomy. If, in fact, some wrestlers are active members of the RSS, how can one say that they subscribe to either one or the other ideology? While I was in Banaras, regional leaders of the RSS asked members of one akhara to put on a demonstration of wrestling techniques to inspire young recruits congregated for a training camp. A local branch of the RSS sponsored a wrestling tournament in Banaras at which pro-Hindu speeches were made. Some wrestlers I knew marched in parades organized by RSS workers. In other words, it should be noted that on some points there is a high degree of overlap between wrestling values and the ideals of Hindu nationalism. Further historical analysis would undoubtedly show that at various times, and in specific parts of the country, the two have converged and diverged to different degrees. My point here is to highlight the distinctive features of the wrestler's nationalistic vision given the nature of the modern world he lives in. In this sense there are enough wrestlers who consciously and exclusively subscribe to a unique way of life that centers on akhara activities to justify speaking of wrestling as a distinct form of nationalism.

Glossary

ACHĀR, spiced vegetable pickle.

ADITI, mother of the gods; earth.

ĀDITYA, sun; son of the earth.

AGNI, fire; god of fire associated with energy on ritual occasions.

AHIMSĀ, non-violence.

AHIR, caste group whose traditional occupation is herding and dairying; synonymous with the label Yadav.

AKHĀṚĀ, any association organized for the practice of a specific art or hobby, most often used to designate a wrestling gymnasium.

AMRIT, elixir.

ĀNAND, satisfaction, peace, contentment.

APARIGRAHA, self-sufficient, independent.

ĀRTĪ PŪJĀ, ritual performed with fire, usually at a designated time.

ĀSAN, yogic exercises.

ĀSHRAM, monastery or hermitage.

ASATYA, falsehood; a lie.

ĀTMĀ, soul.

ĀYURVEDA, science of Hindu medicine (Ayurvedic).

BĀBĀ (BĀBĀ JĪ), title of friendly respect used to refer to a sadhu or holy man.

BAGAL DUBBĀ, wrestling move.

BAJRANG, title given to Hanuman meaning "stout" or "strong."

BAL, physical strength, brute force.

BĀN, pair-exercise done by pushing against a partner's arms.

BANĀRSĪ, person from Banaras or a characteristic trait or fashion of the people from Banaras.

BANYAN, tree (*Ficus indica*) that puts out aerial roots and has religious significance in folk religion; in Hindi, *bargad*.

BARĀT, groom's party in a wedding ceremony.

BATĀSĀ, crystallized, aerated sugar drops used as prasad offerings in religious worship.

BESAN, gram pulse flour.

BEṬHAK, deep knee bends.

BHAGWĀN, generic term for God.

BHAKTĪ (BHAKTA), devotional religion (a practitioner of bhakti).

BHĀKUṚĪ, a wrestling move.

BHĀNG, hashish.

BINDĪ, auspicious mark placed on the forehead.

BRAHMACHARYA, first stage in the fourfold Hindu life cycle scheme of development; celibacy.

BRAHMACHĀRĪ, one who is celibate; a young disciple.

BHŪMIHĀR, landed-gentry caste group.

BRĀHMAN, member of the priestly caste.

BUDDHI, wisdom.

CHAMĀR, low-ranking "untouchable" caste; leather workers.

CHANDĀ, donation; collection.

CHAṆḌĀL, "untouchable" caste group, often those who work at cremation ground.

CHANĀ, chickpeas, a common item in prasad offerings.

CHĀṬ, savory snack prepared in small specialty stores and sold in streetside stalls.

CHAṬNĪ, spicy sauce; condiment.

CHELĀ, disciple or follower.

CHAUK, crossroads or central square.

CHŪRAN, digestive powder sold in herbalist stores and by street vendors; remedy for stomach disorders.

CHŪṚĪDĀR PAYJĀMĀ, loose-fitting, drawstring pants that are tight at the ankle and calf.

DĀDĀ, elder; grandfather; boss.

DĀL, lentils.

DAM KASĪ, stamina.

ḌAṆḌ, jackknifing push-ups.

ḌAṆḌ-ṬHONK, chest beating and arm slapping, the prelude to a competitive bout.

DANGAL, wrestling tournament.

DARBĀR, royal court.

DARSHAN, the visual encounter with god in worship; to do darshan is to go see the image of god in a temple.

DASNĀMĪ, name of the ten monastic orders founded by the followers of Shankaracharya.

DĀW, wrestling move.

DEVTĀ, god.

ḌHĀK, wrestling move.

ḌHĀKULĪ, twists and flips practiced by wrestlers to increase the strength and flexibility of their neck muscles.

DHARMASHĀLĀ, rest house for pilgrims.

DHARMA, religion; moral principle of religious duty.

DHĀTU, primary substance of the body; semen; mineral.

DHOBĪ PAṬ, wrestling move which resembles the movement of a washerman beating clothes.

ḌHOL, drum, the short form of dholak; a two-sided drum beaten with a curved stick.

DHOTĪ, loincloth; long white garment.

DISHĀ MAIDĀN, open plain used for defecation.

DOSH, imperfection, illness, mistake.

GADĀ, weighted club used for exercise.

GADDĀ, mat, as in wrestling mat.

GANESH, elephant-headed god; Shiva's son.

GAR NĀL, circular stone weight hung around the neck for exercising.

GHARĀNĀ, particular substyle of an art form associated with a specific artist and his or her disciples.

GHĀṬ, river bank; usually designated for bathing, ritual performance, or cremation.

GHĪ, clarified butter.

GOD, lap.

GOSHĀLĀ, cow protection shelter; cowshed.

GWĀL, herder, dairyman.

GRIHASTHA, second stage in the fourfold Hindu life cycle scheme; a householder.

GALĪ, narrow lane.

GUṚ, hard molasses.

GURUKUL, traditional school structured around the principles of a guru-chela relationship.

HALDĪ, turmeric.

HAṬHA YOGA, branch of yoga which emphasizes rigorous physical postures.

HĀTH, hand; measure of one swing in exercise.

HIJṚĀ, an Indian gender category which is neither male nor female; full-time female impersonator who is a member of a social group.

ISHṬA DEVTĀ, one's personal god.

ĪSHVAR PRAṆIDHĀN, focused concentration on god; closeness to god through worship.

JAJMĀNĪ, the system of reciprocal exchange that obtains between members of different castes; patron-client relationship.

JĀNGHIYĀ, briefs; wrestling trunks.

JĀṬ, powerful rural caste group in western Uttar Pradesh, Haryana, and Punjab.

JHĀṚ, wrestling move.

JĪVANMUKTI, having left life; a hermit's attitude.

JOR, wrestling when done as a form of exercise.

JOṚĪ, pair of wooden clubs.

KĀLĀJĀNGH, wrestling move.

KALARIPPAYATTU, southwestern Indian martial art.

KALIYUG, dark and final epoch in Hindu cosmology; a time when immorality reigns and social institutions are subverted.

KALĀ, art.

KAMDAMAN, controlled sensuality; continence.

KAPH, phlegm.

KARMA, fate; work; moral work.

KASE LANGOṬ KE, celibate; firm or tight g-string.

KHĀDĪ, rough homespun cotton.

KHĪR, rice-puddinglike drink often served at Yadav weddings.

KHULĀ ḌANGAL, free or open wrestling competition.

KHURĀK, diet.

KRIYĀ, action; work.

KSHATRIYA, varna category used loosely to designate a number of caste groups who identify themselves as warriorlike or of royal heritage.

KUMBHAK, breath control leading to stamina.

KUṆḌALINĪ, the experience of enlightenment achieved through yoga and meditation; vital energy which is "ignited" through disciplined yogic practices.

KUṆḌ, pond; tank.

KURTĀ, a long, loose-fitting, uncuffed shirt.

KUSHTĪ, wrestling in its competitive manifestation.

LAḌḌŪ, besan flour sweets often used as prasad.

LANGOṬ, g-string, worn as an undergarment by men and as a protective covering by wrestlers during practice, worn underneath the janghiya.

LANGŪR DAUṚ, running like a monkey; an exercise done by wrestlers in the pit.

LASSĪ, milkshake made of yogurt, milk, and sugar.

LĪLĀ, divine play.

LINGAM, iconic, phallic form of Lord Shiva.

LOHĀ, iron.

MAHĀDEV, Great God; Shiva.

MAHANT, abbot; head of a monastic order.

MAHĀRĀJ, honorific title used to refer to a holy man or Brahman.

MAHĀVĪR, Great Courageous (or Hero); Hanuman.

MAIDĀN, open plain; central park area.

MALLA, classical term for wrestler.

MALLAYUDDHA, classical wrestling combat.

MALLAVIDYĀ, wrestling knowledge.

MANDIR, Hindu temple.

MANTRA, secret, sacred slogan.

MARĀṬHĀ, term used loosely to refer to the people of Maharashtra.

MASJID, Muslim place of worship; mosque.

MAST, intoxicated with pleasure.

MĀYĀ, illusion.

MAZDŪR (MAZDOOR), laborer.

MEHANDI (MENDĪ), henna; vegetable dye.

MIṬṬĪ, earth.

MOKSHA, release; salvation achieved through self-realization.

MULTĀNĪ, wrestling move.

MŪRTI, image of god.

NĀG, cobra.

NĀGĀ, one of the Dasnami orders known for its martial form of asceticism.

NĀĪ, barber caste.

NĀL, stone weight.

NĀM KAMĀNĀ, to make a name for oneself.

NĪM, margosa tree (*Melia azadirachta*).

NIRODH, retention, control; often used to mean birth control.

NIYAM, rules of right conduct; fundamental principle in yoga.

NŪRĀ, fake; fraud.

OJ (OJAS), the luster of vitality or virility.

PĀN, a betel-leaf, lime-paste, betel-nut, spice, and condiment concoction, mildly narcotic.

PANCHĀYAT, a quorum; council of five.

PAINTRĀ, wrestling stance.

PĀRAS, stone that can turn base metal to gold.

PAW, a quarter of a liter.

PAHALWĀN, wrestler.

PECH, countermove in wrestling.

PHARSĀ, heavy hoe or spade.

PĪPAL, *Ficus religiosa*.

PITTA, bile.

PRADHĀN, chief; head official.

PRĀNA, one of the five vital airs; vital breath.

PRĀNĀYĀMA, disciplined or controlled breathing.

PRASĀD, ritual food offerings.

RAI, gentry caste group.

RĀJĀ, king; lord.

RĀJAS, one of the three "personality" characteristics which also characterizes certain food items; agitated, aggressive, hot.

RĀJPŪT, an encompassing caste category which is roughly equivalent to the varna Kshatriya category; those who belong to a martial caste.

RASA, juice; sauce; soup.

RITU, season.

SĀDHU, mendicant; one who lives on alms and has renounced the world.

SAKHĪ, wrestling move.

SALĀMĪ, salute to the pit.

SAMĀDHI, condition of absolute release from worldly constraints; shrines dedicated to those who have achieved this condition.

SAMĀJ, society; social organization.

SANTOSH, satisfaction, contentment.

SANNYĀS (SANNYĀSI), world renunciation (world renouncer).

SAT GURU, true or great guru.

SATSANG, fellowship; fraternity.

SVAPNA DOSH, wet dream; night emission of semen.

SĀPHĀ, a head cloth.

SARWAJANIK, public.

SĀTTVA, one of the three "personality" characteristics which also characterizes various food items; cool, calm, white, peaceful.

SATYA, truth; truthfulness.

SAWĀRĪ, being a passenger; the superior position in wrestling; type of exercise.

SEER, one-fourth of a given measure.

SHAKTĪ, divine, supernatural energy.

SHAKTĪ SHĀLĪ, an aura of energized strength which characterizes an invigorated wrestler.

SHĀNT, peace and tranquility.

SHARĪR, body.

SHAUK, hobby.

SHĪRSHĀSAN, head stand.

SHAUCH, cleaning out impurities; defecation and urination.

SHŪDRA, varna category designating menial, service castes.

SINDŪR, vermilion.

SUKRAM PAYAS, bright milk; semen.

SŪRYA, sun.

SŪRYA NAMASKĀR, salute to the sun; a type of exercise.

SWĀDHYĀYA, self-control; study.

SWĀGAT, welcome; to honor.

TAMAS, one of the three "personality" characteristics which is also characteristic of various food items; dull, dark, lethargic.

TAP (TAPAS), austerity; sensory control; mortification.

ṬHĀKUR, honorific meaning lord or master; often used as a form of address by wealthy Rajputs.

ṬHANḌĀĪ, a cooling drink.

ṬHEKEDĀR, contractor.

ṬĪKA, mark of vermilion paste placed on the forehead by a priest during rituals and darshan.

TIL, very small seed from the sesame plant.

URAD, type of lentil.

USTĀD, teacher; one who is proficient in a particular art or skill.

VĀNAR, monkey.

VARṆA, color; system of ranked classification which provides the model for caste stratification.

VĀT, one of the humors of the body.

VĀYU, wind, air.

VIBHŪTI, ashes; power; energy.

VĪRYA, semen.

VṚṢṆYAM PAYAS, virile "seedlike" milk.

VYAKTITWA, character; personal identity.

VYĀYĀM, exercise.

VYĀYĀMSHĀLĀ, gymnasium; synonymous with akhara but with a slight connotation of an exercise gym rather than a wrestling gym.

YAM, first principle in yoga; root meaning.

YONI, vagina; base; source.

ZAMĪNDĀR, wealthy landowner; landed gentry of northern India before independence.

Bibliography

Ali, Barkat
    1984   *Pahalwano ki Duniya* [The Wrestlers' World]. New Delhi: Prince Offset Press.

Allchin, F. R. (editor, translator)
    1964   *Tulsi Das Kavitavali*. London: George Allen and Unwin.

Alter, Joseph S.
    1989   Gama the Great: Indian Nationalism and the World Wrestling Championships of 1910 and 1920. Manuscript.

Anderson, W. K.
    1987   *The Brotherhood in Saffron: The Rashtriya Swayamsevak Sangh and Hindu Revivalism*. Boulder: Westview Press.

Anonymous
    1978   "Anar" [Pomegranate]. *Bharatiya Kushti* 16, nos. 7, 8, 9: 17–18.
    n.d.   *Vyayam Shiksha* [Exercise Training]. Delhi: Dehati Pustak Bhandar.

Appadurai, Arjun
    1981   "Gastro Politics in Hindu South Asia." *American Ethnologist* 8, no. 3: 494–511.
    1986   "Is Homo Hierarchicus." *American Ethnologist* 13, no. 4: 745–761.

Areya, Radheshyam
    1978   "Vidhyarti aur Vyayam" [Students and Exercise]. *Bharatiya Kushti* 16, no. 10, 11, 12: 33–34.

Aryan, K. C.
    n.d.   *Hanuman in Art and Mythology*. Delhi: Rekha Prakashan.

Asiaweek
    1989   "Behold the Matman Cometh." June 2: 65.

Atreya, Shanti Prakash
   1965   *Yoga Manovigyan ki Rup Rekha* [A Summary Sketch (lit., Blue-
                 print) of Yoga and Psychology]. Moradabad: Darshan Printers.
   1971   "Gramin Chetron mein Sharirik Shiksha" [Physical Education
                 in Rural Areas]. *Bharatiya Kushti* 8, no. 9, 10, 11: 21–48.
   1972*a*   "Malla Shiromani, Sri Krishna" [That Eminent Wrestler, Lord
                 Krishna]. *Bharatiya Kushti* 9, no. 10, 11, 12: 31–35.
   1972*b*   "Mitti ka Akhara Swarag aur Gadda ka Akhara Narak" [The
                 Earth Pit is Heaven and the Mat Pit is Hell]. *Bharatiya Kushti*
                 10, no. 1, 2, 3: 19–38.
   1972–1973   "Pahalwani mein Guru ka Sthan" [The Place of the Guru in
                 Wrestling]. *Bharatiya Kushti* 10, no. 7, 8, 9: 19–24.
   1973*a*   "Saccha Pahalwan Devta Hota Hai" [The True Wrestler is God].
                 Bharatiya Kushti 10, no. 7, 8, 9: 21–26.
   1973*b*   "Brahmacharya" [Celibacy]. *Bharatiya Kushti* 10, no. 10, 11,
                 12: 21–34.
   1973*c*   "Brahmacharya" [Celibacy]. *Bharatiya Kushti* 11, no. 1, 2, 3:
                 21–30.
   1973*d*   *Health and Yoga*. Varanasi: Sri Hari Press.
   1974   "Pahalwani mein Dand-Bethak Vyayam ka Sthan" [The Place
                 of Dand-Bethak Exercises in Wrestling]. *Bharatiya Kushti* 11,
                 no. 7, 8, 9: 21–26.
   1974–1975   "Pahalwani aur Nasha" [Wrestling and Intoxicants]. *Baharatiya
                 Kushti* 12, no. 4, 5, 6: 17–22.
   1978   "Pahalwani mein Nind awein Vishram ka Sthan" [The Place of
                 Sleep and Rest in Wrestling]. *Bharatiya Kushti* 16, no. 4, 5, 6:
                 17–26.
   1979   "Kalyugi Parashurama: Bhagwan Singh Narayane Walla"
                 [Ram-with-an-Ax of the Dark Age: Bhagwan Singh Narayane
                 Walla]. *Bharatiya Kushti* 17, no. 1, 2, 3: 39–46.
   1981   "Kuthalgate, Rajpur ka Yoga awein Kushti Prashikshan Kendra
                 Chunne ka Vishisht Rahasiya" [The Special and Mystical Rea-
                 sons for Choosing Rajpur's Kuthalgate Yoga and Wrestling
                 Training Center]. *Bharatiya Kushti* 18, no. 10, 11, 12: 62–64.
   1984   "Ghi" [Clarified Butter]. *Bharatiya Kushti* 21, no. 3: 21–36.
   1985   "Pahalwani mein Jor Karne Karane ki Niti" [The Virtue of
                 Doing and Having Jor Done in Wrestling]. *Bharatiya Kushti* 22,
                 no. 4: 23–49.
   1986*a*   "Garibi aur Swasthiya" [Poverty and Health]. *Bharatiya Kushti*
                 24, no. 2: 49–52.
   1986*b*   "Pahalwani Malish ki Niti" [The Virtue of Wrestling Massage].
                 Bharatiya Kushti 24, no. 1: 25–32.
√ Babcock, Barbara
   1980   "Reflexivity: Definitions and Discriminations." *Semiotica* 30,
                 no. 1, 2: 1–14.
√ Babineau, M.
   1979   *Love of God and Social Duty in the Ramacaritamanasa*. New
                 Delhi: Motilal BanarsiDass.

Bahadur, S. P.
  1980   *The Complete Works of Goswami Tulsidas, Vol. VI, Minor Works*. Varanasi: Prachya Prakashan.
Banerjea, J. N.
  1956   *The Development of Hindu Iconography*. Calcutta: University of Calcutta.
Barnett, Steven
  1977   "Identity Choice and Caste Ideology." In *Symbolic Anthropology*, edited by J. Dolgin, D. Keminitzer, and D. Schneider. New York: Columbia University Press.
Barnett, Steven, and Martin G. Silverman
  1979   *Ideology and Everyday Life*. Ann Arbor: University of Michigan Press.
Barth, A.
  1932   *The Religions of India*. Boston: Houghton, Mifflin and Co.
Barthes, Roland
  1972   *Mythologies*. New York: Hill and Wang.
Basu, Birendranath
  1934   *Bharatir Kusti o Tahar Siksa* [Indian Wrestling and its Study]. Calcutta: n.p.
Beals, Alan
  1964   "Conflict and Interlocal Festivals in a South Indian Region." *Journal of Asian Studies* 23: 95–113.
Beck, Brenda E. F.
  1969   "Colour and Heat in South Indian Ritual." *Man* 4, no. 4: 553–572.
  1976   "The Symbolic Merger of Body, Space and Cosmos in Hindu Tamil Nadu." *Contributions to Indian Sociology* 10: 213–244.
Berreman, Gerald D.
  1966   "Caste in Cross-Cultural Perspective." In *Japan's Invisible Race: Caste in Culture and Personality*, edited by G. DeVos and H. Wagatsuma. Berkeley: University of California Press.
  1967   "Caste as Social Process." *Southwestern Journal of Anthropology* 23: 351–370.
  1972   "Social Categories and Social Interaction in a North Indian City." *American Anthropologist* 74: 567–586.
  1973   *Caste and the Modern World*. Morristown: General Learning Press.
  1979   *Caste and Other Inequities: Essays on Inequality*. Meerut: Folklore Institute.
Béteille, André
  1969   *Castes: Old and New*. Bombay: Asia Publishing House.
Beveridge, A. S. (translator)
  1921   *Babur Nama* [Memoirs of Babur]. London: Luzac and Company.

Bhadudi, S. R. (editor)
    1964   *Swastha-o-Shakti* ([Health and Energy] West Bengal Weight-
                  lifter's and Body-Builder's Magazine of Physical Culture and
                  Fitness) 1, no. 1.
Bhagavad Gita
    1945   Poona: Bhandarkar Oriental Research Institute.
Bhagavata Purana
    1929   Bombay: Nirnayasagara Press.
Bhalekar, Basant
    1978   "Parampara Akharon ki: Mitti se Gadde tak" [The Tradition of
                  Akharas: From Earth to Mats]. *Dharmayug* 29, no. 33: 8–10.
Bhattacharya, Sukhmaya
    1966   *Mahabharata Kalin Samaj* [Society in the Mahabharata Era].
                  Allahabad: Lok Bharatiya Prakashan.
√ Blacking, J. (editor)
    1977   *The Anthropology of the Body.* New York: Academic Press.
Blochmann, H. (translator)
    1873–1948 *A'in-i-Akbari of Abu'l Fazal.* Vol. 3 of *Akbar-Nama.* Calcutta:
                  Asiatic Society of Bengal.
    1904   *Akbar-Nama of Abu-L-Fazl.* Delhi: Ess Ess Publications.
                  Symbolic Interactionism. Englewood Cliffs, N.J.: Prentice-Hall.
Bond, Ruskin
    1967   "The Garlands on His Brow." In *The Neighbor's Wife and
                  Other Stories,* by Ruskin Bond. Madras: Higginbothams.
Bose, Dhirendra Nath (editor)
    n.d.   *Harivamsa.* Dum Dum (Bengal): Datta Bose and Company.
Bose, K.
    1967   "Wrestling 'Round Delhi." *Hindustan Times,* November 12: 16.
√ Bourdieu, Pierre
    1977   *Outline of a Theory of Practice.* Cambridge: Cambridge Univer-
                  sity Press.
Brandes, Stanley
√ 1981   "Like Wounded Stags: Male Sexual Ideology in an Andalusian
                  Town." In *Sexual Meanings,* edited by Sherry B. Ortner and
                  Harriet Whitehead. New York: Cambridge University Press.
√ 1985   *Metaphors of Masculinity: Sex and Status in Andalusian Folk-
                  lore.* Philadelphia: University of Pennsylvania Press.
√ Bruner, E. (editor)
    1984   *Text, Play, Story: The Construction and Reconstruction of Self
                  and Society. 1983 Proceedings of the American Ethnological
                  Society.* Washington, D.C.: American Ethnological Society.
√ Bulcke, C.
    1960   "The Characterization of Hanuman." *Journal of the Royal Ori-
                  ental Institute* 10, no. 4: 393–402.
√ Carman, J. B., and F. A. Marglin (editors)
    1985   *Auspiciousness and Purity.* Leiden: E. J. Brill.

✓ Carstairs, G. Morris
    1958   *The Twice-Born*. London: Hogarth Press.
Chajherd, Shantilal
    1972   "Jindadili" [Vital Life]. *Bharatiya Kushti* 9, no. 7, 8, 9: 77.
    1972–1973 "Mashal Tham lo" [Grab Hold the Torch]. *Bharatiya Kushti*
              10, no. 4, 5, 6: 41.
    1973   "Swarag Banainge" [We Will Make it Heaven]. *Bharatiya
              Kushti* 11, no. 1, 2, 3: 30.
Chakravarti, P. C.
    1972   *The Art of War in Ancient India*. Delhi: Oriental Publishers.
Chakravarty, C.
    1900   *Dharmamangala*. Calcutta: Arunodaya Roy.
Chand, D. P.
    1980   "Who's Who on the Indian National Team." In *XXIX National
              Wrestling Championship Souvenir*. Mangalore: South Kanara
              Amateur Wrestling Association.
Changani, S. K.
    1958   *Sharirik Shiksha* [Physical Education]. Bikaner: Navyug Granth
              Kutir.
— Chattopadhyay, A.
    1966   "Martial Life of Brahamans in Early Medieval India as Known
              from the Kathasaritsagara." *Journal of the Oriental Institute,
              Baroda* 16, no. 1: 52–59.
Chaturvedi, Banarsi Das
    1961   "Kushti Kala ki Raksha Kaise Kiya Jai" [How Can the Art of
              Wrestling be Protected]? *Vishal Bharat* 67, no. 2: 101–102.
Chopra, P. N.
    1963   *Society and Culture During the Mogul Age*. Agra: Shivanlal
              Agarwala.
✓ Clifford, James
    1983   "On Ethnographic Authority." *Representations* 2, Spring 1983:
              132–143.
✓ Clifford, James, and George E. Marcus (editors)
    1986   *Writing Culture: The Poetics and Politics of Ethnography*.
              Berkeley, Los Angeles, London: University of California Press.
✓ Cohn, Bernard S.
    1987   *An Anthropologist Among the Historians*. New York: Oxford
              University Press.
Comaroff, Jean
    1985   *Body of Power, Spirit of Resistance: The Culture and History
              of a South African People*. Chicago: University of Chicago Press.
Crapanzano, Vincent
    1980   *Tuhami: Portrait of a Moroccan*. Chicago: University of Chi-
              cago Press.
Craven, G., and R. Mosley
    1972   "Actors on the Canvas Stage: The Dramatic Conventions of
              Professional Wrestling." *Journal of Popular Culture* 6, no. 2:
              326–336.

Crawford, Robert
   1985   "A Cultural Account of Health: Self-Control, Release, and the Social Body." In *Issues in the Political Economy of Health Care*, edited by J. Mckinlay. London: Tavistock.

√ Crooke, William
   1926   *Religion and Folklore of Northern India*. Oxford: Oxford University Press.

√ Daniel, E. Valentine
   1984   *Fluid Signs: Being a Person the Tamil Way*. Berkeley, Los Angeles, London: University of California Press.

Das, Veena
   1968   "A Sociological Approach to the Caste Puranas." *Sociological Bulletin* 17, no. 2: 141–164.
√ 1977   *Structure and Cognition: Aspects of Hindu Caste and Ritual*. Delhi: Oxford University Press.

Datta, K.
   1970   "The Wonder Boy of Wrestling." *Illustrated Weekly of India*, September 6: 4–5.

Davis, M.
   1983   *Rank and Rivalry*. Cambridge: Cambridge University Press.

Dayal, Thakur Harendra
   1981   *Ancient Culture of India*. Delhi: Sandeep Prakashan.

Dehati Pustak Bhandar
   n.d.*a*   *Hanumanbahuk*. Delhi: Dehati Pustak Bhandar.
   n.d.*b*   *Hanumansathika*. Delhi: Dehati Pustak Bhandar.
   n.d.*c*   *Bajrang Ban*. Delhi: Dehati Pustak Bhandar.
   n.d.*d*   *Ekmukhi, Panchmukhi Hanuman Kawach* [One-Faced, Five-Faced, Hanuman Charms]. Delhi: Dehati Pustak Bhandar.

Deopujari, M.
   1973   *Shivaji and the Maratha Art of War*. Nagpur: Vidharbha Samshodan Mandala.

Deshmukh, R.
   1979   "This Kushti Business." *Indian Express*, April 1: 1.

√ De Wachter, F.
   1988   "The Symbolism of the Healthy Body: A Philosophical Analysis of the Sportive Imagery of Health." In *Philosophic Inquiry in Sport*, edited by W. J. Morgan and V. M. Klaus. Champaign: Human Kinetics Publishers.

√ Diehl, C. G.
   1956   *Instrument and Purpose: Studies on Rites and Rituals In South India*. Lund: Gleerup.

Dixit, Rajesh
   1978   *Hanuman Upasna* [Hanuman Worship]. Delhi: Dehati Pustak Bhandar.
   n.d.   *Aunwle ke Gun tatha Upyog* [The Qualities and Use of Gooseberries]. Delhi: Dehati Pustak Bhandar.

Dixit, Ramsanehi
   1967*a*   *Nim ke Gun tatha Upyog* [The Qualities and Use of Nim]. Delhi: Dehati Pustak Bhandar.
   1967*b*   *Ghi ke Gun tatha Upyog* [The Qualities and Use of Ghi]. Delhi: Dehati Pustak Bhandar.
   n.d.   *Badam ke Gun tatha Upyog* [The Qualities and Use of Almonds]. Delhi: Dehati Pustak Bhandar.
Douglas, Mary
   1970   *Natural Symbols: Explorations in Cosmology.* London: Barrie and Rockliff.
Dubois, J. A.
   1906   *Hindu Manners, Customs and Ceremonies.* 3d ed. Oxford: Clarendon Press.
Dumont, Louis
   1960   "Renunciation in World Religions." *Contributions to Indian Sociology* 4: 33–62.
   1970   *Homo Hierarchicus.* Chicago: The University of Chicago Press.
Dundes, Alan
   1980   "Wet and Dry, the Evil Eye: An Essay in Indo-European and Semitic Worldview." In *Interpreting Folklore,* edited by A. Dundes. Berkeley and Los Angeles: University of California Press.
   1985   "The American Game of 'Smear the Queer' and the Homosexual Component of Male Competitive Sport and Warfare." *The Journal of Psychoanalytic Anthropology* 8, no. 3: 115–129.
"Dwivedi"
   1971   "Goshala" [Cowshed]. *Bharatiya Kushti* 8, no. 9, 10, 11: 199.
   1972   "Goshala" [Cowshed]. *Bharatiya Kushti* 10, no. 1, 2, 3: 37.
   1972–1973   "Goshala" [Cowshed]. *Bharatiya Kushti* 10, no. 4, 5, 6: 33.
   1973   "Goshala" [Cowshed]. *Bharatiya Kushti* 10, no. 7, 8, 9: 19.
   1974–1975   "Do Muktak" [Two Stanzas]. *Bharatiya Kushti* 12, no. 4, 5, 6: 33.
Eck, Diana
   1982   *Banaras: City of Light.* New York: Knopf.
Edwards, James
   1983   "Semen Anxiety in South Asian Cultures: Cultural and Transcultural Significance." *Medical Anthropology,* Summer: 51–67.
Embree, Ainslie T. (editor)
   1988   *Sources of Indian Tradition,* Vol. 1. New York: Columbia University Press.
Enthovan, R. E.
   1924   *The Folklore of Bombay.* Oxford: Clarendon Press.
Fabian, Johannes
   1983   *Time and the Other: How Anthropology Makes Its Object.* New York: Columbia University Press.
Farquhar, J. N.
   1918   *Modern Religious Movements in India.* New York: Macmillan.
   1925   "The Fighting Ascetics of India." *Bulletin of the John Rylands Library* 9: 431–452.

Fernandez, James
  1980   "Reflections on Looking into Mirrors." *Semiotica* 30, no. 1, 2:
              27–39.
Flory, C.
  1970   "Wrestling Guru and Successful Proteges (Guru Hanuman and
              Ved Prakash)." *Hindu*, August 30: 6.
Foucault, Michel
  1978   *The History of Sexuality, Vol. I: An Introduction*. New York:
              Random House.
  1979   *Discipline and Punish*. New York: Vintage Books.
  1984a   "Nietzsche, Genealogy, History." In *The Foucault Reader*, ed-
              ited by P. Rabinow. New York: Pantheon Books.
  1984b   "Docile Bodies." In *The Foucault Reader*, edited by P. Rabinow.
              New York: Pantheon Books.
Freitag, Sandria B.
  1989   *Culture and Power in Banaras: Community, Performance, and
              Environment 1800–1980*. Berkeley, Los Angeles, Oxford: Uni-
              versity of California Press.
Freud, Sigmund
  1967   *The Interpretation of Dreams*. New York: Avon Books.
Fruzzetti, Lina, Ákos Östör, and Steven Barnett
  1982   *Concepts of Person, Kinship, Caste and Marriage in India*. Cam-
              bridge: Harvard University Press.
Fuller, Mary
  1944   "Nag Panchami" [Snake's (Cobra's) Fifth]. *Man in India* 24:
              75–81.
Gallagher, C.
  1986   "The Body vs the Social Body in the Works of Thomas Malthus
              and Henry Mayhew." *Representations* 14: 83–106.
Garuda Purana
  1962   2d ed. Varanasi: Chowkhamba Sanskrit Series.
Geertz, Clifford
  1973   *The Interpretation of Cultures*. New York: Basic Books.
Ghose, A. (Sri Aurobindo)
  1949   "On Physical Culture: A Message from Sri Aurobindo." *Advent*
              6, no. 1: 13–15.
  1954   *Physical Education in Sri Aurobindo Ashram*. Pondicherry: Sri
              Aurobindo Ashram.
Ghose, A. (Sri Aurobindo) and The Mother
  1967   *On Physical Education*. Pondicherry: Sri Aurobindo Ashram.
Ghose, J.
  1930   *Sannyasi and Fakir Raiders in Bengal*. Calcutta: Bengal Secretar-
              iat Book Depot.
Ghurye, G. S.
  1953   *Indian Sadhus*. Bombay: Popular Book Depot.

Giddens, Anthony
    1979   *Central Problems in Social Theory: Action, Structure and Con-
                tradiction in Social Analysis*. Berkeley and Los Angeles: Univer-
                sity of California Press.
Goffman, Erving
    1959   *The Presentation of Self in Everyday Life*. Garden City, N.Y.:
                Doubleday.
Gold, Ann Grodzins
    1988   *Fruitful Journeys: The Ways of Rajasthani Pilgrims*. Berkeley,
                Los Angeles, London: University of California Press.
Gotham, Chamanlal
    1980   *Sri Hanuman Charit* [The Acts of Lord Hanuman]. Bareilly:
                Sanskrit Sansthan.
    1983   *Gupt Rog Chikitsa* [The Treatment of Private Ailments]. Bare-
                illy: Sanskrit Sansthan.
Griffith, R. T. H. (translator)
    1963   *The Ramayana of Valmiki*. Varanasi: Chowkhamba Sanskrit
                Series.
Gupta, M. R.
    1973   "Ghas Khaiye, Nirog Rahaiye" [Eat Greens, Stay Healthy].
                Bharatiya Kushti 10, no. 10, 11, 12: 17–20.
Gupta, Rajesh
    n.d.   *Mallayuddha, athwa Akhara Gyan* [Wrestling Combat, or the
                Wisdom of the Akhara]. Delhi: Dehati Pustak Bhandar.
"Guru Hanuman"
    1984   "Pahalwani ki Khurak" [Wrestling's Diet]. *Bharatiya Kushti* 21,
                no. 3: 53–57.
Habermas, J.
    1972   *Knowledge and Human Interest*. London: Heinemann.
"Hans," Rajkumar
    1983   "Tan Durbal Hai to Man Durbal Hai" [If the Body Is Weak, So
                Is the Mind]. *Bharatiya Kushti* 20, no. 1: 17–20.
Hargreaves, Jennifer (editor)
    1982   *Sport, Culture and Ideology*. London: Routledge and Kegan
                Paul.
Hargreaves, John
    1986   *Sport, Power and Culture*. New York: St. Martins Press.
Harivamsa
    1980   West Franklin, N.H.: Amarta Press.
Harper, Edward B.
    1964   "Ritual Pollution as an Integrator of Caste and Religion." In
                Religion in South Asia, edited by E. B. Harper. Seattle: Univer-
                sity of Washington Press.
Hastings, J.
    1979[1908] *Encyclopaedia of Religion and Ethics, Vol 11*. (13 vols.) Edin-
                burgh: T. and T. Clark.

√ Heesterman, J. C.
    1985   *The Inner Conflict of Tradition: Essays in Indian Ritual, King-
                ship, and Society.* Chicago: University of Chicago Press.
Heinemann, William
    1911   *Encyclopaedia of Sport, Vol. 4.* London.
Heinila, K.
    1982   *The Totalization Process in International Sport.* Javaskyala:
                University of Javaskyala.
Hindustan Times
    1969   "Ninety Kilograms of Vegetarian Muscle (Chandagi Ram)."
                March 14: 16.
Hoberman, J.
    1984   *Sport and Political Ideology.* Austin: University of Texas Press.
— Hocart, A. M.
    1950   *Caste: A Comparative Study.* London: Methuen and Company.
Hopkins, E. W.
    1972   *The Social and Military Position of the Ruling Caste in Ancient
                India as Represented by the Sanscrit Epic.* New Haven: Tuttle,
                Morehouse and Tylor.
Hornblower, G. D.
    1928   "Wrestling: India and Egypt." *Man* 43–44: 65–66.
√ Inden, Ronald
    1978   Ritual, Authority and Cyclic Time in Hindu Kingship." In *King-
                ship and Authority in South Asia,* edited by J. F. Richards. Madi-
                son: University of Wisconsin Press.
Irvine, W.
    1962   *The Army of the Indian Moghuls.* New Delhi: Eurasia Publish-
                ing House.
√ Ishwaran, K.
    1968   *Shivapur: A South Indian Village.* London: Routledge and
                Kegan Paul.
√ Jacobs, J.
    1899   *Indian Fairy Tales.* New York: A. L. Blunt and Company.
Jain, Abhya Kumar
    1987   "Kela, Ek Poshtik Phal" [The Banana, A Nourishing Fruit].
                Bharatiya Kushti 24, no. 10: 19–22.
Jain, Hambala
    1973   "Ruchikar Phalse" [Wonderful Rose-apples]. *Bharatiya Kushti*
                10, no. 7, 8, 9: 17.
Jain, Raj Kumar
    1987   "Mas Nahin, Mumphali Khaiye" [Eat Peanuts, Not Meat].
                Bharatiya Kushti 24, no. 6: 19–22.
Jaini, R. N.
    1979   "Amrit Phal Aunwle se Bita Yowan Punhprapt Kariye" [Reju-
                venation with Gooseberries, the Elixir Fruit]. *Bharatiya Kushti*
                17, no. 1, 2, 3: 17.
James, E. O.
    1959   *The Cult of the Mother Goddess.* London: Thames and Hudson.

Jones, Ernest
  1951   *Essays in Applied Psycho-Analysis, Vol. 2, Essays in Folklore, Anthropology and Religion.* London: Hogarth Press.
✓ Juergensmeyer, Mark
  1982   *Religion as Social Vision.* Berkeley, Los Angeles, London: University of California Press.
Kakar, Sudhir
  ✓ 1981   *The Inner World: A Psycho-analytic Study of Childhood and Society in India.* 2d ed. New Delhi: Oxford University Press.
  ✓ 1982   *Shamans, Mystics and Doctors.* New Delhi: Oxford University Press.
  ✓ 1990   *Intimate Relations: Exploring Indian Sexuality.* Chicago: University of Chicago Press.
Kamal, Keshav Dev Mishra
  1971   "Ghar ka Aspatal, Bel" [Wood-apple, the Home Hospital]. *Bharatiya Kushti* 8, no. 9, 10, 11: 17–20.
Karandikar, S. L.
  1957   *Bal Gangadhar Tilak: The Hercules and Prometheus of Modern India.* Bombay: Shirali.
Kaushik, K.
  1979   "Indian Wrestling in Knots." *Times of India,* December 9: 4.
Kesriya, Ram Chandar "Kherawda"
  1972   "Guru Charano mein At Din ka Anubhav" [Eight Days of Experience at the Guru's Feet]. *Bharatiya Kushti* 10, no. 1, 2, 3: 49–54.
  1973   "Kartaviya" [Duty]. *Bharatiya Kushti* 10, no. 7, 8, 9: 25.
  1978   "Bharat ka Shan Barainge" [We Will Advance the Glory of India]. *Bharatiya Kushti* 16, no. 4, 5, 6: 25.
Khare, R. S.
  1976   *Culture and Reality: Essays on the Hindu System of Managing Food.* Simla: Institute of Advanced Study.
  ✓ 1984   *The Untouchable as Himself: Ideology, Identity and Pragmatism Among the Lucknow Chamars.* New York: Cambridge University Press.
Khedkar, V. K.
  1959   *The Divine Heritage of the Yadavas.* Allahabad: Paramanand.
Kitts, E. J.
  1885   "Serpent Worship—Azamgarh." *Panjab Notes and Queries, Allahabad* 3, no. 27: 38.
Klein, M.
  1948   *Contributions to Psychoanalysis, 1921–1945.* London: Hogarth Press.
— Kolenda, Pauline
  1963   "Towards a Model of the Hindu Jajmani System." *Human Organization* 22, no. 1: 11–31.
  1978   *Caste in Contemporary India: Beyond Organic Solidarity.* Menlo Park: Benjamin Cummings Co.

Koshal, Avdesh
　　1972–1973 "Khelkud ka Star Nicha Kyun" [Why is the Position of Sports
　　　　　　and Games so Low]? *Bharatiya Kushti* 10, no. 4, 5, 6: 55–56.
Kumar, Nita
　　1986　　　"Open Space and Free Time: Pleasure for the People of Ba-
　　　　　　naras." *Contributions to Indian Sociology* (n.s.) 20, no. 1:
　　　　　　41–60.
√ 1988　　　*The Artisans of Banaras: Popular Culture and Identity,
　　　　　　1880–1986.* Princeton: Princeton University Press.
Kumawath, Om Prakash
　　1987　　　"Wajan Barane ke liye Shakahari Bhojan" [A Vegetarian Diet
　　　　　　to Increase Your Weight]. *Bharatiya Kushti* 24, no. 3: 11–16.
Kunzle, David
　　1981　　　*Fashion and Fetishism: A Social History of the Corset, Tight
　　　　　　Lacing and Other Forms of Body Scuplture in the West.* London:
　　　　　　Rowan and Littlefield.
La Barre, Weston
　　1962　　　*They Shall Take Up Serpents: Psychology of the Southern Snake-
　　　　　　Handling Cult.* Minneapolis: University of Minnesota Press.
"Lal"
　　1985　　　"Nimbu" [Lemon]. *Bharatiya Kushti* 22, no. 1: 17–20.
Lal, Mohan
　　n.d.　　　*Lathi Shiksha* [Stave Training/Education]. Delhi: Dehati Pustak
　　　　　　Bhandar.
Leach, Edmund
　　1958　　　"Magical Hair." *Journal of the Royal Anthropological Institute*
　　　　　　88: 147–164.
√ 1976　　　*Culture and Communication.* New York: Cambridge University
　　　　　　Press.
Legman, G.
　　1975　　　*No Laughing Matter: Rationale of the Dirty Joke.* 2d ser. New
　　　　　　York: Breaking Point.
√ Lévi-Strauss, Claude
　　1966　　　*The Savage Mind.* Chicago: University of Chicago Press.
Lingis, A.
　　1988　　　"Orchids and Muscles." In *Philosophic Inquiry in Sport*, edited
　　　　　　by W. J. Morgan and V. M. Klaus. Champaign: Human Kinetics
　　　　　　Publishers.
Link
　　1969　　　"Chandagi Ram." May 25: 35.
　　1970　　　"Guru Hanuman and His Wards." August 9: 31–32.
√ Lorenzen, D.
　　1978　　　"Warrior Ascetics in Indian History." *Journal of the American
　　　　　　Oriental Society* 98: 61–75.
√ Lutgendorf, Philip
　　1991　　　*The Life of a Text: Performing the Ramacharitmanas of Tulsi-
　　　　　　das.* Berkeley, Los Angeles, Oxford: University of California
　　　　　　Press.

√Lynch, Owen M.
    1969   *The Politics of Untouchability.* New York: Columbia University Press.
    1990   "The Mastram: Emotion and Person Among Mathura's Chaubes." In *Divine Passions: The Social Construction of Emotion in India,* edited by Owen Lynch. Berkeley, Los Angeles, Oxford: University of California Press.

√ Madan, T. N.
    1987   *Non-Renunciation: Themes and Interpretations of Hindu Culture.* Delhi: Oxford University Press.

Mahabharata
    1925   Poona: Bhandarkar Oriental Research Institute.

Maheshwar, D.
    1981   "Life in Delhi That Was: Golden Era of Wrestling." *Hindustan Times,* July 12: 9.

Maity, P. K.
    1963   "A Note on the Snake Cult of Ancient India." *Folklore* 4, no. 4: 120–129.

Majumdar, B. K.
    1960   *The Military System of Ancient India.* Calcutta: F. K. L. Mukhopadhyay.

Majumdar, D. N.
    1958   *Caste and Communication in an Indian Village.* Delhi: Asia Publishing House.

Malhotra, Govardan Das
    1981   "Uttar Pradesh ke Pahalwan" [Wrestlers of Uttar Pradesh]. *Bharatiya Kushti* 18, no. 7, 8, 9: 17–96.

Malla Purana
    1964   Baroda: Oriental Institute.

Manasollasa
    1959   Baroda: Oriental Institute.

√ Mandelbaum, David G.
    1970   *Society in India.* Berkeley: University of California Press.

Mandlik, V. N.
    1868   "Serpent Worship in Western India: The Nag Panchami Festival as It Is Now Observed." *Journal of the Royal Asiatic Society of Bombay* 9: 169–200.

Manik, G. Y.
    1964   *Bharatiya Vyayam* [Indian Exercise]. Nasik: n.p.

Manik, Kalidas
    1932   *Jujutsu wa Japani Kushti* [Jujitsu and Japanese Wrestling]. Varanasi: Manik Karyalai.
    1939   *Tandrusti aur Takat* [Fitness and Strength]. Professor Ram Murti Vyayam Series, no. 4. Varanasi: Manik Karyalai.

√ Marcus, George E., and Michael M. J. Fischer
    1986   *Anthropology as Cultural Critique: An Experimental Moment in the Human Sciences.* Chicago: University of Chicago Press.

Marglin, Frédérique A.
  1982   "Kings and Wives: The Separation of Status and Royal Power."
            In *Way of Life: King, Householder, Renouncer: Essays in Hon-
            our of Louis Dumont*, edited by T. N. Madan. New Delhi: Vikas
            Publishing House.

Marriott, McKim
  1960   *Caste Ranking and Community Structure in Five Regions of
            India and Pakistan*. Poona: Deccan College Monographs.

Marriott, McKim, and Ronald B. Inden
  1977   "Towards an Ethnosociology of South Asian Caste Systems." In
            The New Wind: Changing Identities in South Asia, edited by
            Kenneth David. The Hague: Mouton.

Mathur, R. W.
  1966   *Saral Vyayam* [Basic Wrestling]. Banaras: Municipal Board.

Minturn, L., and J. T. Hitchcock
  1966   *The Rajputs of Khalapur, India*. New York: John Wiley and
            Sons Inc.

Moffatt, Michael
  1979   *An Untouchable Community in South India: Structure and Con-
            sensus*. Princeton: Princeton University Press.

Mohanty, Gopinath
  1979   "The Somersault." In *A Collection of Oriya Short Fiction*, edited
            and translated by Sitakant Mahapatra. Calcutta: United Writers.

Morgan, W. J., and V. M. Klaus
  1988   *Philosophic Inquiry in Sport*. Champaign: Human Kinetics Pub-
            lishers.

Morton, Gerald W.
  1985   *Wrestling to "Rasslin": Ancient Sport to American Spectacle*.
            Bowling Green: Bowling Green State University Press.

Mujumdar, D. C.
  1950   *Encyclopedia of Indian Physical Culture*. Baroda: Good Com-
            panions.

Mundkar, B.
  1983   *The Cult of the Serpent: An Interdisciplinary Survey of its Mani-
            festations and Origins*. Albany: State University of New York
            Press.

Munna, Rajindar Singh
  1979   "Sarkar, Naujawan, aur Pahalwani" [The Government, Youth
            and Wrestling]. *Bharatiya Kushti* 17, no. 1, 2, 3: 35–37.
  1982   "Bharatiya Kushti ka Patan Kyon" [Why the Demise of Indian
            Wrestling?] *Bharatiya Kushti* 19, no. 4, 5, 6: 21–24.
  1983   "Shakahari Bhojan hi Balshali Banata Hai" [Only a Vegetarian
            Diet Makes You Strong]. *Bharatiya Kushti* 20, no. 1: 37–44.
  1986   "Kaisa Hota hai Pahalwan ki Patani ka Grihastha Jiwan" [What
            is a Wrestler's Wife's Home Life Like?] *Bharatiya Kushti* 23, no.
            5: 83–88.

✓ Nanda, Serena
    1990   *Neither Man nor Woman: The Hijras of India.* Belmont: Wadsworth Publishing.

✓ Narayan, Kirin
    1989   *Storytellers, Saints, and Scoundrels: Folk Narrative as Hindu Religious Teaching.* Philadelphia: University of Pennsylvania Press.

Natanson, M.
    1973   "Introduction." In *Alfred Schutz, Collected Papers I: The Problem of Social Reality,* edited by M. Natanson. The Hague: Martin Nijhoff.

Negi, Sunil
    1987   "Nasha, Mot ka Dusra Rup" [Intoxication, Another Form of Death]. *Bharatiya Kushti* 24, no. 6: 55–60.

Neuman, Daniel M.
    1990   *The Life of Music in North India.* Chicago: University of Chicago Press.

Obeyesekere, Gananath
✓ 1976   "The Impact of Ayurvedic Ideas on the Culture and the Individual in Sri Lanka." In *Asian Medical Systems,* edited by Charles Leslie. Berkeley and Los Angeles: University of California Press.
✓ 1981   *Medusa's Hair: An Essay on Personal Symbols and Religious Experience.* Chicago: University of Chicago Press.

O'Flaherty, Wendy Doniger
✓ 1973   *Asceticism and Eroticism in the Mythology of Siva.* Oxford: Oxford University Press.
✓ 1976   *The Origins of Evil in Hindu Mythology.* Berkeley and Los Angeles: University of California Press.
✓ 1980   *Women, Androgynes, and Other Mythical Beasts.* Chicago: The University of Chicago Press.
✓ 1984   *Dreams, Illusions and Other Realities.* Chicago: University of Chicago Press.

Oman, John Campbell
✓ 1983 [1903] *The Mystics, Ascetics and Saints of India.* New Delhi: Cosmo Publishers.

Oppert, G.
    1967   *On the Weapons, Army Organization and Political Maxims of the Ancient Hindus.* Ahmedabad: New Order Book Company.

✓ Orenstein, H.
    1965   *Gaon: Conflict and Cohesion in an Indian Village.* Princeton: Princeton University Press.

✓ Orr, W. G.
    1940   "Armed Religious Ascetics in Northern India." *Bulletin of the John Rylands Library* 24: 81–100.

✓ Panda, S. C.
    1986   *Naga Cult in Orissa.* Delhi: B. R. Publishing Corporation.

Pandey, Raj Bali
   n.d.   *Yaduvansh ka Itihas* [History of the Yadav Dynasty]. Varanasi:
               Sri Krishna Prakashan.
Pandey, Trilochan
   1964   "Tree Worship in Ancient India." *Folklore in India* 6: 213–218.
Pant, Apa B.
   1970   *Surya Namaskars*. Bombay: Orient Longmans.
Pant, G. N.
   1970   *Studies in Indian Weapons and Warfare*. New Delhi: Army Edu-
               cational Stores.
Parry, Jonathan
   1989   "The End of the Body." In *Fragments for a History of the
               Human Body*, edited by Michel Feher. New York: Zone.
Pathak, Narindar
   1980   "Varsha Ritu mein Swasth Kaise Rahen" [How to Stay Healthy
               During the Rainy Season]. *Bharatiya Kushti* 17, no. 1, 2, 3:
               17–20.
Patodi, Ratan
   1972   "Kushti par se Manoranjan Kar Samapt Ho! Gaon-Gaon mein
               Kushti Pratiyogita Ho" [Stop Assessing an Entertainment Tax
               on Wrestling! There Should be Free and Open Competitions in
               Every Village]. *Bharatiya Kushti* 9, no. 7, 8, 9: 11–14.
   1973*a*   *Bharatiya Kushti Kala* [The Art of Indian Wrestling]. Indor:
               Bharatiya Kushti Prakashan.
   1973*b*   "Kushti ki Unnati ho Rahi hai" [Wrestling is Being Promoted].
               Bharatiya Kushti 11, no. 1, 2, 3: 11–13.
   1982   *Bharatiya Kushti ke Daw Pech* [Moves and Countermoves in
               Indian Wrestling]. Indor: Bharatiya Kushti Prakashan.
   1983   *Bharatiya Kushti* (A Special Volume in Honor of Padama Sri
               Guru Hanuman). *Bharatiya Kushti* 20, no. 1.
   1984   "Akhare ki Hira, Gama" [The Akhara's Diamond, Gama].
               Bharatiya Kushti 21, no. 1: 23–39.
   1985   "Gunga aur Kallu Gama ki [Kushti]" [A Bout Between Gunga
               and Kallu Gama]. *Bharatiya Kushti* 22, no. 1: 43–50.
   1986*a*   "Anubhav Jita, Riyaj Hara" [Experience Won and Practice
               Lost]. *Bharatiya Kushti* 23, no. 1: 81–86.
   1986*b*   "Ye Pahalwan, Ye Maharaja" [This the Wrestler, This the King].
               Bharatiya Kushti 23, no. 5, 53–56.
   1986*c*   "Pahalwano ke Rochak Sansmaran" [Fond Recollections of
               Wrestlers]. *Bharatiya Kushti* 23, no. 5: 57–82.
Philpot, J. H.
   1897   *The Sacred Tree*. New York: Macmillian.
Pollok, F. T.
   1911   "Wrestling—Indian." In *The Encyclopedia of Sport, Vol 4*, ed-
               ited by William Heinemann. London.
Prabhavananda and C. Isherwood (translators)
   1975   *Bhagavad-Gita*. London: Dent.

✓ Prasad, Dharmendra
  1982   "The Naga Sadhus." *Indian Culture* 37, no. 2: 34–42.
  Rabinow, Paul
  1977   *Reflections on Fieldwork in Morocco*. Berkeley: University of California Press.
  1983   "Humanism as Nihilism: The Bracketing of Truth and Seriousness in American Cultural Anthropology." In *Social Science as Moral Inquiry*, edited by N. Haan, R. N. Bellah, P. Rabinow, and W. M. Sullivan. New York: Columbia University Press.
✓ Raghavan, V.
  1979   *Festivals, Sports, and Pastimes of India*. Ahmedabad: B. J. Institute of Learning Research.
✓ Raghaveshananda, S.
  1980   "Hanuman, the Symbol of Service." *Vedanta Kesari* 67, no. 5: 181–183.
✓ Raheja, Gloria Goodwin
  1988   *The Poison in the Gift: Ritual, Prestation and the Dominant Caste in a North Indian Village*. Chicago: University of Chicago Press.
  Rai, Govind
  1976   *Hanuman ke Devtwa tatha Murti ka Vikas* [The Development of Hanuman as Divinity and Icon]. Prayag, Allahabad: Hindi Sahitya Samelan.
  Rai, Indrasan
  1984   "Prachin Bharat mein Mallavidya" [Wrestling Knowledge in Ancient India]. Ph.D. dissertation. Varanasi: Banaras Hindu University.
  Rai, M.
  1956   *Prachin Bharatiya Manoranjan* [Entertainment in Ancient India]. Allahabad: Bharatiya Vidya Bhavan.
  Rajani, S. N.
  1974   "Swasthiya aur Gular" [Fitness and the Wild Fig]. *Bharatiya Kushti* 11, no. 10, 11, 12: 17–18.
  Rajput, A. B.
  1960   "Gama in Retirement." *The Illustrated Weekly of India*, February 7: 8–10.
  Rakesh, "Pandit"
  1986   *Sampuran Vrat aur Tyohar* [Complete (Book of) Fasts and Festivals]. New Delhi: Sadhana Pocket Books.
  Ram, Chandagi
  1982   *Bharatiya Kushti ke Daw Pech* [Moves and Countermoves in Indian Wrestling]. Indor: Bharatiya Kushti Prakashan.
  Ramacaritamanasa
  1913   Poona: Vadyakapatrika Press.
  Ramakrishnan, S.
  1986   "Ghaneshyamdas Birla." *Bharatiya Kushti* 24, no. 2: 19–22.
  Ramayana
  1911–1913 Bombay: Nirnayasagara Press.

Randhir Book Sales
    n.d.   *Sri Hanuman Jiwan Charitra* [The Life and Deeds of Lord Hanu-
                man]. Haridwar: Randhir Book Sales.
Rao, M. S. A.
    1964   "Caste and the Indian Army." *The Economic Weekly* XVI, no.
                35: 1439–1443.
"Ravindranath"
    1975   "Amodh Astra, Brahmacharya" [Brahmacharya, The Infallible
                Weapon]. *Bharatiya Kushti* 16, no. 7, 8, 9: 19–22.
Ricoeur, Paul
    1971   "The Model of the Text: Meaningful Action Considered as a
                Text." *Social Research* 38, no. 3.
    1986   *Lectures on Ideology and Utopia*, edited by G. H. Taylor. New
                York: Columbia University Press.
Rig Veda
    1925–1928 London: W. H. Allen.
Rosaldo, Michelle
    1980   *Knowledge and Passion: Ilongot Notions of Self and Social Life.*
                Cambridge: Cambridge University Press.
Rosaldo, Renato
    1980   *Ilongot Headhunting, 1883–1974: A Study in Society and His-
                tory.* Stanford: Stanford University Press.
Rosselli, John
    1980   "The Self-Image of Effeteness: Physical Education and National-
                ism in Nineteenth-Century Bengal." *Past and Present* 86:
                121–148.
Roy, K. P.
    1967   "Wrestling Past and Present." *Hindustan Times*, November 11:
                10.
Roy, S. N.
    1931   "Herbs and Trees in Worship." *Journal of the Anthropological
                Society, Bombay* 14: 588–604.
Roy, Tridib Nath
    1939   "Indoor and Outdoor Games in Ancient India." *Indian History
                Congress* 3: 241–261.
Sahlins, Marshall
    1981   *Historical Metaphors and Mythical Realities: Structure in the
                Early History of the Sandwich Islands Kingdom.* Ann Arbor:
                University of Michigan Press.
    1986   *Islands of History.* Chicago: University of Chicago Press.
Saksena, Ravindar
    1972   "Chana" [Chickpeas]. *Bharatiya Kushti* 10, no. 1, 2, 3: 17–18.
Sandesara, B. J., and R. N. Mehta (editors)
    1964   *Malla Purana.* Baroda: Oriental Institute.
Sangar, M. S.
    1982   "Pradesh ko Chahiye ek Khel Niti" [The State Needs a Sports
                Policy]. *Bharatiya Kushti* 19, no. 1, 2, 3: 63–68.

Saraswati, Yogananda
  n.d.   *Brahmacharya Raksha hi Jiwan hai* [Celibacy is Life Itself].
                Alwar: Ramji Lal Sharma.
Sarkar, J.
  √ 1950   *A History of the Dasnami Sannyasis.* Allahabad: P. A. Mahani-
                rvani.
Sarkar, J. N.
  1984   *The Art of War in Medieval India.* New Delhi: Munshiram Ma-
                noharlal.
Sarma, G. D.
  1934   *Sharir aur Vyayam* [Body and Exercise]. Allahabad: Chand
                Press.
Satapatha Brahmana
  1890–1912 Calcutta: Asiatic Society of Bengal.
Scarry, E.
  1985   *The Body in Pain: The Making and Unmaking of the World.*
                Oxford: Oxford University Press.
Scheper-Hughes, Nancy, and Margaret Lock
  1987   "The Mindful Body: A Prolegomenon to Future Work in Medi-
                cal Anthropology." *Medical Anthropology Quarterly* (n.s.) 1,
                no. 1: 6–41.
Seesodia, T.
  1915   *The Rajputs: A Fighting Race.* London: East and West Ltd.
Sen, Samer
  1985   *Gharelu Elaj* [Home Remedies]. New Delhi: Sabodh Pocket
                Books.
Sharma, Prayagdatta
  1985   *Sri Hanuman Stuti* [Prayers (to) Lord Hanuman]. Mathura: Sri
                Gopal Pustakalai.
Sharma, Raj Kumar
  n.d.   "Bhumika" [Introduction]. In *Mallayuddha, athwa Akhara
                Gyan* [Wrestling Combat, or the Widsom of the Akhara], by
                Rajesh Gupta. Delhi: Dehati Pustak Bhandar.
Sharma, Rishikumar
  n.d.   *Pipal tatha Bargad Vaksh ke Gun wa Upyog* [The Qualities
                and Use of the Pipal and Banyan Trees]. Delhi: Dehati Pustak
                Bhandar.
Sharma, Sanjay
  1985   "Padama Sri Chandagi Ram Kaite hai ki Kushti ko Sanrakshan
                Chahiye" [Padama Shri Chandagi Ram Says that Wrestling
                Needs a System of Patronage]. *Bharatiya Kushti* 21, no. 10:
                45–52.
Shastri, J. L. (editor)
  1978   *Ancient Indian Tradition and Mythology, Vol. 11, The Bhaga-
                vata Purana.* Delhi: Motilal Banarsidass.
Shastri, Jaganath
  n.d.   *Brahmacharya ke Sadhan* [The Means By Which to Maintain
                Celibacy]. Delhi: Dehati Pustak Bhandar.

Shastri, Jaganath Sharma (editor)
   n.d.   *Hanuman Jyotish* [Hanuman Astrology]. Delhi: Dehati Pustak
                   Bhandar.
Shastri, Shivadatta Mishra
   1982   *Hanumad Rahasyam* [Secrets of Hanuman]. Varanasi: Thakur
                   Prasad Pustak Bhandar.
Shastri, Satyavir
   1986   *Hanuman Upasna* [Hanuman Worship]. Delhi: Sadhana Pocket
                   Books.
Shivananda, "Swami"
   1984   *Brahmacharya hi Jiwan hai, aur Virya Nash hi Mrityu hai* [Bra-
                   hamacharya (Celibacy) is Life, and Sensuality is Death] (English
                   title translation appears in original Hindi text). Allahabad: Ad-
                   hunik Prakashan Grah.
Shukla, Parmanand
   n.d.   "Bharat Vikhyat Malla Shiromani Mangala Rai." [The Famous
                   Mangala Rai: A National Wrestling Treasure.] *Akhare ki Or* 1,
                   no. 1: 10–13.
Shukla, Ramkumar
   1973   "Swami Ustad Fakir Chand." *Bharatiya Kushti* 10, no. 10, 11,
                   12: 43–48.
✓ Singer, Milton
   1963   "The Radha-Krishna Bhajans of Madras City." *History of Reli-
                   gions* 2, no. 2: 183–226.
Singh, Ashok Kumar
   1983   *Vyayam aur Sharirik Vikas* [Exercise and Physical Training].
                   Varanasi: Shyamsundar Rasayanshala Prakashan.
Singh, Balbir
   1964   *Bharat   de   Pahalwan: 1635–1935*   [Indian   Wrestlers:
                   1635–1935]. Jullundur: 103–Basti Nau.
✓ Singh, Damandeep
   1988   "Akharas—Surviving on Faith." *Times of India*, April 27.
Singh, Harphool
   1981   *Adhunik Mallavidya* [Knowledge of Modern Wrestling]. Delhi:
                   Panjabi Pustak Bhandar.
   1984*a*   *Pahalwan kaise Bane* [How to Become a Wrestler]. Delhi: Ar-
                   vind Prakashan.
   1984*b*   *Free Style Kushti* [Free Style Wrestling]. Delhi: Arvind Pra-
                   kashan.
Singh, H. B.
   1972   "Editorial." *Akhare ki Or* [Towards the Akharas] 1, no. 1: 2–6.
Singh, Kamala Prasad
   1972*a*   "Pahalwani aur Pariwar Niyojan" [Wrestling and Family Plan-
                   ning]. *Bharatiya Kushti* 9, no. 7, 8, 9: 25–50.
   1972*b*   "Pahalwani aur Vyaktitwa" [Wrestling and Character]. *Bhara-
                   tiya Kushti* 9, no. 10, 11, 12: 21–25.

1972c   "Mallavidya aur Sarkar" [Wrestling Knowledge and the Gov-
             ernment]. *Bharatiya Kushti* 10, no. 1, 2, 3: 39–48.
1972–1973 "Saccha Pahalwan wah hai jo Dusron ko Pahalwan Banawen"
             [The True Wrestler is One Who Turns Others Into Wrestlers].
             Bharatiya Kushti 10, no. 1, 2, 3: 11–16.
1973   "Vyayam ke Kuch Niyam" [Some Principles of Exercise]. *Bhara-
             tiya Kushti* 10, no. 7, 8, 9: 27–32.
1974   "Daw Pech" [Moves and Countermoves]. *Bharatiya Kushti* 11,
             no. 7, 8, 9: 27–32.
1975   "Pahalwani Prarambh Karne ki Ayu" [At What Age to Begin
             Wrestling]. *Bharatiya Kushti* 12, no. 7, 8, 9: 25–34.
1983   "Guru Hanuman aur Sarkar" [Guru Hanuman and the Govern-
             ment]. *Bharatiya Kushti* 20, no. 1: 23–29.
1986   "Rashtriya Banam Antrashtriya Kushti" [National Alias Inter-
             national Wrestling]. *Bharatiya Kushti* 23, no. 5: 25–28.
Singh, Lallan ji
1982–1983 *Ramayankalin mein Yuddhakala* [Martial Arts in the Ramayana
             Era]. Agra: Abhinava Prakashan.
Singh, Sahadev
1987   "Apna Utsava mein Suresh Kumar Mahan Bharat Kesri Bane"
             [Suresh Kumar won the Mahan Bharat Kesri Title in the Upna
             Utsava (Dangal)]. *Bharatiya Kushti* 24, no. 3: 53–60.
Sinha, Satyadev Narayan
1978   "Ek Shama Raha Gai, Wah Bhi Khamosh Hai" [One Lamp Still
             Remains, It to is Silent]. *Dharmayuga* 29, no. 33: 12.
Sivnathrayji "Taskin"
1955   *Mallayuddha aur Akhara* [Wrestling Combat and the Akhara].
             Agra: Garg and Company.
Soman, V. R.
1963   *Sulabh Kushti (Mallavidya)* [Basic Wrestling]. Satara: Seva Pra-
             kashan.
1974   *Jagatik Kushti.* Satara: Seva Prakashan.
Spratt, P.
√ 1966   *Hindu Culture and Personality.* Bombay: Manaktala.
Sridattasarma, M. V.
√ 1966   "Hanuman." *Vedanta Kesari* 52: 487–491.
Srigondekar, G. K. (editor)
1959   *Manasollasa.* Baroda: Oriental Institute.
Srinivas, M. N.
√1962   *Caste in Modern India and Other Essays.* London: Asia Publish-
             ing House.
√ 1965   *Religion and Society Among the Coorgs of South India.* New
             Delhi: Asia Publishing House.
√1968   "Mobility in the Caste System." In *Structure and Change in
             Indian Society*, edited by M. Singer and B. Cohn. Chicago: Al-
             dine Publishing Company.
√1969   *Social Change in Modern India.* Berkeley and Los Angeles: Uni-
             versity of California Press.

Staal, Frits
    1983–1984 "Indian Concepts of the Body." *Somatics*, Autumn/Winter:
            31–41.
Statesman
    1970   "Akharas Lack Patrons." August 11: 3.
Steed, G.
    1955   "Notes on an Approach to a Study of Personality Formation
                in a Hindu Village in Gujarat." In *Village India*, edited by M.
                Marriott. Chicago: University of Chicago Press.
Sundaracharya, Shyam
    1984   "Hare Shak" [Green Leafy Vegetables]. *Bharatiya Kushti* 19,
                no. 3: 45–55.
    1986a   "Tarbuja" [Watermelon]. *Bharatiya Kushti* 24, no. 1: 21–24.
    1986b   "Malish" [Massage]. *Bharatiya Kushti* 24, no. 1: 33–38.
Suryavamshi, K. G.
    1966   *Bharatiya Mallavidya, Uday ani Vikas* [Indian Wrestling, Its As-
                cent and Development]. Pune: Maharashtra Rajya Kustigir Par-
                ishad.
Suryavanshi, B.
    1962   *The Abhirs, Their History and Culture*. Baroda: Maharaja Saya-
                jirao University.
Swarajya
    1973   "Wrestling, a Neglected Sport." March 10: 30.
Tantras (Mahanirvana)
    1927   2d ed. Madras: Ganesh and Co.
Thompson, Stith
    1955–1958 *Motif-Index of Folk-Literature*. 6 vols. Bloomington: Indiana
                University Press.
Thompson, Stith, and Jonas Balys
    1951   *Oral Tales of India*. Bloomington: Indiana University Press.
Tripathi, R. K.
    1977   "Tulasi's Concept of Bhakti." In *Tulasidasa: His Mind and Art*,
                edited by Nagendra. New Delhi: National Publishing House.
Tripathi, Ramesh Chandar
    1981   "Aunwla, Vitamin 'Si' ka Bhandar" [The Gooseberry, a Reposi-
                tory of Vitamin "C"]. *Bharatiya Kushti* 18, no. 10, 11, 12:
                17–18.
Turner, Bryan S.
    1984   *The Body and Society: Explorations in Social Theory*. New
                York: Basil Blackwell.
Turner, Victor
    1969   *The Ritual Process*. Chicago: Aldine Publishing Company.
Tyler, Stephen A.
    1986   "Post-Modern Ethnography: From Document of the Occult to
                Occult Document." In *Writing Culture: The Poetics and Politics
                of Ethnography*, edited by James Clifford and George Marcus.
                Berkeley, Los Angeles, London: University of California Press.

Uberoi, J.
1967   "On Being Unshorn." *Transactions of the Indian Institute of Advanced Study*, Simla, 4: 87–100.

Vaishya, Amedhi Lal
1975   *Haldi ke Upyog* [Turmeric Remedies]. Varanasi: Shyamsundar Rasayanshala Prakashan.

van der Veer, Peter
1989   "The Power of Detachment: Disciplines of Body and Mind in the Ramanandi Order." *American Ethnologist* 16, no. 3: 458–470.

Vatsyayan, Premlata
1985   *Varsh Bhar ke Vrat aur Tyohar* [Annual Fasts and Festivals]. New Delhi: Hind Pustak Bhandar.

Vedi, Ramesh
1973   "Dudh aur Dehi ki Lassi" [Milk and Yogurt Milkshakes]. *Bharatiya Kushti* 11, no. 1, 2, 3: 17–20.

Verma, Onkar Prakash
1970   *The Yadavas and Their Times*. Nagpur: Vidharbha Samshodan Mandala.

Vishwakarma, Mohan Lal
1974   "Kela, Ek Uttam Pathya" [Banana, A Great Food]. *Bharatiya Kushti* 11, no. 7, 8, 9: 17–28.

Vishnowi, Denesh Kumar
1986   "Rajguru, Sri Guru Hanuman" [The Great Guru, Sri Guru Hanuman]. *Bharatiya Kushti* 24, no. 1: 43.

Vogel, Jean Philippe
1926   *Indian Serpent Lore*. London: Arthur Probsthain.

Vyas, Shanti Kumar Nanooram
1958   *Ramayana Kalin Samaj* [Society in the Ramayana Era]. New Delhi: Satsahitya Prakashan.

Wadley, Susan S.
1975   *Shakti: Power in the Conceptual Structure of Karimpur Religion*. University of Chicago Studies in Anthropology, No. 2.

Willams, Raymond
1977   *Marxism and Literature*. Oxford: Oxford University Press.

Wilson, H. H.
1979   *The Art of War and Medical and Surgical Sciences of Hindus*. Delhi: Nag Publishers.

Wiser, William H.
1950   *The Hindu Jajmani System*. Lucknow: Lucknow Publishing House.

Wolcott, Leonard
1978   "Hanuman, the Power Dispensing Monkey in Indian Folk Religion." *Journal of Asian Studies* 37, no. 4: 653–662.

Woodroffe, J.
1929   *Shakti and Shakta. Essays and Addresses on the Shakta Tantrashastras*. London: Luzac and Co.

Yadav, K. C.
    1957   *Ahiravala ka Itihas: Madhyayuga se 1947 tak* [A History of the
                Ahirs: From the Medieval Period through to 1947]. Delhi: Akhil
                Bharatiya Yadav Mahasabha.
Yadavkumar, Shrimanalal Abhimanyu
    1982   *Ahir-Vansh-Pradip* [The Grandeur of the Ahir Lineage]. Vara-
                nasi: Kali Prasad Yadav.
Yoga Sutra
    1982   3d ed. New Delhi: Oriental Books Reprints Corp.
Yogavasistha-Maha-Ramayana
    1918   Bombay: Nirnayasagara.
Yogi, Kumar
    1986   "Ek Seb Nitya Khaiye" [Eat an Apple a Day]. *Bharatiya Kushti*
                24, no. 2: 23–26.
Zarrilli, Phillip
    1989   "Three Bodies of Practice in a Traditional South Indian Martial
                Art." *Social Science and Medicine* 28, no. 12: 1289–1309.
Zimmer, Heinrich
    1946   *Myths and Symbols in Indian Art and Civilization.* Bollingen
                Series 6. Washington: Pantheon Books.
Zimmer, Henry R.
    1948   *Hindu Medicine.* Baltimore: The Johns Hopkins University
                Press.
Zimmermann, Francis
    1983   "Remarks on the Conception of the Body in Ayurvedic Medi-
                cine." In *South Asian Digest of Regional Writing, Vol. 8 (1979):
                Sources of Illness and Healing in South Asian Regional Litera-
                ture,* edited by B. Pfleiderer and G. D. Sontheimer. Heidelberg:
                South Asia Institute, Dept. of Indology, Heidelberg University.
    1988   "The Jungle and the Aroma of Meats: An Ecological Theme
                in Hindu Medicine." *Social Science and Medicine* 27, no. 3:
                197–215.
Zola, I. K.
    1972   "Medicine as an Institution of Social Control." *Sociological Re-
                view* 20, no. 4: 487–504.

Index

Designer: U.C. Press Staff
Compositor: Maryland Composition Company, Inc.
Text: 10/13 Sabon
Display: Sabon
Printer: Braun-Brumfield, Inc.
Binder: Braun-Brumfield, Inc.